Windows on Japanese Education

Recent Titles in
Contributions to the Study of Education

Diffusion of Innovations in English Language Teaching: The ELEC Effort in Japan, 1956–1968
Lynn Earl Henrichsen

Improving Educational Quality: A Global Perspective
David W. Chapman and Carol A. Carrier, editors

Rethinking the Curriculum: Toward an Integrated, Interdisciplinary College Education
Mary E. Clark and Sandra A. Wawrytko, editors

Study Abroad: The Experience of American Undergraduates
Jerry S. Carlson, Barbara B. Burn, John Useem, and David Yachimowicz

Between Understanding and Misunderstanding: Problems and Prospects for International Cultural Exchange
Yasushi Sugiyama, editor

Southern Cities, Southern Schools: Public Education in the Urban South
David N. Plank and Rick Ginsberg, editors

Making Schools Work for Underachieving Minority Students: Next Steps for Research, Policy, and Practice
Josie G. Bain and Joan L. Herman, editors

Foreign Teachers in China: Old Problems for a New Generation, 1979–1989
Edgar A. Porter

Effective Interventions: Applying Learning Theory to School Social Work
Evelyn Harris Ginsburg

Cognitive Education and Testing: A Methodological Approach
Eugene J. Meehan

American Presidents and Education
Maurice R. Berube

Learning to Lead: The Dynamics of the High School Principalship
Gordon A. Donaldson, Jr.

Windows on Japanese Education

Edited by
EDWARD R. BEAUCHAMP

Contributions to the Study of Education, Number 43

GREENWOOD PRESS
Westport, Connecticut • London

Library of Congress Cataloging-in-Publication Data

Windows on Japanese education / edited by Edward R. Beauchamp.
    p. cm.—(Contributions to the study of education, ISSN
0196-707X ; no. 43)
  Includes index.
  ISBN 0–313–26243–8 (alk. paper)
  1. Education—Japan—Evaluation. 2. Education—Japan—Philosophy.
3. Education and state—Japan. I. Beauchamp, Edward R., 1933–
II. Series.
LA1312.W56   1991
370′.952—dc20   90–45329

British Library Cataloguing in Publication Data is available.

Copyright © 1991 by Edward R. Beauchamp

All rights reserved. No portion of this book may be
reproduced, by any process or technique, without the
express written consent of the publisher.

Library of Congress Catalog Card Number: 90–45329
ISBN: 0–313–26243–8
ISSN: 0196–707X

First published in 1991

Greenwood Press, 88 Post Road West, Westport, CT 06881
An imprint of Greenwood Publishing Group, Inc.

Printed in the United States of America

The paper used in this book complies with the
Permanent Paper Standard issued by the National
Information Standards Organization (Z39.48–1984).

10 9 8 7 6 5 4 3 2

Copyright Acknowledgments

Grateful acknowledgment is given to the following sources: David John Lu, ed.,
Sources of Japanese History, vol. 1 (New York: McGraw-Hill, 1974). Reprinted by
permission of McGraw-Hill, Inc. Solomon B. Levine and Kawada Hisashi, *Human
Resources in Japanese Industrial Development*. Copyright © 1980 by Princeton University Press. Tables, pp. 64, 70. Reprinted by permission of Princeton University
Press.

Contents

Introduction	vii
1. The Historical Context of Japanese Education to 1945 MARK LINCICOME	1
2. The Development of Japanese Educational Policy, 1945–1985 EDWARD R. BEAUCHAMP	27
3. Education Reform in Japan: Goals and Results of the Recent Reform Campaign LEONARD SCHOPPA	51
4. Financing Japanese Education ICHIKAWA SHOGO	77
5. The Japanese Preschool System SARANE SPENCE BOOCOCK	97
6. Task Persistence in Japanese Elementary Schools PRISCILLA N. BLINCO	127
7. Teaching of Mathematics in Japanese Schools NANCY C. WHITMAN	139
8. Japan's Science and Engineering Pipeline: Structure, Policies, and Trends WILLIAM K. CUMMINGS	175

9. The Contribution of Education to Japan's Economic Growth
   ROBERT EVANS, JR. — 209

10. The Education of Women in Japan
    KUMIKO FUJIMURA-FANSELOW and ANNE E. IMAMURA — 229

11. Teacher Education in Japan
    NOBUO SHIMAHARA — 259

12. The Role of Education in Preserving the Ethnic Identity of Korean Residents in Japan
    UMAKOSHI TORU — 281

13. "Examination Hell"
    PETER FROST — 291

14. The Future of Japanese Higher Education
    KITAMURA KAZUYUKI — 307

15. Postscript: What Can We Learn from Japan?
    EDWARD R. BEAUCHAMP — 321

Index — 327

About the Contributors — 333

Introduction

In recent years American interest in Japanese education has grown by leaps and bounds. Japanese education has, indeed, become a growth industry not only among academics, but also in the popular and mass media. Almost without exception articles, books, and television talk shows and documentaries have focused on the strengths of Japan's educational system which can, perhaps, best be summed up in the title of Ezra Vogel's best-selling book, *Japan as Number One*.

We have been told that the performance of Japanese students on international tests of educational achievement is the highest in the world: 99.5 percent of all Japan's youngsters successfully complete the nine years of compulsory education through grade nine, and almost 95 percent actually go on to complete the noncompulsory three years of upper secondary school (as opposed to only 78 percent of their U.S. counterparts); at least 35 percent of Japanese high school graduates go on to some form of higher education; Japan's national curriculum ensures that all pupils are exposed to a rich and challenging curriculum no matter where they live in Japan, and equality of educational opportunity is substantially assured to all; and Japan's smaller population produces approximately twice as many engineers as the much larger United States. One could go on to talk about the diligence of Japanese students, their willingness to attend special after school classes at significant economic costs, and their success in passing through the famous "examination hell."

Early in the Reagan administration, Japan's minister of education visited Washington, D.C., and was told by our then Secretary of Education, Terrel Bell, that the United States "must have *juku* [cram schools] because the Japanese are so productive. What we need is a continuation of your magnificent example."

Bell was reportedly taken aback when his Japanese guest told him that the Japanese would like to do away with *juku*. Bell lamely responded that he did not really know what *juku* were. "I thought," he continued, that "maybe the teachers stayed after school" to hold extra classes for the students. "I was going to ask the minister how he persuaded [the teachers] to do that, since I know that would be a problem in a unionized system."[1] This anecdote illustrates the old adage that "a little knowledge is a dangerous thing" as well as the dangers inherent in advocating educational borrowing.

Americans often view Japanese education as an abstract ideal that we should strive to emulate. Indeed, the American system has been under serious attack, not only by critics at both ends of the political spectrum, but also by many of its traditional supporters. The following quotation will sound familiar:

The . . . education system enjoyed a rapid, unprecedented and continuous expansion of enrollment and financial resources during the 60's followed by a plateau in the early 70's. Recently from the mid-70's and into the 80's, we face a period of no expansion, or decline. A decrease in the age-cohort population has just reached its lowest point at the kindergarten . . . level since the WW II baby boom. . . .

In addition to decreasing enrollment, financial problems are increasing. Before the mid-1970's, "education" and "social welfare" . . . had long been exceptional cases recognized by government treasurers as "sanctuaries" in which budget cuts never occurred. However since the mid–70's these sanctuaries are no longer exempt from cuts due to an increasing deficit in revenue.

Now, many probably think that the above quote comes from the National Commission on Excellence in Education's 1983 *A Nation at Risk* or from one of the other numerous critical reports of recent years that deal with American education. The above quotations, however, are from a distinguished observer of Japanese education, Professor Kitamura Kazuyuki of Hiroshima University.[2] Most scholars, both American and Japanese, tend to see their respective educational situations in terms quite different from those of their counterparts. They tend to evaluate their own system against a highly idealized version of the other, and Professor Kitamura's remarks illustrate the irony of widespread American adulation of Japanese schooling at a time when virtually all Japanese policy-makers, as well as large numbers of the public, are expressing dissatisfaction with what they see as a malaise within the system and a need for fundamental reform.

There is much about Japanese schooling that is excellent and worthy of our closest attention. On the other hand, given the widespread positive view of Japanese education in the United States, we have often neglected to recognize that not even the Japanese argue that their schools are without blemish. This volume of essays on various elements of Japanese education attempts to present a balanced picture of Japan's educational enterprise—its considerable strengths as well as its weaknesses.

All of the contributors, Japanese and American, are well versed in the political, social, and economic contexts within which Japanese schools socialize children and have perceptive insights into the realities of Japanese classrooms. Although each essay represents the individual author's perspective of his or her subject, all the authors write in the context of the larger political, social, and economic dimensions that help shape Japan's society. A careful reading of these essays will result not only in a fund of important data but also in a balanced view of the realities of Japanese education.

Finally, Japanese names are rendered in customary Japanese Style - i.e. family name first.

NOTES

1. "US Educ. Sec. Envies *Juku*," *Mainichi Daily News*, September 13, 1984, p. 1.
2. Kitamura Kazuyuki, "Decline and Reform in Japan" (Paper presented at the Learning from Each Other Conference, Honolulu: East-West Center, August 1984).

1

The Historical Context of Japanese Education to 1945

Mark Lincicome

INTRODUCTION

In the fifth month of 1790, Matsudaira Sadanobu (1758–1829), chief councillor of the Tokugawa bakufu and regent to the shōgun, issued a decree to Hayashi Kimpō, rector of the Shōheikō, where the study and explication of neo-Confucianism had enjoyed official support since 1630. It warned that:

> Since the Keichō era (1596–1614), all generations have put their trust in Neo-Confucianism, and your house has been ordered to support that doctrine. Therefore, you should watchfully encourage that orthodoxy and promote its students. Recently, however, the world has witnessed the rise of several new doctrines; heterodoxy has become a fashion; customs have suffered from it; and orthodoxy [*seigaku*, written with characters, meaning 'correct learning' or 'sacred learning'] has declined. This is a deeply regrettable situation. Even among your pupils, it is said, impure doctrines have spread. I hereby order you to discipline the school strictly.... Regardless of whose students they are, they should study orthodoxy, and in this way you should apply yourself to promoting the formation of talented men.[1]

Matsudaira's ban on heterodox doctrines (*igaku no kin*) was the last in a series of administrative and economic initiatives comprising the Kansei Reform (*Kansei no kaikaku*), undertaken to preserve Tokugawa hegemony over a society undergoing momentous changes in every sphere of human activity. These changes had begun to challenge the boundaries of accepted knowledge, as scholars struggled to account for them without violating doctrinaire explanations based on the commonly recognized philosophical canon. The views branded as heterodox posed a threat to the Tokugawa bakufu because they implicitly questioned the validity of the worldview that served to legitimize its political and moral authority and because they offered the possibility of conceptualizing a different political and social order.

The ban had far-reaching implications, both for politics and for education in Tokugawa Japan:

> Before the ban of 1790 the bakufu had never identified itself in an explicit and exclusive manner with any one ideology.... Nor had the bakufu—its long association with the Hayashi School notwithstanding—ever imposed its control over one institution to foster such ideology to the exclusion of others. Sadanobu changed this situation. Following his pattern of increasing state control, he gave Neo-Confucianism the status of an official ideology and transformed the Hayashi School from a semi-private to a state institution.[2]

But the reason for citing this event is not to depict it as an epochal turning point in the history of Japanese education, foreshadowing more recent efforts by the Japanese state to manipulate education for ideological purposes. For, on the contrary, as will be explained below, Matsudaira's heavy-handed gesture did not silence the Tokugawa period heretics.[3] It merely altered the conditions under which competing interests subsequently contested bakufu power and authority and eventually helped topple it less than eighty years later.

What this episode does illustrate is the critical link between social relations and education, which must be addressed in any historical account of education. Education reflects a society's capacity to produce, reproduce, adapt, and consume itself[4] because it is both an agent and a product of those pursuits. Diverse and often complex educational formations—each one distinguished by its own particular configuration of accepted knowledge, theory, practice, and institutions—that appear and disappear over the course of a society's history as it attempts to act upon itself and its environment, reproduce itself, and endow itself with meaning are neither created nor sanctioned by metasocial, evolutionary forces acting upon that society. Rather, they are produced *by* that society, within a "field of conflictive creation" that is marked by competing class interests and animated by "debates and conflicts, political initiatives and claims, ideologies and alienations."[5]

The following historical survey of Japanese education begins, therefore, with the premise that for any society, in any age, efforts to articulate, build, and sustain a viable educational formation confront a common set of fundamental problems—concerning the definition of knowledge, access to knowledge, and the uses to which it is put—that lacks a common set of corresponding answers. Resolution of these problems must occur historically, through the action of that society upon itself.

Consequently, this particular interpretation of the activity guiding the development of Japanese education resists the common tendency simply to plot its trajectory as a smooth and orderly path along an evolutionary continuum. Instead, an attempt will be made to analyze that activity, both diachronically and synchronically, as a product of social relations subject to tension, confusion, contestation, and discontinuity.

THE CLASSICAL PERIOD (7TH TO 12TH CENTURIES)

Ever since the introduction of writing from the Asian mainland first prompted the formation of an educational system in Japan, the pursuit of literacy and learning was monopolized by the ruling class. Indeed, the link between knowledge and power was established partly through the introduction of literacy since the Chinese writing system that was brought to Japan was not fully separable from its content, which centered on Confucian ideas of political organization and practice as well as Buddhist theology.[6]

Not only did familiarity with the classical Confucian and Buddhist texts come to be regarded as a prerequisite for leadership during this period, but so, too, the ability to prepare, issue, and implement written edicts based on the principles contained therein.[7] Confucianism also imposed other stipulations on claimants to power, including familiarity with rites, music, and poetry, while early Buddhist sects developed elaborate rituals catering to the aristocracy. In addition, Confucian respect for historical precedent, coupled with the Chinese practice of preparing official histories to glorify dynastic accomplishments, presented new opportunities for the ruling elite in classical Japan to construct and sanction a putative record of the past that would explain and legitimize existing political arrangements.

Little wonder that, from early in the period, members of the court aristocracy took steps to endow themselves and their posterity with at least the trappings of continental culture through the formation of both secular and religious educational arrangements. Passing references to specific schools can already be found in seventh-century literature, although little is known about them. The first extensive evidence of secular education in classical Japan appears in the Taihō Code (*Taihō ritsuryō*) of 701 and in a revision to that code, promulgated in 718, which mandated the creation of the Imperial University (*daigakuryō*).[8]

These laws outlined both the administrative structure and the composition of the faculty of the university. Instruction was to be provided in the Confucian canon, the spoken and written sound system, writing, and mathematics. Law and letters were added to the curriculum in 728, as was history in 735. Enrollment, initially set at 430, was restricted to the children of high-ranking families between the ages of thirteen and sixteen, although others from designated lower ranks could petition for entry.[9]

In addition to the university located in the capital, Heian-kyō, provision was made in the code for the establishment of provincial schools called *kokugaku*. Their major function was to groom the children of provincial government officials to succeed their fathers, although graduates were also eligible to petition for service in the central government. Another possibility for accomplished students at these schools was entry into the university. Standard enrollment at these schools varied between twenty and fifty students.[10]

Supporting the university was a second tier of schools knows as *zōshi*,[11] which housed students enrolled at the university and supplemented their education with training in other facets of their future official duties. One of these schools, the *Monjōin*, was directly affiliated with the university; others were supported by high-ranking noble families.[12]

Long before the Taihō Code had designated the education of the ruling class to be a function of the government, Buddhist adherents were sponsoring their own educational activities, often with official support and encouragement. By the time that Shōtoku Taishi (574–622), regent to the emperor and an early champion of Buddhism, passed away, there were nearly fifty monasteries and nunneries in Japan, supported by assigned lands and sustaining more than 1,000 monks and nuns. In these institutions the sutras were studied, the religion was propagated, and the education of the aristocracy was advanced.[13]

Through such arrangements, the intellectual and cultural line of demarcation separating the rulers from the ruled was drawn and reinforced, since no comparable educational opportunities existed for the latter, at least not for very long. Briefly, during the seventh and eighth centuries, when their own social and political positions were still in flux, the rulers permitted various schools of Buddhist thought to flourish, encouraged the construction of monasteries for families and even commoners, and allowed unlicensed as well as licensed monks to teach. But as they tightened their grip on power, the elite moved to channel and restrict Buddhist thought and practice.[14] Over time, this led to a marked distinction between what Conrad Totman calls "aristocratic Buddhism" and "plebeian religion." The former, catering to a literate elite, was expounded by formally educated monks familiar with sophisticated religious thought. The latter, appealing to a largely illiterate mass, was communicated by unlettered practitioners professing magicoreligious insights borrowed from folk wisdom and custom rather than the study of sophisticated texts.[15]

Ironically, however, it was the very success of the ruling class in fashioning for itself a privileged world of political order and cultural refinement, isolated from the lower classes on whom it depended for economic survival, that precipitated its gradual stagnation and decline. That trend is clearly reflected in the educational institutions and practices just described. By the end of the tenth century the university had lost much of its former luster. In a memorial he submitted to the throne in 904, one distinguished scholar, whose career included professor of literature, provincial governor, rector of the university, and state councillor, observed that students had come to regard the university

> as the place to meet unfulfilled dreams and disappointment. To them it also becomes a place of poverty, hunger and cold. Parents admonish each other not to send their sons to school. Thus the quadrangle between the south and north halls is overrun by wild grass, and there is no one in the east and west study halls. At the time of making

recommendations, professors do not take into account the talent of the candidates, but simply glance at a list of students. In this manner the labors of many are wasted, and favoritism arises, causing the unqualified to prosper.[16]

Education at the university had become formalistic, antiquated, and increasingly irrelevant to a student's prospects for entering government service.[17] Little wonder that after fire destroyed the school in 1177 it was never rebuilt.

The *kokugaku* had disappeared entirely from the provincial landscape long before as the ancient system of laws that had reinforced the power of the central government slowly crumbled.[18]

Similar problems beset the educational activities of the established Buddhist monasteries. The priesthood became an accepted career alternative for aristocratic family members who found the door to secular positions closed to them. Within the Buddhist establishment they maintained their aristocratic orientation. Such an outlook was actually encouraged by the administrative structure of the monasteries: "as the education of promising acolytes progressed, they were steadily promoted upward from provincial monasteries toward the main monastery of their sect. They were inevitably absorbed into the aristocratic milieu rather than forming an effective outward-oriented linkage between metropolis and hinterland."[19]

But even as the social relations between patrician and plebian led to the eventual stagnation of aristocratic education by the end of the classical age, they simultaneously prompted new educational initiatives among those whom the elite institutions had failed to serve. This trend became more pronounced once political and economic power had fully passed into the hands of the newly ascendent warrior class, inaugurating the medieval age.

THE MEDIEVAL PERIOD (12TH TO 16TH CENTURIES)

The collapse of aristocratic hegemony toward the end of the twelfth century had begun long before with the gradual accumulation of economic and military power by the provincial samurai. Many of these samurai were themselves of aristocratic lineage but had been forced by law or by circumstances to abandon their hereditary claims. Commissioned to protect the interests of the nobility from encroachment by rivals, they succeeded in establishing their own economic and political bases outside the capital at the same time. Once the center collapsed, the stability that had characterized Japanese society in the classical age gave way to an era of fluidity in which politics and culture were decentralized, along with education.

The absence of a strong central government discouraged the organization of a common, secular school system. Rather, it was in religious, chiefly Buddhist, institutions that the greatest educational opportunities continued to be found.[20] A major difference between the classical and medieval periods, however, was that such opportunities were no longer limited to the nobility.

According to William LaFleur, "In many ways Buddhism performed in medieval Japan much of the role now customarily assigned to science. It did so by giving to the epoch a basic map of reality, one that provided cognitive satisfaction not only to learned monks in monasteries but also to unlettered peasants in the countryside."[21]

The older established sects, whose emphasis on textual study and elaborate rituals had appealed to an aristocratic class with sufficient wealth and time to pursue them, failed to meet the worldly needs of the samurai. Furthermore, in many cases, these monasteries represented substantial bases of economic and military power rivaling that of the samurai. These conditions encouraged the adoption of newer doctrines, such as Zen and Amidism, that eschewed heavy dependence on texts as sources of knowledge in favor of knowledge grounded in individual being and action. In addition, efforts were made to harmonize Shintō, Confucian, Taoist, and Buddhist perspectives through a discursive process that not only broadened the appeal of Buddhism among literate and illiterate alike, but also enabled its purveyors to cast Buddhism (and themselves) in a superior light vis-à-vis its rivals.[22] Some of the resulting sects attracted substantial followings, not only among the samurai but also among commoners.

Temples were established in towns and villages throughout the country. In exchange for economic support from members of the surrounding community, they offered basic, practical instruction in reading, writing, and mathematics—skills demanded by an expanding and diversifying economy—in addition to religion and ethics. They were the forerunners of the *terakoya* (writing schools) that were a mainstay of education for commoners during the Tokugawa period.[23]

To reinforce their position as legitimate heirs to the power they had expropriated from the nobility, the samurai exhibited a similar propensity to assert class privilege. This led to the outward preservation of the court structure and institutional arrangements centered around the emperor, as well as the appropriation of certain cultural forms developed by the nobility.

This growing interest in the amenities and privileges of rank may have been behind the establishment of the *gakumonjo*, which were schools located within the residences of certain noble and upper samurai families. In most cases, these consisted of exclusive, private arrangements between the teacher and his students. However, at least one of these, the Ashikaga School (*Ashikaga Gakkō*), founded by the Ashikaga family at the beginning of the Kamakura period (1185–1382), was revitalized in 1439 by the warrior Uesugi Norizane (1411–1466), who opened it to monks and other samurai occupying local positions of authority. Uesugi reformed the school's course of instruction, commended land to support it, enriched the library, and appointed as its director a Zen monk. The curriculum concentrated on Confucian learning, with particular emphasis placed on divination studies based on the Book of Changes (*I Ching*). However, in the 1570s, during the civil war period, the school also began to offer lectures on military science and medicine, and many of its graduates became military advisers.[24]

Christianity, another catalyst for the spread of education in the medieval age, would become a growing source of suspicion and consternation during the Tokugawa period, for it represented a new source of authority and a new body of knowledge that competed with accepted doctrines for popular allegiance. Shortly after their arrival from Portugal in 1549, the first Jesuit missionaries began establishing not only churches but also primary schools throughout the country in order to serve the children of the faithful and to strengthen their base of community support. Two hundred such schools were opened between 1561 and 1583 where, in addition to religious instruction, children might be taught reading, writing, composition, singing, and perhaps Latin or mathematics. Some of them recorded enrollments as high as forty, fifty, even seventy students.[25]

Beginning in 1580, these missionaries took the next step of opening a small number of seminaries offering secondary and higher educational opportunities to those willing to follow them into the priesthood. Students at the secondary level received training in Japanese, Latin, Christian doctrine, Buddhism, history, composition, and singing. To the regular curriculum was added instruction in painting, copperplate sculpture, printing, and the manufacture of organs, watches, and instruments used in astronomy. Enrollment at these schools averaged between twenty and thirty students. At the institutions of higher learning the principal subjects of study were theology and philosophy.[26]

This diversity of educational options did not simply reflect the broader distribution of, and competition for, economic and political power that characterized social relations in medieval Japan, but also helped perpetuate it. On the other hand, as contending groups resorted increasingly to military force in order to settle disputes and gain advantage, the resulting unrest and instability hampered the further development of education in Japan. That had to await the succeeding Tokugawa period, when a strong measure of central authority was restored.

THE TOKUGAWA PERIOD (1600–1868)

From the latter part of the fifteenth century throughout the sixteenth, Japan was racked by persistent warfare between rival domains seeking to extend their power. Indicative of the fluidity of social relations during this period was a process known as *gekokujō*, literally "those below toppling those above," in which "local warrior leaders overthrew their lords, forged larger domains, and, in turn, were overthrown by some of their own vassals and other challengers."[27]

Battlefield victories were likewise responsible for Tokugawa Ieyasu's eventual ascension to power in the late sixteenth century, but consolidating and maintaining that power in the seventeenth demanded more than the threat of further military action. Ending the cycle of *gekokujō* required the creation of new political, social, and economic arrangements supported by a commonly accepted form of authority. Education was again to be both a product of, and an influence on, this process.

Long before Matsudaira Sadanobu had issued his aforementioned ban on heterodox doctrines, the Tokugawa bakufu moved to check the spread of certain rival systems of thought that posed a challenge to its authority. The magnitude of that challenge is suggested by the severity with which they were dealt.

The strong following that Buddhist institutions enjoyed among all social classes in medieval Japan made them early targets of regulation. Already by the 1580s, Ieyasu's predecessors had recognized this threat and had dealt with it harshly by ruthlessly attacking and destroying the headquarters of the most militant Buddhist sects, together with their supporters. To prevent their revival, the bakufu restricted the authority of the imperial court to grant the highest Buddhist ranks after 1615, eroded the financial bases of the major temples, and transformed them into administrative subdivisions of the bakufu government by imposing on them the function of keeping census records. Furthermore, it issued periodic regulations limiting the activities of monks. One such document, dated 1665, enjoined monks from mixing and disarranging the doctrines and rituals established for different sects and from preaching unorthodox doctrines if a new rite was established. It also determined criteria for entry into the priesthood, cautioning the clergy not to allow anyone "who is not of good lineage" to become a disciple. "If there is a particular candidate who has an improper and questionable background," it warned, "the judgement of the domainal lord or magistrate of his domicile must be sought and then act accordingly."[28]

Christianity met an even harsher fate. By the beginning of the seventeenth century it, too, had attracted a measure of support among the population: mostly poor peasants as well as smaller numbers of samurai and urban dwellers. Hence, an uneasy tolerance at the beginning of the Tokugawa period soon gave way to a series of stern edicts and extreme government actions: from the first order calling for the expulsion of foreign missionaries in 1614 to occasional mass executions of Japanese Christians and foreign priests beginning in 1618. By 1639, the year of the third and final expulsion order, and two years after their largest and most prolonged antigovernment revolt, Christian churches and schools were closed, and the small body of faithful who remained were reduced to practicing their faith in secret or renouncing it entirely.[29]

Although their religious authority was thus emasculated, it is important to note the contributions that Buddhism and Christianity each made to the subsequent development of secular education during this period. Buddhism had provided training in literacy and learning to many of the early Tokugawa political leaders and scholars who would help to shape educational policy in the new era. And the study of medicine, astronomy, navigation, and other scientific subjects, introduced by Christian missionaries to Japan, provided the foundation for the so-called barbarian studies (*nambangaku*) which, in turn, encouraged the development of Dutch studies (*rangaku*). These would gain increasing respect throughout the period, as rulers and ruled alike embraced and exploited the call for "practical study" (*jitsugaku*).[30]

Meanwhile, the bakufu slowly moved to define a distinct canon of knowledge and belief that would legitimize its authority and a new political order, while making access to that knowledge a prerogative of the ruling class. As noted earlier, it was not until Matsudaira issued his decree to the Shōheikō in 1790 that neo-Confucianism was belatedly identified as the doctrine that "all generations have put their trust in." Nevertheless, through its provision of financial and political support to Hayashi Razan, founder of the school, and his descendants ever since Razan's appointment as Ieyasu's adviser in 1607, the bakufu had helped to make possible the emergence of neo-Confucianism as an independent system of thought, expropriating it from its medieval custodians, the Buddhist clergy.

Neo-Confucianism had a pervasive impact on education throughout the Tokugawa period. Initially, it inspired the creation of a recognized intellectual class, composed of individual scholars who enjoyed considerable freedom to develop their own competing analyses and interpretations of the Confucian texts. To propound those views, a number of them established independent schools—of which the Shōheikō under the Hayashi family was but one example—which brought together interested students for organized study of those texts. Others found employment in the various domains (*han*) where, in addition to serving as advisers to the domainal lords, many provided instruction in the classics—and the attendent skills of reading and writing—to their retainers. Eventually, out of this intellectual and pedagogical ferment emerged a common discourse concerning education itself, which defined its purpose, specified its content, designated a methodology, established certain broad criteria for the evaluation of its purveyors, and identified its legitimate recipients. As summarized by Ronald Dore:

[T]he means of education were provided by Chinese writings, especially the Confucian classics; its purpose was primarily to develop moral character, both as an absolute human duty and also in order to better fulfill the samurai's function in society; a secondary purpose was to gain from the classics that knowledge of men and affairs and of the principles of government which was also necessary for the proper performance of the samurai's duties. Certain other technical vocational skills were necessary which could not be gained from classical Chinese study. Also, classical Chinese study itself brought certain legitimate fringe benefits in the form of life-enhancing aesthetic pleasures.[31]

Thus, the political utility of neo-Confucianism for the bakufu was partly a function of its concurrent development as a comprehensive educational doctrine. That doctrine held sway until the end of the eighteenth century, not only within the schools supported by the bakufu, but in many of the domain schools (*hankō*) established by its rivals.

In contrast, the attitude of Tokugawa neo-Confucianism toward education for members of the lower classes—peasant, artisan, and merchant—might be described as one of benign neglect. At one extreme were those who argued that too much education among the lower classes would invariably breed arrogance and disrespect for authority.[32] Furthermore, it would distract them from much more important tasks. The latter concern was especially acute in the case of farmers, whose production of rice provided the major source of tax revenue upon which the samurai class depended for its survival.

Accordingly, the bakufu promulgated a series of edicts that carefully identified the rights and duties of each strata in a carefully defined class hierarchy, along with numerous laws designed to regulate nearly every aspect of their daily lives, from work habits to food and clothing. In effect, these regulations constituted a surreptitious educational policy. On one hand, they were intended to instill complete acceptance of the feudal order.[33] In one set of injunctions, for example, peasants were admonished to "Consider the Lord of your domain the sun and the moon. Respect your fief holder (*jitō*) or magistrate (*daikan*) as the patron diety (*uji gami*) of your place. Treat your village head (*kimoiri*) as if he were your own father."[34]

On the other hand, these regulations mandated no time for educational pursuits. Instead, almost every waking hour was to be devoted to some aspect of their livelihood as farmers.[35] With or without such official injunctions, it would appear that the working lives of the peasants made acquiring an education a formidable prospect.

Other members of the ruling class held that a certain amount of education for the moral refinement of the lower classes was desirable, in the belief that it would make them more obedient and loyal, more devoted to their superiors, more efficient and diligent producers, and more tractable subjects.[36] Even so, throughout most of the Tokugawa period, it was rare for domainal authorities who might have been persuaded by this opinion to permit the enrollment of commoners in the official domain schools, and it was just as rare for them to establish special schools for commoners. Instead, they might employ the occasional services of a Confucian scholar to travel to different villages for the purpose of lecturing adults and children on proper morality, or simply post on town and village notice boards a list of moral precepts for them to follow.[37]

In spite of, or perhaps because of, samurai attitudes and policies concerning commoner education, the lower classes were largely free to provide for their own educational needs within the limits of their individual resources. For most parents and their children, the impetus to acquire at least a rudimentary education was economic demand for training in the three Rs, together with practical information relevant to their hereditary occupations. As such, a good deal of this training continued to take place in the home, under the guidance of one's own parents or at the direction of another family to whom one might be apprenticed.

As time went on, however, more and more families, particularly those of the merchant class, began delegating some of the responsibility for their children's education to teachers operating small writing schools known variously as *terakoya* and *tenaraisho*. A wide variety of institutional arrangements were covered by these terms. For example, not all schools served commoners exclusively; some were designed primarily for the children of lower samurai who were not admitted to the domain schools. Some were established by charitably disposed priests, doctors, or well-to-do farmers or village officials who considered it their paternalistic duty to share their learning with villagers or townsmen, while others were run by scholars or *rōnin* samurai on a tuition basis, which was often paid through in-kind gifts.[38]

The power of neo-Confucian discourse to guide the formation of this elaborate hierarchical system of education could be sustained only so long as it satisfied the particular educational requirements of Tokugawa society in general and the samurai ruling class in particular. Over time, however, those requirements changed faster than the system could adjust to them. This prompted both criticism of the existing system and the efforts to reform it.

A number of factors combined to render its emphasis on moral training obsolete. Foremost among them was the transition from an agrarian to a mixed economy, which brought about a gradual redistribution of financial resources into the hands of the merchant class at the expense of both the peasants and the samurai. At the same time, with the onset of peace following centuries of intermittent warfare and with their removal from the land to the castle towns that now functioned as administrative centers overseeing domainal affairs, the samurai themselves underwent a metamorphosis from warriors to bureaucratic functionaries, facing new responsibilites that an orthodox Confucian education did not fully prepare them to assume.[39]

According to Tokugawa neo-Confucianism, the purpose of studying the Chinese classics was to discover the eternal, unchanging moral principle governing both the natural world and human society. Thereafter, maintaining peace and harmony in society was largely a matter of the ruler applying that knowledge to rectify his own inner mind and outward conduct, thereby serving as a compelling example of virtue for others to follow, each according to his own proper position in the social hierarchy. When changing circumstances rendered this doctrine problematic, others arose to challenge it.

One of the earliest and most devastating critiques was put forward by proponents of ancient studies (*kogaku*), which, not surprisingly, was the principal target of Matsudaira's ban on heterodox views in 1790.[40] Ancient studies rejected neo-Confucianism's moralistic and naturalistic assumptions as a basis of government. Instead, it argued that the real purpose of study was to acquire a practical knowledge of the techniques of government that were invented by the sages and used in ancient China prior to the time of Confucius.[41] Furthermore, one must learn the art of modifying and applying those techniques, or even inventing new ones, since they were not immutable, anymore than society was.

The appearance of ancient studies and its considerable following during the eighteenth century came in response to dramatic economic and social changes which implicitly questioned the bakufu's moralistic claim to political authority, which was based on orthodox neo-Confucianism. Although the aim of the scholars who propagated ancient studies was to preserve the bakufu-domain order (*bakuhan seido*), its long-term effects on Tokugawa period politics and education were truly revolutionary. In the political realm, ancient studies implicitly denied the bakufu's claim that the Tokugawa distribution of power and the institutions (including education) which maintained it were ordained by nature for all time.

In the educational realm, ancient studies emphasized the promotion of talent (*jinzai*), and practical training in the techniques of statecraft, over the cultivation of one's moral nature.[42] Furthermore, it implicitly questioned the claim that learning was exclusively a hereditary privilege of the samurai. In principle, anyone could govern, provided he had acquired the requisite knowledge of the Way of the Ancient Sages and had demonstrated superior talent.

While the immediate effect of the ban on heterodox doctrines appears to have been a decline in enrollment at even the most popular schools of ancient studies, it clearly did not lay to rest the issues that had been raised, since the problems stemming from economic and social change were not resolved by Matsudaira's Kansei Reform program. This provided fertile ground for the cultivation of other heterodox doctrines that all contributed to the late Tokugawa discourse on politics and education. Among the most influential were (1) Western studies (*yōgaku*), including Dutch studies, formerly the preserve of private scholars, doctors, and *rōnin* samurai, which gained stature during the nineteenth century as the threat of Western military encroachment loomed larger; (2) nativism (*kokugaku*), which rejected slavish imitation of Chinese institutions and adherence to Chinese texts in favor of rediscovering the superior essence or spirit of native culture manifested in the ancient Japanese texts; (3) Mito learning (*mitogaku*), which combined neo-Confucianism's belief in a natural social order with nativism's elevation of Japanese culture over Chinese culture and advocated propagating this native cultural and spiritual essence as a national religion, equal in power to that of Christianity in the West.[43] Each of these doctrines was developed and propagated through educational channels—private academies (*shijuku*) in the case of Dutch studies and nativism, and the Mito domain school in the case of Mito learning—and each found its way into the curricula of bakufu and domain schools around the country during the final years of the Tokugawa period.[44]

Contrary to conventional accounts of this period, the often contentious discursive activity that engaged the advocates of these doctrines during the late Tokugawa period did not end with the Meiji Restoration in 1868. Competing political activists and educators representing diverse interests all proclaimed the restoration a victory for their views.

THE POST-RESTORATION PERIOD (1868–1945)

The legacy of Tokugawa education for the Meiji era (1868–1912) encompassed more than just the high rate of literacy, the development of national consciousness, and the propensity to view education as an avenue to personal as well as national improvement that scholars such as Ronald Dore and Herbert Passin have documented in their classic studies.[45] In addition to these attributes, which they assert were partly responsible for Japan's rapid achievement of political independence, industrialization, and economic growth, there was another side to the legacy, wherein knowledge itself had become a problem with far-reaching implications.

By the end of the Tokugawa period, neo-Confucianism was being openly challenged and with it the bakufu's claim to authority, not only through the political rhetoric of ideologues like Yoshida Shōin (1830–1859), who inspired a generation of samurai activists who studied at his private school, but also through the introduction of nontraditional subjects into the curricula of both private and domain schools.

At the same time, the weakening of the Tokugawa class hierarchy, purportedly part of the neo-Confucian natural order, raised questions about who should have access to knowlege and, by extension, to positions of power.

In this sense, the overthrow of the bakufu was a referendum on the conception of knowledge and the worldview defined as "orthodox" by Matsudaira's ban in 1790, along with the institutions that perpetuated them. The verdict, as interpreted by those whom events brought to power in 1868, was more than simply a repudiation of the recent past. It was a mandate for change, albeit draped in the mantle of "imperial restoration." However, this slogan accommodated a variety of conflicting opinions about precisely what kind and degree of change was called for. These disagreements were not limited to the political sphere, but they spilled over into educational discourse and action, as well.

The uneasy alliance between court nobles, domainal lords, and lower samurai that was responsible for defeating the bakufu showed continued volatility even after the restoration. Early signs suggested a victory for nativist ideologues and the court nobility, who took their own calls to "restore antiquity" literally by proposing to resurrect the eighth-century university (*daigakuryō*) under imperial aegis in Kyoto. The difference was that the curriculum would be based on Shintō and nativism, rather than on Confucian thought. At the same time, the Peer's School (*gakushūin*) was reopened in Kyoto for the purpose of preparing members of the nobility to assume positions in the restoration government.[46]

In opposition to this interpretation of the restoration as a literal return to a pristine, prefeudal past stood the Imperial Oath of Five Articles (*gokajō no goseimon*), which was drafted by samurai members of the ruling alliance and promulgated with imperial sanction in the spring of 1868. Perhaps because of its obvious political importance,[47] little attention has been paid to the educational significance of this document. Yet, whatever may have been its authors' intent, once it entered public discourse several of its famous articles could be, and were, interpreted by some educators as the new government's response to the fundamental problem of knowledge outlined above. The oath's promise that government policy would be decided on the basis of public opinion, expressed through deliberative assemblies, implied that knowledge and information would also be public and therefore accessible to all. Its vaguely worded assurance that all classes of people shall be allowed to achieve their aspirations could be taken to include the pursuit of knowledge, for personal as well as national advancement.

At the same time, uncivilized customs of former times were to be abolished through the impartial application of universal principles of justice and equality. And finally, the search for knowledge would no longer be confined to national borders or the bounds of canonical taste but would be extended throughout the world.

It is a reflection of the magnitude of the problem it inherited that the new Meiji government was compelled to offer, with imperial endorsement, such a radical solution: mandating the production of new social relations, institutions, and a supporting ideology. And it is a reflection of the nature of the problem that the process through which society produced itself following the restoration was frequently animated by tension and conflict in the educational sphere. The dialectics of this process, whereby the actions of competing interest groups both inside and outside the government continuously influenced each other, can be appreciated by reviewing some of their specific manifestations.

The first major educational debate in this period focused on the curriculum of a newly established, government-support university (*daigaku*), which was formed by merging together three bakufu institutions: the Shōheikō, with its tradition of Confucian and, more recently, Japanese studies; the Kaiseijo, which had been a center of Western learning; and the Igakujo, or medical school. During 1869, debate raged among the faculties of nativism and Chinese studies over the proper direction of education at the university and, by implication, throughout the country, since the university at this time also functioned as the administrative center for the nation's fledgling educational system. Later that year the debate shifted to the Shūgiin, a government advisory body, which sparked further rhetorical clashes among the teachers and students.[48]

In the end, neither party claimed victory, for the very next year the campus where both doctrines were being taught was closed, leaving only the faculties and students of Western studies and medical learning to gain dominance.[49] However, neither Confucian nor nativist rhetoric was completely expunged from educational discourse between 1868 and 1945. Elements of both were periodically reintroduced by different factions of the ruling class, either to challenge those government officials and advisors pushing for the adoption of Western educational theory and teaching methods, or to counter public opposition to government authority and policies.

One of the best examples of this internal struggle afflicting the ruling elite occurred in 1879 as the government prepared to revise Japan's first universal, compulsory education law, the Fundamental Code of Education (*gakusei*), which had been promulgated seven years earlier. This ordinance mandated central government control and authority over the rapid proliferation of schools that was occurring independently in regional centers around the country, such as Kyoto.[50] As will be discussed below, these expressions of local autonomy must have been disconcerting to a fledgling, self-appointed oligarchy that only the year before had finally gained the grudging compliance of former domainal lords with its 1869 order to return their lands to the emperor. The new education ordinance quickly came under fire from different quarters for a variety of reasons. Some complained that its overly ambitious plan to establish 53,760 elementary schools, 256 middle schools, and 8 universities created a heavy tax burden on local governments and the people. Others pointed out that the four years of compulsory education it stipulated was onerous for families dependent on the labor of their children for economic survival.[51]

What prompted the most vociferous debate among contending factions of the ruling elite, however, was the ideological emphasis of the curriculum under the Fundamental Code of Education. In a document known as the Great Principles of Education (*kyōgaku taishi*), which was issued as an imperial rescript in 1879, Motoda Nagazane (1818–1891), who held the post of Confucian lecturer to the emperor, complained that education under this law overemphasized the acquisition of Western knowledge and Western ways, to the neglect of the great principles governing education that were established by the nation's ancestors. According to those principles, the aim of education is to pursue the Way of Man by clarifying benevolence, justice, loyalty, and filial piety and by mastering knowledge and skills. The danger of indiscriminate emulation of the West is that the principles governing relations between ruler and subject, father and son, will be forgotten. To remedy this condition, Motoda specifically called for the study of morality (*dōtoku no gaku*) based on Confucius.

Motoda's observations were vigorously rebutted by Itō Hirobumi (1841–1909), in his capacity as home minister, in a document drafted by Inoue Kowashi (1844–1895) and known as the Opinion on Education (*kyōiku gi*). While acknowledging the deterioration of traditional customs and manners since the restoration, it maintained that this was not attributable to the government's educational policies, which had not been given enough time to prove their effectiveness. Instead, it argued that this condition was an inevitable consequence of sweeping social reforms instituted by the government which were necessary to correct the evils of the past. Hence, the solution did not lie in establishing a single national doctrine based on the Confucian classics, which is not a proper area of government control. Rather, it was best to patiently continue on the present course, which meant encouraging the development of individual talents through practical instruction, less for the sake of the individual than in order to strengthen and modernize the nation.

This dispute over educational doctrine concealed a struggle for political power within the Meiji government that continued interminably for over a decade. Its immediate effect on educational policy, however, was the abrupt promulgation in 1879 of a new Education Law (*kyōikurei*) in place of the Fundamental Code of Education, and its equally abrupt replacement by the Revised Education Law (*kaisei kyōikurei*) the very next year.[52] The Education Law, championed by Itō, responded to complaints that its predecessor had unduly burdened the people by mandating a reduction in the duration of compulsory education and the decentralization of educational control. The Revised Education Law reversed this liberalizing trend, in response to the concerns expressed by Motoda in the Great

Principles of Education. Among other things, it reasserted central government control over education, emphasized moral instruction in the curriculum, and made "proper character" a requirement for anyone wishing to become a teacher.[53]

While these polemical exchanges and strategic machinations were clearly directed against opposing factions within the ruling alliance, they were also jointly directed against other political forces outside the government known collectively as the freedom and popular rights movement (*jiyū minken undō*). This movement was initiated in 1874 by a handful of disgruntled government leaders who resigned their positions over policy differences. In a bid to regain a share of power, they formed political parties that rallied around calls for a constitutional, popularly elected form of government. By the end of the decade, however, the movement began to broaden its base of support, as other segments of society found in it an opportunity to voice their own criticisms of the government. One of their major concerns was education.

For example, in an 1877 memorial to the emperor from the Self-Help Society (*risshisha*) advocating the formation of a representative assembly, it was noted that establishing schools is "no doubt necessary and excellent, but when the ideas are carried out to an extravagant extent at the expense of the people, the only effect is to create a great deal of bitter feeling among the people, who complain that they are not profited by these new measures."[54] In 1882 Itagaki Taisuke (1837–1919), one of the founders of the movement, observed:

Public opinion is the axis round which should revolve government policy. On its prosperity or decay depends the prosperity or decay of the government. For its promotion and simultaneous inauguration of a beneficial policy we must educate the people in politics. A good administration and the felicity of the commonwealth are dependent upon public opinion, insomuch as the government can prevent their rulers from making arbitrary use of political power. If those who are governed are wholly ignorant and unable to impose any check upon their rulers by the expression of public opinion, even a good and perfect polity may degenerate into selfishness and tyranny, and the people will be deprived of all the benefits designed for them.[55]

Among those attracted to the freedom and popular rights movement were many teachers and students. Indeed, some of these political associations, including the Self-Help Society, formed their own private academies, where the curricula centered on English and French works on law, politics, and economics. Students would travel among these schools for debates and discussions.[56]

Both the educational and the political dimensions of this struggle between the new government and the freedom and popular rights movement centered on competing views of knowledge and its relationship to power. As aptly described by Horio Teruhisa (1933–), "The major difference between these interpretations was that the advocates of enlightenment from above sought to separate politics from scholarship and education, while those who supported enlightenment from below tried to make scholarship and education the foundation of a new kind of politics."[57] To the leaders of the movement, including Nakae Chōmin (1847–1901) and Ueki Emori (1857–1892), individual liberty and equality were sine qua non not only for a new kind of politics, but a new kind of education as well.[58]

The Education Law and the Revised Education Law each represented different responses to the threat posed by the freedom and popular rights movement: the former was one of mitigation, through the relaxation of central government control over education; the latter, one of confrontation, through the expansion of that control. Other laws dealt specifically with the political involvement of teachers and students through a policy of censorship and suppression. In April 1880, for example, eight months before the enactment of the Revised Education Law, the government issued an ordinance prohibiting teachers and students, together with soldiers, sailors, and police officers, from participating in political meetings.[59] And in December 1881, the Ministry of Education moved to curtail the use of school facilities for political speech gatherings; a tougher law expressly forbidding their use was announced in June 1883.[60]

In their accounts of educational and social development in Japan between 1868 and 1945, historians frequently cite the 1880 Revised Education Law as a watershed separating an initial period of unabashed enthusiasm for Western political and educational theories emphasizing individualism, natural rights, positivism, and utilitarianism from a subsequent period of conservative reaction to these "Western excesses." The chronology of events they usually cite proceeds from the Revised Education Law to the statist policies enacted by Mori Arinori (1847–1889) during his tenure as minister of education (1885–1889), and from there to the promulgation of the Imperial Rescript on Education (*kyōiku chokugo*) in 1890. According to these historians, the Rescript on Education provided an ideological foundation upon which the government formulated an educational policy of intense nationalistic indoctrination. As further proof of this, they frequently allude to the establishment of such celebrated school rituals as the principal's solemn reading of the Rescript on Education before the student body on national holidays and the imposition of complete government control over the production of textbooks in 1903. Ultimately, many of them conclude that the pervasive emphasis on emperor-centered nationalism throughout the school curriculum and the authoritarian nature of school life, coupled with the government's program of thought control outside the schools, made Japan's involvement in World War II inevitable. Ienaga Saburō (1913–), for example, writes:

The prewar state kept the populace in a powerful vise: on one side were the internal security laws with their restrictions on freedom of speech and thought; on the other side was the conformist education that blocked the growth of a free consciousness and purposive activity for political ends. The vise was tightened whenever any individual or popular resistance challenged reckless military action. These laws and public education, used as instruments of coercion and manipulation, were the decisive factors that made it impossible for the Japanese people to stop their country from launching the Pacific War.[61]

Unquestionably, education in Japan from the 1930s until 1945 was manipulated as an instrument of domination by the military government and its civilian supporters in order to avert public opposition to the Pacific War. But is it accurate to speak of a historical continuum linking this outcome to a series of unilateral government actions beginning in the 1880s? This view ignores the historical context of education, especially the social relations prompting the dialectical process through which education becomes an agent of its own development. This process can proceed, in spite of education's link to the dominant ideology, because education is "never reduced to that ideology completely, because it is the vehicle for knowledge, not just values, because it is dependent on a state in which nondenominant categories exert an influence, because its professional rhetoric remains distinct from the ideology of the ruling class, because the age groups within it put up a resistance to authority and its norms."[62]

Indeed, there is abundant evidence after 1880 to suggest that teachers and students were capable of challenging the government's ideological and organizational attempts to secure its domination over them and that, over time, the government was obliged to resort to harsher, more overt tactics of coercion and suppression precisely because small but vocal numbers of teachers and students did not readily succumb to its ideological domination.

Furthermore, in apposition to the purported connection between state control of education beginning in 1880 and Japan's "inevitable" entry into the Pacific War, it is possible to reconstruct concurrent links between the aforementioned freedom and popular rights movement and subsequent popular movements for educational reform. At different times, supporters of these movements ranged from local teachers and students to political parties and labor unions.

In a way, the government itself armed Japanese teachers in the post-Restoration period with their principal defense against passive ideological subjugation by encouraging them to develop a professional consciousness. This fostered their active and energetic participation in educational discourse through such vehicles as professional associations and publications. That discourse incorporated elements of educational philosophy, psychology, history, and methodology.

One of the earliest chapters in this saga concerns the doctrine of developmental education (*kaihatsushugi*) which was introduced into Japan during the 1870s and was initially disseminated among teachers around the country through government-sponsored normal schools and in-service training programs. Inspired by the American Pestalozzian movement, developmental education eventually cast a long shadow of influence over educational theory, teaching methods, curricula, and textbooks in Japanese primary and normal school between 1872 and approximately 1895. Its appeal for Japanese teachers lay in its positivistic approach to teaching and its opposition to the traditional teaching methods of rote memorization and "pouring in" (*chūnyū*) knowledge.

Developmental education carried with it a number of potentially revolutionary implications, both for Meiji education and for society in general. It challenged orthodox conceptions of education, knowledge, and the process by which children learn, which, in turn, cast doubt upon the suitability of existing primary school curricula and textbooks, which ultimately broached the issue of who— teachers, school administrators, government bureaucrats—should be empowered to create, inspect, and authorize new ones. By insisting upon a child-centered approach to education, in place of the earlier teacher-centered one, developmental education actually enhanced the position and responsibilities of the teacher vis- à-vis the work of schooling. Consequently, it provided teachers with a legitimizing claim to professional authority and autonomy and also lent support to the concept of a decentralized educational system, at a time when the state was moving in precisely the opposite direction by attempting to consolidate its power over teachers, students, and virtually every major facet of the Japanese school system.[63]

Developmental education was the prototype for a succession of educational movements that engaged educators intellectually, pedagogically, and on occasion politically to the great consternation of government officials and school administrators. A cursory look at the nomenclature developed in conjunction with them gives some hint of their antiauthoritarian appeal: liberal education (*jiyū kyōiku*), new education (*shinkō kyōiku*), proletarian education (*puroretaria kyōiku*), life-in-education (*seikatsu kyōiku*) and creative writing movement (*seikatsu tsuzurikata undō*).[64]

These movements prompted educators to seek new ways to resist government interference in education. For example, as part of the liberal education movement (*jiyū kyōiku undō*) that took place during the Taisho period (1912–1926), a small band of educators organized the Japan Teachers Union Association for Enlightenment (Nihon Kyōin Kumiai Keimeikai) in 1919. Its Program for Educational Reform, announced the following year, called for the creation of an educational system that would cultivate the democratic spirit and emphasize the good of the individual rather than the good of the state; grant all qualified students an equal opportunity to receive an education, at public expense, up to the university level; abolish bureaucratic control over education by, among other things, providing for the popular election of elementary school principals; and abolish uniformity and standardization in the curriculum, through such measures as allowing educators to select their own textbooks.[65]

To disseminate its views, the association sponsored meetings of elementary school teachers and produced several publications, including the periodical *Enlightenment* (*Keimei*), the magazine *The Cultural Movement* (*Bunka Undō*), and a series of pamphlets. Although government harassment of its members, who numbered 1,500 teachers at its height, and periodic suppression of its publications eventually led to the dissolution of the association in 1928, a number of its leaders went on to head other teachers' organizations during this period, such as the Young Educators' League (Seinen Kyōikuka Remmei), which later became the League of Elementary School Teachers (Shōgakko Kyōin Remmei),[66] and the Education Century Society (Kyōiku no Seki Sha). The latter promoted its program of educational reform by founding a private elementary school, the

Children's Hamlet (Jidō no Mura Shōgakkō), as an alternative to state-controlled education. The libertarian doctrine of this school placed managerial control in the hands of a parents' organization. Students were given the right to choose their teachers, as well as what they studied, so the curriculum could change daily. No rankings were assigned based on students' grades.[67]

The liberal education movement and its successors in the early years of the Shōwa period (1926–1989) were influenced by larger mass movements that sought political solutions to social problems. In practice, however, this approach did not bring about lasting educational reforms of the sort envisioned by their supporters, in large part because the government retained firm control over the schools while successfully employing the tactics of harassment and censorship to undermine the union activities of teachers.[68]

Thereafter, proponents of educational reform adopted a different stance. Rather than attempt to politicize education, they turned to the goal of liberating popular thought from political control. To this end, they advocated a scientific approach to education, wherein each subject in the curriculum—morals, Japanese language and literature, history, mathematics, and so on—would be taught in a pure and objective manner, free of dogma and oversimplification. At the same time, they hoped to overcome persistent class distinctions by instructing all children in the same manner, thereby granting them equal access to the same knowledge and an equal opportunity to become independent, self-governing individuals. Eventually, the demands of war undermined this effort, as science education was forced to respond to the need for increased production and national defense. Even so, teachers active in the creative writing movement (*seikatsu tsuzurikata undō*) continued to promote the teaching of science to all citizens even during the war.[69]

Among students, there is also evidence that the Imperial Rescript on Education, military style physical training and discipline, and other forms of indoctrination did not always achieve their desired effect. Between the Russo-Japanese War (1904–1905) and World War I, many educated youth exhibited a new consciousness of the individual. The Ministry of Education attempted to counter this trend by placing even greater emphasis on ethical education, through such means as public admonitions and the formation of provincial youth organizations (*seinendan*).[70]

Meiji-period youth were even prone to militant expressions of discontent. Admittedly, these acts were generally nonideological, being directed instead at some specific grievance, such as disciplinary action taken by school authorities that students considered unjust, curriculum changes, or dislike of a particular teacher. However, these incidents created a tradition of action against established authority which convinced students "that they had the right to a voice in school administration." From there it was but a short step to protest activities founded on broad concepts of political and social reform during the succeeding Taishō period.[71] And far from quelling these disturbances, government suppression for a time only succeeded in further aggravating them since "[t]he prevalence and variety of government control gave to the students a wide array of issues and incidents on which to further build their movement in the name of academic freedom and student autonomy."[72]

The conflict, confusion, and contradictions characterizing the social construction of education in post-Restoration Japan are captured in Carol Gluck's description of the process of ideological formation and transmission during the late Meiji period:

> Existing social relations continually interfered with the smooth transmission of messages from the government through its putatively subordinate hierarchy. Moreover, new institutions, once in existence, created their own demands and ideological strategies for self-preservation. The much-extolled organs of local self-government (*jichi*) possessed ideological concerns of their own, some reinforcing, others conflicting with those of the central government. Schoolteachers in charge of creating the 'next Japanese' (*daini no kokumin*) soon acquired as strong an allegiance to their profession as to the government whose citizen-making interests they were hired to serve....
>
> Nor were government-sponsored institutions the only purveyors of ideology to the late Meiji population.... Increased literacy, a result of the national compulsory education system established in the 1870s, meant that growing numbers of younger Japanese were exposed to a wide diversity of opinion. Travel broadened, entertainment beckoned, and the sources of 'education' proliferated.... These institutional channels for the dissemination of ideology were thus multiple in number and conflicting in interest. Partial proof of this was the perennial preoccupation with ideological unity. Like sumptuary laws in the Tokugawa period, which were promulgated so often that their reiteration alone casts doubt on their effectiveness, the continued concern with ideology suggests that had the efforts at influence (*kyōka*) gone smoothly, no one need have dealt so copiously with the matter.[73]

In the post-Restoration period, then, the history of Japanese education is marked by a long, circuitous path between the ruling alliance's initial "conservative reaction" in the early 1880s, and the government's recourse to harsher measures of coercion and repression in the 1930s and 1940s. It is as much a record of forceful subjugation dictated by the state as one of nationalistic indoctrination orchestrated by the state; a record punctuated by occasional acts of resistance by various segments of the population.

Indeed, through the government's unwitting support, education itself had become a major field of political, economic, and social contestation. Such innovations as universal compulsory education and a highly developed teaching profession were double-edged swords, making possible not only the dissemination of doctrinaire notions of national essence (*kokutai*) and loyalty and patriotism (*chūkun aikoku*), but also the formation of a critical historical consciousness.

NOTES

1. Herman Ooms, *Charismatic Bureaucrat: A Political Biography of Matsudaira Sadanobu (1758–1829)* (Chicago: University of Chicago Press, 1975), pp. 133–34.

2. Ibid., p. 122.

3. During the last decade of the Tokugawa period such doctrines as nativism (*kokugaku*) and Western studies (*yōgaku*), once considered unorthodox, even found their way into the curriculum of the Shōheikō. Umihara Tōru, *Gakkō [Schools]* (Tokyo: Kondo Shuppansha, 1979), p. 49.

4. Alain Touraine, *The Self-Production of Society*, trans. Derek Coltman (Chicago: University of Chicago Press, 1977), pp. 1–64. See also Peter L. Berger and Thomas Luckman, *The Social Construction of Reality* (New York: Anchor Books, 1967), pp. 49–51.

5. Touraine, *The Self-Production of Society*, pp. 30, 59.

6. Conrad Totman, *Japan before Perry: A Short History* (Berkeley: University of California Press, 1981), p. 21.

7. Ibid., p. 26.

8. Umihara, *Gakkō*, pp. 18–19; Naka Arata, *Gakkō no rekishi* [The History of Schools], 2 vols. (Tokyo: Dai Ichi Hokki Shuppan Kabushiki Gaisha, 1979), 1:43–44.

9. Umihara, *Gakkō*, pp. 18–19; Naka, *Gakkō no rekishi*, 1:44. Separate facilities provided medical care and training; research on divination, astronomy, and calendar making; and guidance in court music and dance.

10. Umihara, *Gakkō*, pp. 22–23; Naka, *Gakkō no rekishi*, 1:44–45.

11. The names *zōsha*, *zōshisha*, and *bessō* were also used.

12. Umihara, *Gakkō*, pp. 20–21; Naka, *Gakkō no rekishi*, 1:45.

13. Totman, *Japan before Perry*, p.22.

14. Ibid., pp. 32–33.

15. Ibid., pp. 60–61.

16. David John Lu, ed., *Sources of Japanese History*, 2 vols. (New York: McGraw-Hill Book Company, 1974), 1:64.

17. See Ivan Morris, *The World of the Shining Prince* (New York: Alfred A. Knopf, 1975), pp. 171–77.

18. Umihara, *Gakkō*, p. 23; Naka, *Gakkō no rekishi*, 1:44–45.

19. Totman, *Japan before Perry*, pp. 59–60.

20. William LaFleur views the "intellectual hegemony" that Buddhism enjoyed at this time as *the* defining characteristic of Japan's medieval period: an "epoch during which the basic intellectual problems, the most authoritative texts and resources, and the central symbols were all Buddhist." William R. LaFleur, *The Karma of Words: Buddhism and the Literary Arts in Medieval Japan* (Berkeley: University of California Press, 1983), p. 9.

21. Ibid., p. 27.

22. Ibid., pp. 41–46.

23. Ibid., pp. 93–118. See also Umihara, *Gakkō*, pp. 36–37.

24. Umihara, *Gakkō*, pp. 40–41; Naka, *Gakkō no rekishi*, 1:45–46; *Kōdansha Encyclopedia of Japan*, s.v. "Ashikaga Gakkō," by Etō Kyōji, and s.v. "Uesugi Norizane."

25. Umihara, *Gakkō*, p. 42; Naka, *Gakkō no rekishi*, 1:46–47.

26. Umihara, *Gakkō*, pp. 42–43.

27. Totman, *Japan before Perry*, p. 84.

28. Lu, *Sources of Japanese History*, 1:214–15.

29. George Sansom, *A History of Japan, 1615–1867* (Stanford, Calif.: Stanford University Press, 1963), pp. 39–44.

30. Katsuta Moriichi and Nakauchi Toshio, *Nihon no gakkō* [Japanese Schools] (Tokyo: Iwanami Shinsho, 1964), pp. 7–13.

31. Ronald Dore, *Education in Tokugawa Japan* (Berkeley: University of California Press, 1965), p. 59.

32. Ibid., pp. 214–18.

33. Uchiyama Katsumi, Kumagaya Tadayasu, and Masuda Shiroichi, *Kinsei Nihon kyōiku bunkashi* [The History of Educational Culture in Early Modern Japan] (Tokyo: Gakugei Tosho Kabushiki Gaisha, 1961), pp. 15–16.

34. Lu, *Sources of Japanese History*, 1:207.

35. These laws governing the work of the peasants could be extraordinarily detailed:

During the first five days of the new year, pay respect to those around you in accordance with your position. Within the first fifteen days, make more than enough ropes needed to perform your major and minor public services.... After the first fifteen days, when mountains and fields are covered with snow, accumulate all the firewood needed for the year. Use a sleigh to pull nightsoil on the fields. At night make sandals for horses. Daughters and wives must sew and weave Chinagrass to make clothing for their menfolk....

During the fourth month, men must work in the fields from dawn to dusk and make furrows as deep as the hoe can penetrate. Wives and daughters must make meals three times, put on headbands and take the meals to the fields....

Near the end of the fourth month, put a harrow on the horse and rake the fields. Cut miscanthus grass from the nearby mountains and put them on the China-grass field.... If time is appropriate, sew millet, barley and wheat seeds. Ibid., 1:207–8.

36. Dore, *Education in Tokugawa Japan*, p. 214.

37. Ibid., pp. 219–42.

38. Ibid., pp. 252–70.

39. Kokuritsu Kyōiku Kenkyūjo, ed., *Nihon kindai kyōiku hyakunenshi* [One Hundred Years of Modern Japanese Education], 10 vols. (Tokyo: Kyōiku Kenkyū Shinkōkai, 1974), 1:6–7.

40. Ironically, the most provocative exponent of ancient studies, Ogyū Sorai, had earlier served as an advisor to the bakufu, and even lectured before the shōgun. See Yoshida Noboru, Nagao Tomiji, and Shibata Yoshimatsu, ed., *Nihon kyōikushi* [The History of Japanese Education] (Tokyo: Yūhikaku, 1979), p. 31.

41. Dore, *Education in Tokugawa Japan*, pp. 42–44.

42. Ibid.

43. Bob Tadashi Wakabayashi, *Anti-Foreignism and Western Learning in Early-Modern Japan* (Cambridge, Mass.: Harvard University Press, 1986), pp. 3–57.

44. Ishikawa Matsutarō, *Hankō to terakoya* [Domain Schools and Writing Schools] (Tokyo: Kyōikusha, 1978), pp. 96–106; Richard Rubinger, "Education: From One Room to One System," in *Japan in Transition*, ed. Marius B. Jansen and Gilbert Rozman (Princeton, N.J.: Princeton University Press, 1986), p. 198. See also Richard Rubinger, *Private Academies of Tokugawa Japan* (Princeton, N.J.: Princeton University Press, 1982).

45. Dore, *Education in Tokugawa Japan*, pp. 291–316; Herbert Passin, *Society and Education in Japan* (New York: Columbia University Press, 1965), pp. 50–61.

46. Rubinger, "Education: From One Room to One System," in *Japan in Transition*, pp. 202–3.

47. George Sansom deems it part of the "first Constitution of Modern Japan." *The Western World and Japan* (New York: Vintage Books, 1973), pp. 317–18.

48. Kuki Yukio, Suzuki Eiichi, and Imano Yoshikiyo, ed., *Nihon kyōiku ronsō shiroku* [Historical Records of Debates on Japanese Education], 2 vols. (Tokyo: Dai Ichi Hōki, 1980), 1:22–30.

49. Rubinger, "Education: From One Room to One System," in *Japan in Transition*, pp. 203–4.

50. For a firsthand description of the Kyoto school system in 1872 by Fukuzawa Yūkichi as it existed on the eve of the announcement of the *Gakusei*, see Nakayama Kazuyoshi, trans. and ed., *Fukuzawa Yūkichi on Education* (Tokyo: University of Tokyo Press, 1985), pp. 73–78.

51. For a description of the practical difficulties of incorporating regular school attendance into the working lives of Japanese peasant children, see Mikiso Hane, *Peasants, Rebels, and Outcastes: The Underside of Modern Japan* (New York: Pantheon Books, 1982), pp. 51–54.

52. The debate between Motoda and Itō and its relationship to the *Kyōiku rei* is analyzed in Kuki, Suzuki, and Imano, *Nihon kyōiku ronsō shiroku*, 1:41–50; relevant documents, including the *Kyōiku taishi* and *Kyōiku gi*, are reprinted on pp. 50–64. See also Passin, *Society and Education in Japan*, pp. 82–84, 226–33.

53. Kokuritsu Kyōiku Kenkyūjo, *Nihon kindai kyōiku hyakunenshi*, 1:98–119.

54. Centre for East Asian Cultural Studies, comp. and pub., *Meiji Japan through Contemporary Sources*, 3 vols. (Tokyo, 1970), 2:195.

55. Ibid., pp. 232–33.

56. Rubinger, "Education: From One Room to One System," in *Japan in Transition*, p. 221.

57. Teruhisa Horio, *Educational Thought and Ideology in Modern Japan*, ed. and trans. Steven Platzer (Tokyo: University of Tokyo Press, 1988), p. 39.

58. For a brief description of the educational views of Ueki and Nakae, see Sakamoto Tadayoshi, "Tennosei kyōiku taisei seiritsuki no minshū kyōiku no shisō to isan" [The Ideology and Legacy of Popular Education during the Formative Period of the Educational System under the Emperor System], in Shiromaru Fumio and Kawai Akira, eds., *Nihon no kyōiku* [Japanese Education], vol. 2: *Minshū kyōiku no undō to isan* [Popular Educational Movements and Their Legacy], 11 vols. (Tokyo: Shin Nihon Shuppansha, 1975), pp. 44–45.

59. Ishitoya Tetsuo, *Nihon kyōinshi kenkyū* [A Study of the History of Japanese Teachers] (Tokyo: Kōdansha, 1967), pp. 102–3; Tsuchiya Tadao, *Meiji zenki kyōiku seisakushi no kenkyū* [A Study of the History of Educational Policies in the Early Meiji Period] (Tokyo: Kōdansha, 1962), p. 377; Horimatsu Buichi, *Nihon kindai kyōikushi* [The History of Modern Japanese Education] (Tokyo: Risōsha, 1981), pp. 76–77.

60. Ishitoya, *Nihon kyōinshi kenkyū*, pp. 64–65; Tsuchiya, *Meiji zenki kyōiku seisakushi no kenkyū*, pp. 390–91.

61. Ienaga Saburō, *The Pacific War* (New York: Pantheon Books, 1978), pp. 31–32.

62. Touraine, *The Self-Production of Society*, p. 59.

63. For an analysis of developmental education, both its role in stimulating the professional and political consciousness of educators and its influence on school curricula, see Mark Lincicome, "Educational Discourse and the Dimensions of Reform in Meiji Japan" (Ph.D. diss., University of Chicago, 1985).

64. For information on the etymology of these terms, see Minkan Kyōiku Shiryō Kenkyūkai, Ōta Takashi, and Nakauchi Toshio, eds. *Minkan kyōikushi kenkyū jiten* [Research Dictionary on the History of Popular Education] (Tokyo: Hyōronsha, 1976).

65. Donald R. Thurston, *Teachers and Politics in Japan* (Princeton, N.J.: Princeton University Press, 1973), pp. 31–33; Katsuta and Nakauchi, *Nihon no gakkō*, pp. 222–24.

66. Thurston, *Teachers and Politics*, pp. 33–35; Benjamin C. Duke, *Japan's Militant Teachers: A History of the Left-Wing Teachers' Movement* (Honolulu: University Press of Hawaii, 1973), pp. 14–15.

67. Katsuta and Nakauchi, *Nihon no gakkō*, pp. 224–26.

68. Ibid., p. 238.

69. Ibid., p. 239–41.

70. Oka Yoshitake, "Generational Conflict after the Russo-Japanese War," in Najita Tetsuo and J. Victor Koschmann, eds., *Conflict in Modern Japanese History: The Neglected Tradition* (Princeton, N.J.: Princeton University Press, 1982), pp. 197–225.

71. Henry DeWitt Smith II, *Japan's First Student Radicals* (Cambridge, Mass.: Harvard University Press, 1972), pp. 21–26.

72. Ibid., p. 186.

73. Carol Gluck, *Japan's Modern Myths: Ideology in the Late Meiji Period* (Princeton, N.J.: Princeton University Press, 1985), pp. 11–12.

2

The Development of Japanese Educational Policy, 1945–1985

Edward R. Beauchamp

The appointment of an Ad Hoc Reform Council, or Rinkyoshin, on 21 August 1984 was a logical culmination to a lengthy period of concern in Japan over a set of widely perceived educational problems and the future prospects for Japanese education. The charge given to the council by Prime Minister Nakasone Yasuhiro was clear: "to consider basic strategies for necessary reforms ... so as to secure such education as will be compatible with the social changes and cultural developments of our country." The prime minister went on to remind council members that "if our nation is to build up a society that is full of vitality and creativity as well as relevant to the 21st century, it is a matter of great urgency to design necessary reforms."[1]

The Ad Hoc Council's final policy recommendations make several things clear. First, their proposals have elicited both intense interest and comment both within Japan and abroad. In addition, the problems that the recommendations are designed to alleviate are not recent ones but have their roots in earlier phases of Japan's postwar educational development. Finally, this systematic attempt to institute fundamental educational reforms is not a new phenomenon in Japan. Indeed, major attempts to implement basic educational reforms occurred in the 1870s and again following World War II. In the first instance, the reform movement was initiated by the new Meiji government, in reaction to a perceived external threat, as a means of building a modern state as quickly as possible; in the latter case, the reforms were imposed by a powerful Occupation force which intended to transform Japan from a military dictatorship into a democratic society. In both cases the initial sweeping reforms were followed by more conservative reactions which tempered the earlier changes.

JAPANESE EDUCATION, 1868–1945

The first of these reforms occurred in the early Meiji period (1868–1880) when Western education was introduced for the purpose of modernizing the nation. The Japanese approach was a pragmatic one, based on the Imperial Charter Oath of April 6, 1868, which called on the people to eschew old-fashioned ways, insisting that "knowledge shall be sought throughout the world." The major criterion used by the Meiji reformers was simply to borrow the best features of several Western educational systems and adapt them to the Japanese situation. As a result, a highly centralized administrative structure with an emphasis on state-run normal schools was borrowed from France; a system of higher education rooted in a handful of elite public universities was the German contribution; the English model of Spartan-like, character-building preparatory schools stressing moral discipline fit nicely into the Japanese context; and from the United States came the model for elementary education, a number of practical pedagogical approaches, and an interest in vocational education.

Another important element in Japan's rush to reform was the policy of sending promising young students abroad for study while at the same time hiring foreign experts, the so-called *oyatoi gaikokujin* (foreign employees) as teachers and advisors until enough young Japanese could be trained to replace them. The best estimates of the numbers of these foreign employees in Japan between 1868 and 1912 range from 3,000 to 6,000. Whatever the number, these foreign educators were instrumental in introducing Western educational thought, practice, textbooks, and equipment into the country.[2]

From 1868 to about 1875, the Meiji reformers pursued modernization in a pell-mell fashion. By the latter date, however, they began to believe that events were moving too rapidly, that certain Western ideas (e.g., individualism) were not well suited to the Japanese environment, and they systematically began to slow down the process. By 1880 a widespread attitude had emerged that the reforms of the previous decade had gone too far, and steps needed to be taken to recapture the essence of such traditional values as Confucianism which, in the view of one leading scholar, "taught that the meaning of social life lay . . . in cultivating relationships among members of society built on trust, a fundamental sense of one's humaneness, and above all, a commitment to loyal action on behalf of others." This, its advocates insisted, "should be reintegrated as a nutritive value into modern Japanese life."[3]

The success of the Meiji educational strategy is affirmed by the noted historian and former U.S. ambassador to Japan, Edwin O. Reischauer, who concludes that this policy was "closely tailored to national needs as the leaders saw them. It eventually created a literate mass of soldiers, housewives, and workers with ample middle-level technical skills—an aspect of education that many of today's modernizing countries have failed adequately to appreciate—and a thin stream of highly talented young men emerging from the universities to occupy positions of leadership in government and society."[4]

Before and during World War II, American policymakers saw Japanese education as a conscious vehicle for carrying out the intent of the 1890 Imperial Rescript on Education. This document promulgated by the Emperor Meiji on October 30, 1890, remained the official statement of the principles underlying Japanese education until it was scrapped by the Occupation authorities. The rescript gave both legal form and, perhaps more significantly, moral force to an educational system that supported the rise of militarism and ultranationalism during the late 1920s and 1930s.

The Imperial Rescript is a key document from several points of view. It paraphrases the acceptable and highly moralistic Confucian virtues to which all loyal Japanese were expected to adhere and sets down the principles from which much of the militaristic and ultranationalistic emphasis in education developed. Along the latter lines it clearly subordinates the individual to the good of the state and promotes unthinking acceptance of, and blind obedience to, instructions from above. An Office of Strategic Services (OSS) document on Japanese education, prepared during World War II, concludes that "the attitude that education should be for the purposes of the State rather than for the liberation of the individual has permeated the entire system. Elementary school instruction has been dedicated to the development of unquestioning loyalty. The Department of Education's exclusive copyright over textbooks held since 1903, has made it possible to intensify this process of indoctrination." The minister of education, in a 1941 speech, called for the eradication of thoughts based on individualism and liberalism, and the firm establishment of a national moral standard with emphasis on service to the state.[5]

THE OCCUPATION OF JAPAN, 1945-1952

A second major set of reforms took place immediately following World War II as a key element in the Allies' determination to transform Japan from an aggressive military dictatorship into a peace-loving democracy.[6] When Japan surrendered to the Allies in August 1945, those Americans charged with planning the eventual occupation of Japan shared an essentially common view of prewar and wartime Japanese education and the role it had played in Japan's military expansion into much of Asia and Oceania.[7] Since the Meiji Restoration of 1868, they believed that education had been consciously used by Japan's political leaders as an instrument to advance the ends of the state, including economic development, national integration, and military power and conquest.

When the emperor's representatives formally signed the instrument of surrender, Japan lay numbed and prostrate before a conquering army. The country's educational system was in shambles; capitulation found 18,000,000 students idle, 4,000 schools destroyed, and only 20 percent of the necessary textbooks available.[8] In addition, large portions of many of those textbooks contained unacceptable nationalist propaganda which had to be removed before they were suitable for pedagogical purposes. Finally, more than one of every three institutions of higher education lay in ruins; thousands of teachers were homeless, hungry, and dispirited; and many of their pupils had been moved to safer areas. In short, a functioning educational system was virtually nonexistent.[9]

The major goals of the Occupation of Japan can be simply stated as the democratization, demilitarization, and decentralization of Japanese society. The Americans recognized that a new orientation of the educational system was an indispensable element in achieving these objects, especially that of remaking Japan into a functioning democracy.

Having surrendered its sovereignty to the Allies, Japan entered a period in which the policymaking function was no longer in its control. As an occupied nation, all Japan could hope for was that through persuasion and political skill it could at least have an influence on the educational policy that the Americans formulated and had the power to force a defeated people to implement. It was during this time that the process of transforming Japan's prewar system proceeded apace. This was a dual process in which the terrible scars of war led the Japanese people to acquire a strong aversion to their military establishment while, simultaneously, the Occupation authorities systematically dismantled the prewar institutions and structures which they saw as causing Japan's slide into the abyss of militarism and nationalism. The Japanese commitment to peace was evidenced by the widely accepted Article 9 of the 1946 Constitution which forever renounced war as an instrument of the national policy; the emergence of the so-called nuclear allergy which has made discussions of national defense and American nuclear forces in Japan a politically explosive subject; and the increasingly left-of-center political ideology of intellectuals, university students, and the Japan Teachers Union (JTU).[10]

This new situation, reinforced by surviving remnants of the prewar Japanese willingness to accept and obey instructions from above, enabled the American authorities to use the existing instruments of government to implement educational reforms. The Occupation proceeded to censor textbooks, magazines, and films as well as to purge teachers whose pre-Occupation activities were deemed to be either undemocratic or actively supportive of the military's policies.[11] Thus, one of the great ironies of this period was that, in encouraging the democratization of Japanese education, the actions of the all-powerful Occupation forces were often not democratic.

What appeared to be wrong with Japanese education, in the eyes of most American policymakers, was that it was not like the American system. American-initiated educational reforms were, therefore, designed to reform Japanese education along the lines of the American model. This meant that the Occupation authorities would have to transform the prewar orientation of the Japanese people (characterized by an emphasis on filial piety, the perfection of moral powers, group cohesion and harmony, and loyalty and obedience to the emperor and the nation) into one that would be congruent with the goals of the United States in Japan.

To assist in carrying out this transformation, the First United States Education

Mission, composed of twenty-seven prominent American educators, was invited to spend a month in Japan examining the educational system for the purpose of making recommendations for the reform of that system. True to their American heritage, they rejected most of the elements of prewar Japanese education and insisted on the democratization of Japan's highly centralized enterprise into a system in which the centralized power of the powerful Ministry of Education would be broken and local communities would control their own educational destinies. The American reformers also suggested the dismantling of the highly differentiated multitrack system of prewar days in favor of a nine-year compulsory single track as part of an American-style 6-3-3-4 school ladder, along with steps designed to foster greater individuality, freedom of inquiry, development of the "whole child," coeducation, greater flexibility in the curriculum, and a radical reform of Japan's written language.[12]

As a number of scholars, Japanese and American, have pointed out, many of these reforms, such as coeducation, comprehensive schools, and local control, were deeply rooted in the American democratic model but were dysfunctional when transported to the Japanese context. The Japanese educational authorities, however, had little choice but officially to accept the recommendations of the mission's report, and, indeed, these recommendations became the basis for a series of important educational laws implemented between 1947 and 1949. The most important of these were the Fundamental Law of Education and the School Education Law which were promulgated in 1947.[13] The former represented a 180-degree change from the 1890 Imperial Rescript, declaring that "education shall aim at the full development of personality, striving for the rearing of the people sound in mind and body, who shall love truth and justice, esteem individual value, respect labor and have a deep sense of responsibility, and be imbued with the independent spirit, as builders of a peaceful state and society." It also established the important principle that all major educational regulations would be made by parliamentary procedure. The latter, on the other hand, established a new educational structure in which a 6-3-3 school ladder was created, the school-leaving age was raised to fifteen, and coeducation was legitimated. These two basic pieces of education legislation still form the legal underpinnings of Japanese education.

By 1949 the major accomplishments of the Occupation had been completed. The political and strategic imperatives of the emerging Cold War caused American policymakers to reassess their plans for the future of Japan and to ally themselves more closely with conservative Japanese interests.[14] The reforming zeal of the Americans had abated, and the environment in Japan underwent an important change. Before American control was withdrawn in the spring of 1952, the American reformers had succeeded in clearing away the old undemocratic structures and replacing them with ones more to their liking; they had replaced those individuals identified as hostile to democracy with Japanese who seemed committed to democratic values; and they had provided the Japanese educators with new curricula, textbooks, and methodologies.

THE POST-OCCUPATION PERIOD, 1952–1960

April 28, 1952, the day on which the San Francisco Peace Treaty took effect, marked the official end of the American Occupation of Japan. For the first time since its surrender, sovereignty was returned to the Japanese government. In the six years and eight months separating these two watershed events the social and political systems of the Japanese nation had been dramatically transformed into an essentially democratic pattern, albeit not into a mirror image of the American model of democracy. Most Japanese preferred the new postwar environment to that which had brought them such destruction, but there were many who felt that the Occupation reforms had gone too far and, indeed, had often done considerable violence to cherished Japanese values and traditions.

Given the new political and social systems existing in 1952, it should not be surprising that the Japanese government undertook a careful reassessment of the recent reforms with an eye to correcting what were widely viewed as excesses. Education did not escape the government's reassessment, and during the post-1952 period the Japanese authorities scrapped a number of the American-initiated reforms and modified others to fit traditional Japanese models more closely. For example, the 1948 Board of Education Law, designed to implement the Occupation policy of transferring power from the centralized Ministry of Education to local communities through locally elected boards of education, was abolished, and since 1956 board members have been appointed by the prefectural governors or local mayors with the approval of the appropriate legislative body, thereby making the school board an integrated part of local administration.

The Occupation-imposed abolition of *shushin* (moral education), seen by the Americans as a primary vehicle for inculcating prewar ideas of racial supremacy, the righteousness of Japanese overseas expansion, and the divinity of the emperor, was viewed by many Japanese as having thrown out the baby with the bathwater, leaving public education without a spiritual backbone. In fact, in 1949, even before the Occupation ended, Prime Minister Yoshida Shigeru advocated the creation of an educational statement on morality that would replace the discredited Imperial Rescript. The Japanese left immediately denounced Yoshida's proposal as an attempt to reinstitute prewar thought control. The following year Amano Teiyu, then minister of education, provoked charges of a rebirth of militarism by proposing to celebrate national holidays by raising the rising sun flag and playing the national anthem. He also echoed Yoshida's call for a new ethical code to replace the discredited Imperial Rescript. By 1958, the Ministry of Education's required "course of study" included one hour per week for moral education, called *dotoku* in place of the disreputable term, *shushin*. This reintroduction of moral education has not led to the evils predicted by critics. A leading American specialist on Japanese education, William K. Cummings, after observing several lessons in the mid-1970s, concluded that "I quickly overcame my bias against moral education and looked forward to each week's new drama." Rather than finding right-wing patriotic themes in these lessons, Cummings was surprised to see that the lessons "emphasized fundamental matters such as the value of life, the foolishness of fighting, the importance of friendship, the problems of old people."[15]

The conservative Ministry of Education also began to challenge another legacy of the Occupation, the powerful Japan Teachers Union. Organized in the early days of the Occupation, primarily by a minority of militant communists and socialists (the only groups having "clean hands" following the war), the Japan Teachers Union was quickly recognized by MacArthur's headquarters. As the result of the union's close ties with the political opposition, and the beginnings of the Cold War in the early 1950s, the conservative Ministry of Education refused to have anything to do with the JTU, claiming that it was devoted to fomenting a communist revolution and that its members were, therefore, unfit to teach Japan's youth. Relations between these two major educational forces have not improved significantly in recent years, and prospects for real understanding and cooperation are not yet on the horizon.[16]

This Japanese counterreformation received strong support from the business community. Indeed, as early as 1952, Nikkeiren, an influential federation of some of Japan's largest industrial firms, issued a statement on education policy that bluntly expressed the unhappiness in industrial circles with the democratically oriented schools and called for an educational system that was more closely allied to the needs of industry. In practice this meant more and better vocational courses and a higher degree of professionalization at the university level. This salvo would not be the last fired by the big guns of Nikkeiren (Japan Federation of Employers).

Certainly big business favored much of the reverse course, but the more important meaning of that phenomenon was that it clearly demonstrated a broadly based Japanese conviction that, if they were to have democracy (and there was widespread agreement that they would), they were determined to have a variant of it that was more-or-less consistent with their traditions and culture. As one distinguished Japanese scholar explained, "it was easy for liberty to become license," and the "incompatibility of American-style democracy with Japanese traditions was [clear], and the process of developing an amended Japanese version of democratic ideals was pushed forward."[17] The Japanese preference for centralization reasserted itself, but centralization was not necessarily undemocratic. One can make the argument, and many Japanese do, that their centralized system ensures that every child—from Okinawa to Hokkaido—enjoys "equality of opportunity" because of substantially equal physical facilities throughout the archipelago, a uniform curriculum administered by a single Ministry of Education, equal access to the same textbooks, teachers of relatively equal competence, and a uniform set of national standards.

As governmental authorities turned to "fine tuning" the new system to reflect more faithfully the Japanese cultural environment and the spirit of the nation's new democratic ideology, they also began to expand the net of educational opportunity more widely than ever before in Japanese history and to improve the quality of the education offered to students. Reinforcing these essentially political decisions was the reality of a postwar baby boom which began in 1947, after large numbers of military and civilian personnel returned from wartime assignments overseas. The birthrate rose sharply after 1945. For example, the number of births soared from 1,576,000 in 1945 to 2,718,000 in 1947. This resulted in a virtual flood of children reaching elementary school age in 1953, along with the certain knowledge that the same children would enter junior high school in 1959, senior high school in 1962, and the university in 1965.

This trend required the government to expand rapidly educational facilities systematically beginning with the elementary grades, and continuing through the university level as the youngsters wended their way through the system. Providing the necessary facilities would have been difficult enough in normal times, but Japan still suffered from the loss of educational facilities in World War II. The problem was exacerbated by an expansion in educational opportunity and by a significant rise in the percentage of students continuing beyond the elementary and secondary levels. "The new 6-3-3-4 system established in the late 1940's gave people much easier access to higher levels of education than the old system, and an economic revival in the late 1950's followed by a period of high economic growth in the 1960's and the first half of the 1970's, made educational opportunity which had been institutionally offered feasible."[18]

There is no doubt that postwar Japan has made enormous strides in providing expanded educational opportunities for its young people. In the thirty-five years between the end of World War II and 1980, the number of students attending school in Japan increased over 80 percent, from 15 million to over 27 million. Virtually all youngsters complete the nine years of compulsory education (99.98 percent), and an impressive 94.2 percent of these graduates go on to a noncompulsory senior secondary school. Perhaps most significantly, the Japanese have persuasively demonstrated that mass education does not have to be purchased with diluted standards. International achievement tests have consistently placed the Japanese at, or close to, the top in a variety of subjects. Furthermore, in 1980, 37.4 percent of the senior high school graduates attended some kind of institution of higher education.[19]

Prior to 1945, Japanese females had very limited access to advanced education, especially that of an academic type. The secondary education alternatives that were available to them heavily favored domestic education, while university preparatory schools were a male preserve. It has only been recently that educational opportunities for women have improved in Japan. In 1970, for example, "the proportion of Japanese women with an education beyond high school constituted a fraction of the United States distribution, particularly among women between the ages of 35 and 44."[20] Today, although things have changed for the better, much remains to be done. In 1983, 94.5 percent of the female college-age cohort attended the noncompulsory senior high school as opposed to 93.1 percent of the male cohort. In addition, one out of every three female graduates advances to some form of higher education, but the vast majority of these female graduates enroll in junior colleges, and most of those who attend four-year schools major in English literature, home economics, and other subjects that prepare better for homemaking than for business or professional pursuits.

The slow progress of women is rooted in part in deeply held attitudes about their proper role in both education and society. A 1973 government survey "found only 14 percent of mothers wanting their daughters to have a university education, in contrast to 49 percent for sons."[21] Still another example of the lingering bias against the education of women is reflected in a 1983 decision by the administration of the Kyoto Pharmaceutical College that it would give preference to male applicants. It seems that the number of young men successfully passing the entrance examination had been declining for several years and more women than usual were accepted. The university officials felt threatened by what they called the "feminization" of their institution and sought to reverse this trend. They justified their decision on the grounds that Japanese companies overwhelmingly prefer to hire men and that the university sees no point in producing female graduates who will not be hired by the industry. It is clear that, although Japanese women have made important educational strides since 1945, they have a long way to go to achieve equality with their brothers.

As the government has grappled with the problem of creating expanded educational opportunities, it also has worked hard to provide the resources and teachers needed to improve the quality of education. The Ministry of Education has issued four five-year plans, beginning in 1958, designed to address problems of class size, staffing needs, and other technical issues. Since 1980, an ambitious twelve-year (1980–1992) plan has been in operation. Perhaps one of the most effective activities of the Ministry of Education is the preparation of official revised courses of study, which serve as guides for the various curricula. The first of these was undertaken in the late 1950s in an attempt to evaluate the quality and effectiveness of postwar education. A second revision occurred in 1968 and focused on providing a higher level of study in mathematics, science, and other subjects. These decennial revisions ensure that the curriculum is kept up to date and, indeed, provide at least a partial explanation for the success of Japanese students in the International Survey of Educational Achievement (IEA) Project, the first large-scale, systematic attempt to measure achievement in mathematics, science, social studies, and so on, across national boundaries.

EXPANSION IN THE 1960S AND 1970S

No less important for Japanese education than the Occupation reforms of the immediate postwar years was the unprecedented period of high economic growth triggered by the restoration of sovereignty and accelerated by the outbreak of the Korean War, continuing unabated until the first oil crisis of 1973. Enjoying a steady accretion of her growth rate of over 10 percent yearly (in real terms), Japan experienced rapid changes not only in her economy but also in the political and social arenas. It was not so much that the democratizing themes of the

Occupation were forgotten—the more democratic segment of the population would not allow that to happen—but after years of economic hardship there was a wide consensus on the need for economic reconstruction. Educational policy during the 1960s and much of the 1970s was consciously designed to foster economic development. Indeed, there is little doubt that since the middle of the 1950s the interests of industry have been extremely influential in shaping educational policy.

Almost immediately after Japan's reassertion of her sovereignty in 1952, the recognition of a serious shortage of scientific and technical manpower emerged as a major educational problem. Major special interest groups, such as Nikkeiren, had aggressively begun to urge the government to play a major role in overcoming the problem. Industry spokesmen generally agreed on the need for the "functional differentiation of the higher educational structure, and . . . increased specialization in courses and the graduation of more science and engineering specialists."[22]

There had existed in prewar Japan a system of single faculty technical schools providing subprofessional training (roughly comparable to that offered by American community colleges but of a generally higher quality) to those either unable to pass the university entrance examination or without the necessary economic means to attend a university. Students could enter technical schools directly from the lower middle school and graduate with certification in a wide variety of technical fields, including drafting, accounting, architecture, engineering, and, in some cases, even medicine or dentistry. Although such graduates did not enjoy the same level of professional status as university graduates, "they provided the important battalions that filled the growing needs of Japanese industry."[23]

Many major firms were nostalgic for the prewar multitrack system which had enabled them to make "use of a status system based on the academic background of their employees. Within companies one found multiple tiers and compartments divided along school-affiliation lines. The school one had been graduated from would determine one's type of job within the organization and the highest position one could hope to reach." In addition, there were complaints from industry about the quality of the graduates entering the work force. Viewed from this perspective, the postwar reforms had been a disruptive force within corporate culture. As the new system's considerable strengths began to be appreciated, however, members of the corporate world "began to use the system to their advantage." They began, for example, "using the rankings into which the new schools were eventually classified," and "a hierarchy among universities took shape in line with the caliber of each university's student body, and companies shifted their internal organization to match the structure of the university hierarchy."[24] This reality was not lost on high school graduates who, quite naturally, saw their futures best served by attending a university in the upper reaches of the new hierarchy. This, in turn, reinforced and expanded the importance of university entrance examinations.[25]

In an extraordinary policy statement, issued shortly after assuming office as prime minister in 1960, Ikeda Hayato announced his intention of doubling Japan's national income in a ten-year period. This, in effect, required an annual growth rate of about 7 percent. In the late 1950s Japan's share of the world gross national product stood at about 3 percent, but by the time of the first oil crisis of 1973 it had grown to a remarkable 10 percent. Japan had, in fact, achieved an average annual growth rate of about 11 percent between 1961 and 1969, attaining Ikeda's ambitious target in just five years. By 1969 Japan's gross national product was 3.7 times that of 1960.

Increases in per capita income kept pace with this dizzying trend and soon Japan's standard of living reached new levels of prosperity. Per capita income, which had stood at barely $200 in the early 1950s, rocketed to $2,300 per year in 1972.[26] Several important consequences flowed from Japan's newfound economic cornucopia, including increased social mobility, a quickened flow of young people from rural to urban centers, a declining birthrate, and an unprecedented expansion of employment opportunities. An increasing demand for formal education reflected these economic and social developments, and educational officials were hard pressed to keep up with it.

In 1957, the recently established Economic Planning Agency, the coordinating body for overall governmental economic planning, had issued a long-range plan establishing guidelines for economic development and education's role in achieving it. The Ministry of Education contributed a five-year plan designed to accommodate 8,000 new university places annually for science and technology students and by 1960 was close to achieving its target. Prime Minister Ikeda's scheme to double the national income in a decade, however, required the production of an additional 170,000 scientists and engineers. The Ministry of Education planned to meet this need with a seven-year plan that added 16,000 places annually, but it was subsequently replaced with a four-year plan that added 20,000 new places yearly.

Perhaps the single most influential educational document of this period was the "Report on the Long-Range Educational Plan Oriented toward the Doubling of Income." Prepared by a technical subcommittee of the Economic Planning Agency's Economic Council in 1960, this document stressed the importance of education as an investment in developing human resources. It argued for more and better science and technical education to meet industry's need for skilled workers and intoned that "future progress in economics and social welfare depends largely on the effective use of the human resources of the nation."[27] It insisted, in the view of one close observer, on the necessity of "extending upper secondary education to most adolescents, shaping the motivational and cognitive orientations of adolescents toward a complex society through upper secondary education, and training talented human resources to compete economically in the international domain."[28]

In 1962 the government passed legislation creating a system of nineteen technical colleges, designed "to train [middle-level] technicians with well-rounded general knowledge and a thoroughly specialized knowledge in technology."[29]

These institutions, offering a five-year curriculum in a variety of industrial (and sometimes merchant marine) studies, are open to graduates of the lower secondary school. As of May 1983 there were sixty-two technical colleges with a total enrollment of 47,245 students, of whom 97.2 percent were male.[30]

This law, along with subsequent actions of the Ministry of Education, resulted in a highly differentiated system of technical education. The universities, at the apex of this system, provided both undergraduate and graduate education for scientists and high-level technical personnel. The elite nature of this arrangement can be seen in the decision to concentrate advanced courses in a handful of important universities. The technical schools described above were designed to train the large numbers of middle-level technicians needed to operate a sophisticated scientific and technical economy. In addition, specialized technical high schools, and high-quality technical courses in general high schools, produced large numbers of lower-level technicians. Finally, there was created a variety of miscellaneous schools outside the formal system of education which provided technical education. Many of these offer short-term courses in a wide variety of fields, including electronics. A sophisticated set of public and private industrial training centers to train skilled workers was also developed. The School of Education Law of 1961 allowed, under certain circumstances, for work done in them to be credited toward high school graduation. This differentiation, clearly, served the interests of those industrial interests who, as early as 1952, had severely criticized the new educational system.

In the decade between 1960 and 1970 the government had succeeded in more than doubling the number of university science and engineering faculties and increasing the number of science and engineering graduates by more than 2.5 times. This, however, tells only part of the story. "In 1960, 18.2 percent of the total [university] student enrollment was in the fields of science and engineering; by 1975 this figure was up to 23.2 percent. Even more significant, within the national universities, where the government efforts were most direct, the figure rose from 24 percent to 33 percent in these fields."[31]

Early on, educational planners had identified secondary education as a critical factor in human resource development, and, although they recognized the long-term need for overall improvement in general secondary education, they opted to give priority to science and technical education in the short term. The same study that called for the training of 170,000 scientists and engineers also insisted on the need for 439,000 technical school graduates in the same period. This goal could not, of course, be met without a substantial increase in the number of technical teachers available, so a number of temporary three-year teacher-training institutes, tied to nine major national universities, were created. In the next seven years 800 future teachers were admitted to these schools.[32]

As noted earlier, the postwar period was one of quantitative expansion, but the need for a similar qualitative improvement remained. The amount of public money devoted to education rose from 159,818 million yen in 1950 to 372,006 million yen in 1955; to 1,057,070 million yen in 1963; and to 5,060,245 million yen in 1973. This money went not only toward providing better teachers but also better facilities (including laboratories and libraries), smaller classes, inservice training for teachers,[33] and a system of Science Education Centers in each prefecture where "teachers at all precollege levels received inservice training in the use of the latest materials and methods for science and mathematics teaching."[34]

The widespread acceptance of higher education as prerequisite to maintaining Japan's newly acquired affluence sent increasing numbers of high school graduates through the narrow gates of the universities. The gatekeepers, however, insisted that those admitted first demonstrate their merit by successfully passing rigorous entrance examinations.[35] Ezra Vogel has suggested that "no single event, with the possible exception of marriage, determines the course of a young man's life as much as entrance examinations, and nothing, including marriage, requires as many years of planning and hard work."[36]

A bizarre but true example of the kind of horror stories associated with entrance examinations is recounted by Ronald Dore. In describing how a preoccupation with these examinations at higher educational levels tends to create a "backwash" into the lower levels of the educational system, he describes its logical conclusion in "a pre-pre-kindergarten which was reported in 1970 to have failed to devise adequate tests for 2 year olds and decided to test their mothers instead."[37] Although an admittedly extreme case, there are few Japanese who would be overly surprised upon hearing about this case. Thomas Rohlen characterizes this kind of "obsession with entrance examinations" as "a dark engine powering the entire school system" and, if anything, he understates the case.[38]

Most Japanese seem to think that entirely too much emphasis is placed on examinations, but very little has been done to change this situation. What obstacles prevent a change that most thoughtful people seem to favor? At least three possible answers, in no particular order of importance, suggest themselves: (1) a deeply ingrained Confucian legacy, (2) powerful vested interests, and (3) too few places for too many applicants.

The Confucian legacy stresses the efficacy of memorizing the classics, and a number of scholars have pointed out how deeply inbred this approach seems to be in the Japanese psyche. One distinguished student of Japan has written that Japan's "ferocious race and competition for the best possible places at the best universities, is simply the ancient Chinese system of state examinations to accede to the class of *jugakusha* (literati) in a modern context. Today one may gloss Karl Marx instead of Mencius, or write an essay on spherical trigonometry instead of defining filial piety, but the terms, rules and outcomes of the game have changed very little."[39] Whoever learns the most facts and best develops test-taking skills is most likely to be successful.

The entrance examinations of today are still shaped by this attitude, but it may not be quite as absurd as it sounds. There is a widely held view among many Japanese that the value of entrance examinations is not in the information memorized and regurgitated upon command, but rather in the intense, difficult, and often lonely experience of preparing for those examinations. This, we are told, strengthens one's character and moral fiber and prepares the individual for the arduous challenges lying ahead. Interestingly enough, Thomas Rohlen lends support to this view when he suggests that, although intelligence is needed to pass the exams, "self discipline and willpower are equally essential."[40]

A second obstacle to reforming the examination system lies in the powerful vested interests which might suffer economically if significant changes were to be made in existing arrangements. A visit to virtually any bookshop in Tokyo, or any other large urban center, will illustrate the profitability of the current examination system to publishers. These bookshops are usually crowded with students of all ages who flock to the shelves appropriate to their needs. Shelves are conspicuously marked with signs such as "For Secondary School Entrance Preparation."

In addition, most students preparing for entrance examinations attend voluntary, often expensive, supplementary or cram schools. Many of these are part of major nationwide chains and have made many an entrepreneur affluent. There are also the fat fees charged students for the privilege of taking a university's entrance examination—fees that can make a considerable difference to the financial health of many private institutions. These are not the only ones to benefit from the examination system which is so widely criticized. Manufacturers of specially designed student desks and worktables, desk lamps, and so on, would also suffer economically from a weakening of the examination system. Ironically, even many of the victims of this system would still be victims should entrance examinations lose their centrality to the Japanese educational experience. One of the easiest and often lucrative sources of income for Japanese students who have successfully entered university is to tutor students preparing to take the examinations themselves.

A third obstacle to examination reform is a simple one. Over 90 percent of the relevant age cohort graduate from high school in Japan, and almost two-thirds of them have taken a college preparatory curriculum. "There were," in 1980, "590,000 places in higher education available and about 636,000 senior applying." At first glance, this appears to be a reasonably close fit, but this overlooks another 200,000 applicants, called *rōnin*. These high school graduates from earlier years had failed in earlier attempts to enter their university of choice, and rather than admit failure, they continued their studies in preparation for another try at the examination.

Expanded enrollments for a limited number of university places have inevitably meant increased competition for those relatively few places that were perceived to be of the greatest value. Thus, with more and more applicants striving to attend a handful of famous national universities, and an even smaller number of prestigious private universities, the existing hierarchy was not only maintained but also strengthened. This trend also reinforced the power of the entrance examination system, and not only for its importance as a sorting device. Every student who takes the university entrance examination, and most take the examination for more than one institution, pays a fee ranging from about US$65–100 (based on an exchange rate of 150 yen to a dollar). Thus, the money-starved private universities have come to depend on the income to help meet their operating expenses.

This changed academic environment of the post-Occupation years was one in which students found the realities of university life disappointing. After working exceptionally hard for many years to pass the examination for a prestigious university, the reality of large classes, rigidly prescribed curricula, disinterested lecturers, seldom-seen professors, and a Byzantine bureaucratic structure clashed with their image of a university. The postwar educational system and its left-of-center teaching force had encouraged students to question both society's materialism and the political assumptions underlying the conservative government's apparent repudiation of the antiwar constitution and attempts to return Japan to a more authoritarian society.

Student radicals were an important part of the 1945–1960 intellectual ferment in Japan, but during the 1960s their numbers proved to be the heart of the great student protest that shook the nation over the ratification of the revised United States–Japan Security Treaty of June 1960. The movement continued on, using the American intervention in Vietnam as an emotional focus and culminated in the great Tokyo University protest of 1968. This event marked the high point of the student movement, and student occupation of Todai's physical facilities not only forced the university's closure for several months but was directly responsible for suspending the 1969 entrance examinations.

The government of Prime Minister Sato Eisaku accepted the challenge and rammed through the Diet a "Bill for Emergency Measures of University Administration," in August of the same year. The significance of this bill, which broke the back of the student movement, was that it gave university presidents and, if necessary, the minister of education extraordinary powers to supersede the authority of the faculty, and even to suspend teaching and research functions. Despite spirited opposition from those supporting traditional faculty autonomy, and although this legislation was never applied, its mere existence changed the academic environment and the traditional relationship between government and university. The result was that, with occasional exceptions, campus unrest subsided, and the student movement broke up into increasingly rival factions, each claiming to be more ideologically pure than its opponents. They still visited violence upon one another, but their challenge to the state had been successfully met.

Somewhat like the aerodynamics of the gooney bird, the marvel of Japanese higher education is not that it fails to perform as well as critics would like, but that it works at all. Harvard sociologist Nathan Glazer's generalized characterization of Japanese education seems to be most applicable to higher education. Seemingly puzzled, Glazer has noted:

The basic paradox of Japanese education is that underfunded. . . . devoid of any marked evidence of innovation, [and] sharply criticized for its enormous emphasis on examinations, under attack from business for the quality of its college graduates, with limited research facilities, and a modest system of graduate education, torn by conflict between an alienated and radicalized teaching force in the elementary and secondary schools and a firmly conservative Ministry of Education, characterized by a college and university intelligentsia most of whom are opposed to the national government and unsympathetic to the emphasis on economic growth—it manages nevertheless to educate a labor force that serves the needs of Japanese business, industry and government.[41]

THE THIRD MAJOR REFORM PERIOD, 1978–PRESENT

The late 1970s and early 1980s served as a "run up" period to Japan's current educational reform movement. In the early 1970s, several important reports calling for educational reforms of various types stirred widespread discussion among thoughtful Japanese and contributed to the ferment that resulted in the appointment of the Ad Hoc Reform Council, or *Rinkyoshin*, in 1984. The first of these early documents, published in 1970, was the Ministry of Education's *Educational Standards in Japan* which provided a comparative framework within which to evaluate Japan's educational achievements. This was soon followed by a report of one of the ministry's advisory organs, the Central Council for Education, which caused a considerable stir and provoked the Japan Teachers Union to undertake its own study, which was published in 1975.

The Central Council for Education document took a swipe at both conservative apologists of the existing system and the radical Japan Teachers Union when it warned that "education is rapidly falling behind the times because vested interests protect the status quo, because idealists oppose reforms without paying attention to their actual contents, and because much time is spent wastefully on the discussion of reforms which have no possibility of being implemented."[42] The report advocated "long-range fundamental policies and measures for developing the educational system, basing these proposals on an examination of the educational system's achievements over the past twenty years and on its understanding of the system of education appropriate for the years to come in which rapid technological innovations and national and international changes are anticipated."[43] The then minister of education, Michita Sakata, was impressed enough by this analysis to refer to it as a plan "for the third major educational reform in Japan's history."[44]

Among its proposals, all of which carried hefty price tags, were extending free public education to four- and five-year-olds, providing teachers with large salary increases, allowing teachers more time to teach by shifting paperwork to an expanded clerical staff, expanding special education programs, and increasing subsidies to private universities. One could probably characterize this report as recognizing that educational expansion had run its course and that there was now a need to move in the direction of improving the quality of education. As was to be expected, reactions to specific proposals depended upon whether one's ox was being gored or not.

Still another important document feeding the reform debate was the analysis of Japan's educational policies conducted by the Organization for Economic Cooperation and Development (OECD). Falling back on its traditional practice of actively seeking outside advice, Japan invited the OECD to send a team of education experts to advise it on future directions. The 1971 OECD report, on balance, was probably the clearest view of Japan's educational problems. It praised the role played by education in the nation's industrial development, but strongly criticized the conformist nature of the Japanese system, overcentralized control, and an overemphasis on standardization in the name of egalitarianism. Instead it recommended that the time seemed to be ripe "for some practical measures aimed at the development of students' personalities through a more flexible and less pressured scheme of education, with more free time, more curricular freedom, more diversity in extra-curricular activities and more cooperation among pupils. The time may have come," the OECD examiners continued, "to devote more attention to such matters as *co-operation*, in addition to discipline and competition, and *creativity*, in addition to receptivity and imitation."[45]

Finally, after several years of careful study, the Council on Education Reform of the Japan Teachers Union published its own view of the correct path to educational reform. Arguing that Japanese education "is circumscribed" by the government's "high economic growth policy nationally, and Security Treaty setup with the United States internationally," the JTU report suggests that this has resulted in "environmental destruction, soaring prices, housing problems, [a] traffic mess and energy crisis."[46]

While the reform ferment of the early 1970s was at its height, Japan was hit by the first oil crisis in 1973. As a result of this international economic dislocation, Japan's economy sputtered to a virtual halt and, for a brief period, experienced a negative growth rate. After this sharp decrease in the growth rate, which had averaged 9.1 percent between 1959 and 1973, to a mere 4.0 percent between 1974 and 1980, the government was hard put to provide the resources needed by the education sector and, indeed, has had to find ways to reduce its financial support.

For the reverse of many of the reasons that educational enrollments expanded rapidly during the economic boom of the 1960s, the system began to contract after 1973. The birthrate has dropped sharply in recent years, and there appears to be no good reason to anticipate a turnaround in the near future. The school-age population has been decreasing since 1979 at the kindergarten level and since 1981 at the lower elementary level, and this negative wave is gradually making its way through the entire system. Attendance rates among school-age children in the noncompulsory sector have stabilized since the 1970s, suggesting that demand may have peaked. Further, "Japan's birth rate for 1980 equaled the record low level for 1966," and, according to a government spokesman, "the proportion of women of childbearing age will decline during the next four or five years."[47] Also, the percentage of Japan's under-fifteen population decreased from 22.3 percent in 1984 to 21.8 percent in 1985, which represents 105.3 boys for every 100 girls.[48]

Although Japan's commitment to education as an escalator for success is still very high, cracks in that commitment are beginning to appear. Professor Amano Ikuo of Tokyo University presents a persuasive argument in which he refers to a "crisis of structuration." Amano argues that postwar Japan was successful in creating a society that was both egalitarian and mobile, but, since the slowdown of the economy after the oil crisis of 1973, opportunities for mobility have been significantly reduced. He believes that the Occupation's attempt to dismantle the prewar hierarchical system of higher education failed and that a stable hierarchy of high schools, dominated by the relatively few serving as feeder schools to the top universities, has emerged. "The opportunities to the top universities are virtually monopolized by the top high schools," he writes, and graduates of these top schools tend to secure jobs leading to the elite positions in society. In the earlier stage of rapid expansion of secondary and higher education, Amano contends, there existed a healthy competition, but, as a result of the kinds of changes described above, the number of places in elite universities has decreased, and the number of desirable jobs available upon graduation are fewer. Although it is still true that a majority of young people continue to play this game, there are increasing numbers who are unwilling to participate.[49]

Amano's assertion that most Japanese youths continue to play the competition game is undoubtedly accurate, but, for the first time, an increasing number of young people are dropping out of that game. In the past, one of the things that distinguished Japanese schools from their American counterparts was their miniscule number of dropouts. In 1983, the latest year for which figures are currently available, 111,531 students of public and private senior high schools in Japan dropped out, an increase of 5.2 percent over the preceding year. These figures constituted only 2.4 percent of all senior high school students. This figure is quite low, especially when compared to the United States where 23 percent of senior high school students drop out before graduation. What is troubling, however, is that the Japanese figure has shown an increase every year since 1974 when relevant statistics were first collected.[50]

One of the most interesting dimensions of this phenomenon is the so-called school refusal syndrome, which, in the view of the Ministry of Education, is caused by "the rapidity of social change, the proliferation of the nuclear family, loss of community feelings, affluence and urbanization." Another view, however, "blames the school system which is theoretically designed so that all children of the same group stay at the same level and work at the same pace." When reality intrudes on this Pollyannish assumption, however, the result is "great strain on the slower children." These children's complaints of physical ailments that keep them home from school are neither truancy nor delinquency, but "a cry of silence" against the terrible pressures placed upon them by an unyielding system.[51]

Others see the problems emerging in today's Japan as nothing more than what they call "advanced nation disease" (*senshinkoku-byo*), in other words, the inevitable, if alarming, results of modern industrial society—"increases in the rates of divorce, juvenile crime, school violence and other social ills associated with countries like the United States."[52] It is undeniable that school violence, although still a minor problem when compared to that in the United States, is seen by most Japanese as simply unimaginable. The actions of this still tiny minority have shocked adult Japan because "their behavior violates the most fundamental code of Confucian-influenced traditional educational values—namely, respecting and obeying teachers."[53]

There is no doubt that the socioeconomic environment of contemporary Japan is very different from that of a decade ago. Young people today are growing up in an affluence that is in stark contrast to that of previous generations. They are living in a more universal culture; the music which they listen to on their Walkman is the same as their counterparts in Düsseldorf or Detroit hear. They are sensitive to changing youth culture trends abroad, and it is not uncommon for them to have travelled overseas. They spend much of their time shopping for the latest fashions, playing video games, and even driving automobiles in increasing numbers. In summary, the consumer orientation of young people in the late 1980s is a far cry from that of the 1960s youth. Whereas politically active students a quarter of a century ago were committed to idealistic goals and were intensely interested in building what they perceived to be a better society and a majority of those in the 1970s worked hard to become "salarymen" and share in the nation's economic prosperity, today's youth pursue personal pleasure with a single-minded devotion reminiscent of their older brother's loyalty to his company.

The combination of a rigid and inflexible educational system, along with this new orientation of students, has led not only to an increase in dropouts, but also a great increase in school violence. For example, the first half of 1983 saw a 26 percent increase over violent school incidents in 1982. A bewildering increase of violence against teachers occurred and, to the suprise of many, more and more females are becoming violent; the National Police Agency (NPA) reported that in 1984 almost one out of every five youngsters taken into custody by the police was a female.[54]

Both 1983 and 1984, however, saw a slight decline in school violence according to NPA reports, but the violence that occurred has been characterized by authorities as more "vicious" than in the past; indeed, the NPA recorded an increase "in such crimes as kidnapping, arson, and assaults by minors."[55] The category showing the greatest increase, however, is that of *ijime*, or school bullying, and both the vernacular and English-language press have been filled with reports, editorials, and letters to the editor describing it and analyzing its causes. It has become so serious a problem that the Tokyo Metropolitan Police Department has recently created "a special unit for taking into public custody tormentors in school bullying cases." They report that in the period 1–18 November 1985 they received forty calls from victims, and "14 [of them] were taken up as criminal cases." The complaints included inflicting bodily injuries, blackmailing, being burnt with cigarette butts and a cigarette lighter, forcing victims to drink large quantities of sour milk, poking hot needles under a victim's fingernails, and forcing victims to eat insects.[56] Another recent article reports that a significantly large group of children "who are apparently victims of bullying at schools have been admitted to . . . a mental hospital for children in Tokyo." The hospital reports that "many admitted children not only refuse to go to school but also show symptoms of obsessional neurosis . . . out of fear of bullying."[57]

It is important to understand that, as disturbing as such uncivilized behavior may be, bullying is a tragic phenomenon that occurs at schools in all countries and, indeed, it is nothing new in Japan.[58] In fact, one cannot be sure that its practice today is of greater magnitude than it was in the past. The argument can be made that, because of changes in society, bullying and school violence are now regularly reported whereas in the past they went unreported for a variety of reasons. Donald Roden argues, for example, that in the elite prewar higher schools upperclassmen "customarily intimidated" new students, and "any sign of annoyance could lead to more severe forms of harassment." This behavior was not described as bullying, however, but merely as "initiation." More serious were the so-called welcome storm (*kangei sutomu*) in which new students "would be attacked in their sleep by a roving band of upperclassmen"; while terrified, they "quivered in huddled masses."[59]

A number of other issues are relevant to the policy process, but lack of space precludes a discussion of them. There is little doubt, however, that the most important policy issues include the examination system, centralized control over the educational system, the role of education in fostering economic development, and the knotty problem of how to reform Japanese education to meet the challenges of the twenty-first century while, at the same time, taking care that reforms take a form that is harmonious with Japanese traditions and values. If the two previous major reforms, in the early Meiji period and following World War II, are any guide, we can expect reforms of a rather sweeping nature to be made in the next few years, to be followed shortly by a period of reflection in which modifications of the original reforms are made to bring them into closer conformity with the realities of Japanese life.

One of the major differences between the 1980s and the two earlier reform experiences is that in both the Meiji and the Occupation periods there were foreign models available that most Japanese agreed were worthy of emulation. The foreign models, whether English, French, German, or American, were models with which their creators were reasonably satisfied. Today, however, there is no foreign model that stands out as an obvious candidate for adaptation. Virtually all of the countries to which Japan has traditionally looked for educational ideas are themselves engaged in reform efforts to salvage inadequate educational systems. Perhaps the question that ought to be posed is, "Can the Japanese reformers *create* a new model which will not only meet their needs in the twenty-first century, but will also serve as a model from which the rest of the world might learn?''

NOTES

This chapter was originally commissioned by the National Institute of Education (Contract No. NIE-P-85-3206) as part of the U.S. Study of Japan Project. It was originally published in the *History of Education Quarterly* 27, 3 (Fall 1987), pp. 299–324. The author wishes to thank Richard Rubinger and Shimahara Nobuo for helpful comments on early drafts.

    1. Provisional Council for Educational Reform, *First Report on Educational Reform* (Tokyo: Ministry of Education, 1978), pp. 66–67.
    2. Ardath W. Burks, ed., *The Modernizers: Overseas Students, Foreign Employees, and Meiji Japan* (Boulder, Colo.: Westview Press, 1985); Foster Rhea Dulles, *Yankees and Samurai: America's Role in the Emergence of Modern Japan, 1791–1900* (New York: Harper, 1965); Robert Schwantes, *Japanese and Americans: A Century of Cultural Relations* (New York: Harper, 1955); Hazel J. Jones, *Live Machines: Hired Foreigners and Meiji Japan* (Vancouver, B.C.: University of Bristish Columbia Press, 1980).
    3. Najita Tetsuo and Irwin Scheiner, eds., *Japanese Thought in the Tokugawa Period, 1600–1868: Methods and Metaphors* (Chicago: University of Chicago Press, 1978), pp. 98–99.
    4. Edwin O. Reischauer, *The Japanese* (Cambridge, Mass.: Harvard University Press, 1977), p. 169.
    5. United States, Department of War, Office of Strategic Services, "Japanese Education" (Washington, D.C.: National Archives of the United States, n.d.), p. 2.
    6. Nishi Toshio, *Unconditional Democracy: Education and Politics in Occupied Japan, 1945–1952* (Stanford, Calif.: Hoover Institution, 1982); Robert E. Ward and Frank Joseph Shulman, eds., *The Allied Occupation of Japan, 1945–1952: An Annotated Bibliography of Western Language Materials* (Chicago: American Library Association, 1974).
    7. Hugh Borton, *American Presurrender Planning for Postwar Japan*, Occasional Papers for the East Asian Institute, Columbia University (New York: 1967); Hugh Borton, "Preparation for the Occupation of Japan," *Journal of Asian Studies* 25 (February 1966): pp. 203–12; Thomas W. Burkman, ed., *The Occupation of Japan: Educational and Social Reform* (Norfolk, Va.: The MacArthur Foundation, 1982); Marlene J. Mayo, "American Wartime Planning for Japan: The Role of Experts," in *Americans as Proconsuls: United States Military Government in Germany and Japan, 1944–1952*, ed. Robert Wolfe (Carbondale: Southern Illinois University, 1984), pp. 3–51.
    8. Robert King Hall, *Education for a New Japan* (New Haven, Conn.: Yale University Press, 1949), p. 2.
    9. Nishi, *Unconditional Democracy*, pp. 176–80.
    10. Benjamin C. Duke, *Japan's Militant Teachers: A History of the Left Wing Teachers' Movement* (Honolulu: University of Hawaii Press, 1973); Donald R. Thurston, *Teachers and Politics in Japan* (Princeton, N.J.: Princeton University Press, 1973).
    11. Ronald S. Anderson, *Education in Japan: A Century of Modern Development* (Washington, D.C.: U.S. Government Printing Office, 1975), p. 63. See also Hans H.

Baerwald, *The Purge of Japanese Leaders under the Occupation* (Berkeley, Calif.: University of California Press, 1959).

12. Edward R. Beauchamp, "Educational and Social Reform in Japan: The First U.S. Education Mission," in Thomas W. Burkman, ed., *The Occupation of Japan*, pp. 175–92. It should be pointed out that a Japanese scholar, Satow Hideo, has found evidence in the National Archives to suggest that the 6-3-3 system was not imposed on the Japanese but was instituted at the request of a committee of Japanese educators. See "6-3-3 System Not Imposed by GHQ," *Japan Times*, September 15, 1986, p. 2.

13. Herbert Passin, *Society and Education in Japan* (New York: Teachers College Press, Columbia University, 1965), pp. 293–304.

14. John W. Dower, *Empire and Aftermath: Yoshida Shigeru and the Japanese Experience, 1878–1954* (Cambridge, Mass.: Harvard University Press, 1979), pp. 369–470; Michael Schaller, *The American Occupation of Japan: The Origins of the Cold War in Asia* (New York: Oxford University Press, 1985).

15. William K. Cummings, *Education and Equality in Japan* (Princeton, N.J.: Princeton University Press, 1980), p. 116.

16. There is evidence to suggest that the power of the Nikkyoso (Japan Teachers Union) is on the decline. "Only 50% of Teachers in JTU, Says Ed. Ministry," *Asahi Evening News*, August 27, 1985, p. 2; "Nikkyoso Teachers Less Than Half of Total for First Time," *Japan Times*, October 1, 1986, p. 3; "Teachers' Union Membership Falling," *Mainichi Daily News*, October 1, 1986, p. 12.

17. Fukatake Tadashi, *The Japanese Social Structure: Its Evolution in the Modern Century*, trans. Ronald P. Dore (Tokyo: Tokyo University Press, 1982), p. 70.

18. Ichikawa Shogo, "Japan," in *Educational Policy: An International Survey*, ed. J.R. Hough (New York: St. Martin's Press, 1984), p. 105.

19. Japan, Ministry of Education, Science and Culture, *Statistical Abstracts of Education, Science, and Culture* (Tokyo: Ministry of Education, 1983).

20. Samuel Coleman, *Family Planning in Japanese Society: Traditional Birth Control in a Modern Urban Culture* (Princeton, N.J.: Princeton University Press, 1983), p. 150.

21. Ibid., p. 151.

22. T.J. Pempel, *Patterns of Japanese Policymaking: Experiences in Higher Education* (Boulder, Colo.: Westview Press, 1978), p. 163.

23. Passin, *Society and Education in Japan*, p. 97.

24. Amano Ikuo, "Educational Crisis in Japan," in *Educational Policies in Crisis: Japanese and American Perspectives*, ed. William K. Cummings et al. (New York: Praeger, 1986), pp. 23–43.

25. Edward R. Beauchamp, "Shiken Jigoku: The Problem of Entrance Examinations in Japan," *Asian Profile* 6 (December 1978), pp. 543–60; William K. Cummings, *Education and Equality in Japan* (Princeton, N.J.: Princeton University Press, 1980), pp. 206–34; Thomas P. Rohlen, *Japan's High Schools* (Berkeley, Calif.: University of California Press, 1983), pp. 77–110; Shimahara Nobuo, *Adaptation and Education in Japan* (New York: 1979), pp. 77–126.

26. Ardath W. Burks, *Japan: A Postindustrial Power* (Boulder, Colo.: Westview Press, 1981), p. 157.

27. Kobayashi Tetsuya, *Society, Schools, and Progress in Japan* (New York: Pergammon, 1976), p. 93.

28. Shimahara, *Adaptation and Education in Japan*, p. 133.

29. Anderson, *Education in Japan*, p. 201.

30. Japan, Ministry of Education, *Outline of Education in Japan, 1985* (Tokyo: Ministry of Education, 1985), p. 13.
31. Pempel, *Patterns of Japanese Policymaking*, p. 180.
32. Ichikawa, "Japan," in *Educational Policy*, p. 115.
33. Japan, Ministry of Education, *Educational Statistics, Japan* (Tokyo: 1976), p. 73.
34. Anderson, *Education in Japan*, p. 98.
35. Beauchamp, "Shiken Jigoku," *Asian Profile*, pp. 243–60.
36. Ezra P. Vogel, *Japan's New Middle Class: The Salary Man and His Family in a Tokyo Suburb* (Berkeley, Calif.: University of California Press, 1965), p. 40.
37. Ronald P. Dore, *The Diploma Disease: Education, Qualification, and Development* (Berkeley, Calif.: University of California, 1976), p. 49.
38. Thomas P. Rohlen, "Japanese Education: If They Can Do It, Should We?" *American Scholar* (Winter 1985–1986), pp. 29–43.
39. Fosco Maraini, *Japan: Patterns of Continuity* (Tokyo: Kodansha, 1971), p. 27.
40. Rohlen, "Japanese Education," *American Scholar*, pp. 29–43.
41. Nathan Glazer, "Social and Cultural Factors in Japanese Economic Growth," in Hugh T. Patrick and Henry Rosovsky, eds., *Asia's New Giant: How the Japanese Economy Works* (Washington, D.C.: Brookings Institution, 1976), p. 821.
42. *Basic Guidelines for the Reform of Education: On the Basic Guidelines for the Development of an Integrated Educational System Suited to Contemporary Society; Report of the Central Council for Education* (Tokyo: Government of Japan, 1972), p. 2.
43. Ibid.
44. *Mainichi Daily News*, June 12, 1971, p. 8.
45. Organization for Economic Cooperation and Development, *Reviews of National Policies for Education: Japan* (Paris: OECD, 1971).
46. Japan Teachers Union, *How to Reform Japan's Education* (Tokyo: Japan Teachers Union, 1975), p. 30.
47. *Japan Times*, February 26, 1981, p. 2.
48. *Mainichi Daily News*, May 5, 1985, p. 12.
49. Amano Ikuo, "Educational Reform in Historical Perspective," *Japan Echo* 11 (1984), p. 12.
50. *Japan Times*, April 7, 1985, p. 2; *Asahi Evening News*, April 5, 1985, p. 4.
51. Margaret Lock, "Plea for Acceptance: School Refusal Syndrome in Japan," *Social Science and Medicine*, Fall 1987.
52. G. Cameron Hurst III, "Japanese Education: Trouble in Paradise?" *Universities Field Staff International Reports*, no. 40: Asia (1984), p. 10.
53. Nishimura Hidetoshi, "Educational Reform: Commissioning a Master Plan," *Japan Quarterly* 37 (January–March 1985), pp. 18–22.
54. *Mainichi Daily News*, December 30, 1984, p. 12.
55. Ibid.
56. *Japan Times*, November 19, 1985, p. 3.
57. *Mainichi Daily News*, November 13, 1985, p. 13.
58. Murakami Yoshio, "Bullies in the Classroom," *Japan Quarterly* 32 (October–December 1985), pp. 407–11.
59. Donald T. Roden, *Schooldays in Imperial Japan: A Study in the Culture of a Student Elite* (Berkeley, Calif.: University of California Press, 1980).

3

Education Reform in Japan: Goals and Results of the Recent Reform Campaign

Leonard Schoppa

Given the positive publicity that Japan's education system has enjoyed in the United States and other nations of late, it may be difficult for anyone who was not in Japan in 1983–1986 to understand the sense of crisis that dominated talk about education in that country at that time. Stories of students attacking teachers were featured regularly in the press; the Ministry of Education reported an epidemic of bullying in the nation's elementary and junior high schools; and the nightly news told the stories of tormented young students who blamed bullies and examination pressure before committing suicide.

These were the circumstances that surrounded the initiation of Japan's recent education reform campaign. In the spring of 1984, Prime Minister Nakasone Yasuhiro responded to this perceived crisis by announcing his intention to establish a cabinet-level advisory council, the Ad Hoc Council on Education (AHCE, *Rinkyoshin*), which was to be charged with the task of examining the nation's educational system and proposing solutions to its problems. Following debate in the Diet, such a council was formed in August of that year and proceeded to spend the next three years deliberating and issuing proposals. Reflecting concern about education in Japan, the council's every move was followed closely by the media. Especially in the first year, even closed-door debates within the council were the subject of numerous front-page headlines and extensive television coverage. The education system seemed headed for significant change.

By 1987 when the council issued its final report, however, much of this initial momentum was lost. Stories of educational crisis were less often in the news, and many of the bolder proposals which had been discussed early in the reform debate had run into opposition from entrenched interests. While the reform campaign resulted in the enactment of a range of programs and statutes, most represented minor changes along the established line of educational policymaking.

While the results of this reform campaign were therefore quite limited, it nevertheless provides an interesting opportunity to examine the Japanese educational system. The debate produced volumes of commentary on Japanese education by Japanese involved in all aspects of the education system: business groups concerned about whether the education system was producing the kind of workers needed for the next stage in Japan's economic advancement, traditional conservatives concerned about the decline of the Japanese work ethic, a teachers' union concerned about government efforts to reduce teacher autonomy, and local grass roots organizations and social commentators concerned about the effects of examination pressure on the nation's youth. In short, the reform campaign points out those aspects of Japan's internationally acclaimed education system about which Japanese themselves have doubts. It provides an opportunity for outsiders to see the Japanese education system through Japanese eyes. This chapter summarizes the main arguments, proposals, and results of this recent reform campaign.

THE PROBLEM

Although Japan's recent education reform debate came to focus eventually on complex issues such as the education system's perceived failure to foster creativity and its perceived lack of an international outlook, it began with a concern about more tangible problems: school violence, bullying, and suicides. It is therefore these aspects of Japan's educational "problem" which we must examine first.

The immediate problem most responsible for making education reform a leading political issue in the 1980s was that of school violence and delinquency (*konai boryoku to hiko*). These phenomena had started to make headlines in 1980 when, in that year, the city of Tokyo reported a 44-percent increase in cases of school violence.[1] The next year, the National Police Agency (NPA) reported a similar increase in the number of cases nationwide, and figures continued to grow for the next two years, reaching a peak in 1983 (see Tables 3.1 and 3.2). By 1984 when Nakasone embarked on his reform initiative, therefore, incidents of school violence were receiving nationwide publicity in a way which created the feeling of a real educational crisis. Two incidents within the period of a week in February 1983 particularly served to focus national attention on problems in the schools. In the first, a group of junior high and senior high school youths in Yokohama were arrested after they attacked a number of sleeping vagrants, killing three.[2] Just three days later, the media headlined reports that a Tokyo junior high school teacher had stabbed a student in the chest, resorting to the use of a knife in order to protect himself from his violent students.[3] Both stories received wide media attention and served to dramatize what statistics

Table 3.1
Incidents of School Violence in Japan

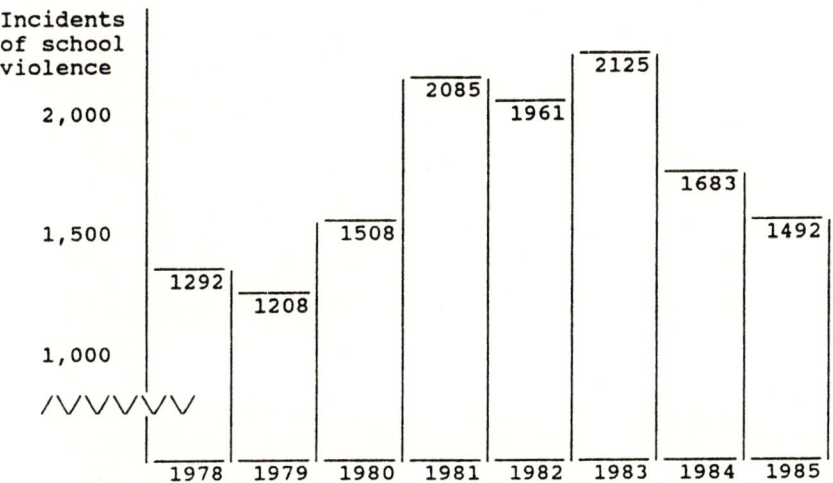

Source: Keisatsucho, *shonen no hodo oyobi hogo no gaikyo*, September 1986, p. 63.

Table 3.2
Incidents of Attacks on Teachers

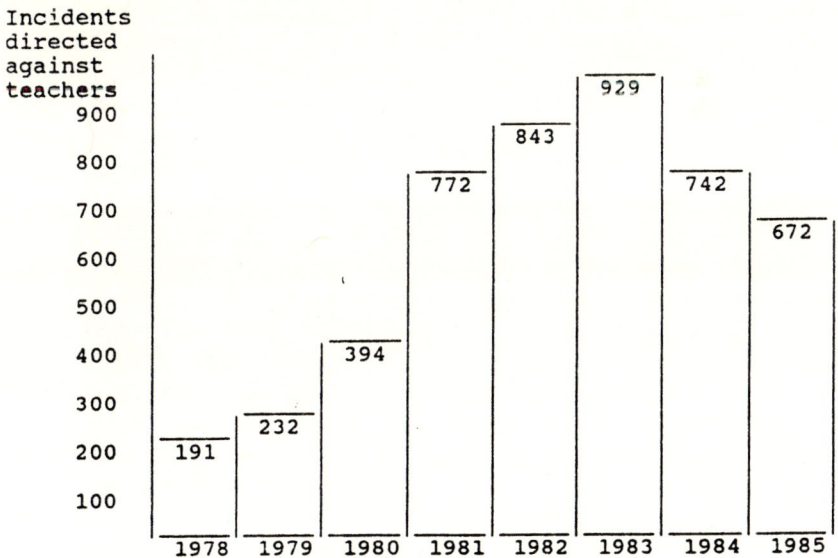

Source: Keisatsucho, *shonen no hodo oyobi hogo no gaikyo*, September 1986, p. 63.

showed was a rapidly growing problem in the schools. Shortly after the above incidents, Prime Minister Nakasone spoke for the first time about the need for a "radical solution" to deal with problems in the schools.[4]

Of course, Japan's school violence problem, even at its peak, was statistically insignificant compared to the situation in U.S. schools. In the peak year of 1983, there were 2,125 incidents of school violence reported in Japan. In contrast, in a peak year in the United States, 282,000 students were physically attacked and 1,000 teachers were assaulted seriously enough to require medical attention *each month*.[5] While the U.S. statistics thus dwarf the numbers for Japan, one must realize that Japanese reports of rising school violence did not refer to such comparative data. The emphasis was on the rising tide of indiscipline in Japan. The media stories about case after case of violence in the schools simply shattered the popular image of the schools as being uniformly peaceful and orderly places of learning.

After 1983, the reported incidence of school violence declined—soon reaching a level not very different from that of the pre-1980 period.[6] Concern about problems in the schools, however, did not diminish. In place of school violence, the media and pundits now directed their attention to a new set of problems: bullying, suicides, and refusal to attend school.

Of particular concern was an apparent epidemic of *ijime*, "the physical or psychological harassment of a weaker party by a stronger party or of a minority by a majority"—or just plain bullying.[7] Again, there were celebrity cases. In November 1984, two high school victims of *ijime* killed their persecutor and dumped his body in a river. In January 1985, a bullied junior high school girl committed suicide in order to escape the pain. The following February, a junior high school boy chose the same method of escape, leaving a suicide note in which he expressed the hope that his death would spur action that would prevent others from suffering as he had suffered.[8] The incidents received nationwide coverage in the media and prompted volumes of analysis by social commentators. In 1986, the Ministry of Education released a document that reported that 55 percent of the nation's schools were experiencing outbreaks of *ijime*; a total of 155,066 incidents had been reported in a seven-month period.[9] Table 3.3 reproduces one table in this Ministry of Education report. The degree of detail as to types of bullying indicates the seriousness with which this problem was treated.

Closely related to this problem of bullying was that of student suicides. According to the National Police Agency, fifteen student suicides in the 1984–1985 period could be attributed to bullying.[10] While the NPA reported that the total number of suicides for youths nineteen or younger was down in 1985, the number of cases it attributed to school-related causes was up from 124 to 136.[11] While the issue of suicides was of significant concern in Japan at this time, these statistics should again be put into perspective. Contrary to what is commonly believed in Japan (and the United States), Japan does not have an astronomical youth suicide rate—relative to its own historical rates or to the rates of other nations. As reported by Thomas Rohlen in his recent book *Japan's High Schools*,

Table 3.3
Incidents of *ijime* by Type*

(Incidents reported between 4/1/1985 and 10/31/1985)

Type of Bullying	Element.	Jr High	Sr High	Total
Verbally abused	18,561 (19.2%)	14,517 (27.4%)	1,754 (30.7%)	34,832 (22.5%)
Ridiculed / teased	29,698 (30.8%)	18,117 (34.3%)	1,680 (29.4%)	49,495 (31.9%)
Had personal possessions hidden	15,869 (16.5%)	7,036 (13.3%)	600 (10.5%)	23,505 (15.2%)
Had friends taken away	28,118 (29.2%)	12,169 (23.0%)	877 (15.3%)	41,164 (26.5%)
Ostracized by the group	7,673 (8.0%)	6,185 (11.7%)	436 (7.6%)	14,294 (9.2%)
Physically abused	20,990 (21.8%)	13,068 (24.7%)	1,743 (30.5%)	35,801 (23.1%)
Blackmailed	2,572 (2.7%)	4,257 (8.0%)	799 (14.0%)	7,628 (4.9%)
Annoyed by ** imposing kindness	3,761 (3.9%)	1,442 (2.7%)	149 (2.6%)	5,352 (3.5%)
Other	3,456 (3.6%)	2,386 (4.5%)	452 (7.9%)	6,294 (4.1%)
Total incidents	96,457 (100 %)	52,891 (100 %)	5,718 (100 %)	155,066 (100 %)

* Individual incidents included some in which two or more types of bullying had occurred. Totals of types therefore exceed total incidents. Percentages given indicate the proportion of incidents for the given group which included the particular type of bullying.

** Japanese children (and adults) generally do not like to be placed under obligation to another person who, without prompting, gives them gifts or offers them assistance. Children would consider it bullying, therefore, if their peers repeatedly gave them pencils and paper and offered to help them with their homework.

Source: Mombusho, *Jido seito no mondai kodo no jittai to mombusho no shisaku ni tsuite*, December 1986, p. 33.

Japan's youth suicide rate has fallen sharply since the 1950s when it did indeed have the highest rate.[12] By the 1970s, its rate had fallen behind many other nations, and today Japan's youth suicide rate is substantially lower than that of the United States.[13] As in the case of school violence, however, comparative statistics for youth suicide rates in other nations were not included in media reports in Japan. There were also few references to the fact that the overall youth suicide rate was actually declining. Rather, saturation reporting of each new suicide case created the popular perception of an unprecedented suicide "crisis."

A final related problem causing concern during this period was the growth in the number of students who refused to go to school. In this case, there was more statistical evidence of a growing problem. According to the Ministry of Education, the number of chronically absent junior high school students (those absent fifty days or more in a year) giving the reason "I hate school" for their absence rose steadily from 7,704 in 1975 to 27,926 in 1985. Though not as marked, the elementary schools also reported an increase in "school hating" chronic absenteeism.[14] Many of these students were suffering from what Japanese experts labeled school refusal syndrome, a psychosomatic condition sometimes associated with stomach aches, vomiting, and ulcers.[15] As in the case of the violence, bullying, and suicide problems, reports of this rise in school refusal caused a great deal of concern in a nation which prided itself on its educational system.

While these tangible education problems received a great deal of popular attention during the course of the recent reform initiative, they were not the only educational problems which caused concern in Japan. The educational, business, and political communities in particular were also worried that the nation's education system—though successful in turning out large numbers of workers with a uniform level of basic skills—might not be able to produce the kinds of workers needed to power the nation's continued advance into the twenty-first century. They were concerned that the strictly regulated and examination-oriented education system might not be able to produce workers who were more creative, more able to adapt to fast-changing technology, and more internationalist in their outlook. In short, these elites worried that Japan's educational system might not be able to adapt to the needs of its changing economic environment.

That Japanese education fails to nurture creativity is often asserted but is much more difficult to prove. What is true is that the content of Japanese education is subject to central curricular control and is dominated by an entrance-examination system which tests factual knowledge. These two features of the system clearly do inhibit creativity in some ways. The Ministry of Education's national curriculum guidelines specify in detail the body of information that a student is expected to master at each stage. Thus the guidelines for the elementary Japanese language arts course, for example, list exactly which ideographs (*kanji*) each student is expect to learn each year. The process through which the ministry approves textbooks for each course guarantees that this detailed plan is actually followed in the nation's schools. This central curricular control tends to have a dampening effect on creativity because the factual orientation of the curriculum and textbooks encourages teachers to emphasize learning by rote (*anki kyoiku*). Teachers tend to say, "this is the answer; learn it," rather than teach in a way which calls on students to think creatively about a problem.

Although central control of the curriculum does seem to limit creativity in this way, its effect is difficult to separate from that of Japan's entrance-examination system. Under the system, access to the nation's high schools and universities is governed by examinations which test each student's mastery of detailed facts and methods. Attainment rather than aptitude is measured. In a nation which assigns social status and employment prospects largely on the basis of where one went to high school and university, these examinations exercise enormous influence over the content of what is taught throughout Japan. Secondary school teachers in particular tend to teach to the test rather than to inspire their students to think creatively.[16] Those teachers who try to downplay the test are quickly forced to fall in line by parents who realize that the future prospects of their children depend not on their ability to think for themselves but on their ability to reproduce for the examiners a set body of knowledge.[17] In cases where teachers refuse to respond to such parent pressure, parents simply discount the class and encourage their children to concentrate on the exam preparation offered by private after school cram courses (*juku*).[18] Faced with this potential loss of their role, most teachers and public schools give in and concentrate on the skills needed to pass the exams. The examination system thus strongly reinforces the tendency of central curricular control to encourage rote learning.

Of course, to point out that education in Japan tends toward rote learning does not necessarily lead to the conclusion that the Japanese system has a creativity problem. It is not clear, first of all, whether creativity can actually be fostered through the formal educational process. A strong case can be made that the Japanese system—by providing large numbers of students with a solid fact- and mastery-based education—prepares the gifted few to build on that base with truly creative innovation. After all, one must learn to walk before one can attempt to run. Furthermore, there are elements in the Japanese curriculum (required art and music classes) which do allow and encourage creative expression.[19]

Nevertheless, the creativity problem was one which has increasingly concerned Japanese education policymakers and was one of the leading issues going into the recent reform initiative. Typical of this concern was a report published by the Committee for Economic Development (CED, Keizai Doyukai), a leading organization of businessmen, in 1984. In it, the businessmen argued that Japan needed the next generation of workers to be "creative, diverse, and internationally-minded," adding that foremost emphasis should be placed on the first of those three qualities.[20] The Study Group on Culture and Education, set up by Prime Minister Nakasone to set the stage for his reform initiative, echoed these concerns when it concluded that Japanese education had come to be characterized by a spread of "cramming, uniformity, and neglect of each student's abilities and individuality."[21] When Nakasone put the Ad Hoc Council on Education to work in 1984, therefore, he gave it clear instructions to shape a new educational system "full of the vitality and creativity relevant to the twenty-first century." Whether or not it can be demonstrated empirically that Japanese education suffers from a creativity problem, it is clear that many in Japan perceive it to have shortcomings in that area.

Many of those concerned about creativity in Japanese education have also been worried about two related problems: the weakness of Japanese universities and the failure of Japan's educational system to provide lifelong learning opportunities. These problems are related to the creativity issue because they too are a function of the nation's examination system. As noted above, the job prospects of a young Japanese person are largely determined by how he or she performs on entrance examinations, which decide where he or she will go to high school and university. An individual who gains admission to the University of Tokyo, regardless of how he or she performs there, can be quite sure of finding a job in a prestigious government ministry or with a well-regarded firm. An individual who is only able to obtain admission to a lower-ranking national university can expect to find a job only in local government or in a middle-ranking firm. Once placed in these jobs, the social status and life course of these individuals are largely set. There is very little social mobility—up or down— once young people settle into their jobs at the age of twenty-two. Japanese do not go back to graduate school in order to improve their social or professional position. While the linkage between entrance examinations and job prospects creates a powerful motivation for educational dedication in the preexamination years (up through age eighteen), the lack of any link between job prospects and education after the exams means Japanese have little incentive to dedicate themselves in their university years or to go back to graduate school in the years that follow.

This system was acceptable when the vast majority of jobs required skills that could be learned in the first eighteen years of life. It has increasingly come to be questioned, however, at a time when growing numbers of jobs require specialized knowledge and when fast-changing technology and lengthening career spans have created the need for lifelong learning opportunities. More and more Japanese, therefore, have come to question the nation's *gakureki shakai*—its social system which allocates life chances based on where one went to school rather than on what one learned there or what one has learned since then. They have come to question the quality of the education being received by the nation's university students in such a social system. Business groups in particular worry that too many students treat their university years as a vacation period between cramming for exams and their return to the grind of the work force. One recent business report called higher education—particularly the humanities programs— "a waste of public monies."[22] Also of concern has been the weakness of the nation's graduate programs, few of which are set up to offer programs for mid-career workers. As the Ad Hoc Council on Education noted in its 1986 midterm report, such a deficiency is a serious problem at a time when the average worker in Japan works for more than forty years in a fast-changing world.[23]

As the changing demands of the marketplace have given rise to such concerns about creativity and the weakness of Japanese university and graduate programs, they have also drawn attention to the need for a stronger international component in Japanese education at a time when the nation is becoming increasing integrated into the world economy. "Internationalization" (*kokusai-ka*) was Japan's buzzword for the 1980s, and its proponents were particularly interested in the internationalization of Japanese education. The report of Japan's Committee for Economic Development, cited above, wanted future workers to be "internationally-minded" (*kokusaisei*) as well as creative. The following specific proposals were outlined by this business group in its discussion of the need to internationalize education: (1) a strengthening of English education in the schools; (2) a shift in the school year from an April start to a September start to make it easier for students, teachers, and professors to participate in international exchanges; and (3) the hiring of more foreigners in Japan's universities and firms.[24] While it is difficult to determine objectively the degree to which Japanese education had an internationalization problem, the demands of the CED and other groups indicate that there was definitely a perception in Japan that the established educational system was failing to meet the need for a new generation of more internationally aware and trained workers.

INTERPRETATIONS AND PROPOSALS

The above analysis has identified a number of problems (as perceived by various groups and individuals in Japan) which gave rise to the recent reform initiative: rising school violence, an epidemic of bullying, suicides, a rise in absenteeism, the weakness of the system in developing creative thinking skills, the weakness of the universities, the absence of lifelong learning opportunities, and the need for internationalization. Clearly, not all Japanese regarded all of these as problems. Some put emphasis on a few problems and played down the rest. Different segments of the political community interpreted the problems in different ways. The analysis which follows presents three basic schools of thought based on different interpretations of the same problems. Although all three schools agreed on the need for education reform, the analysis makes it clear that there was great disagreement regarding the nature of the change that was necessary.

The Traditional Conservatives

The "traditional conservative" segment of the political community, including Nakasone and most of the Liberal Democratic Party (LDP) as well as many business leaders, argued that the most significant of Japan's education problems was the rise in school violence and delinquency. Although it recognized the importance of other problems, this set of elites was most concerned that the rise in indiscipline posed a threat to Japan's fabled work ethic. Not surprisingly, the Japanese Federation of Employers' Association (JFEA, Nikkeiren) was one group which was particularly concerned about this perceived threat to the work ethic. In a 1983 report on the school violence problem, it argued that the "disrespect for rules inherent in school violence" could not be tolerated, adding that the schools should guide students toward a "proper outlook on society and work" in an effort to "maintain the Japanese worker's diligence and group-consciousness which have been so crucial in helping to propel the nation's economy."[25] Nakasone echoed similar concerns in his speeches, expressing his intention to refocus the education system on "the training of 'sympathetic hearts' (*omoiyari no kokoro*) and the training of internationalists who love their country and are willing to work hard for its development."[26]

These quoted remarks also suggest the source of the problem as interpreted by the traditional conservatives. In speaking of guiding students toward a proper outlook and training students to love their country, Nakasone and Nikkeiren were making it clear that they blamed the schools' problems chiefly on a weakness in moral education. Nakasone was most explicit in his criticisms. Recalling the American role in shaping Japan's education system under the Occupation, he argued that schools in the postwar period had come to put too much emphasis on the Western ideal of individual autonomy at the expense of "traditional Japanese values" emphasizing responsibilities to the community and the nation. He thus called for changes in the education system which would reemphasize Japanese values and encourage young people to rededicate themselves to their nation.[27] He wanted to strengthen the moral education curriculum and he wanted schools to be forced to display the national flag and play the national anthem at official functions.

The traditional conservatives also blamed teachers for the rise in school violence. If the schools were failing to instill moral values in the nation's youth, that failure not only was a function of the curriculum but also reflected what they saw as a decline in the "quality" of teachers. The quality which concerned the conservatives was not, strictly speaking, the academic quality of the young people being drawn into teaching. Attracted by relatively high wages and social status, most new teachers were graduates of top-ranking universities with strong academic records. Rather, what concerned the conservatives was what they perceived to be a weak commitment to teaching on the part of new teachers. Many seemed to lack the selfless dedication to teaching that had characterized earlier generations of teachers, and too many seemed to buy into the teachers' union's argument that teachers should spend only as much time on the job as was specified in their contracts.

The traditional conservatives' proposal for dealing with this perceived problem was their plan to require all new teachers to undergo a probationary year of training. Originally referred to as the *shiho* (probationary) system, the proposal was later modified to be called the *shoninsha kenshu* (new teacher training) system in order to play down the probationary aspect in favor of an emphasis on the training aspect of the proposal. In both forms, the plan called for all new teachers—traditionally given job security from the date of employment—to be employed on a special basis for one year. During this time, they would teach a full load of classes but would also be required to attend training workshops and (in various versions of the proposal) would be assigned a mentor from among the staff or from among the ranks of retired principals.[28]

The probationary training year proposal was aimed at a clear weakness in the established teacher-training system. Under the established rules, the university courses leading to teaching certificates require only a minimal period of practice teaching in an actual classroom. Government regulations require only four weeks of teaching practice for elementary school teachers and only two weeks for secondary school teachers. Although some state institutions specializing in teacher training require a somewhat longer period of practice, the bulk of secondary school teachers (most of whom are trained in education departments of regular universities) undergo only two weeks of practice—part of which is devoted to observation.[29] This lack of practical experience in the classroom clearly made it more difficult for new teachers to deal with problems in the classroom of the type that proliferated in the 1980s.

It should be noted that, given this concern about the weakness of university teacher-training courses, the traditional conservatives could have addressed the problem by forcing universities to require prospective teachers to spend more time in the classroom during their university course. They chose, however, to emphasize the *shoninsha kenshu* system because it promised to give the government (rather than university education faculties) control over the training process. The government could control the content of the training seminars and could encourage teachers to adopt their ideology of selfless dedication. Furthermore, through the review process leading to a decision on permanent employment, the government could discourage teachers from joining the teachers' union. Given the conservatives' view that the problems of the educational system were at least partly to blame on the corrupting influence of the teachers' union, this system in particular was their ideal.[30]

The Progressives

Not surprisingly, the Japan Teachers Union (JTU, Nikkyoso) and the rest of the progressive segment of the political community did not agree with the conservatives' interpretation of Japan's educational problems or with their proposals for change. They too saw the rise in school violence as a significant problem, but rather than blame it on a lack of moral education or weak teachers, they attributed it to the pressures of the nation's competitive examination system and on the where-you-went-to-school social system (*gakureki shakai*) that lay behind that competition. Not only the school violence problem but also the problems of bullying, the rise in the dropout rate, the rise in absenteeism, and the whole "desolation of education" were blamed on examination competition.[31]

The root of the problem, according to the teachers' union, lay in the *selective* nature of the system. Thus, they pointed out, the greatest growth in violence and absenteeism was at the junior high school level—the years building up toward the first selective examinations which determine where young people will go to high school (and ultimately to university). As one Japanese university professor who examined the pattern of school violence argued, "the established order of the middle school, where this process of evaluation and selection takes place, becomes the target for student violence."[32]

Given this interpretation of the problem, the JTU's education reform proposals differ significantly from those of the traditional conservatives. If selection is the problem, the solution is to eliminate (or at least delay) the process of tracking students by ability. Their reform plan outlined in 1985 called for the state to extend the period of compulsory education to include the high school years and proposed that the high school entrance examination be abolished as a means of selection. They proposed, furthermore, that the rank stratification of the high schools be ended through the introduction of "small-district high schools" (comprehensive neighborhood schools). Finally, in order to reduce the pressures of the university entrance examinations, they argued that the government should build more "universities open to the people" and specifically proposed that it should establish "regional comprehensive junior colleges" to provide greater opportunities for more young people to receive post-secondary education.[33]

The JTU and the progressive camp in general did not have the opportunity to participate directly in the recent education reform initiative. No official teachers' union representative was included on the prime minister's Ad Hoc Council.[34] Nevertheless, their perspective is representative of a significant segment of the political community and contrasts interestingly with the view of the conservatives. In terms of their actual influence, however, the JTU's proposals for positive change are probably less important than the union's opposition to the changes advocated by the other two schools of thought outlined here. Blaming the school system's problems on competition, the union had no use for the traditional conservatives' proposals for more moral education or a probationary training year for new teachers. Likewise, given its advocacy of a move *away* from selection by ability, the JTU strongly opposed the neoconservative call for increased and earlier tracking aimed at providing diverse students with education matched more closely to their diverse abilities and interests. The union labeled all such proposals "discrimination by ability" and strongly opposed them.

The Neoconservatives

For most of the postwar period, the debate over education policy has been dominated by the above two groups: the traditional conservatives and the progressives. The conservatives have tried to impose tighter controls over the curriculum, textbooks, and teachers in order to make sure that young people are taught traditional moral and patriotic values while the progressives have tried their best to stop them. In recent years, however, a new school of thought has emerged, one which I call the "neoconservatives." Not having been around for very long, this interpretation of the problems plaguing the nation's education system has been less clearly defined, and the associated proposals have not always been consistent. Still, the neoconservative view does represent a distinct interpretation which was quite important in the most recent round of the reform debate.

For the neoconservatives, the nation's biggest education problem was not school violence, bullying, or absenteeism, and the solution was not to be found in Ministry of Education guidelines calling for more moral education or more teacher training. According to this view, the most important problem was the rigidity and standardization of the educational system, and the solution was to be found in *less* Ministry of Education control. Nothing better illustrates the difference between the traditional and neoconservative views than the contrast between the two education reports issued at about the same time (1983–1984) by the Japan Federation of Employers' Association and the Committee for Economic Development. The JFEA's report, devoted entirely to the problem of school violence, emphatically called on the government to bring the schools back under control.[35] The CED's report, which did not once mention the issue of school violence, emphasized instead the need for a relaxation of government control in order to allow greater diversity, creativity, and internationalization.[36] For the neoconservatives, the future economic need for workers possessing these qualities was the greatest educational challenge.

In order to meet this challenge, the neoconservatives called for a very different set of educational reforms than those advocated by either of the other two schools of thought. The CED, in its report, blamed the rigidity and standardization of the education system on the way in which employers and universities select their students and employees. Both, it argued, should reduce their emphasis on standard criteria. Employers should recognize diverse sources of specialized talent— and not just hire the best generalists coming out of the top-ranked universities. The universities should each develop their own strengths and develop diverse selection criteria emphasizing those strengths, thereby replacing a system in which all universities (and all students) compete for their ranking on a single exam-based pyramid with a system composed of diverse universities less clearly stratified on a topography of multiple pyramids.

The chief spokesman for the neoconservative line in the recent reform debate was Koyama Kenichi, a close adviser of Prime Minister Nakasone who was named to the Ad Hoc Council. Like the CED, he too considered "eliminating uniformity in education" to be the top priority. He attacked "the disproportionate reliance on the standard criteria of entrance examination scores" as one source of excessive uniformity, but he also pointed to several other causes: the uniform, single-track 6-3-3-4 system which did not allow any alternatives to a progression of six years of elementary school, three years of junior high school, three years of high school, and four years of college; the excessive devotion in elementary and secondary education to standardized and egalitarian teaching methods and materials; strict and standard regulations for school accreditation which leave little room for schools to develop their individuality; and the maintenance of school zones and strict rules limiting school choice for parents of elementary and junior high school students.[37] The final two items on Koyama's list were also targeted by another neoconservative group, the Kyoto Group for the Study of Global Issues, which issued a widely publicized report in March 1984 just as Nakasone was embarking on his initiative. "Ideally," the group argued, "education should be free and independent of constraints and interference from public authorities. In particular, we would like to see as much decontrol as possible—if not the outright abolition of restrictions—in the education system."[38]

The neoconservative reform agenda thus contrasted sharply with the changes advocated by the traditional conservatives. The neoconservatives wanted to *reduce* regulation of educational content and textbooks; they wanted to allow schools and teachers to cater to the individual abilities and interests of students by allowing tracking and greater course specialization at lower levels of schooling; they wanted to allow diverse kinds of private and public schools by liberalizing school establishment standards and the rigidity of the 6-3-3-4 framework; and they wanted to encourage schools at lower levels to improve by allowing greater parental choice and introducing free market competition into the education sphere. In the education debate which ensued, "liberalization" (*jiyuka*) and "flexibilization" (*junanka*) became the slogans of the neoconservatives.

The Debate

The above three schools of thought certainly do not exhaust the categories of opinions on education which were expressed during the course of the recent debate in Japan. First, it should be noted that not all opinions were negative. Many Ministry of Education (MOE, Mombusho) bureaucrats and many of the LDP politicians with years of experience of working in the education sphere emphasized the strengths of the current system and opposed many of the reform ideas outlined above. While public opinion polls at the time Nakasone set off on his reform initiative indicated that nearly 80 percent of the public supported the idea of education reform, there can be no doubt that many individuals also recognized certain strengths in the system.[39] The recent education reform debate—growing in volume as Nakasone established his council in 1984 and continuing through the end of the council's term in 1987—provided a forum for all of the above voices to be heard. While the actual course of the council's debate is the subject of a much longer work, an outline of the way in which this debate took shape provides a basis for understanding the results of the reform initiative which are summarized below.[40]

Nakasone, the dominant force in initiating the reform offensive in 1984, set the tone for a confused debate with a series of pronouncements in the early months which were a curious mix of all of the reformist views outlined above. On the one hand, the prime minister served as chief spokesman for the traditional conservative view, blaming school violence on a decline in traditional morality as noted above. Nakasone also responded to progressive criticism of the examination system, however, and promised in an election speech to revise both the high school and university entrance-examination systems.[41] At the same time, the prime minister echoed the advice of close neoconservative advisors like Koyama when he remarked that "it is important that we introduce an element of competition into the whole school system through policies of liberalization and flexibilization."[42]

The MOE and the LDP's educationist Diet members responded with alarm, in particular, to Nakasone's neoconservative line. None of these members of the education establishment wanted to sacrifice their control of the system, and all resented the criticism of an education system which they had devoted their careers to building. The progressives similarly opposed the prime minister's call for the introduction of free market competition and greater diversity (which they read as "elitism") in the education system as well as his call for more moral education and stricter teacher training. Even before the Ad Hoc Council was established, therefore, the three reformist schools of thought began a fierce argument over the direction of change.

While the prime minister was not required to compromise with the progressive opposition, he needed the support of the education establishment (in particular his own party's educationists) in order to win passage of the law establishing his Ad Hoc Council. The compromise which he was forced to accept perpetuated the disagreement it had been meant to solve. In agreeing to share his power to appoint the reform council's members, Nakasone guaranteed that the membership would replicate the divisions within the conservative camp. Nakasone helped ensure that the council included neoconservatives like Koyama, CED leader Nakayama Sohei, and Kyoto Group members Amaya Naohiro and Ishii Takemochi. The MOE and the LDP's educationist Dietmen helped ensure that traditional conservatives like JFEA member Arita Kazuhisa and leaders of the education establishment such as former MOE vice minister Saito Sei and Nagoya University president Iijima Soichi were also named to the council. Although this appointment process ensured that the Ad Hoc Council would serve as a forum for a vigorous debate on the direction of educational reform, it was not particularly conducive to the formation of a consistent and concrete plan.

THE RESULTS

The reform proposals of the Ad Hoc Council, published in a series of four reports between 1985 and 1987, touched on most of the problems and proposals discussed above. Moral education and teacher training were given attention, but so were examination reform, liberalization, and internationalization. The degree of specificity of the proposals and the subsequent commitment to implement the proposals, however, varied widely—and looking back at the results three years after the dissolution of the council, it is clear that only a few areas have seen substantial change. This final section reviews, briefly, the fate of some of the most important reform ideas.

Moral Education

Prime Minister Nakasone's aim had been to instill in the nation's young people a greater sense of responsibility to their nation and a greater sense of patriotism through the educational system. He and some members of his council had wanted to go so far as to rewrite Japan's Basic Law on Education, a statement of the nation's educational goals written during the U.S. Occupation, which reflects a strong emphasis on what traditional conservatives saw as Western, individualistic values. The traditional conservatives also wanted to use the schools' moral education courses to instill traditional Japanese values and wanted to require schools to display the national flag and to play the national anthem at school functions.

The Ad Hoc Council decided early in its tenure that it would not seek to rewrite the Basic Law.[43] It did, however, devote a great many pages of its reports to the discussion of Japan's educational goals, concluding that education in Japan should play a special role in cultivating "a proper national awareness," teaching students about social responsibilities, and preserving "the unique culture and traditions of Japan."[44] The council also responded to conservative pressure and proposed that students be trained to respect and understand the flag and anthem—a proposal which was subsequently written into MOE guidelines for the nation's schools.[45] Finally, the council called for a "substantialization" (*jujitsuka*) of moral education in the schools, proposing specifically that the government develop official supplemental teaching materials and encourage teachers to use them.

Whether or not moral education classes, as they are conducted in the schools, have changed noticeably is difficult to judge. It is a fact that a completely rewritten moral education curriculum was adopted by the MOE in 1989. The guidelines do not call for any decisive return to traditional moral values, however, but merely for the morals courses to emphasize manners (*shitsuke*) and "an attitude of upholding social norms in daily behavior."[46] The MOE did follow through on the Ad Hoc Council's recommendation to develop supplemental teaching materials and is now distributing these free of charge to teachers. Given the hostile attitude of the teachers' union toward government efforts to dictate the content of moral education classes, though, it is unlikely that many teachers are picking up these free materials and changing the content of their morals classes to please the ministry.

Teacher Training

The traditional conservative proposal calling for a training year for new teachers was endorsed by the Ad Hoc Council. The conservatives were largely frustrated, however, in their aim of making this a probationary year. The council proposed that the "conditional employment period" for new teachers (usually a mere formality given the sacrosanct nature of the lifetime employment system

Education Reform in Japan 67

in Japan's public sector) be extended from six months to a full year in recognition of their trainee status. It also recommended, however, that "consideration be given in order to avoid causing new or prospective teachers to feel anxiety," a cautious tone which was echoed by a subsequent MOE council which laid out the proposal in greater detail.[47] The emphasis in the recommendations, therefore, was on practical training rather than on the establishment of a system for reviewing the actual aptitudes and abilities of new teachers.

The final plan calls for all new teachers, while carrying a full load of classes, to undergo a year of training composed of at least sixty days of in-school training and thirty days of off-campus training. The in-school training is conducted by a senior member of the faculty who offers advice to the new teacher on class management and teaching techniques. The off-campus training includes an array of activities such as lectures, overnight training camps, and visits to other schools. The training system was implemented for all new elementary teachers in 1989 and is due to be implemented for other levels in the near future.[48]

Reduced Uniformity of Educational Content

Going into the council's deliberations, the neoconservatives had advanced a whole set of proposals aimed at reducing the uniformity of schooling in Japan. They wanted to change the way in which businesses and universities choose their employees and students in order to reduce the emphasis on standard entrance examinations, to relax school establishment standards to allow diverse kinds of schools and universities, and to relax curricular control to allow schools and teachers to aim their teaching at the individual interests and abilities of students (through earlier tracking and specialized courses of instruction as well as within the classroom). These policies were designed to help the Japanese system produce a new generation of workers who were more creative and more diversely talented.

The council spent most of its first year dealing with this issue at the philosophical level, arguing over whether the goal of education in the twenty-first century should be "the promotion of individuality-ism" (*koseishugi*) or "an emphasis on individuality" (*koseijushi*). It finally settled on the latter.[49] At a more concrete level, its first proposals related to this goal were proposals to alter the structure of the 6-3-3 system and to reform the university entrance examination. The first, a proposal that six-year secondary schools (a "6-6 track") be established parallel to the mainstream 6-3-3 system, was never picked up by the Ministry of Education and seems to have died.

The debate over examination reform produced a curious compromise. Nakasone had vowed to abolish the Joint First-Stage University Entrance Examination (the *kyotsu-ichiji*) and seems to have wanted to replace it with a system which allowed a great deal more diversity in the ways in which universities selected their students. The education establishment strongly opposed this idea, however, and succeeded in blocking any radical change. The final proposal called for the *kyotsu-ichiji* to be replaced by a new nationwide entrance examination, the *kyotsu tesuto*. This test would be different from the old one in two ways. First, private universities would be allowed to participate as well (the old test was limited to the public universities). This change can hardly be described as contributing to diversity; more colleges using the same standard test would only further contribute to the uniformity of Japanese education. Second, universities would be allowed to choose to test as few as one subject, rather than the previously required five subjects.[50] The actual change has been even less significant than the already limited proposal. As of the 1990 test, only 16 private universities had joined the test, and only a token 2 out of 148 participating universities had reduced the number of tested subjects below the previously required (now optional) five.[51]

This failure of the initiative to produce more significant changes in the examination system was probably the most important of the many failures recorded here, for the lack of change in this crucial area doomed to irrelevance many of the other changes proposed by the council. As is discussed in more detail below, among the other proposals advanced by the council was one which proposed that curricular guidelines be made more flexible so that teachers and schools would be able to offer education more closely matched to the interests of their students. In the absence of examination reform, however, teachers are unlikely to be able to resist parent pressure and take advantage of any new flexible guidelines. Secondary school teachers in particular will still be expected to teach to the test. Likewise, while secondary schools might be expected to use their new leeway under such flexible guidelines to develop new specialized courses of instruction, they will not do so as long as high school and university entrance examinations require knowledge of a broad range of subjects.

For the record, the council did make recommendations in several other areas aimed at "emphasizing individuality." First, the council endorsed the principle that employers should reduce their emphasis on school background and examinations in selecting their new employees: their catchphrase called for "the pluralization of evaluation." The council left the actual adoption of reformed hiring criteria by private employers to the voluntary cooperation of numerous individual employers. In the one area in which the government had authority to change hiring practices (the public sector), the council made no specific proposal, despite the fact that the government ministries are among the most extreme in their emphasis on school background.

In addition, the council called for "regulatory relief" in a number of areas identified by the neoconservatives as contributing to uniformity: it called for the MOE to rewrite its curricular guidelines in "a broader, outline form" (*taikoka*) and called on it to relax standards for school establishment. These phrases were qualified, however, by a clause noting that the government retained the responsibility to "ensure certain standards and maintain the quality of education."[52] The implementation of these measures, having been left to the MOE with its interest in preserving its authority over public education, has been uneven. The new curriculum for junior high and high schools, adopted in 1989 and scheduled to be implemented over the next several years, is aimed at providing schools with a greater choice in terms of which courses they may offer and require. Nevertheless, at the high school level, for example, the number of specific courses required has actually been increased. At the junior high school level, the "optional" courses include such subjects as English which, because they are included on the high school entrance exam, are really not optional at all.[53] It is not at all clear, therefore, that the new curriculum will actually lead to greater diversity by encouraging students to specialize at an earlier point in their studies. As for the neoconservative call for education more closely matched to the abilities of individual students, it remains to be seen whether junior high schools will take advantage of their new opportunity to track students by ability—something which will be allowed for the first time under the new curricular guidelines to be implemented over the next several years.[54]

School Choice

Koyama and the neoconservatives on the Ad Hoc Council pushed hard for changes which would have allowed parents greater choice in choosing elementary and junior high schools. Under the established system, the 99 percent of elementary school parents and 90 percent of junior high school parents who send their children to public schools had no option other than to send them to their neighborhood school. The education establishment opposed the introduction of school choice, however, primarily because of its fear that such a system would be an administrative nightmare and would introduce inequalities into an egalitarian system. In the end, Koyama was able to win council approval only of a proposal suggesting that localities create *some* means by which to respect the wishes of parents. The proposal was qualified, however, by a clause specifying that such changes should be introduced only in such a way that they would not create inequality or administrative problems.[55] In response, the MOE issued a directive to local authorities suggesting that they study how they might go about responding more flexibly to parental requests.[56] In practice, little has changed.

Internationalization

The concern was that Japanese in general needed a greater international awareness and, specifically, that the nation needed a growing number of workers able to work in an international environment. The council addressed this issue, too, at the philosophical level, identifying the training of "Japanese within the world" (*sekai no naka no nihonjin*) as one of the goals of future education policies. Even in emphasizing the importance of international understanding, however, the philosophical section of the council's final report ends up sounding peculiarly nationalist. The document speaks of the importance of understanding and appreciating foreign cultures, but seems to advocate this international exposure primarily as a means of helping young people come to "lay claim to the uniqueness of Japanese culture." It argues that young people should not limit themselves to viewing things from the narrow perspective of their own nation, but adds in the same paragraph that young people should remain patriotic and should learn to understand and respect their national flag and national anthem.[57]

This ambivalent attitude toward internationalization is reflected as well in the specific policies proposed by the Ad Hoc Council. The main policies are designed to preserve and utilize the international experience enjoyed by the children of Japanese workers posted abroad by the government or the private sector. Special programs have been created in schools designed to help these "returnee children" (*kikokushijo*) maintain the English-speaking ability they acquired while abroad. Special rules of high school and university admission have been created to ensure that the special talents of these young people are recognized. And a New International School has been set up to allow returnees to attend school with foreigners and a few ordinary locals.[58]

All of these policies do nothing to internationalize the school system as a whole. They are mainly designed to train an elite but compartmentalized corps of workers able to work in the *English* language and in *Western* culture. While these returnees may supply the needs of businesses which need internationally capable workers, they are but a tiny fraction of Japanese children. As for policies aimed at *all* school children, the council did also recommend an upgrading of English language education in the schools through greater emphasis on communicative teaching methods, exams which do more than test grammar and reading comprehension, and the employment of foreigners and foreign-trained teachers. These policies will perhaps help future generations of Japanese feel more comfortable in their contacts with the outside world (or at least the English-speaking world).

CONCLUSIONS

It is fitting that this survey of Japan's recent education reform policies finishes with a look at its internationalization effort, for the tensions visible in the way in which the Ad Hoc Council tried to balance nationalism and internationalism on this issue reflect a deeper ambiguity in the way Japanese see their education system. A serious effort to achieve internationalization in Japan—requiring not just the ability to use English and not just the training of a tiny corps of internationalists—would have the schools nurture in all Japanese an ability to understand, appreciate, and even empathize with the diverse cultural values found in the world. It would require an appreciation, in other words, of a broad diversity of outlooks. The council members recognized that there was a fundamental tension between this kind of internationalization and the traditional conservative call for a return to traditional Japanese values. The tension was seen to be particularly serious given the traditional conservative view that "Western individualism" threatened "the Japanese emphasis on responsibilities to the group." The effort to develop an internationalization policy therefore required the balancing of two opposing views about exactly what was wrong with Japanese education.

This fundamental conflict also dominated the broader education reform debate. While one group of reformists argued that the need was for a greater emphasis on teaching children to live according to social norms and to be responsible to the group, another group of reformists called for a greater emphasis on diversity and creativity. While one group wanted to maintain government regulatory control over the schools, another group wanted to loosen these controls. Preoccupied and immobilized by this debate, the Ad Hoc Council was in the end able to put into effect only very limited changes. Very little was done to reform the examination system, despite the fact that both the neoconservatives and the progressives saw this system as a source of many of the problems in Japanese education. The whole problem of Japan's weak universities was put off and delegated to a subsequently established University Council. The degree of government control over the education system, on balance, does not seem to have been increased or decreased.

The fact that little changed as a result of this reform initiative, however, does not diminish its value in shedding light on Japan's education system and Japanese views of that system. Even though no group of reformists succeeded in achieving its reform agenda, it remains the case that a substantial cross-section of the Japanese elite (and apparently a substantial share of the public) is not happy with the present education system. Although the problems they identify and their interpretations of those problems are different, they nevertheless offer the observer a wealth of criticisms to examine and analyze. This chapter has not attempted to evaluate the alternative views presented here. It is hoped, however, that the presentation of Japanese views on their own system—as revealed in a very interesting education reform debate—has provided the reader with a reason to reexamine for him or herself the widely acclaimed Japanese education system.

NOTES

1. *Asahi nenkan*, 1982, p. 474. Although these early statistics showing an increase in the number of reported incidents of school violence probably did reflect an increase in the actual number of such cases, some of the subsequent rise in the statistics probably reflected the increased *reporting* of such incidents as the problem received massive media attention. Likewise, some of the subsequent decline probably reflected decreased reporting as school violence became less of a media concern.

2. *Asahi shimbun*, February 13, 1983.

3. *Asahi shimbun*, February 16, 1983.

4. Yagi Atsushi, *Mombu daijin no sengoshi* [The Postwar History of Ministers of Education] (Tokyo: Bijinesusha, 1984), p. 211.

5. Figures reported by Benjamin Duke, *The Japanese School: Lessons for Industrial America* (New York: Praeger, 1986), p. 188.

6. See qualifier about "reported incidence" in note 1. These school violence statistics are compiled by the National Police Agency based on information gathered from local

police. The local police in turn rely on schools to report specific incidents. While some cases, such as a stabbing, would almost certainly be reported and investigated by the police, many other incidents (a physical threat or a fight between students) might or might not be reported. Whether or not schools report such discretionary incidents depends on many factors, one of which is the degree of attention given to the problem by the media (see note 1). In addition, schools must consider whether reporting the incident would result in help from prefectural authorities or would cause the reputation of the school to suffer. My evaluation, based on discussions with teachers, reporters, and government officials, is that these factors together exaggerated both the peak and the subsequent decline in the school violence figures.

7. The definition is given by Iwao Sumiko, "Bullying in the Schools," *Japan Echo* 8, no. 2 (1986), p. 54.

8. Ibid., pp. 54–55. See also Murakami Yoshio, "Bullies in the Classroom," in James J. Shields, Jr., ed., *Japanese Schooling: Patterns of Socialization, Equality, and Political Control* (University Park: Pennsylvania State University Press, 1989), pp. 145–51.

9. Mombusho, Shoto chuto kyoiku kyoku, Chugakko ka, *Jido seito no mondai kodo no jittai to mombusho no shisaku ni tsuite* [Ministry of Education, Elementary and Secondary Education Bureau, Middle School Division, Regarding the Actual Condition of Student Problem Behavior and Ministry of Education Policies] (Tokyo: Mombusho, December 1986), p. 31.

10. Keisatsucho, *Shonen no hodo oyobi hogo no gaikyo* [National Police Agency, The General Condition of Youth Guidance and Protection] (Tokyo: Keisatsucho, September 1986), p. 62.

11. Ibid., pp. 98–100.

12. Thomas Rohlen, *Japan's High Schools* (Berkeley: University of California Press, 1983), p. 328.

13. While Japan's suicide rate for youths aged fifteen to nineteen dropped from 9.7 per 100,000 in 1975 to 5.5 per 100,000 in 1984, the U.S. index for the same age group rose from 7.5 to 9.0, almost double Japan's rate. Figures reported in Cynthia Hearn Dorfman, ed., *Japanese Education Today* (Washington, D.C.: U.S. Department of Education, 1987), p. 79.

14. Mombusho, Shoto chuto kyoiku kyoku, Chugakko ka, *Jido seito no mondai kodo no jittai to mombusho no shisaku ni tsuite*, p. 24.

15. See Margaret Lock, "Plea for Acceptance: School Refusal Syndrome in Japan," *Social Science and Medicine*, Fall 1987.

16. For an excellent description of the style of instruction in Japanese secondary schools, see Rohlen, *Japan's High Schools*, pp. 241–47.

17. Many parents criticize Japan's examination system and the pressures it puts on their children. Nevertheless, given the system as it is, few Japanese parents are willing to sacrifice their children's chances by allowing teachers to stray too far from examination preparation. See comments by Merry White, *The Japanese Educational Challenge* (New York: The Free Press, 1987), pp. 177–78. From my own experience, I recall the efforts of an energetic junior high school English teacher I worked with in Kumamoto who sought to incorporate a new method of English teaching into her classes. Parents immediately became concerned that their children would suffer on the high school entrance exam. The teacher had to promise the parents that she would conduct orthodox exam preparation as well as her new method and that she would not allow their scores to suffer.

Only after her first group scored well on exams did other teachers in the school and in neighboring schools attempt to sell *their* parents on the new method. Unfortunately, few teachers will make the effort to overcome parental conservatism in this way.

18. A quarter of the elementary school students and almost half of all junior high school students attend *juku*. See Mombusho, "Jido seito no gakkogai gakushu katsudo ni kansuru chosa" [Ministry of Education, "Research Regarding the Out-of-School Learning Activities of Students"], reprinted in *Gendai kyoiku kagaku*, no. 355 (June 1986), pp. 104–7. While these *juku* usually supplement and support what is taught in the regular classroom, they can also *replace* the regular classroom in the eyes of parents and students when teachers are seen as failing to prepare students for their examinations.

19. See the argument made by White, *The Japanese Educational Challenge*, pp. 78–81.

20. Keizai Doyukai, *Sozosei, tayosei, kokusaisei o motomete* [Committee for Economic Development, Demanding Creativity, Diversity, and Internationalism] (Tokyo: Keizai Doyukai, July 1984), p. 1.

21. Koyama Kenichi, "An End to Uniformity in Education," *Japan Echo* 12, no. 2 (1985), p. 44.

22. Japanese Federation of Employers' Association [Nikkeiren], *Report of the Committee for the Study of Labor Questions: Toward a More Vital Society* (Tokyo: Nikkeiren Publicity Division, 1985), p. 17. For an academic's description of higher education in Japan, see John F. Zeugner, "The Puzzle of Higher Education in Japan," *Change* (January/February 1984), pp. 24–31.

23. Ad Hoc Council on Education, *Summary of Second Report on Educational Reform*, April 23, 1986, p. 34.

24. Keizai Doyukai, *Sozosei, tayosei, kokusaisei o motomete*, pp. 1, 7–8.

25. Nikkeiren, *Kinnen no konai boryoku mondai ni tsuite* [Japanese Federation of Employers' Association, Regarding the Recent Problem of Violence in the Schools] (Tokyo: Nikkeiren, May 7, 1983), pp. 6–7.

26. Nakasone quoted from "Sengo kyoiku tenkan to chukyoshin: 'atarashi hoshu' no ronri" ["The Reform of Postwar Education and the Central Council on Education: The Arguments of the 'New Conservatism' "], *Nihon kyoiku shimbun*, April 23, 1984.

27. See, for example, Nakasone's answers to parliamentary questions about the need for an Ad Hoc Council, contained in Rinji kyoiku shingikai jimukyoku, *Rinkyoshin setchico-hoan shingi toben no gaiyo* [Ad Hoc Council on Education Office, A Summary of Answers Given in Parliamentary Debate Regarding the Bill and Law Establishing the Ad Hoc Council on Education] (Tokyo: Ministry of Education, September 14, 1984, section 1). The LDP as a whole endorsed the prime minister's emphasis on moral education in its 1986 election platform: Jiyu minshuto, *Wagato no koyaku* [Liberal Democratic Party, Our Party's Platform] (Tokyo: Jiyu minshuto shuppankyoku, 1986), p. 80.

28. The *shiho* version of the proposal has long been pushed by the LDP, most recently in 1983 when it was endorsed as a long-term goal by the Subcommittee on Teacher Problems of the party's Policy Affairs Research Council Education Division: *Kyoin no yosei, menkyo ra ni kansuru teigen* [Proposals Regarding Such Matters as the Training and Licensing of Teachers] (Tokyo: Jiminto, May 19, 1983), p. 4. The 1986 party platform of the LDP called for a *shoninsha kenshu* system aimed at "improving the quality of teachers": *Wagato no koyaku*, p. 81.

29. Committee for Facilitating Research, Japan Association of Universities of Education, *Teacher Training in Japan* (Tokyo: Daiichi Hoki, 1986), pp. 21–22.

30. The LDP has in recent years also pushed to upgrade the university teacher-training courses. It chose not to push for an actual lengthening of the period in the classroom, however, with the argument that such an increase would place too great a burden on the schools. At present, despite the fact that only 40,000 new teachers are employed each year, 170,000 university graduates participate in practice teaching and receive a teaching certificate. When so few who practice teach actually end up teaching, schools do not like to devote so much time and energy to the shepherding of practice teachers. At least, that was the LDP's excuse for not pursuing more fundamental reforms in the university training programs. See Subcommittee on Teacher Problems, *Kyoin no yosei, menkyo ra ni kansuru teigen*, p. 3. I would argue that, if university courses required longer periods of practice teaching, only those most interested in teaching would seek to earn a teaching credential.

31. Nihon Kyoshokuin Kumiai Kyoiku Kaikaku Kenkyuiinkai, "Nihon no kyoiku o do aratameruka" [Japan Teachers Union Research Committee on Education Reform, "How Shall We Reform Japanese Education"], *Minna de kyoiku kaikaku o* no. 5 (December 1, 1985), p.4.

32. Soeda Yoshiya, "Changing Patterns of Juvenile Aggression," *Japan Echo* 10, no. 3 (1983), p. 15.

33. Nihon Kyoshokuin Kumiai Kyoiku Kaikaku Kenkyuiinkai, "Nihon no kyoiku o do aratameruka," pp. 10–13.

34. One elementary school teacher who happened to be a dues-paying member of the JTU served on the Ad Hoc Council. She was not chosen as a JTU representative but, rather, because her prior cooperation with a Ministry of Education moral education project suggested that she would work well with the ministry. Omori Kazuo, "Sutato shita rinkyoshin" ["The Ad Hoc Council on Education Began Its Work"] *Asahi nenkan*, 1985, p. 208.

35. Nikkeiren, *Kinnen no konai boryoku*.

36. Keizai Doyukai, *Sozosei, tayosei, kokusaisei o motomete*.

37. Koyama Kenichi, "An End to Uniformity in Education," *Japan Echo*, pp. 44–45.

38. The Kyoto Group, "Seven Recommendations to Revitalize School Education, March 13, 1984," in *Discussions on Educational Reform in Japan* (Tokyo: Foreign Press Center, 1985), p. 31.

39. Harada Saburo, "Mombu kanryo no tanagokoro no ue de: maboroshi ni owatta kyoiku kaikaku" ["With Little Effort on the Part of Ministry of Education Officials: Education Reform Which Ended as Nothing More Than a Bad Dream"], *Sekai*, no. 500 (April 1987), p. 95.

40. For a detailed account of the reform debate, see Leonard Schoppa, *Education Reform in Japan* (London: Routledge, 1991).

41. Nakasone, "Seven Point Proposal on Educational Reform, December 10, 1983," *Discussions on Educational Reform in Japan*, p. 13.

42. Remarks on the NHK program "Ask the Prime Minister," quoted from "Daisan no kyoiku kaikaku: jiyukaron" ["The Third Education Reform: The Liberalization Argument"] *Nihon kyoiku shimbun*, September 3, 1984, p. 3.

43. The law establishing the Ad Hoc Council actually specified that the council would "respect" the Basic Law—a compromise Nakasone agreed to in order to win the support of moderate parties in the Diet. Nevertheless, some members of the council expressed an interest in rewriting the Basic Law despite the statute, and it was not until several months after the council's establishment that members finally put the issue behind them.

44. Rinkyoshin, "Kyoiku kaikaku ni kansuru dainiji toshin" [Ad Hoc Council on Education, "The Second Report Concerning Education Reform"], April 23, 1986, in *Rinkyoshi dayori*, Special Edition 5 (April 1986), pp. 18–21.

45. As of 1990, MOE regulations require that all schools display the national flag and play the national anthem at official school ceremonies (such as the opening and closing ceremonies). There is in fact no legal basis for calling the flag and anthem "national," but conservatives in Japan have long endeavored to use them to promote Japanese nationalism. For background on this issue, see Nishimura Hidetoshi, "Flag and Anthem, Symbols of Distress," *Japan Quarterly* 35, no. 2 (April–June 1988), pp. 152–56.

46. Mombusho, *Wagakuni no bunkyo shisaku: heisei gannendo* [Ministry of Education, Our Nation's Education Policies: 1989] (Tokyo: Okurasho Insatsukyoku, 1989), pp. 80–81.

47. Rinkyoshin, "Dainiji toshin," p. 41. Mombusho kyoiku shokuin yosei shingikai, Kyoin shishitsu noryoku no kojo hosakura ni tsuite [Ministry of Education Advisory Council on Teacher Training, Regarding Measures to Improve the Ability and Quality of Teachers], December 18, 1987, in *Nihon kyoiku shimbun*, December 26, 1987 (pullout section), p. 5.

48. Mombusho, *Wagakuni no bunkyo shisaku: heisei gannendo*, pp. 145–46.

49. See Schoppa, *Education Reform in Japan*, for a complete discussion of the debate.

50. "Kyotsu tesuto: Yonbukaicho: Yokisemu hantai iken" ["The Kyotsu Tesuto: The Unanticipated Opposition of the Chairman of the Fourth Subcommittee"], *Nihon kyoiku shimbun*, September 2, 1985, p. 1; "Anrakushi: Seihi, shidai no 'fusanka' " ["Mercy Killing: Success or Failure, the 'Nonparticipation' of Private Universities"], *Nihon kyoiku shimbun*, September 9, 1985, p. 1.

51. "College Entrance Tests Start," *Japan Times Weekly*, January 27, 1990.

52. Rinkyoshin, "Dainiji toshin," p. 71.

53. For a summary of the curricular changes, see Mombusho, *Wagakuni no bunkyo shisaku: heisei gannendo*, pp. 70–76.

54. Previously, the egalitarian philosophy underlying compulsory education in Japan required that all students in elementary schools and junior high schools (grades 1–9) be educated strictly as equals, no "gifted" track; no "basic" track. The new curriculum, adopted in 1989 and due to be phased in over the next several years, allows junior high schools to implement tracking by ability. Given strong teachers' union opposition to tracking at this level and probable opposition from many parents, it remains to be seen how many schools will actually implement tracking at that level.

55. Rinkyoshin, "Kyoiku kaikaku ni kansuru daisanji toshin" [Ad Hoc Council on Education, "The Third Report Concerning Education Reform"], April 1, 1987, in *Rinkyoshin dayori*, Special Edition 7 (April 1987), pp. 32–33.

56. *Nihon kyoiku shimbun*, May 25, 1987.

57. Rinkyoshin, Kyoiku kaikaku ni kansuru daiyoji toshin (saigo toshin), [Ad Hoc Council on Education, The Fourth Report Concerning Education Reform (The Last Report)] (Tokyo: Ministry of Education, August 7, 1987), p. 11.

58. The proposals are spelled out in Rinkyoshin, "Dainiji toshin," pp. 59–61. Mombusho offers the latest status report on the implementation of these ideas in *Wagakuni no bunkyo shisaku: heisei gannendo*, pp. 491–93. For a thorough discussion of the returnee issue in Japan, see Merry White, *The Japanese Overseas: Can They Go Home Again?* (New York: The Free Press, 1988).

4

Financing Japanese Education

Ichikawa Shogo

NATIONAL ECONOMY AND EDUCATIONAL OUTLAYS

Modernization and Education

The predominant view among overseas specialists is that education has been one of the greatest interests to the Japanese people and that some historical evidence for their lavish spending on education proves their enthusiasm.[1]

During the Tokugawa period (1603–1867), local feudal lords took an active role in establishing academies (fief schools). In the meantime, ordinary people, including farmers, craftsmen, and merchants as well as samurai in the ruling class, tended to spare no expense to equip their children with a good education. By the end of the Tokugawa period in 1867, boys and girls attending *terakoya* (temple schools, the most widespread type of elementary schools for commoners) had amounted to 79 percent and 21 percent, respectively.[2] As a result, Japan was reasonably competitive in the literacy rate with European countries in those days: 40 or 50 percent of men and about 15 percent of women were literate.[3]

Although Japan had fallen far behind European civilization in the field of science and technology, the people were richly cultivated in artistic and spiritual culture. Afterward, this background enabled the country to learn efficiently from advanced countries and to catch up with them within a short period. One of the main strategies used to accomplish this was making a large investment in education.

It was about 120 years ago during the Meiji Restoration in 1868 when Japan abolished the feudal Tokugawa regime and launched the task of modernizing society on a Western model. The new government established a modern school system in 1872, only a few decades after advanced European countries had instituted national school systems. Since that time, efforts have been made to expand and improve the system's quality in order to catch up with the more advanced countries of the West.

Generally speaking, educational expenditures, as a percentage of national income, become greater as per capita national income increases. In the share of public expenditure on education, however, Japan surpassed many Western countries having a much higher national income in the late nineteenth century.[4] This demonstrates that Japan made education an exceptional priority in her quest for development.

Thus, the enrollment rate in primary schools exceeded 90 percent in 1902, only thirty years after the establishment of the school system, and reached nearly complete attendance in 1920.[5] Subsequently, the proportion of pupils going on to secondary education began to increase, reaching 25 percent in 1940.

When Japan, in the late 1950s, had virtually recovered from the effects of World War II, an age of high economic growth began which enabled the country to extend opportunities for secondary and higher education to more and more of her population. This trend has continued; by 1985, the upper secondary school enrollment rate had exceeded 94 percent and that of higher education, approximately 37 percent.[6]

Resource Allocation to Education

During the postwar period, Japan lost its position as the leader in the proportion of public educational expenditure to national income. This occurred partly because Japan's national income expanded very rapidly and partly because many other countries increased their levels of public expenditure on education.

The Ministry of Education, Science and Culture (hereafter referred to as the Ministry of Education) reports that 16,568 billion yen, or 5.2 percent of Japan's gross national product (GNP) and 6.5 percent of Japan's national income, were allocated to education in 1985. Those figures could, however, be rather misleading as they include loan charges and are expressed in nominal terms.[7] According to Unesco statistics, Japan's share of public educational expenditure in Gross Domestic Product (GDP) (excluding loan charges in real terms) was 6.0 percent in 1981, enabling her to occupy an intermediate level among advanced countries.[8]

A fairer comparison of the share of educational expenditures in various national economies would be possible if data on their private expenditure on education were available. However, even if these statistics could be produced, Japan would undoubtedly record one of the highest values in the proportion of national economy reflecting private expenditure on education.

For example, 5,947,000 students participated in the private sector in 1985, constituting 21 percent of total enrollment of 27,763,000 pupils and students from primary to tertiary education. Another factor is the disbursement of 5,183 billion yen by the private educational institutions, accounting for 1.6 percent of the GNP and 2.0 percent of the national income.[9] Therefore, educational expenditures by both public and private sectors (excluding overlapping government subsidies toward private education) total 21,080 billion yen, or 6.6 percent of the GNP and 8.3 percent of the national income in the same year.

In addition, funds spent on a variety of "cram schools" (*juku*) and supplementary lessons in traditional arts and activities, as well as funds for adult education, must be included in any economic analysis of educational spending. Taking such nonformal types of education into account, Japan is clearly one of the world's most lavish countries in terms of educational expenditures.

As mentioned earlier, although it is true that Japan's current public educational expenditure is rather small in comparison to the national economy, this is partly explained by the fact that the public sector does not play as great a role in Japan's national economy as it does in many other advanced countries. In fact, the Ministry of Education statistics suggest that the share of education was 18.4 percent of the total government expenditure of 90,050 billion yen in 1985.[10] With reference to data released by the Organization for Economic Cooperation and Development (OECD), Japan is second only to Australia among member countries in the proportion of resources devoted to education.[11]

Based upon total expenditure reflected in the System of National Accounts, Japan's educational expenditure reached 9,849 billion yen, or 37.0 percent in 1983.[12] Only Belgium, among OECD members, spent as high a percentage of her resources as Japan in 1983.[13]

These data support the popular image that Japan is "a society mobilized for education."[14] Both the government and the Japanese people have willingly devoted a large proportion of their resources to education.

PUBLIC OUTLAYS ON EDUCATION

Allocation in Favor of Compulsory Education

The proportion of public resources devoted to education is impressively large. The net total educational expenditures by central and local governments amounted to 16,568 billion yen in 1985. Out of the total, 13,731 billion yen, 82.9 percent, was spent on national and local public schools; public subsidies to private schools amounted to 671 billion yen in the same year. This means that school education costs (including higher education) reached 14,402 billion yen, or 86.9 percent of Japan's total public educational expenditure. On the other hand, the expenditure on education of adults and out-of-school youths (hereafter referred to as adult education) remained as low as 1,225 billion yen, or 7.4 percent, although its share recently has been increasing rapidly. The remainder, including expenses for educational administration, took up only 5.7 percent.

In the breakdown among school levels in 1985, the largest share of 36.8 percent went to primary education, the second largest share of 23.4 percent went to lower secondary education (grades 7–9), and the third largest share of 19.8 percent went to upper secondary education (grades 10–12). A smaller share of 14.8 percent went to higher education in the same year.

The allocations for special schools for the handicapped, for kindergartens, and for special training and miscellaneous schools were even smaller—3.0 percent, 1.9 percent, and 0.3 percent, respectively. This means that primary and secondary education took up 72.1 percent of the total public educational expenditure, in other words, 83.0 percent of the public outlay on school education. What is more striking is that more than one-half of the former and nearly two-thirds of the latter were devoted to compulsory education (ages 6–15), provided by primary and lower secondary schools and by the departments at the corresponding levels of special schools for the handicapped.[15]

For more than a century Japan has consistently given top priority to compulsory education in the allocation of public resources, and this tendency continues to characterize the structure of educational outlays in Japan. As a result, its primary and secondary education, especially compulsory education, has not only become universal, but also has acquired a high standard of unit cost by international standards. This approach has, however, resulted in financial sacrifice by both ends of Japan's educational spectrum—preprimary and higher education.

Private Preprimary and Higher Education Expansion

The proportion of five-year-olds enrolled in kindergartens was 63.7 percent, in 1985, and the proportion of those in preprimary education, or both in kindergartens and in day nurseries (catering to infants from birth to five years including those who are in need of institutional care offered by national and local welfare authorities rather than educational authorities), reached nearly 90 percent. On the other hand, 37.6 percent of secondary school graduates chose to pursue some form of higher education. Although these figures suggest that both preprimary and higher education have already been popularized, the private sector has played the more important role in these educational levels. It is very rare to find the private sector with such a large share of students or children in a homogeneous and relatively egalitarian country such as Japan.[16] In fact, 76.3 percent of the children in kindergartens and 75.2 percent of the students in higher education were in private institutions in 1987.[17]

In the breakdown of expenditures by private institutions, higher education constituted 52.1 percent; upper secondary education, 20.3 percent; special training and miscellaneous schools, 13.5 percent; and kindergartens, 10.6 percent in 1985. In contrast to public educational expenditure, compulsory education constituted only 3.3 percent of the private sector total.[18]

On the other hand, public subsidies of education in the private sector developed rapidly during the period from 1970 to 1981, and these subsidies covered nearly 30 percent of current private higher education expenditures. Since 1981, however, the total amount of subsidies has increased only slightly, and their share of current expenditures has declined to below 20 percent.[19] Accordingly, the private sector depends on tuition and fees paid by the students for more than one-half of its budget, and the cost to families has reached a point where the financial burden is often heavier than a household can afford. Therefore, the only path open to the private sector is to admit more fee-paying students at the cost of raising the student-teacher ratio.

Financial problems facing the private sector have, thus, prevented it from improving the educational standards of both preprimary and higher education. As shall be discussed below, the unit costs at those levels of education have remained low in comparison with other advanced countries.

Educational Outlays by Local Governments

Except at the higher education level, responsibility for the organization of both formal pretertiary and nonformal adult education rests with local governments. Therefore, it disbursed 14,335 billion yen, or 86.5 percent of the total public outlay, on education in 1985. This educational expenditure accounted for the largest part, 25.5 percent of the total local expenditure amounting to 56,293 billion yen.[20]

Statistics published by the Ministry of Home Affairs indicate that personnel expenses and facility costs accounted for 65.6 percent and 17.9 percent of local educational expenditures, respectively. Moreover, the proportion of salaries for staff of local educational authorities and educational institutions amounted to 48.8 percent of the total local personnel expenses. This occurs partly because nearly one-half, or 46.5 percent, of the local civil servants work for educational institutions and in education boards, and partly because the salary level for teachers is approximately 10 percent higher than that for the staff of general administrative offices, fire brigades, or police forces.

Statistics from the Ministry of Home Affairs also demonstrate that 66.6 percent or two-thirds of the local educational expenditure was related to the prefectures and that the amount of educational expenditure by the municipalities was only one-half of that by prefectures in 1986. The share taken by education in the total expenditure of the municipalities was 15.5 percent, while the percentage was 28.4 in the total expenditure of the prefectures.[21] The difference in the amount and the proportion of educational expenditure between the two levels of local government results from the fact that prefectures play an important role in providing educational services at the local level.

In Japan, the law prescribes that the task of establishing and maintaining public educational institutions, and of operating and financing them, should be assigned to a particular level of government by school level. Thus, the central government is responsible for higher education, the prefectures for upper secondary education and special education for the handicapped, and the municipalities for compulsory, kindergarten, and adult education. The law does not, however, prohibit the central government from providing primary or lower secondary education or the prefectures and municipalities from providing higher education or, indeed, any type of education. Nevertheless, it does not require them to do so either, and in practice there are few cases of such diversification.

An important exception to this "division of labor" occurs in the municipal schools of compulsory education (including those for the handicapped and excluding those in ten designated metropolitan areas). In this case, the responsibility of covering most of the personnel expenses and the authority to appoint personnel to schools rest with prefectures instead of municipalities. The share, therefore, of personnel expenses in the prefectural total educational expenditure has been as high as 84.4 percent. This figure covers salaries for the above mentioned municipal school staff in addition to the staff of the prefectural schools.

On the other hand, municipalities must bear the entire cost for kindergartens and adult education facilities. At the compulsory education level, however, they are responsible only for buildings, equipment, and the salaries of lunch workers, caretakers, and janitors. The prefectures contribute the salaries of the teaching staff, clerks, nutritionists, and nurse teachers. Accordingly, in 1986, the proportion of personnel expenses remained 30.5 percent of the total municipal educational expenditure, while the cost of facilities accounted for 40.1 percent and the equipment cost for 21.2 percent of the total.[22]

Educational Outlays by the Central Government

According to statistics published by the Ministry of Education, its budget for 1985 was 4,627 billion yen (8.7 percent of the total expenditure in the General Account), and the Special Account Budget for National Schools was 1,613 billion yen (including transfer of 1,076 billion yen from the General Account Budget); the net total of these two budgets amounted to 5,164 billion yen. In addition, various grants toward local school activities from other government ministries (e.g., the Ministry of Agriculture) totalled 38 billion yen. This resulted in a total central government outlay on education of 5,202 billion yen.[23]

The Ministry of Finance, on the other hand, released figures showing that the amount and share of expenses for education and science in a breakdown by major expenditure programs of the General Account in 1985 was 4,883 billion yen, or 9.2 percent of the total.[24]

The two calculations concur in demonstrating that the central government allocates to education as little as 9 percent of its total budget, and its total educational outlay is around one-third of that contributed by local government in both absolute and relative terms.

According to the Ministry of Education statistics, the central government made grants of 2,969 billion yen, or 57.1 percent of its outlay on education, to local governments in 1985. This accounted for 20.7 percent of the local public educational expenditure. In addition, a part of the local allocation tax grants given by the central government,[25] 1,984 billion yen, was spent on education. Taking into consideration these allocation tax grants devoted to education, the grand total of educational outlay by the central government amounted to 7,186 billion yen, with 4,953 billion yen out of this going to the local government, or 34.6 percent of local educational expenditures.[26]

Meanwhile, statistics published by the Ministry of Home Affairs show that the local government received educational grants of 3,074 billion yen from the central government, or 63.0 percent of the national educational expenditures in the General Account. This means that nearly two-thirds of central government educational expenditure is constituted by grants to the local government. The statistics also demonstrate that these grants accounted for 22.8 percent of the local public educational expenditure, 13,456 billion yen.[27]

The outlay on national public schools (including higher education institutions) by the central government was 1,613 billion yen in 1985. This constitutes only 31.0 percent of its educational expenditure and 22.4 percent of its total educational outlay (including local allocation tax grants spent on education).[28] The overwhelming proportion of resources for national public schools go to higher education, especially four-year university education. The rest of the educational expenditure by the central government, 620 billion yen, mainly consists of subsidies to private educational institutions (324 billion yen) and scholarships (83 billion yen).

Thus, in Japan, local governments administer most of the educational activities in the public sector except those at the higher education level, and the primary function of the central government is to prescribe standards and to make grants for such activities.

RESPONSIBILITY FOR FUNDING EDUCATION

Burden Sharing between the Central and Local Governments

Although local governments appear to cover most of the public educational expenses, the central government heavily subsidizes local governments, and, therefore, the resources supplied for education by the former are only slightly smaller than those supplied by the latter.

As mentioned earlier, local governments spent 14,335 billion yen on education, accounting for 86.5 percent of the total public educational expenditure in 1985. However, it received 2,969 billion yen, or 20.7 percent of its finances, from the central government as specific grants to education. Furthermore, the central government gives local allocation tax grants (see note 25) to prefectures and municipalities through the Ministry of Home Affairs. These grants are not earmarked for a specific purpose, but they are often used for education. These block grants totalled 8,881 billion yen in 1985. The amount distributed to education is estimated to have been 1,984 billion yen, 22.3 percent of these tax grants, which accounted for 13.8 percent of the total educational expenditure by the local government.

Thus, specific grants and block grants to education from the central government, in 1985, totaled 4,953 billion yen and constituted 34.6 percent of the local educational expenditure. This means that local government was responsible for the remaining 9,382 billion yen, 65.4 percent of the total local expenditure for education. In other words, the local government received one-third of its educational financial needs from the national treasury. From their own resources, prefectures provided 5,175 billion yen (55.2 percent), and municipalities provided 4,207 billion yen (44.8 percent) in the same year.

In conclusion, the breakdown of the total public resources devoted to education by various levels of governments, in 1985, was 43.4 percent (including grants to the local government of 29.9 percent) by the central government, and 56.6 percent (31.2 percent by prefectures and 25.4 percent by municipalities) by the local governments.[29]

Increase in Funding by the Central Government

It was not until the 1940s that the central government began to share the responsibility of financing education on an almost equal basis with the local government. Just prior to 1920, local governments had been charged with providing nearly 90 percent of the public educational expenditures; the share assumed by prefectures was less than 20 percent and that by municipalities as high as 70 percent. The reason for this was that municipalities shouldered the responsibility of covering almost all the expenses of primary education. In those days, secondary and higher education had not yet become popular, and students at the compulsory education level accounted for nearly 95 percent of the participants in formal education.

From the 1920s to 1940s, however, profound changes occurred in responsibility for funding education. For one thing, the local governments came to have generous financial support from the central government. In 1918, the government promulgated a Law Concerning the National Treasury's Share of Municipal Compulsory Education Expenses, and the subsidies grew so fast that by 1940 they covered about one-half of the personnel expenses connected with primary education.[30] The share of national subsidies in local public educational expenditure, which had been less than 1 percent, grew to 8 percent in 1918 and continued to rise until it reached 40 percent in 1941.[31]

A state-aid system relating to primary education was established because of the spread of local public schooling. The local government suffered from financial difficulties in the early twentieth century because education's share of the budget rose to a quarter of the total expenditure and municipalities had to spend between one-third and one-half of their total outlay on education. Subsidies from the national treasury relieved local governments (especially municipalities) from the intolerable burden, but the funding burden laid on the central government naturally grew much heavier. The share of the total budget claimed by education reached 2 percent in 1918 and swelled to more than 9 percent in 1930.[32]

Personnel Expenses Borne by Prefectures

Another noteworthy change in public educational finance took place during the period between the 1920s and 1940s, when the chief responsibility for financing education shifted from the municipalities to the prefectures. This occurred partly because the above mentioned subsidies from the central government to primary education removed a heavy burden from the municipalities and partly because the rapid spread of secondary education in the 1920s resulted in more expense for the prefectures. The number of secondary school students increased from less than 5 percent in 1910 to 8 percent in 1925 and again to more than 11 percent in 1940.[33]

By the 1920s, serious differences had arisen in the financial capacity of business and manufacturing cities, which had kept up with the swift pace of modernization, and that of rural farming and fishing villages, which lagged behind the impressive economic development of the larger urban areas.

As a result, the unit cost for pupils and the salary standard for teachers remained inconsistent among municipalities. Some poverty-stricken towns or villages were unable to pay their teachers' salaries, with the onset of an economic recession which negatively impacted on their finances. Despite the central government's payment of one-half of their personnel expenses for primary education, the financial problem remained a serious one.

Under these circumstances, in 1940, the prefectures came to assume responsibility for providing personnel expenses (the largest part of the compulsory education expenditures). In sharing the financial burden for education, the prefecture and the municipality then reversed their positions, and the former came to surpass the latter. At the same time, the proportion of total prefectural expenditures devoted to education increased to a point where it exceeded 20 percent, while that of the total municipal expenditures devoted to education dropped to less than 30 percent.[34]

UNIT COST OF EDUCATION

International Survey of Expenditure Levels

It is particularly difficult to discuss Japan's level of educational expenditure in an international perspective. Differences in currency between various countries make accurate comparisons extremely difficult. The official exchange rate for U.S. dollars, for example, does not faithfully reflect purchasing power and fluctuates frequently. Fortunately, the OECD has recently developed new conversion factors known as purchasing power parities (PPPs) which are comparatively free from the flaws found in the ordinary exchange rates.[35]

In a comparison of primary and secondary per pupil expenditures in the public sector (adjusted for the purchasing power parity exchange rate), Japan ranks slightly above West Germany, the United Kingdom, and France but slightly below the United States. In other words, it compares favorably with other advanced countries in unit cost for primary and secondary education.

On the other hand, the unit cost of Japanese higher education remains surprisingly low, which reflects the Japanese government policy of giving priority for financial resources to the compulsory education sector. In addition, serious inequalities exist between the public and private sectors in higher education. Leaving aside the private sector, in which the unit cost is very low, higher education in the public sector permits a ready comparison with that in other countries.[36]

Level of Teachers' Salaries

The nominal average salary of Japanese teachers, converted by using present market exchange rates of currencies, surpasses that in any Western country, but it is approximately equal to Western salaries in real terms, that is, when one factors in Japan's exceptionally high commodity prices.

A comparative analysis of Japanese and American public school teachers' salaries demonstrates that their average salaries were nearly equal in purchasing power during 1983–1984. It is estimated that the average salary of a Japanese teacher in that year, converted into "equivalent dollars" according to a PPP exchange rate, was $20,775 as compared with a U.S. average of $21,476 during the same period. However, this equivalency needs to be analyzed in light of other factors.

For example, teachers' salaries are linked more to seniority in Japan than they are in the United States. A Japanese teacher is paid about 76 percent as much as his or her U.S. counterpart upon entry into teaching, but this pay differential disappears around the twentieth year of teaching, and Japanese salary levels are significantly higher from then on. At the retirement age of sixty, Japanese teachers earn about 40 percent more than comparable teachers in the United States.

In Japan, both the workweek and the work year are longer than they are in the United States; the pupil-teacher ratio is higher; and the availability of nonteaching staff is less. Retirement benefits and pensions in the Japanese system are generous by U.S. standards. In this context of responsibilities and fringe benefits, a determination of which country's working conditions are superior is a subjective judgment.

Finally, the average 1983 teacher's salary in Japan was 2.4 times as great as the nation's per capita national income, as compared with 1.7 times per capita national income in the United States. In addition, comparisons of teachers' salaries with those in other occupations support the finding that Japanese teachers are better paid. The ratio of the average teacher's salary to average wage in manufacturing is only 1.2 in the United States but 1.6 in Japan.[37]

The economic status of teachers in both countries is more a matter of relative than absolute earnings. What counts is how teachers' salaries compare with pay levels in other occupations and with general levels of income and consumption in the national economy. Therefore, it seems fair to conclude that the relative economic status of teachers is higher in Japan than in the United States.

Little Imbalance among Local Entities

In the level of educational spending, Japan comes close to achieving national uniformity, and so the differences found among local districts is trifling. Specifically, the coefficient of variation of unit cost for public primary and secondary schools, among forty-seven prefectures, is only from 0.12 to 0.18, and the cost per class is even lower.[38] This slight variation in educational outlay among districts results partly from the uniform criteria prescribed by the central government for school facilities and accommodation, class size, number of staff members, teaching materials and aides, and teacher salary schedules.[39]

For instance, it is up to the prefectures to decide annually on teacher salary schedules for local public schools under their authority by following the recommendations of their personnel commissions. Nevertheless, the law provides that prefectural salary schedules shall be modeled after those of their national schools' counterparts, which depend upon the Recommendation on Pay Revisions released by the National Personnel Authority (NPA) every August.[40] In fact, prefectural personnel commissions make recommendations of the same sort as the NPA, except in some prefectures containing large cities which tend to recommend a slightly higher salary level.

Another factor contributing to salary uniformity is the role played by national funding in levelling the differences in financial capacities among local governments. The system of local allocation tax grants (see note 25), for example, plays a central role in adjusting imbalances by distributing a part of the national tax revenue to individual local governments in proportion to the shortage of their revenues.[41]

In addition, educational subsidies to local governments from the Ministry of Education have been working well. The strategy that the government took in 1940, shifting the responsibility for personnel expenses at the compulsory education level from municipalities to prefectures, and at the same time covering one-half of the expenses through national funding, has proved to be remarkably efficient in achieving an equitable educational standard among local districts. This can be shown by the ratio of the highest prefectural unit cost to the lowest prefectural unit cost at the primary school level. It had been about four times in 1928; it declined to less than two times after action was taken in 1940. As a result, there is little significant difference today in salaries for school staff or facilities and accommodations throughout the country.

BUDGETARY SYSTEM FOR EDUCATION

National Treasury

The central government allocates resources for educational and cultural activities, one of the major items in the General Account Budget, to the Ministry of

Education. There are three basic steps in the budgetary process. First, the various ministries submit their respective budgetary needs to the Ministry of Finance. Second, the Ministry of Finance studies these estimates, formulates a draft of the next year's overall government budget, and opens negotiation with each ministry over its proposed share of the budget. Third, after this process is completed, the Ministry of Finance prepares the government's proposed budget which goes to the Diet where it is deliberated prior to approval. As can be observed in these steps, Japan does not follow a top-down system of budget formulation, but rather a bottom-up process within the individual ministries.

In May, a month after the beginning of the fiscal year, each ministry prepares estimates of its revenues and expenditures for the following fiscal year. The budgeting and accounting division of each minister's secretariat takes the initiative in adjusting the requests advanced by the various divisions within the ministry, local branch offices and attached organizations, following the budget drafting policy that previously has been agreed upon by the cabinet. The individual ministries then submit their budget estimates to the Ministry of Finance by the end of August.

Assessing their estimates, the Budget Bureau of the Ministry of Finance begins budget hearings in September. The Ministry of Finance formulates a tentative government budget draft and conducts negotiations with individual ministries. When the Cabinet Council has finally agreed upon a budget draft, the Ministry of Finance submits a budget proposal to the Diet. The Diet begins deliberations on the proposal in January and, after it finishes, passes the proposed budget from the budget committee to a plenary session in the House of Representatives. The same process occurs in the House of Councilors. Upon the approval of a plenary session of the House of Councilors, the budget proposal becomes law and takes effect on April 1.

After the closing of the fiscal year on March 31, each ministry prepares a report on its revenues and expenditures, based on data presented by individual divisions and attached organizations, and the minister submits this report to the Minister of Finance. Following the Cabinet Council's decision, the settlement of accounts is passed to the Board of Audit which inspects and confirms the settlements. Then the board returns it to the cabinet, and the cabinet lays it before the Diet with an inspection report attached. In the Diet, settlement of accounts committees and plenary meetings of both houses deliberate upon these documents to determine government responsibility in the event of injustice or factual distortion.[42]

In summary, in regard to educational finance, planning is left to the Ministry of Education; adjustment, to the Ministry of Finance and the cabinet; control, to the Diet; and inspection, to the Board of Audit.

Please note here that the finance of national schools and research institutes is separately dealt with in a special account. Accordingly, the Ministry of Education prepares a budget estimate for this account which passes through the same process as General Account budget before the budget for the National Schools Special

Account is carried into effect. The Ministry of Education allocates current expenditure in the appropriate budget to each university and school or research institute in proportion to its number of staff or students.

Local Treasury

As of April 1988, there were 47 prefectural governments and 3,440 municipal governments (including 23 special wards in Tokyo). These local governments individually carry out the task of financing education. Nevertheless, local public entities concur in planning along the lines laid down in the central government's budget. The cabinet publishes a model plan, Plan for Local Finance, from the viewpoint of the national financial situation, and this document influences the actions of local public entities.

Basically, there is no special account relevant to education established in local finance, and accordingly all budgeting for education is included in the Ordinary Account. A local board of education compiles an initial estimate of revenues and expenditures for the coming year (except for university and junior college education and for subsidies to private educational institutions which are under the jurisdiction of a general affairs division of the local entity). Subsequently, the chief executive (governor or mayor) adjusts this draft to estimates for other fields, and the local assembly votes on it.

In regard to settled accounts, the chief accountant coordinates and the auditors of the local government examine his work. In addition, the Ministry of Education, the Ministry of Finance, and the Board of Audit supervise and examine how the grants given by the central government have been used.

As mentioned earlier, the prefectures pay the salaries of most of the staff members of municipal compulsory schools. Therefore, the amount of salary, the number of positions, and the length of working hours are prescribed by prefectural ordinances and not by municipal ones.[43]

Private Sector

In 1985, there were 18,356 private schools including kindergartens as well as universities and colleges. These are established and operated by nonprofit school corporations (*gakko hojin*). These corporations, in principle, are independent from government control and are responsible for financing the schools they have founded. The corporation consists of a board of directors headed by a chairman, a board of trustees, and auditors.

A board of directors compiles a budget, hearing the advice of the board of trustees in advance. When a corporation runs some profitmaking business to support school expenses, its earnings and expenses are separately handled in a special account. In regard to settled accounts, after a statement of accounts is audited by two or more auditors, the chairman of the board of directors reports the settlement of accounts to the board of trustees and requests their advice.

Although a school corporation has the final decision in its budget, it is laid under government intervention as far as it receives public support. The Ministry of Education and the Board of Audit have the authority to examine the accounts of schools receiving grants from the central government. The private school section and the auditors of prefectural governments are also allowed to examine the accounts of those private schools that have received grants from the prefectures.

In addition, government control has become tighter on the private schools receiving government subsidies for current expenses under the Private School Subsidy Law. The minister of education can suggest revisions in the budget of such private universities and colleges, and prefectural governors can give advice to private schools under their care.

POLITICS OF EDUCATIONAL FINANCE

Liberal Democratic Party

The government's budget for educational and cultural activities passes through the Ministry of Education, the Ministry of Finance, and the Diet. This budgetary route often results in direct and indirect influences on the part of various interest groups. The ruling conservative Liberal Democratic Party (LDP), by virtue of being in power, has the preponderant influence in the budgetary process. Since both the minister of education and the parliamentary vice minister are appointed from among sitting Diet members in the dominant party, the LDP can exert a dominant influence during the course of deliberations and usually can ensure that legislation reflecting the party's educational policy is passed into law.

However, the LDP's primary influence is not the result of its Diet members' control over the cabinet, but in the intervention of LDP Dietmen in policymaking in administrative affairs. As the LDP has held the reins of government for virtually the entire period since 1955, it has usually been able to transform its goals into government policy. This has been true not only in education policy but also in a range of other fields including public works, defense, governmental pensions, and annuities.

The Education Committee in the Policy Affairs Research Council of LDP acts as liaison with the Ministry of Education. The ministry is obliged to discuss its budget estimate with this committee and cannot submit its budget estimate to the Ministry of Finance until both parties agree on the scope of that estimate. In this way, the LDP Education Committee plays a crucial role in the formulation of an education budget. This process ensures the ministry's officials that they can rely upon the Dietmen from the committee for active support during their negotiations with the Ministry of Finance. This is particularly important because the eventual budget allocation depends upon negotiations between the Minister of Finance and the leaders of the LDP.

In actual fact, the LDP Education Committee has taken the initiative in carrying out most of the major postwar educational policies which have entailed great expense for the government.[44] These include the free supply of textbooks at the compulsory education level since 1963, public subsidies toward current expenses of private educational institutions since 1970, and a 25-percent salary increase for public schoolteachers since 1973. The members of the LDP Education Committee and former ministers and parliamentary vice ministers of education are therefore recognized as the *bunkyozoku* (a group of Dietmen with special interest in education) and wield great power in formulating the educational budget. Today, people concerned with education plead for a greater share of public resources with those LDP Dietmen as often as they do with the officials from the Ministries of Education, Finance, or Home Affairs.

Opposition Parties and the Japan Teachers Union

On the other hand, the opposition, such as the Japan Socialist Party (JSP), the Democratic Socialist Party, the Clean Government Party (Komeito), and the Japan Communist Party (JCP), are far less influential in educational policy than the ruling party. The budget process is carried out under the supervision of the National Diet where the dominant LDP commands a majority. Therefore, the government's budgetary proposal is usually adopted in its entirety.

The opposition parties sometimes display their power by using delaying tactics to prevent the passage of the budget until after the beginning of a new fiscal year. In this situation, the government is compelled to bring a provisional budget into effect and to postpone new policy initiatives contained in its original budget. In order to push through a proposed budget, the government party sometimes attempts to compromise on some details of the tax reduction bill or to shelve a bill about which the opposition feels strongly. Even in this case, however, a substantial portion of the budget remains unchanged.

Two of the major opposition parties, the JSP and the JCP, are intimately linked with the Japan Teachers Union (JTU), Japan's second largest trade union. About two-thirds of the members support the JSP and the other one-third the JCP. The union has, since its creation during the Occupation, been in virtually constant conflict with the government concerning most of its educational policies, but it is usually not strong enough to force the central government to alter its education budget. Nevertheless, in some local governments where the JSP or the JCP is in office, the JTU has an influential voice in educational affairs. In the late 1960s and the first half of the 1970s, a number of local left-wing governments came to power, and some educational policies of the central government were rejected or crippled at local levels.

Recently, however, the influence of the JTU over local governments has been waning. In addition, the central government succeeded in weakening the JTU's influence over education when it made provision for teachers to enjoy a higher salary standard than general civil servants. The very existence of the JTU is, however, still of major concern to the government.

Other Pressure Groups in Education

Various other groups exerting pressure on the government over its educational policy represent the worlds of education, economics, and local communities.

In the educational world, a number of nationwide associations have been formed by people holding particular positions or holding common views. These include organizations of chairmen of prefectural or municipal education boards, superintendents of local education boards, principals or vice principals of similar kinds of schools, teacher specialists of the same subject, clerks, nutritionists, nurse teachers, and the staffs of private schools. Each of these, and other, groups are constantly pressing their requests for improvements in school facilities, salary standards, or various types of subsidies.

On the other hand, the commercial world's interest in the education budget results from its profit motive in the fields of school architecture, school textbooks, teaching materials, and aides. Groups such as the Federation of Economic Organizations, the Japan Committee for Economic Development, the Japan Federation of Employers' Associations, and the Japan Chamber of Commerce and Industry also attempt to influence educational policy when they see their interests at stake. Their requests usually reflect their interest in manpower planning and employment stabilization, promotion of science and technology, preservation of the social order, and administrative reforms designed to decrease the size of governments. Owing to its financial contributions to the LDP, the world of commerce and industry enjoys a close intimacy with the ruling party, resulting in its having an important voice in the formulation of educational policy.

Most of the requests presented to the government by local entities fall into two categories. The national associations of governors, mayors, or chairmen of local assemblies always favor an increase of national subsidies for local educational activities. Also, groups from particular local communities, concerned over a particular problem or issue, often petition the ministry to situate a national university in their hometown, to favor a specific district in their region with exceptionally generous education grants, or to approve their opening a fund for new school building.

Centralization and the Financing of Education

Although their resource bases are not uniform, the various prefectures and municipalities compile their own education budget. It should be pointed out, however, that the quantitative differences among them are not terribly large in terms of their expenditure on education in spite of considerable inequality of social environment or economic development.

This is because, as the Ministry of Home Affairs points out, 7.9 percent of local public resources for education are provided by the sale of public bonds which a local entity is supposed to ask the Ministry of Home Affairs for permission to issue.

In addition, grants toward education from the central government account for nearly a quarter of their educational expenditures, although the categories on which these grants may be expended are specified by the central government. Furthermore, most of these categorical grants are given as percentage grants to cover from one-half to one-third of the cost of specified educational activities. Thus, the local governments must bear the remainder of the expenses. As a result, more than one-half of local educational expenditures are not controlled by the local entities.

Meanwhile, according to the statistics from the Ministry of Education for 1985, the local allocation tax grant (see note 25) constituted 13.8 percent of the local educational expenditure. The purposes for which these grants can be used are not specified and therefore constitute general revenue in the same way as local tax revenue. This block grant system performs an important function not only in securing local governments a certain provision of resources, but also in enabling them to carry out rationalized and appropriate administrative activities under certain standard discretionary conditions. Nevertheless, to work out an allocation to each local government requires an estimate of its basic financial needs in which the contents of the activities are presumed. Therefore, in one sense, this block grant also partly deprives local governments of autonomy.

Excluding the allocation tax grants, the amount of general unspecified resources that local governments are allowed to spend freely on education is quite modest. It is often suggested that local governments have, in practice, 30-percent autonomy because of their limited control over their finances,[45] but their autonomy in financing education is even narrower, roughly estimated at only 10 percent, mostly because grants from the central government come with strings attached.

NOTES

1. U.S. Department of Education, *Japanese Education Today* (Washington, D.C.: Government Printing Office, 1987), p. 3; Merry White, *The Japanese Educational Challenge: A Commitment to Children* (New York: The Free Press, 1987), p. 11; William K. Cummings, *Education and Equality in Japan* (Princeton, N.J.: Princeton University Press, 1980), p. 273; Ronald P. Dore, *Education in Tokugawa Japan* (London: Routledge & Kegan Paul, 1965), p. 292.

2. Herbert Passin, *Society and Education in Japan* (New York: Teachers College Press, 1965), p. 44. (cf. Dore, *Education in Tokugawa Japan*, pp. 317–21); Richard Rubinger, *Private Academies in Tokugawa Japan* (Princeton, N.J.: Princeton University Press, 1985).

3. Herbert Passin, "Japan," in James S. Coleman, ed., *Education and Political Development* (Princeton, N.J.: Princeton University Press, 1965), p. 276.

4. Michael C. Kaser, "Education and Economic Progress: Experience in Industrialized Market Economies," in R.A.G. Robinson and John E. Vaizey, eds., *The Economics of Education* (London: Macmillan & Co. 1966), pp. 89–173.

5. Ministry of Education, Science and Culture (hereafter MESC), *Japan's Modern Educational System: A History of the First Hundred Years* (Tokyo: MESC, 1980), p. 106.

6. MESC, *Statistical Abstract of Education, Science and Culture: 1986* (Tokyo: MESC), p. 24.

7. MESC, *Report on Local Educational Expenditures: 1984* (Tokyo: Government Printing Office (hereafter GPO), 1988). [In Japanese]

8. Unesco, *Statistical Yearbook: 1984* (Paris: Unesco, 1984).

9. MESC, *Report on Survey of Financial Conditions of Private Schools: 1985* (Tokyo: MESC, 1987). [In Japanese]

10. MESC, *Report on Local Educational Expenditures: 1985*.

11. OECD, *Educational Costs, Expenditures and Financing: An Analysis of Trends* (Paris: OECD, 1986).

12. Economic Planning Agency, *Annual Report on National Accounts* (Tokyo: GPO, 1986). [In Japanese]

13. OECD, *National Accounts: 1971–1983* (Paris: OECD, 1985).

14. White, *The Japanese Educational Challenge*, p. 9.

15. Calculations made by the author, based on data from MESC, *Report on Local Educational Expenditures: 1985* and *Report on Survey of Financial Conditions of Private Schools: 1985*.

16. Estelle James and Gail Benjamin, *Public Policy and Private Education in Japan* (London: Macmillan & Co., 1988), pp. xvi–xvii.

17. MESC, *Statistical Abstract of Education, Science and Culture: 1988*.

18. MESC, *Report on Survey of Financial Conditions of Private Schools: 1985*.

19. Japan Association of Private Colleges and Universities, *Japan's Private Colleges and Universities* (Tokyo: JAPCU, 1988), pp. 164–67.

20. MESC, *Report on Local Educational Expenditures: 1984*.

21. Ministry of Home Affairs, *White Paper on Local Finance: 1986* (Tokyo: GPO, 1988). [In Japanese]

22. Ministry of Home Affairs, *White Paper on Local Finance: 1986*.

23. MESC, *Report on Local Educational Expenditures: 1985*.

24. Ministry of Finance, *Financial Statistics* (Tokyo: GPO, 1987). [In Japanese]

25. The system of local allocation tax grants is a financial method which adjusts imbalances in tax resources among local governments and attempts to maintain governmental services at a certain level throughout the country.

The grants come from national tax revenues and claim 32 percent of the total corporate taxes, income taxes, and liquor taxes collected. The amount of ordinary allocation tax grants distributed to each local government is determined by subtracting the basic financial revenues (BFR) of each government from its basic financial needs (BFN). The BFR are 80 percent (in the case of a prefecture) or 75 percent (in the case of a municipality) of its estimated tax revenues, calculated by using the standard tax rate plus its estimated revenues from local transfer taxes. The BFN are the cost to the local government of carrying out rationalized and appropriate administrative activities under certain standard conditions.

Special allocation tax grants, which account for 6 percent of the total allocation tax grants, are provided to those local governments that have special financial needs owing to natural disasters or other unexpected emergencies that occur during a fiscal year. (Ministry of Home Affairs, "Local Administration and Finance," in Tsuji Kiyoaki, ed.,

Public Administration in Japan (Tokyo: University of Tokyo Press, 1984), pp. 101–2, 117–18.

26. MESC, *Report on Local Educational Expenditures: 1985*.
27. Ministry of Home Affairs, *White Paper on Local Finance: 1986*.
28. MESC, *Report on Local Educational Expenditures: 1985*.
29. Ibid.
30. MESC, *Japan's Modern Educational System*, pp. 193, 220.
31. Ichikawa Shogo, and Hayashi Takehisa, *Educational Finance* (Tokyo: Tokyo University Press, 1972), p. 61. [In Japanese]
32. MESC, *Japan's Growth and Education: Educational Development in Relation to Socio-economic Growth* (Tokyo: MESC, 1963), p. 126.
33. MESC, *Japan's Growth and Education*, p. 120.
34. Ibid., p. 126.
35. Michael Ward, *Purchasing Power Parities and Real Expenditures in the OECD* (Paris: OECD, 1985).
36. Ichikawa Shogo, "Financial Aspects of Higher Education in Japan," in *Comparative Study on University Finance in Asia* (Seoul: Korean Council for University Education, 1986), pp. 72–74.
37. Stephen M. Barro et al., *A Comparison of Teachers' Salaries in Japan and the United States* (Washington, D.C.: SMB Economic Research, Inc., 1986).
38. Calculations made by the author, based on data from MESC, *Report on Local Educational Expenditures: 1985*.
39. MESC, *Education in Japan: A Graphic Presentation* (Tokyo: Gyosei, 1982), pp. 54–68.
40. National Personnel Authority, "The Civil Service System," in Tsuji, ed., *Public Administration in Japan*, pp. 53–69.
41. Ministry of Home Affairs, "Local Administration and Finance," in Tsuji, ed., *Public Administration in Japan*, pp. 101–2.
42. Ministry of Finance, "The Budgetary System," in Tsuji, ed., *Public Administration in Japan*, pp. 156–58.
43. Ichikawa Shogo, "Japan," in J R Hough, ed., *Educational Policy: An International Survey* (London: Croom Helm, 1984), p. 122.
44. T.J. Pempel, *Patterns of Japanese Policymaking: Experiences from Higher Education* (Boulder, Colo.: Westview Press, 1978), p. 78.
45. Shindo Muneyuki, "Relation between National and Local Government," in Tsuji, ed., *Public Administration in Japan*, p. 109.

5

The Japanese Preschool System

Sarane Spence Boocock

It comes as a surprise to many people to learn that Japan, a society that has been viewed as antifeminist and family oriented in the extreme, has one of the world's most highly developed preschool systems. In the past decade, while discussions of primary, secondary, and higher education in Japan have appeared with increasing regularity in the American mass media and scholarly literature, relatively little attention has been given to Japan's equally impressive achievements in early childhood education and child care. Total enrollments in licensed, government-subsidized preschool programs have doubled every decade since 1960, to the extent that the majority of Japanese children between the ages of three and six, and substantial numbers of younger children as well, are now enrolled (Fuse, 1984: 4; Koseisho, 1984; Mombusho, 1982, 1985). Precise international comparisons of preschool enrollment rates are difficult because of the differences in the composition of preschool systems in different societies, as well as the differences among scholars and practitioners in the definition of a preschool. If "preschool" is narrowly defined to include only institutions guided primarily by educational goals (thereby excluding day care and other programs which serve custodial as well as educational functions), Japan in 1980 ranked twenty-seventh among the ninety nations for which Unesco data were available, with an enrollment rate close to that of the United States but less than half of that of the highest ranking nations, namely, France, West Germany, and Belgium (O'Connor, 1988). If, however, one includes all programs that have at least some educational component (thereby including day care centers), then Japan has one of the world's highest—perhaps *the* highest—rates. For example, a 1982 study of child care arrangements of working mothers in six nations (Japan, Korea,

United States, Great Britain, West Germany, and France) showed that Japan was the only nation in which the majority of children aged five or younger was enrolled in an organized preschool program, although France had the highest proportion of children in *public* kindergartens and nursery schools. By contrast, the modal form of care for American children was the babysitter (Youth Development Headquarters, 1982; Mombusho, 1985).

Japan's relatively high preschool enrollments seem less surprising when viewed in a broader context of worldwide trends. Throughout the world, but especially in industrialized societies, the preschool level is expanding faster than any other level of the educational system although there is considerable variation among societies and between geographical regions of the world. While various hypotheses have been offered to explain the explosion of preschool enrollments and the differences among societies in preschool development, crosscultural empirical research indicates that expansion of national preschool systems is greatest in societies in which: (1) economic development is high enough to support extensive preschool services; (2) a high proportion of women is employed in the industrial and service sectors of the labor market (women's participation in agricultural work, like nonemployment in the labor market, is negatively correlated with preschool enrollment rates); (3) there is widespread acceptance of the idea of women's right to full participation in society, including the right to work; and (4) there is widespread recognition of the developmental needs of children, and their status is relatively favorable. Concerning the third and fourth points, it should be noted that regardless of their status as citizens, women in all societies are still assigned the primary responsibility for the care of children (O'Connor, 1988; Kamerman and Kahn, 1981; Semonyenov, 1980; Mialaret, 1976; Koseisho, 1980).

In this context, the high level of development of the Japanese preschool system is not so surprising. Currently one of the world's most highly developed nations economically, contemporary Japanese society is also characterized by high and growing rates of female employment with decreasing proportions of that employment in agriculture and family-based businesses. By almost any indicator of health, welfare, or educational attainment, the state of children in Japan today is unusually favorable.[1] Finally, as we shall see, the conceptualization of high-quality outside-the-home child care services as a right of women and children alike—to ensure the all-around development of children and at the same time to guarantee their mothers the freedom to work and to participate in the life of the community—is relatively well developed in Japan.

This chapter attempts to present as comprehensive a picture as possible in a short space of Japanese preschool policy and practice. Following a brief overview of the preschool system, in which the major types of preschool institutions are identified and described, consideration is given to the *naiyo*, or content, of preschool programs and the social organization of preschool settings, including major points of debate or disagreement over substance and methodology. Next to be examined are the roles of and relations between the major groups or actors that have an interest in preschool education—in particular, teachers or caregivers, parents, the government, and the community or citizenry. Finally, some of the major unresolved issues concerning early childhood education and child care in Japan are discussed, and the outlook for the future is considered.

OVERVIEW OF THE JAPANESE PRESCHOOL SYSTEM

It has been argued that Japan as a society is characterized by such a high degree of homogeneity and consensus regarding important cultural goals and values that there is an unusually high degree of uniformity in the structure of social institutions and in the modes of socialization and social control. For example, in her recent study of early childhood socialization in Japan, Joy Hendry justified the conclusions she drew from a rather small and selective sample of preschools on the grounds that:

there were enough common features to make possible a considerable amount of generalisation about pre-school establishments in Japan. Much of this may be due to national concern and the legally sanctioned standards, which make the whole educational system remarkably comprehensive and uniform compared with that found in other nations. (Hendry, 1986b: 128. See also Reischauer, 1978: 196)[2]

On the other hand, some scholars feel that there is greater flexibility and innovativeness at the preschool level than at the higher levels of the educational system, that Japanese preschools are worth studying *because* they are less tightly controlled than most other Japanese social institutions (Professor Hara Hiroko, personal communication).

In the following analysis, three types of preschools are considered: (1) establishments under the auspices and control of the Ministry of Education (Mombusho) as opposed to the establishments under the auspices and control of the Ministry of Welfare (Koseisho), (2) public as opposed to private establishments, and (3) licensed as opposed to unlicensed establishments.[3] These three types are examined as well as regional variations in the Japanese preschool system.

Mombusho vs. Koseisho Control

The majority of preschoolers—over 70 percent of all Japanese children between the ages of three and five—are enrolled either in *yochien* or in *hoiku-en*. *Yochien*, which are under the authority of the Mombusho, cannot be exactly compared to any one type of American preschool because they combine elements of the kindergarten and the nursery school. Most *yochien* accept children from age three until six, when they enter elementary school. Most programs run for four hours a day, although some have now extended their hours in response to the demands of working mothers. *Hoiku-en*, which are under the authority of the Koseisho, are comparable to American day care centers. Although most of the children in day care are between the ages of three and five, many *hoiku-en* now accept younger children, some as young as six weeks (when the national maternity leave program expires). The standard *hoiku-en* program is for eight hours a day, six days a week, although again some now offer extended hours to accommodate parents with irregular working hours or long commutes.

Yochien and *hoiku-en* each enroll a total of more than 2 million children. Total enrollments have nearly doubled each decade since 1960—from 1.430 million (27 percent of all three to five-year-olds) in 1960, to 2.8 million (52 percent of all three- to five-year-olds) in 1980. Although the total number of children accommodated in *yochien* and *hoiku-en* is roughly the same, all preschoolers under the age of three are enrolled in *hoiku-en*, but the majority of preschoolers enter, or transfer into, a *yochien* by the age of five, the last preprimary year. By 1980, almost 80 percent of all four-year-olds and over 90 percent of all five-year-olds were in one of these two types of preschool programs.[4] Although still only a fraction of infants and very young children attend *hoiku-en*, the fastest rates of growth are occurring at these younger ages.

Japanese kindergartens and day nurseries, like their American and European counterparts, had very different historical origins. The first *yochien*, established in 1876, was attached to the Tokyo Women's Normal School. Its first head teacher, born in Berlin and trained in a school established by Froebel, was typical of *yochien* founders, many of whom had traveled abroad and had observed European and American kindergartens. As time went on, however, *yochien*, like *hoiku-en*, were also utilized for the transmission of traditional, especially Confucian, values. The early *yochien* were held primarily for the children of the wealthy. Even after the Ministry of Education created by the Meiji government officially recognized the kindergarten as an institution—to supplement home training, to prepare children for elementary school, and to provide moral education—and introduced (in the Act of Content and Facilities of Kindergarten Education, 1899) the first national standards for preschool education, the spread of *yochien* was gradual, reaching a total of about 2,000 establishments by the beginning of World War II (Ichibangase et al., 1978; Early Childhood Education Association of Japan, 1979).

Hoiku-en, begun around the turn of the century, were initially designed for the children of the poor. There had been some earlier day nurseries in rural areas to care for farmers' children during the busiest periods of the agricultural year, but, as in the United States, day care was primarily a reformers' response to the problems of industrialization and urbanism. Some early *hoiku-en* were subsidized by the Ministry of Home Affairs, and some attempted to incorporate some of the pedagogical content of the *yochien*, but since the children came from urban slum homes and most required all-day care, there was also a strong emphasis upon improving the children's eating habits, personal hygiene, and morals which is reminiscent of Jane Addams and Hull House. (The best study in English on the historical development of day care in Japan is Uno, 1987.)

The spread of *hoiku-en* was even slower than the spread of *yochien* until World

War II, when, as a result of the conscription of women for factory work, new facilities for the care of children sprang up all over Japan, in temples, shrines, libraries, schools, and any other space that could be converted into a child care facility (Early Childhood Education Association of Japan, 1979: 17–19). At the end of the war, many of these temporary preschools were closed, just as the end of the war saw the end of Lanham Act funding for child care facilities in the United States. In contrast to the United States, however, the drop in Japan was only temporary. A series of ambitious national plans for postwar recovery and industrial development, coupled with a continuing labor shortage, resulted in a continuing demand for female labor. In 1947, the new Japanese government created under the American Occupation promulgated the School Education Law, which made *yochien* part of the school system, and the Child Welfare Law, which established ten different kinds of institutions, including *hoiku-en*, under the auspices of the Ministry of Health and Welfare. Thus, ironically, the American Occupation set in motion a national system of early childhood education and child care which has yet to be realized in the United States itself. From 1947 on, the system expanded steadily, reaching a total of over 20,000 *hoiku-en* and over 15,000 *yochien* in the 1980s. Overall, the empirical evidence supports the contention of one specialist that preschool has acquired the state of "semi-compulsory education" for four- and five-year-olds—and, increasingly, for three-year-olds as well—and even for younger children; group care outside the home has become "socially established" (Murayama, 1983: 16–17; see also Early Childhood Education Association of Japan, 1979; Ichibangase et al., 1978).

There is considerable disagreement over the degree of differentiation that exists—and should exist—between Mombusho- and Koseisho-sponsored preschools. Probably the greatest distinction is in the relative centrality of the educational function. As a Koseisho official I interviewed put it: "The curriculum is the center of kindergarten education, but *hoiku-jo* is not just curriculum." In the latter, daily health checks, meals, and naps are as much a part of the daily routine as songs, games, and art projects. The hours are longer (twice as long on the average), and the groups are generally smaller (classes of forty children with one teacher are common in *yochien*, whereas day care groups are seldom larger than thirty children and usually have more than one nurse or caretaker).

In the case of *yochien*, parents apply directly to the establishment of their choice (*yochien* may also set their own entrance requirements), and they pay their fees to the establishment in which their child is enrolled. There is considerable variation in fees—some elite private kindergartens cost more than private universities. A parent wishing to enroll a child in *hoiku-en* applies not to a particular establishment but to the local municipal office. Acceptance is determined by the degree to which the child is defined as "in need of care" by a set of categories used nationwide, as well as by the availability of places. For example, children of working mothers, disabled or seriously ill parents, and single parents are given priority over other children. The fee, also paid to the municipality, is based upon family income, more precisely upon the amount of income tax the parents or guardians pay. For *hoiku-en*, both public or private, operating expenses are divided about evenly between parents and the government, with the national government assuming until recently 80 percent of the government burden and the remainder shared by prefectural and local governments. Building, remodeling, and equipment expenses are also subsidized (about half from the national government). In the case of *yochien*, public and private establishments have separate funding systems; all public but only some private establishments receive subsidies for operational expenses. (Differences in the funding of public and private establishments are discussed further in the next section. Recent shifts in government policy regarding support of preschool programs are discussed in a later section on the governmental role.)

The Ad Hoc Council on Educational Reform, appointed by Prime Minister Nakasone, recommended greater "coordination" of kindergarten and day care programs (Takahashi, 1985), although it is difficult to see how this could be brought about administratively given the stake the two government ministries, not to mention a host of officials at lower levels of government, have in protecting their "territory" and the substantially different financing, staffing, and application procedures that exist for *yochien* and *hoiku-en*. There are, however, some indicators of convergence between the two institutions. In the opinion of a Koseisho official:

The view that at the basic level both *hoiku-en* and *yochien* are the same is getting more prevalent. In the countryside, the kindergarten is still considered to be more prestigious, but this view is changing. The situation of working mothers makes *hoiku-jo* indispensable. (Interview with S. Matsuda, Koseisho, Mother-Child Welfare Section, December 16, 1985)

Moreover, the level of governmental subsidizing of day care in Japan has made licensed day care, especially in places like Tokyo which subsidize *hoiku-en* at a level well above the national standard, such an obvious bargain that the sorts of people who do not generally use day care in the United States (e.g., professional women) are much more likely to do so in Japan. A postwar shift in the term used for day care center—from *hoiku-sho*, or "car-place," to *hoiku-en*, or "care-garden"—may also have helped to reduce the association of day care with poor children (interview with Shigefune Nagano, Kokusai Kyoiku Kenkyu-sho, June 22, 1987).[5] In any case, both the stigma of day care and the actual correlation of enrollments in *yochien* vs. *hoiku-en* with family status appear to be considerably less in Japan than in the United States, even though, as we have seen, the origins of the two kinds of institutions were very similar in the two societies.

Public vs. Private Preschools

The majority of *hoiku-en* (60 percent) are public, while almost 60 percent of *yochien* are private. (Over three-fourths of the children enrolled in *yochien* attend private ones, reflecting the higher average enrollment at private than public establishments.) The correlation between social class and the use of public vs. private preschool facilities, so strong in the United States, appears to be much less significant in Japan. Indeed, in the case of *hoiku-en*, some would claim that the only difference between public and private establishments is whether the founder was a governmental agency or a private person or association. In all other respects—how they are financed, what kind of children are enrolled, and what minimum standards are observed—public vs. private is a distinction without a difference (interview with Toyoma Yoichi, Zenkoku Shiritsu Hoiku-en Remmei [National Association for Private Day Nurseries], July 1985).

Distinctions between public and private *yochien* are more readily acknowledged. Parents' fees are on the average much higher in private kindergartens than they are in any other type of preschool: about four times higher than public kindergartens nationwide (Early Childhood Education Association of Japan, 1979). In 1972, the national government initiated a ten-year program designed to promote kindergarten education, which included subsidizing the construction of 6,000 new *yochien* and the addition of 42,000 classes to existing ones. During that period efforts were made to provide financial aid to private kindergartens comparable to that given to public ones. Current support to private establishments, however, depends upon their form of administration. In particular, as part of a government policy to encourage incorporation of private kindergartens, those that become incorporated as educational foundations (*kyoiku hojin*) become eligible for subsidies, while those run by individuals or by groups that are not incorporated as *kyoiku hojin* are not subsidized.

There is disagreement about the results of this policy. Some claim that it has led to destructive competition among *yochien* to attract children from the shrinking pool of three- to five-year-olds and to economies that lower the quality of the educational program. Many classes now exceed forty children; many schools now exceed 400 children, double the total enrollment recommended by Koseisho and Unesco guidelines. Busing is more frequent, as schools seek enrollments from a larger area (at least 70 percent of all children in private *yochien* commute by school bus). The tactics of some establishments remind one more of college athletic recruiting than of programs oriented to the welfare of young children:

Some kindergartens try to collect children by eliminating day care fees, luring parents by premiums and giving 1,000 yen in cash to those who introduce children to the kindergarten. Some kindergartens even withdraw from the private kindergarten association in order to evade the association's prohibition of "luring." (Murayama, 1983: 100)

Licensed vs. Unlicensed Establishments

The distinction which is probably even more significant today than the two already discussed is that between licensed, or legally established and government-subsidized, facilities and unlicensed facilities, or *muninka*. The diversity of unlicensed establishments is only suggested in Figure 5.1. Some are pioneering experiments, such as the nurseries established in the textile mills which employed so many women during Japan's rush to "overtake the West" industrially during the Meiji period. Some are cooperative ventures initiated by parents or teachers with innovative or politically radical pedagogical theories which could not be accommodated within the more mainstream government-supported institutions, although it appears that most cooperative establishments are patronized by parents who do not qualify for, cannot afford, or are on a waiting list for a licensed day care program. Some establishments meet all of the national minimum standards but do not meet the criteria of "need" defined by prefectural or other authorities. Finally, there are commercial establishments, among which the establishments known as *bebi hoteru* (baby hotels) have come to symbolize the underclass of the Japanese preschool system. Many *bebi hoteru* operate twenty-four hours a day, charge by the hour, have no formal application procedures, and are not covered by liability insurance.

Theoretically, only licensed establishments are subsidized by the government, and many cooperative child care centers stave off insolvency with bazaars and other fund-raising activities and various add-ons to the fees paid by parents. There are, however, circumstances under which *muninka* establishments receive government funds. For example, in an effort to ease the shortage of nurses, the government subsidizes nurseries in hospitals for the children of hospital employees, although such facilities do not come under the national child welfare law. Similarly, some establishments for infant care in localities where the demand for this kind of care has greatly outstripped the supply of licensed places available receive temporary funding from municipal governments.

Reliable statistics on enrollments in unlicensed establishments do not exist. A Koseisho survey in 1980 located 587 baby hotels caring for some 12,000 children, but the report acknowledged that there were probably two to three times that number of establishments in operation (Suzuki, 1984: Chapter 2). Among children under the age of three, it is estimated that as many or more are cared for in unlicensed as in licensed establishments (TBS Hodo-kyoiku, 1981).

The research on baby hotels has also indicated that they are meeting a demand not met by most licensed establishments. Many users of commercial child care are parents whose hours do not fit the eight-hour daytime schedules of most licensed establishments (e.g., beauticians, sales clerks, and waitresses), who live in areas where there is a scarcity of licensed facilities, or whose children are under the age of three (there is a scarcity of places for infants and very young children). Some are housewives who simply need a temporary baby-sitter (still a rare service in Japan). A high proportion of users are bar hostesses or waitresses in the large entertainment districts found in all Japanese cities (TBS Hodo-kyoiku, 1981; Kawashima, 1984; Suzuki, 1984).

Public attention was drawn to the problems of unlicensed establishments in the early 1980s when the death of several children in baby hotels precipitated a flood of newspaper and magazine articles, an influential television documentary,

Figure 5.1
Major Types of Japanese Preschools

	LICENSED ESTABLISHMENTS		UNLICENSED ESTABLISHMENTS
	-UNDER MONBUSHO JURISDICTION	-UNDER KOSEISHO JURISDICTION	
PUBLIC ESTABLISH-MENTS	Public <u>yochien</u>	Public <u>hoiku-en</u>	– – – –
PRIVATE ESTABLISH-MENTS	Private <u>yochien</u>	Private <u>hoiku-en</u>	Cooperative nursery schools and day nurseries
			Establishments operated by companies, hospitals, and other employer or labor organizations
			Commercial establishments (e.g., "baby hotels")

and several empirical research studies. It was learned, for example, that of the 130 deaths that occurred in child care establishments between 1968 and 1982, 90 percent occurred in unlicensed establishments, and 85 percent occurred when a caretaker was not present (Kawashima, 1984: 117). Empirical investigations have also revealed that, although some commercial establishments have programs that truly meet the needs of infants and very young children or children suffering from the stress of unusually long or irregular hours in group care, the treatment of children in many establishments leaves much to be desired. In many baby hotels, the care is purely custodial with little or no educational content, meals are haphazard, sleeping quarters are crowded and unsanitary, and a disturbing number of caretakers are not only untrained but often indifferent, and sometimes abusive, toward the children under their care. Observers saw children scolded, threatened, hit, and locked in closets or bathrooms. Crying, vomiting, and other signals of distress were often ignored or even punished. In one baby hotel, a row of ten infants was fed by one employee with a single spoon; the author noted that the babies who ate faster and made more noise got more to eat than the slower or quieter babies (Kawashima, 1984: 42, 46).

These investigations not only raised the obvious issues of child abuse and neglect, they also pointed to potential cleavages in a society that likes to think of itself as classless or, more precisely, as uniformly middle class. Government agencies tend to ignore them—and the unmet needs they represent—until some mishap focuses public attention on them.[6] Until then, both the public and private sectors of the preschool system tend to distance themselves from the problem and from the large number of mothers who are employed in work that is viewed as not entirely respectable by many Japanese. A prefectural official, discussing the problems of unlicensed child care, summed up a prevailing attitude in saying: "I would really like to help nurses, but I certainly wouldn't want to bother to help those women whose job is to flirt with drunkards."

Regional Variations

Although the stigma of day care and some of the inequities in the distribution of resources within the preschool system do seem to have decreased during the postwar period, regional differences in preschool enrollments remain large. The total proportion of children enrolled and the relative enrollments in *yochien* versus *hoiku-en*, in all of the prefectures and autonomous metropolitan areas (Tokyo, Osaka, and Kyoto), suggest considerable variations from one area to another. At one extreme is Okinawa, in which virtually all three- to five-year-olds are in preschools, all of them in *yochien*. At another extreme is Kochi, in which the total number of children enrolled is about the same as Okinawa, but less than 20 percent are in *yochien*. In Aomori less than 60 percent of the children are enrolled, but enrollment is about evenly divided between *yochien* and *hoiku-en*. My interviews revealed similarly large variations in enrollment rates *within* prefectures and metropolitan areas (e.g., between central city areas and their surrounding suburbs).

Some of these variations are related to regional differences in demographic characteristics and family structure. In general, areas in which three-generation families still exist in large numbers tend to have fewer *hoiku-en*, since children of working mothers may be cared for by grandparents or other relatives. Other variations are explained by special historical circumstances. For example:

Okinawa is special. It was under American supervision, and all preschools were called kindergartens. Also in Okinawa, the extended family still exists, and it is rare that a child is left without anybody to look after him.... In the postwar period, when assistance to kindergartens began, many were attached to elementary schools, and they tend to be public. Around here [downtown Tokyo], and in Osaka and Kanagawa—being old districts—private kindergartens are numerous. Nagano is the opposite. Especially in Kochi, there was a switching from kindergarten to day care because the government will assist with building and maintaining Nagano also. Also there used to be day care centers attached to elementary schools. Thus it differs according to the place—and in some places day care centers may be doing the same thing as kindergartens. (Interview with Matsuda, Koseisho, 1985)

The historical circumstances related to regional variations in the preschool system have not, however, been systematically analyzed.

Conclusions about the uniformity and egalitarianism in the Japanese preschool system are difficult to draw since neither data on the effects of preschool experiences (including comparisons of different kinds of programs) nor data on the family background of children in the various types of preschools are systematically gathered by any Japanese ministry or research organization. I found that the staff of a particular preschool usually knew a great deal about the families of the children enrolled, and the amount of note taking by teachers and caretakers, on the physical and social development of the children under their care, was prodigious. Parents applying to *hoiku-en* must, of course, provide information about their occupation and income to establish eligibility and the amount of the fee. But, although the government officials and researchers whom I queried all claimed that allocation of children to preschools was no longer related to social class, as it was in the past, no one I interviewed could cite research evidence for this claim nor did any of their agencies have plans for conducting such an investigation.

One study (Nitta and Nagano, 1975) has attempted a relatively rigorous evaluation of preschool effects, controlling for both social class background and type of preschool program. This study was based upon a sample of 4,000 subjects, in three different prefectures, who graduated from elementary school in 1968, about evenly divided between students who had attended *yochien*, who had attended *hoiku-en*, and who had not attended preschool. Nitta and Nagano's findings showed that students' scores on the fifth grade national achievement tests were correlated with their type of preschool experience. Generally, children who attended *yochien* performed better than those who attended *hoiku-en* or who did not attend preschool. However, this relationship was itself affected by family economic status.[7] Children's success in elementary school was greater if their preschool program was compatible with their home environment. For example, lower class children benefited more from *hoiku-en*—indeed, they did less well if they had attended kindergarten than if they had had no preschool experience. Higher fifth grade achievement scores were, as might be expected, associated with higher IQ scores, although this relationship did not wash out the effects of social class and preschool experience. Finally, there were significant differences in mean scores among the three prefectures, and region was also correlated with the independent variables of social class background, IQ, and type of preschool experience.

Admittedly, this is a single study, published over a decade ago and perhaps now out of date, and the measurement of key variables is open to question, but it does suggest that the Japanese preschool experience is not uniform. On the contrary, variations in types of preschools and in their external environments, as well as variations in the types of experiences children bring with them when they enter preschool, may all affect the outcomes of preschool education.

It should also be noted that none of the data discussed above contained information about the preschool enrollments or the experiences of minority group children, in particular, Burakumin, Ainu, or Korean children. Shimahara's pioneering research on the Burakumin indicates that there have been substantial improvements in school integration and educational attainment during the past fifteen years. At the elementary and secondary levels, overt discrimination against Burakumin students has diminished, but poor academic performance, behavior problems, truency, and dropping out of school are still more frequent among the Burakumin than among the majority students (Shimahara, 1984). At the preschool level, there are fewer indications of integration. In Tokyo, Osaka, and other large cities, Korean and Burakumin organizations have built day care centers of their own, some but not all of which are licensed. (For example, 40 of the 1,000 licensed *hoiku-en* in Osaka are operated by Burakumin organizations.) Virtually all minority children who attend preschool are enrolled in segregated establishments. Only one of my interviewees, the founder and codirector of a large league of day care organizations in Osaka, discussed the issue of minority children at any length. She acknowledged that the efforts of her organization to incorporate minority preschools or preschool organizations within her league had not been successful, although she remains committed to conducting "research to find ways to bring up children strong enough to fight against discrimination" (interview with Yokota Masako, Osaka Hoiku-undo Center, November 5, 1985). In sum, from the little evidence available, it appears that preschool-aged minority children are largely confined to their own ghettos. Shimahara's observation that survey data are sporadic and that "few Japanese scholars, except those affiliated with Burakumin organizations, study this minority group, considering the subject too sensitive and difficult" (Shimahara,

1984: 339), clearly applies to research on minority education at the preschool level as well.

THE CONTENT AND SOCIAL ORGANIZATION OF PRESCHOOL SETTINGS

There are lively debates in Japan today about preschool *naiyo*, that is, the content or substance of the preschool program, generally broadly defined to include the social organization of the preschool setting and the scheduling of the daily routine as well as the content and methodology of specific activities.

Operation of a licensed *yochien* or *hoiku-en* requires adherence to national minimum standards which specify in some detail requirements with regard to the size of classes or groups, the numbers and qualifications of personnel, the number of hours per day and days per year of operation, physical space, and equipment. For example, licensed *yochien* must have slides, swings, pianos or organs, equipment for breeding animals, and a number of other specific kinds of equipment. Mombusho has also established guidelines for the content of kindergarten programs in Yochien Kyoiku Yoryo, put into effect in 1964 and currently under revision. The guidelines spell out 137 different recommended activities, grouped in six basic content areas: health, society, nature, language, music and rhythm, and arts and crafts. The goals and content of day care programs are contained in a 1965 Koseisho ordinance, and it is also now Koseisho policy that *hoiku-en* use the Yochien Kyoiku Yoryo, shortening and simplifying the guidelines for children under age three (Early Childhood Education Association of Japan, 1979: 22–27; interview with Matsuda, Koseisho, 1985). The extent to which these comprehensive guidelines is followed in actual practice appears to vary considerably from one establishment to another. Comparing the uniformity of preschool vs. elementary school *naiyo*, a staff member of a national child care movement commented that although Mombusho sets the curriculum for both: "In elementary schools, you are punished for not following the fixed curriculum, so people follow it, but in preschools, nobody follows it."

The Japanese literature on preschool education and preschool *naiyo* is highly eclectic, reflecting the influences of Froebel, Kodai, Montessori, and Rousseau, as well as the Confucian, Buddhist, or Christian principles upon which many private preschools were founded. The individual preschools I visited represented considerable variation in their theories of education (underscoring the importance of internal as well as crosscultural comparisons). The government officials I interviewed cited Froebel, Montessori, and Piaget as theorists who had influenced their own and their agency's thinking about early childhood education, but all hastened to assure me that their agency does not adhere to any particular theory of human development and early childhood education.

Japan has also produced some true pioneers in preschool theory and practice, little known outside of Japan but highly influential within, many of whom acknowledge their intellectual debts to socialist and Marxist thought. For example,

Saito Kimiko, the energetic, charismatic, and controversial founder of Sakura-Sakurambo Hoiku-en, regarded by some Japanese as the best in Japan, has created a highly original preschool *naiyo* which draws from the ideas of education reformers like Ellen Key, the Swedish feminist, and Nadezhda Konstantinova Krupskaya, the Russian revolutionary leader who helped form the modern Soviet educational system, from biological research, from the folklore and children's literature of many societies, and from her own critique of contemporary Japanese culture and society. The daily and seasonal routines at Sakura-Sakurambo are designed to nurture physical vitality, simple and direct interpersonal communication, and the personal qualities—will power (*iyoku*), concentration (*shuchuryoku*), and perseverance (*nebari-tsuyosa*)—needed to carry out complex, demanding tasks. Saito claims not to have a fixed curriculum, and children are allowed to roam freely over the four and one-half acres of the preschool grounds. They are, however, responsible for tending gardens and cleaning animal pens and barns as well as their own classrooms, and they also participate daily in a series of rhythmic exercises developed by Saito which call for coordination, concentration, timing, and a considerable amount of courage. Few toys are bought. Children collect stones, leaves, twigs, and other things they find outdoors, and they make their own tops and jump ropes. Art and music are important parts of the *naiyo*. Most children produce literally hundreds of drawings and paintings per year, all of which are carefully stored and are studied by staff and parents in order to understand each child's development. There are also joint art projects which require groups of children to work cooperatively for extended periods of time. Though now in her sixties and recently retired as director, Saito still publishes voluminously, conducts workshops (attended by teachers from all over Japan), travels widely, and remains deeply involved in the lives of the children who are or have been enrolled in Sakura-Sakurambo.[8]

Visits to a number of preschools and an examination of the statements of purpose, curriculum materials, newsletters, and other materials prepared by preschool associations and individual preschools do leave the impression that there is considerable flexibility and innovativeness within the preschool system. At the same time, there seem to be some common themes in the Japanese preschool *naiyo*, based upon underlying assumptions about the nature of children and the purposes of socialization and education, that seem to be widely shared among Japanese. I shall mention just three of these themes.

1. *Children are viewed as inherently good, and childhood is defined as a special, and especially vulnerable, stage of life.* While the presence of evil in the world is acknowledged, it is connected to adults and events in the adult world which corrupt the originally pure and good nature of children (Kojima, 1986; Yamamura, 1986). A number of Japanese proverbs or popular sayings refer to the goodness and specialness of children, for example, *Ko ni sugitara takaranashi* (There is no treasure that surpasses a child); *Tsumi mo kegare mo nai kodomo* (In children there is neither sin nor pollution); and *Nanatsu made wa kami no uchi de aru* (Until seven, children are with the gods).

Foreign visitors to Japanese schools are often impressed by the students' quiet, attentive demeanor and self-disciplined behavior, and crosscultural comparisons of American and Japanese elementary school classrooms have shown that Japanese students spend more time than their American counterparts listening to their teachers, less time in "inappropriate" behavior, such as talking to other students, or wandering around the room (Stevenson, 1983; Stevenson, Stigler, and Lee, 1986). Observational studies at the preschool level, however, indicate that the Japanese preschoolers are as noisy and active as American preschoolers, perhaps more so (presentations by Harold Stevenson, by Fujita Mariko, and Sano Toshiyuku, and by James Tobin at a conference on Social Control and Early Childhood Education in Japan, held in Muir Beach, California, in October 1987).

Observational research also indicates that preschool teachers' handling of children presumes that the children are basically good. One such study, of fifteen *hoiku-en*, found that not only did many teachers tolerate a noise level and a latitude of behavior that few American teachers would define as acceptable, but also they tended to attribute aggressive or mischievous acts (e.g., one child hiding another's shoes; or several children dropping clay "bombs" on the fish in the aquarium) to a *lack of understanding* on the children's part rather than to intentional misbehavior (Lewis, 1984. Similar anecdotal evidence is reported in Tobin 1987; Fujita and Sano, 1988).

The perception of children as inherently good and especially vulnerable is coupled with child-rearing techniques that seem very lenient, even indulgent, by Western standards. Traditional care of babies and young children emphasized "skin-ship," that is, physical and emotional contact between child and caretaker. Even today weaning, toilet training, sleeping alone, being disciplined for temper tantrums, aggression against parents and other adults, even for misbehavior in public all begin on the average later in Japan than in the United States (DeVos, 1974; Lebra, 1976; Smith and Wiswell, 1982). It is only after they reach elementary school that adults demand and children acquire the adultlike decorum which so impresses foreign visitors. (The most comprehensive study to date on the transition from home to preschool is Peak, 1987).

2. *Group life and harmonious group relations are highly valued, and group tasks which promote sensitivity toward and cooperation with others tend to be emphasized more than individual tasks which promote self-discovery and self-realization.* Observational studies of Japanese preschools usually conclude that, compared to preschool programs in most Western societies, the proportion of the day spent in structured group activities is high, the time in undirected free play low. Joy Hendry describes a number of ways in which preschool teachers inculcate a sense of collective identity in their students:

> First of all, considerable attention is devoted to creating a new inside group for these children to identify with. As children arrive at kindergarten they may play freely in the playground for a while, but at an appointed hour each day the class gathers in its own

room and goes through an important greeting sequence.... Similar routines accompany the serving of meals, and break, and separation at the end of the day....

Each child in the room will be wearing the same uniform, or at least a smock or apron to make them alike, and every child is provided with identical sets of equipment. During the course of the day, many activities will be carried out together, each child being instructed to make the same preparations as the others, and following the teacher's demonstration in drawing, folding or constructing some chosen item. Singing or dancing is often carried out in unison, again with a clear demonstration from the teacher to follow....

Forms of address and reference used with the children reinforce this emphasis on equality within the group. All the children in the same class are referred to as "friends" by parents and teachers alike, and children are not encouraged to seek out special friends for themselves. There is a collective term of address, *mina-san*, which literally means everyone *(mina)*, with a polite suffix *(san)* used also for individuals. Addressed in this way, the children are expected to chorus their reply. Used in its possessive form, it denotes the collective ownership of classrooms and kindergarten equipment, for which everyone is therefore responsible. (Hendry, 1986a: 55. Lewis, 1984, also contains multiple examples of the sort of cooperative group activities favored in Japanese preschools.)

Group care, even for very young children, may be more acceptable in Japan than in the United States because it is not basically incompatible with traditional Japanese culture or Confucian ethics. As one observer has commented, group care outside the home may be viewed as simply reinforcing the group consciousness already acquired in the home (Christopher, 1983: 76). The traditional saying that "A child cannot be raised by mother's love alone" is echoed in Saito Kimiko's criticism of contemporary Japanese society, where so many young families are isolated in tiny apartments, far from their relatives and without real links to their communities, that children "grow up in a vacuum where only mother and child exist." In such a society, group child care, in which the child is surrounded by many loving adults as well as by a children's peer group, is absolutely essential for the child's development as a human being (Saito, 1982: Chapters 1 and 3).

The relative congruence of group care with traditional Japanese values *and* contemporary child-rearing expertise may explain why the spread of government-subsidized preschool programs has proceeded rather more quickly and smoothly in Japan than in the United States, why Japanese scholars and educators have paid so little attention to the huge body of American research attempting to measure the "effects" of day care, and why almost no research on this topic has been conducted in Japan (interviews with K. Nakanishi, Mombusho, Yochien Section, December 9, 1985, and Matsuda, Koseisho, 1985. American research on the effects of day care is summarized in Belsky and Steinberg, 1978; Bradley, 1982). It is probably not coincidental that the best-selling handbook for parents, by Dr. Matsuda Michio (1967), often referred to as Japan's Dr. Spock, espouses both prolonged breast feeding and early group socialization and that many of the photographs in Dr. Matsuda's book are of children in *hoiku-en*.

3. *Socialization in the home and school emphasizes doing one's best and doing things correctly. Differences in children's behavior and accomplishments are viewed as stemming not from significant differences in natural talent, but from differences in effort.* The Confucian model of education taught that there is a correct way to carry out any task and that, if the learner is taught the correct way, she or he will do it freely, without external constraints. In the preschools I observed, a good deal of time was spent in teaching children the "correct" way to do many things—how to sit in a chair, to hold a fork or chopsticks, to fold up a *futon* after a nap, to arrange chairs for an assembly.

Good preschools throughout the world provide warm, supportive environments for young children and are solicitous of children's overall well-being. Good Japanese preschools are no exception in this regard. What does seem to distinguish Japanese preschools from their Western counterparts is the portion of the *naiyo* given to activities which require concentration and attention to details for long periods of time. Japan's Nobel Prize winner, Yukawa Hideki, is often held up as a role model to Japanese school children, not so much for his natural talents and the originality of his work, but primarily for his comment that success in any endeavor comes through continuous repetitive practice until one masters every detail (Cummings, 1980: 108).

It is also believed, however, that children learn better through observation and imitation (a process the Japanese term *minarai*, which was used in the teaching of many traditional arts and crafts) than through abstract verbal instruction. The Suzuki method of music instruction is exemplary in this regard. The Suzuki method requires the beginning student, who may be as young as two, simply to observe more experienced students' lessons, quietly but with full concentration, for a period of weeks or even months, then to spend more weeks or months learning to stand in front of the teacher and to bow properly, before ever picking up the instrument let alone attempting to play it. When the student finally begins to make music, she or he will already have correct habits as well as tremendously high motivation, and progress will be rapid (Peak, 1986).

TEACHER AND CARETAKER ROLES

Studies of Japanese elementary and secondary schools have generally concluded that Japanese teachers enjoy higher status, better salaries, greater job security, and better working conditions than their American counterparts and that these advantages help to explain the relatively higher academic achievement of Japanese students (Shimahara, 1986; Cummings, 1980; Rohlen, 1983; White, 1987). This conclusion applies to preschool personnel to some degree, but preschool teaching is more distinctly a female occupation, and there is greater variation in teacher qualifications at the preschool than at the elementary and secondary levels.

The typical kindergarten teacher or day care *hobo-san* (caretaker or nurse) is a young woman in her twenties with two years of post–high school training.

(*Hobo-san* are on the average somewhat older and more experienced than *yochien* teachers, who are, theoretically, certified in the same way as elementary and secondary teachers.) There are, however, two paths to certification. A first-class certificate requires a BA from a four-year college; a second-class certificate may be obtained after two years of study at a college or teacher-training institution (often a junior college) approved by the Ministry of Education. Not surprisingly, most of the graduates of four-year colleges go on to teach in elementary or secondary schools, while 90 percent of *yochien* teachers are graduates of two-year programs. *Hobo-san* qualify by graduating from a training school approved by Koseisho (most are junior colleges) or by passing an examination offered by prefectural governments (Mombusho, 1981: 15–16). The latter option is a sore point with many professionals who complain that even two years are not sufficient to train properly.

As a result of a recent shift in government policy, in the direction of greater emphasis on the educative function of day care, there is now more overlap in the certification requirements for all preschool positions. Some institutions may now train staff for both *yochien* and *hoiku-en*. Currently, about 80 percent of *hobo-san* are certified to teach in *yochien* as well (Early Childhood Education Association of Japan, 1979: 78–81; interviews with faculty at Shiraume Gakuen College).

For both *yochien* and *hoiku-en*, salaries tend to be higher and working conditions better in public than in private establishments. The staff of public licensed *hoiku-en* enjoy the same salaries as other municipal employees, but in private *hoiku-en*, salaries tend to be lower, hours of work longer, child-to-staff ratios higher, working conditions more stressful, and, predictably, turnover rates higher. In one survey of *hobo-san* employed in private establishments, it was found that almost half worked nine or more hours a day; less than a third said that they were able to take a rest sometime during each day. A majority reported occupationally related health problems, in particular, back, shoulder, arm, or neck pain, and a disproportionate number of female staff had suffered miscarriages or childbirth complications. Studies of kindergarten staff have also reported larger classes, longer hours, and lower pay in private than in public facilities. Not surprisingly, professional commitment is also lower—the majority of teachers in private *yochien* teach for less than five years, and few are members of a teachers' union or professional association (Murayama, 1983: Chapter 1).

PARENT ROLES AND RELATIONS BETWEEN THE HOME AND THE PRESCHOOL

It has been posited by a number of scholars that a major difference between Japanese nuclear families on the one hand and American and Western European families on the other is that in the latter, the husband-wife relationship takes precedence over parent-child relationships, whereas in the former, the parent-child (especially mother-child) bond is the central one (e.g., Befu, 1986; Lebra,

1984). Although child rearing in Western industrialized societies is now defined as the responsibility of both parents (however much the ideal may be honored in the breach and despite the growing number of single-parent households), changes in Japanese family structure and functioning have, if anything, reinforced sex role differentiation. As a consequence, in most households, the day-to-day responsibilities of parenting fall on the mother:

In general mothers act as disciplinarians, often completely replacing their husbands as authority figures. The traditional images of the stern father and the protective mother (*gempu jibo*) are apparently no longer the acknowledged reality in many homes: the Japanese father seems to have become "insignificant." (Wagatsuma and Lanham, 1983: 278)

The very intensity of many Japanese mothers' involvement with their one or at most two children has received considerable recent attention. The phenomenon of the *kyoiku mama* (education mother), who devotes herself single-mindedly to her children's academic career, is, on the one hand, lauded as the source of Japanese students' impressive scholastic successes, and, on the other hand, criticized for depriving children of their childhood (Simons, 1987; Vogel, 1978). The following passage describes the efforts of one such mother to prepare her four-year-old son for the entrance examination to a prestigious elementary school which usually accepts about 125 first graders from some 1,200 applicants:

[A]fter nursery school, I go to *juku* or *okeiko goto* with my son from 2:00 until 6:30 or 7:00 P.M. I watch and watch and make notes about his weak points. . . . Today is Wednesday, so the children will be doing active work. They'll be using wooden blocks to make animals . . . and the more pieces the children use the better. For instance, the child who uses all fifty pieces to make a crocodile does better than the narrow-minded child who uses just ten pieces to make a giraffe.

Then on Thursdays, the children are divided into groups of ten or less, so that the teachers can watch the children more closely and give the kids more individual attention. The teacher might ask each child how many insects he can name. Some can give the names of ten insects, and some can say twenty-six in one minute.

After a two-hour session like this, the mothers are gathered together and told: "Your boy should study more" or "Your boy shouldn't study so much because he's nervous." . . .

Besides Wednesdays and Thursdays, my boy has writing practice on Saturdays. The children listen to tapes so that they can practice giving answers. All exams are on tape now. . . .

We also send him to two other optional classes: Monday music lessons and Friday drawing lessons. A Sunday run in the park is recommended too. . . . Tuesday is the only afternoon that he has free. (Condon, 1985: 130–31)

Even though the number of employed mothers continues to increase, the expectation of what Hendry calls a mother's "general availability" remains strong in Japanese culture. *Yochien* have rather short hours, and school is often called off for a variety of reasons (including annual visits by teachers to each child's home). Mothers, and increasingly fathers, are expected to participate in PTA, which organizes bazaars, festivals, and outings and, in the case of private *yochien*, raises a substantial portion of the school's income (Hendry, 1986b: 24). As the Mombusho official I interviewed put it: "If the parent wants to work, we like her to take the child to a day care center. Kindergarten presupposes a 'home.'" Day care does not assume a stay-at-home mother, but there is still a great deal of ambivalence about mothers not taking care of their own children, particularly when the children are under the age of three. A case study of a day care center by Eyal Ben-Ari (1988) reported considerable conflict between mothers and staff, not only over the mother's role, but also over the extent to which the institution was to intervene in the lives of the mothers and children.

At the same time, Japanese preschools seem to have gone far in breaking down the barriers of mutual suspicion which characterize teacher-parent relations in many societies.[9] One device which I have observed in no other nation is the daily exchange of notes. In all of the licensed and some of the unlicensed *hoiku-en* I visited, caretakers took notes on each child every day (eating and sleeping patterns, favorite activities, relations with other children, developmental turning points, and possible health or behavior problems were common topics). These notes are given to the person who comes to pick up the child at the end of the day, and whoever brings the child in the morning is expected to bring a similar note describing the child's activities at home. I suspect that few American parents or teachers would be willing to spend so much time recording the mundane details of children's everyday lives and that many would consider such record keeping an invasion of privacy, but it does encourage adults to become more observant of young children, and it provides a regular channel of communication between home and school.

THE GOVERNMENTAL ROLE

Preschools may be established by a variety of agents: public agencies at the city (*shi*), ward (*ku*), town (*machi*), or village (*mura*) levels; religious organizations (mainly Christian or Buddhist—many preschools are operated in and constitute a major source of income for Buddhist temples); private social service corporations or foundations; private employers, especially in organizations which hire many women (e.g., department stores and hospitals); labor unions; and associations based upon a particular pedagogical theory (e.g., Montessori preschools). Anyone wishing to establish a *yochien* or *hoiku-en* must, however, seek authorization at the prefectural (*ken*) or, in the case of Tokyo and Osaka, at the metropolitan (*to* or *fu*) level. (There are a few exceptions to this rule, for example, a handful of national *yochien* and *hoiku-en*.) Public establishments need, in addition, approval of the mayor (in the case of *hoiku-en*) or the board of education (in the case of *yochien*) of the municipality where the new facility would be located (Early Childhood Education Association of Japan, 1979; Hendry, 1986b: 120–21; Mombusho, 1981; interviews with K. Nakanishi, Mombusho, 1985, and S. Matsuda, Koseisho, 1985).

How the decision whether or not to approve an application is actually made is somewhat of a mystery—or so it seemed to many of my interviewees, and I have not found a clear published explanation of the process. Applicants must, of course, meet the national standards mentioned above, but in addition prefectural officials use criteria relating to the "needs" of the area, for example, evaluating the location of the proposed new establishment relative to other establishments; the mix of *hoiku-en* and *yochien*, public and private, in the district; and the correlation of preschools' capacity (*tei-in*) to actual enrollments and the current and projected numbers of children of preschool age. For example, the director of an unlicensed day care establishment who has been trying unsuccessfully to obtain licensing described her dilemma as follows:

We want to be authorized and have asked the prefectural administrative body, but the law doesn't allow more than three day care centers within the radius of three kilometers. We really wanted to make this center solely for babies, but an existing *hoiku-en* is already registered as a concurrent babies' center. Even if they don't take any babies there, another babies' center will not be allowed. We asked the head of this town in person, but in vain.

The national, prefectural, and local levels of government are bound to each other not only by complementary (sometimes competing) policymaking and supervisory functions, but also by the complex system of financing preschool institutions. There have been rather frequent shifts in governmental funding patterns during the postwar period, reflecting shifts in political power and in the relative effectiveness of lobbying activities on behalf of children's programs. For *hoiku-en*, both public and private, working expenses are divided about evenly between parents and government, with the national government assuming (until recently) 80 percent of the government burden and the remainder shared by prefectual and local governments. Building, remodeling, and equipping *hoiku-en* are also subsidized (about 50 percent from the national government and 25 percent from prefectural authorities). Public and private *yochien* have separate funding systems, and, although both receive financial assistance for buildings and equipment, the responsibilities for current operational expenditures in private establishments fall mainly on the "beneficiaries" (i.e., the parents).

Some metropolitan and municipal governments have chosen to support day care at a level higher than the national minimum standards and to subsidize private as well as public kindergartens in order to provide higher quality care, to ease the financial burden on parents, and to achieve greater equity in staff salaries. Tokyo is exemplary in this regard. When I was conducting field work in 1985, the maximum fee paid by Tokyo parents, including affluent professional families with two working parents, was equivalent to about U.S. $150 per month, which was about half of what parents at the same income level in Fukui City, a prefectural capital on the Sea of Japan, paid for the same type of care. Within the Tokyo metropolitan area, moreover, certain wards or towns prided themselves upon being in the "top class" in support of day care, which meant that they supplemented further the already high Tokyo City (*to*) contributions (Murayama, 1983; Early Childhood Education Association of Japan, 1979: 81; interviews with Takenai Minoru, director, Child Care and Women's Programs, Koganei-shi, Tokyo, June 1984, and Nishizawa S., Child Care Section, Shinagawa-ku, Tokyo, December 1985).

There is at present considerable pressure at the national level of government to cut back on funding for preschool programs. As part of the administrative reforms initiated by the Nakasone government, the national budget for 1985 reduced the contribution of the national government to all welfare and education programs including day care by 10 percent, leaving the lower levels of government to cover the shortfall, and further cuts have been announced. In addition, national governmental policy now favors greater efficiency in the operation of preschools, for example, by consolidating smaller facilities, raising fees, and encouraging the growth of private and nonlicensed facilities. Such measures are defended as being in keeping with a "Japan-style welfare society" in which responsibility for human services would be shifted back to the local level and the private sector (Zenkoku Hoiku Dantai Renraku-kai, 1985; Murayama, 1983; Yokota, 1984a, 1984b).

The next section considers the sources of opposition to the Japan-style welfare society model and examines an array of organizations committed to the maintenance and extension of quality preschool programs.

PROFESSIONAL ORGANIZATIONS AND CITIZENS' MOVEMENTS

During the later 1940s and 1950s, numerous organizations devoted to extending and improving the preschool system were established in Japan. In addition to national and local associations of public *hoiku-en*, private *hoiku-en*, public *yochien*, and private *yochien*, there are separate associations for principals or directors of these various institutions, for Buddhist and Christian establishments, for unlicensed establishments, for preschools operated by labor organizations, for women's organizations and mothers' organizations, and for institutions specializing in the care of infants and of handicapped children, to name just a few. All hold annual meetings as well as intermittent lectures, workshops, and symposia. Most are involved in research and publication activities—the sheer volume of publications on every aspect of early childhood education and child care is daunting. The majority are also involved in lobbying and currently cite "fighting the Nakasone reform" as one of their major objectives (Zenkoku Hoiku Dantai Renraku-kai, 1984: 284–302; Early Childhood Education Association of Japan, 1979: 87).

Of particular interest is the role of child care movements (*hoiku undo*) and education movements (*kyoiku undo*), which have created a core of politically sophisticated children's advocates. Just as citizens' movements have been credited with providing the impetus for creating the world's strictest and most comprehensive antipollution legislation (McKean, 1981), so the convergence of professional and citizen activism in large-scale child care movements has played a major role in the expansion of government-subsidized preschool programs during the past two decades. While children's advocates borrowed some of their principles and tactics from American and European protest movements, they also drew much of their strength from their appeal to widely shared Japanese values, for example, the high value placed upon children as "society's treasure" (*kodakara*). At the same time they have achieved widespread acceptance—or at least tolerance—of political positions which are still highly controversial in the United States, for example, that high-quality group care is a right both of parents and children and that the state should share with families the responsibility for children's well-being (Zenkoku Hoiku Dantai Renraku-kai, 1985; Yokota, 1984a). Some activists have argued that participation in collective action on behalf of children can strengthen the entire society as well as enrich children's lives—as one put it, "The day care movement is the locomotive for the development of our society" (Yokota, 1984b: 140).

On the practical level, the child care movements have been remarkably successful in resisting governmental efforts to raise preschool fees, to lower the government's contributions, and to impose administrative reforms designed to lower operating costs (e.g., by closing smaller centers or by amalgamating them into larger "unified" systems). Movement members have on occasion obtained the signatures of a third or more of the registered voters in a city or have mobilized thousands of parents and teachers to march on government offices to protest some government economy move.[10]

DISCUSSION

During a recent visit to Japan, Ernest Boyer, president of the Carnegie Foundation for the Advancement of Teaching, described life in a Japanese kindergarten as "heaven before reality sets in." Certainly many preschools strike the visitor as extremely pleasant places. Ruth Benedict's characterization of the years up to about age seven as "the privileged life of little children" seems as applicable to present day Japan as it did to the prewar society she examined in *The Crysanthemum and the Sword* (1946: 279).

Japan's preschool system is also of interest because the Japanese have been particularly innovative with respect to some of the problems that have plagued preschool systems in other industrial societies, for example, how to design outside-the-home environments for young children which are both interpersonally warm and educationally rich; how to achieve greater equity in the distribution of resources among various kinds of preschool facilities; how to organize parents, teachers, and concerned citizens on behalf of high-quality preschool programs;

and how to enhance communication between parents and teachers. Because Japanese scholars and practitioners have been relatively successful in articulating an ideology of group child care as meeting both the developmental needs of children and the citizen rights of women, even full-day care does not raise the spector of poverty, neglect, and maternal deprivation which it often connotes in the United States.

This is not to say that the Japanese preschool system is without problems. The greatest weaknesses are in the unlicensed sector which constitutes a growing portion of the total system. It is ironic that national government policy is actually contributing to the growth of this sector—and to the declining supply of high-quality public preschools—at a time when the importance of early childhood education is almost universally acknowledged and when changing family and employment patterns create an ever greater demand for outside-the-home child care.

Another weakness is the lack of evaluative research. While governmental and other agencies maintain very accurate records of enrollments, staff, and equipment, and although there is a veritable flood of theoretical and philosophical works on child rearing and early childhood education, virtually no systematic research has been conducted on the effects of the various types of preschool programs or relating preschool enrollment and experiences to characteristics of children and their families. Social class and racial or ethnic differences are generally ignored, although it is clear that minority children and children placed in baby hotels or other commercial forms of child care are less likely to enjoy a "privileged" childhood than are most other children in Japan.

Concerning the operation of the preschool system, conflicts remain over the basic question of who is to bear responsibility for the care and education of young children, more specifically, what portion of the responsibility is the family to share with the state? The main protagonists in this conflict are the national government, on the one side, and a variety of parent, teacher, and citizen advocates, on the other side. In the 1980s, the advocates are up against demographic trends as well as strong political counterforces. The birth rate has dropped so precipitously that, even though the proportion of children of a given age cohort attending preschool continues to increase, occupancy rates, based upon the number of children enrolled in licensed establishments relative to the number of places available (*tei-in*), has fallen to between 80 and 90 percent nationwide. This demographic change has occurred in an era of government cutbacks in support for human services of all sorts. Clearly the teachers' and caretakers' unions and the citizens' movements face an uphill battle as they try to prevent further decline in the quantity and quality of preschool programs.

A second kind of conflict within the preschool system is that between mounting pressures to make all kinds of preschool programs more academic versus the efforts to maintain the "specialness" of early childhood. Although the prevailing professional opinion is that preschool programs ought to be different from regular school, many people acknowledge, as my Mombusho informant put it, that too much is being taught. Ideally kindergarten should be fostering the spontaneous development of the child The problem is that the teachers want to teach "intellectual content," and the parents encourage this. (Interview with Matsuda, Mombusho, 1985)

By this official's estimate, 98 percent of *yochien* teachers were teaching letters and numbers. Some prestigious *yochien* accept fewer than one in five of the three-year-olds whose parents apply, and the competition for entrance, viewed by many parents as necessary to ensure ultimate acceptance into a major university, has spawned a new generation of cram schools specializing in the preparation of one- and two-year-olds and their parents for kindergarten entrance interviews and exams (*Japan Times*, November 24, 1985).

The Japanese preschool system contains much to be studied and at least some things to be emulated. The societal level of commitment to children and their education is impressive, and the extent to which the state has shared responsibility with the family for the care of young children is rare in a nonsocialist society. Whether the privileged world of little children in Japan will survive the large-scale social and economic changes that are transforming contemporary Japanese society in many regards remains to be seen.

NOTES

The research reported in this chapter has been supported by a Fulbright research fellowship and by grants from the Spencer Foundation, the Social Science Research Council, and the Rutgers University International Center. Earlier versions of this chapter were presented at the Annual Meetings of the Comparative and International Education Society, Washington, D.C., March 1987, and the Association for Asian Studies, San Francisco, March 1988. I am deeply indebted to Professor Yamaguchi Hiroko, of Shiraume Gakuen College, Tokyo, to Professor Yamamura Yoshiaki, Rikkyo University, Tokyo, to Professor Kuse Tacko, Aichi University of Education, Aichi Prefecture to President Shimada Tadashi, Professor Koboyashi Tsuyoshi, and the late Professor Yamazaki Aisei, of Fukui University, for facilitating my work during the data gathering phase. Professor Yamazaki's untimely death, while I was revising this chapter for publication, reminded me afresh how much I owed to his friendship and to his extraordinary helpfulness, and the chapter is dedicated to his memory. I am also grateful to Catherine Lewis, Lois Peak, Nobuo Shimahara, Koya Azumi, and Tsuneyoshi Ryoko for their helpful comments on earlier drafts of the chapters, and to Okuda Yoshiko, Ishii Noriko, Shimada Hiroko, Takinami Keiko, and Atarashii Sumi for assistance in translating and interpreting my voluminous data.

1. For example, Japan has the world's lowest infant mortality rate, and virtually no children suffer from malnutrition, low birth weight, or other health problems associated with poverty or environmental pollution. Japan has the world's highest high school graduation rate and close to 100 percent literacy. In international comparisons of academic achievement carried out since the 1960s, the average scores of Japanese students were at or near the top in virtually all subjects studied (UNICEF, 1985; Rohlen, 1983; Steen, 1987; Crosswhite et al., 1986; Boocock, 1988).

2. The view that the commonalities outweigh the variations in the educational system appears to be rather widely held. Several of the scholars and officials I interviewed in Tokyo, upon learning that I was planning to collect comparable data in other parts of Japan, advised me that this would be unnecessary because their child care programs are much the same everywhere.

3. This analysis includes preschool institutions that combine an educational component with "care" or custodial functions—in particular, day care centers—rather than limiting the discussion to programs under the auspices of the Ministry of Education which have purely educational objectives. I include both because, at the preschool level, it is often difficult to place clear boundaries between educational and other functions and because there is, in fact, a growing overlap between these two types of preschools.

4. By comparison, the proportion of American children enrolled in formal preschool programs in 1980 was as follows: 25 percent of three-year-olds, 43 percent of four-year-olds, and 92 percent of five-year-olds (Center for Education Statistics, 1986).

5. Note that the *kanji* for the *en* in *hoiku-en* is the same as the *en* in *yochien*, thus providing a closer association with the middle-class institution of the kindergarten.

6. Prefectual and metropolitan governments now have the right to "control" unlicensed as well as licensed establishments, but my informants indicated that supervision was limited to occasional visits to a few facilities.

7. As judged by the teacher—a problematic measure, since the criteria for judgment were likely to vary from one school or class to another.

8. Probably the best statement of Saito's theory and methods is Saito, 1982. Unfortunately, none of Saito's writings—or those of most other major Japanese preschool innovators—have been translated into English, though one can gain some idea of life at Sakura-Sakurambo from some books that combine essays by Saito with extensive sections of photographs, in particular, Saito and Kawashima, 1976; and Kawashima and Saito, 1984. For a collection of brief "profiles" of a cross-section of Japanese *hoiku-en* and *yochien*, also accompanied by photographs, by another distinguished scholar and practitioner, see Shirai, 1985.

9. I am grateful to Professor Hara Hiroko for pointing out that this may be easier in Japan than in many other societies because of the generally high level of respect for and trust in education and educational institutions.

10. There is an extensive literature on *hoiku* and *kyoiku undo*, although almost none of it has been translated. General accounts include Ichibangase et al., 1978, pp. 106–25; Murayama, 1983; Yokota, 1984a. A moving personal account of the development of the Osaka Hoiku Renmei, a league of child care movements which is one of the largest and most effective in Japan, can be found in Yokota, 1984b. For an example of the kind of pamphleteering activity engaged in by these movements, see, for example, Zenkoku Hoiku Dantai Renraku-kai, 1985.

REFERENCES

Befu Harumi. 1986. "The Social and Cultural Background of Child Development in Japan and the United States." Pp. 13–27 in *Child Development and Education in Japan*, edited by H. Stevenson, H. Azuma, and K. Hakata. New York: Freeman.

Belsky, J. and L.D. Steinberg. 1978. "The Effects of Day Care: A Critical Review." *Child Development* 49: 929–49.

Ben-Ari, Eyal. 1988. "Disputing about Day-Care: Care-taking Roles in a Japanese Day Nursery." *International Journal of Sociology of the Family* 17: 197–216.
Benedict, Ruth. 1946. *The Chrysanthemum and the Sword: Patterns of Japanese Culture*. Boston: Houghton Mifflin.
Boocock, Sarane Spence. 1988. "Social Treasure: Changing Definitions of Childhood in Japan and the United States." Paper presented at University Seminar on Modern Japan, Columbia University, April 1988.
Bradley, R.H. 1982. "Socialization within Day Care: A Brief Review." *Infant Mental Health Journal* 3: 156–61.
Center for Education Statistics. 1986. *Pre-School Enrollment: Trends and Implications*. Issue paper. Washington, D.C.: U.S. Department of Education, Office of Educational Research and Improvement.
Christopher, Robert C. 1983. *The Japanese Mind: The Goliath Explained*. New York: Linden Press/Simon & Schuster.
Condon, Jane. 1985. *A Half Step Behind: Japanese Women of the '80s*. New York: Dodd, Mead.
Crosswhite, F.J. et al. 1986. *Second International Mathematics Study: Detailed Report for the United States*. Champaign, Ill.: Stipes.
Cummings, William K. 1980. *Education and Equality in Japan*. Princeton, N.J.: Princeton University Press.
DeVos, George. 1974. "The Relation of Guilt toward Parents to Achievement and Arranged Marriage among the Japanese." Pp. 117–41 in *Japanese Culture and Behavior: Selected Readings*, edited by T.S. Lebra and W.P. Lebra. Honolulu: University of Hawaii Press.
Early Childhood Education Association of Japan, ed. 1979. *Early Childhood Education and Care in Japan*. Tokyo: Child Honsha.
Fujita Mariko and Sano Toshiyuku. 1988. "Children in American and Japanese Day Care Centers: Ethnography and Reflective Cross-cultural Interviewing." Pp. 73–97 in *School and Society: Learning Content through Culture*, edited by H.T. Trueba and C. Delgrade-Gaitan. New York: Praeger.
Fuse Akiko. 1984. "The Japanese Family in Transition. Part I." *Japan Foundation Newsletter* 12, 3: 1–11.
Hendry, Joy. 1986a. "Kindergartens and the Transition from Home to School Education." *Comparative Education* 22: 53–58.
———. 1986b. *Becoming Japanese: The World of the Pre-School Child*. Honolulu: University of Hawaii Press.
Ichibangase Yasuko et al. 1978. *Nihon no Hoiku* [Japanese Child Care]. Tokyo: Domesu.
Kamerman, Sheila B., and Alfred J. Kahn. 1981. *Child Care, Family Benefits, and Working Parents: A Study in Comparative Policy*. New York: Columbia University Press.
Kawashima Hiroshi and Saito Kimiko. 1984. *Hito ga ningen ni naru* [Becoming a Human Being]. Tokyo: Ayumi Shuppan.
Kawashima Shizuyo. 1984. *Yami ni tadayou kodomotachi* [Children Who Float in the Dark]. Tokyo: Kaisosha.
Kojima Hideo. 1986. "Child Rearing Concepts as a Belief-Value System of the Society and the Individual." Pp. 39–54 in *Child Development and Education in Japan*, edited by H.W. Stevenson, H. Azuma, and K. Hakuta. New York: Freeman.
Koseisho (Japan Ministry of Health and Welfare). 1980. *Welfare White Paper for 1978*

Fiscal Year (Summary of General Review): Japanese Children—Their Present State and Future. Tokyo: Foreign Press Center.

———. 1984. A Brief Report on Child Welfare Services in Japan, 1982. Tokyo: Japan Research Institute on Child Welfare.

Lebra, Takie Sugiyama. 1976. Japanese Patterns of Behavior. Honolulu: University of Hawaii Press.

———. 1984. Japanese Women: Constraint and Fulfillment. Honolulu: University of Hawaii Press.

Lewis, Catherine C. 1984. "Cooperation and Control in Japanese Nursery Schools." Comparative Education Review 28: 69–84.

McKean, Margaret A. 1981. Environmental Protest and Citizen Politics in Japan. Berkeley: University of California Press.

Matsuda Michio. 1967. Ikuji no hyakka [Handbook of Child Rearing]. Tokyo: Iwanami Shoten.

Mialaret, G. 1976. World Survey of Preschool Education. Education Studies and Documents, no. 14. Paris: Unesco.

Mombusho (Japan Ministry of Education, Science and Culture). 1981. Preschool Education in Japan. Tokyo: Ministry of Education, Science and Culture, Research and Statistics Division.

———. 1982. Education in Japan. Tokyo: Ministry of Education, Science and Culture, Research and Statistics Division.

———. 1985. Monbu tokei yoran [Handbook of Education Statistics]. Tokyo: Ministry of Education, Science and Culture.

Murayama Yuichi. 1983. Gendai no hoiku-sho/yochien [Today's Day Care Centers and Kindergartens]. Tokyo: Aoki Shuten.

Nitta Noriyoshi and Nagano Shigefumi. 1975. "The Effects of Pre-School Education." Research Bulletin of the National Institute for Educational Research 13: 17–19.

O'Connor, Sorca M. 1988. "Women's Labor Force Participation and Preschool Enrollment: A Cross-National Perspective, 1965–80." Sociology of Education 61: 15–28.

Peak, Lois. 1986. "Training Learning Skills and Attitudes in Japanese Early Educational Settings." Pp. 111–23 in Early Experience and the Development of Competence, edited by W. Fowler. San Francisco: Jossey-Bass.

———. 1987. "Learning to Go to School in Japan: The Transition from Home to Preschool." Ph.D. diss., Harvard University.

Reischauer, Edwin O. 1978. The Japanese. Cambridge, Mass.: Belknap Press.

Rohlen, Thomas P. 1983. Japan's High Schools. Berkeley: University of California Press.

Saito Kimiko. 1982. Kosodate [Raising Children]. Tokyo: Rodojunpo-sha.

Saito Kimiko and Kawashima Hiroshi. 1976. Asu o hiraku kodomo-tachi [Children Who Uncover Tomorrow]. Tokyo: Ayumi Shuppan.

Semonyenov, M. 1980. "The Social Context of Women's Labor Force Participation: A Comparative Analysis." American Journal of Sociology 86: 534–50.

Shimahara Nobuo. 1984. "Toward the Equality of a Japanese Minority: The Case of Burakumin." Comparative Education 20, no. 3: 339–53.

———. 1986. "The Cultural Basis of Student Achievement in Japan." Comparative Education 22: 19–26.

Shirai Tsune. 1985. Sekai no yoji-kyoiku: Yochien/hoiku-en/hoiku-sho. #12. Nihon [Early Childhood Educational Institutions of the World. No. 12. Japan]. Tokyo: Maruzen.

Simons, Carol. 1987. "They Get by with a Lot of Help from Their *Kyoiku Mamas.*" *Smithsonian* 17: 44–52.
Smith, Robert J. and Ella Lury Wiswell. 1982. *Women of Suye Mura*. Chicago: University of Chicago Press.
Steen, L.A. 1987. "Mathematics Education: A Predictor of Scientific Competitiveness." *Science* 237, 4812: 251–2, 302.
Stevenson, Harold W. 1983. "Making the Grade: School Achievement in Japan, Taiwan, and the United States." Pp. 41–51 in *Annual Report 1983*. Palo Alto, Calif.: Center for Advanced Study in the Behavioral Sciences.
Stevenson, Harold W., James W. Stigler, and Shin-ying Lee. 1986. "Achievement in Mathematics." Pp. 201–16 in *Child Development and Education in Japan*, edited by H. Stevenson, H. Azuma, and K. Hakuta. New York: Freeman.
Suzuki Masao, ed. 1984. *Bebi hoteru: Jittai to mondai* ["Baby Hotels"—The Reality and the Problems]. Tokyo: Sasara Shobo.
Takahashi Mamoru. 1985. *Discussions on Educational Reform in Japan*. Tokyo: Foreign Press Center.
TBS Hodo-kyoiku. 1981. *Bebi hoteru ni kansuru TBS chosa: Sogo hokokusho* [The TBS Study of "Baby Hotels": Comprehensive Report]. Tokyo: TBS Information Office.
Tobin, Joseph. 1987. "Controlling Hiroki." Paper presented at conference on Social Control and Early Childhood Education in Japan, Muir Beach, California, October 1987.
United Nations Children's Fund (UNICEF). 1985. *The State of the World's Children*. Oxfordshire, U.K.: Oxford University Press.
Uno, Kathleen. 1987. *Day Care and Family Life in Late Meiji-Taisho Japan, 1900–26*. Ph.D. diss., University of California, Berkeley.
Vogel, Suzanne H. 1978. "Professional Housewife: The Career of Urban Middle Class Japanese Women." *Japan Interpreter* 12: 17–43.
Wagatsuma Hiroshi and Betty B. Lanham. 1983. "Childhood and Child Rearing." P. 278 in *Kodansha Encyclopedia of Japan*, 1983 ed., vol. 1. Tokyo: Kodansha.
White, Merry. 1987. *The Japanese Educational Challenge: A Commitment to Children*. New York: Free Press.
Yamamura Yoshiaki. 1986. "The Child in Japanese Society." Pp. 28–38 in *Child Development and Education in Japan*, edited by H. Stevenson, H. Azuma, and K. Hakuta. New York: Freeman.
Yokota Masako. 1984a. *Hoiku no ayumi to hoiku undo no wadai* [The Story of Child Care and Child Care Movements]. Tokyo: Ayumi Shuppan.
———. 1984b. *Kosodate no daichi o tagayasu* [Cultivating the Fields of Childhood]. Tokyo: Ayumi Shuppan.
Youth Development Headquarters. 1982. *International Comparison: Children and Their Families, Summary Findings*. Tokyo: Prime Minister's Office, Youth Development Headquarters.
Zenkoku Hoiku Dantai Renraku-kai. 1984. *Hoiku hakusho* [Child Care White Paper]. Tokyo: Sodo.
———. 1985. *Mirai o hiraku minna no hoiku-en* [Opening the Future: Everyone's *Hoiku-en*]. Tokyo: Zenkoku Hoiku-en Renraku-kai.

6

Task Persistence in Japanese Elementary Schools

Priscilla N. Blinco

INTRODUCTION

Persistence permeates all of Japanese society. The foundation for the ability to survive and endure in spite of adversity begins in the home and continues in early childhood education in Japan. This chapter examines the persistence element in the behavior of Japanese elementary school children.

The discussion is divided into two sections. The first examines the persistence behavior of the Japanese from historical and cultural perspectives. The second compares the persistence phenomenon in the behavior of Japanese elementary school children with their peers in the United States. The latter discussion is based on my earlier comparative study of task persistence in Japan and the United States.[1]

HISTORICAL AND CULTURAL PERSPECTIVES

The influence of the civilization of China played an important role in the development of Japan's culture. Buddhism arrived in Japan in the sixth century A.D., at the same time as the Chinese writing system. During this period, Confucianism, with its high respect for learning, achievement, Confucian classics, and philosophical traditions of Confucian beliefs, took firm roots in Japan. A hierarchical system of relationships, with emphasis on group harmony and respect for one's family members and country, are all attributed to the Confucian tradition.

Between approximately 1540 and 1640, when European colonial powers penetrated the Asian continent, Japan already had close relationships with the West.

Japan enjoyed limited trade with England, Spain, Portugal, and The Netherlands, nations with great traditions of overseas trade and the colonial leaders of the period. The Japanese adopted and adapted new techniques from the West and used them for their own purposes. Along with the Portuguese traders came Jesuit missionaries with their printing skills which were used to print Japanese books for use in schools maintained by the church.[2]

The Tokugawa family unified Japan in 1603 and set up the shōgun (military ruler) as head of the government. Tokugawa Ieyasu wanted to develop foreign trade and for some thirty years remained quite friendly with the Christian missionaries. However, his concern to obtain full control of the country and to assure complete loyalty to his regime led toward the adoption of a policy of strict seclusion and isolation from the outside world. Historian John Whitney Hall points out that the history of the adoption of the seclusion policy by the Tokugawa Ieyasu "shows an intermingling of three strands of concern: (1) the Tokugawa effort to secure internal political stability, (2) the Tokugawa desire to secure a monopoly of foreign trade, and (3) fear of Christianity."[3] By 1641 the seclusion policy adopted by the Tokugawa was fully executed. Christianity was outlawed, trade with foreign countries was prohibited, and the Japanese were forbidden from traveling abroad. This period of domestic isolation lasted over 200 years.

The warrior samurai, the most powerful class in feudal Japan, placed great importance on education.[4] As head of the other three classes of society (peasant, artisan, and merchant), the samurai was expected to be well educated in order to carry out his administrative duties. Responsibility was assigned to the parents for ensuring that he was well educated. The samurai curriculum focused primarily on military training and studies of the Confucian classics.

Education for the common classes was held in the temple schools (*terakoya*) and consisted of reading, writing, and mathematics. These schools were operated by the local citizenry without official support. They evolved because of the need for education in all areas of the country. The *terakoya* provided merchants, town residents, and farmers with the necessary skills to be successful members of a developing nation. There were more than 8,000 *terakoya* schools founded after 1830 and at one time there were over 10,000 of these schools in Japan.[5]

In 1868, after more than two centuries of total isolation from the outside world, the new Meiji government decreed that "Knowledge shall be sought throughout the world."[6] Thus, many Japanese students studied in the United States and Western Europe to learn the ways of the West. In the first twenty years of the Meiji era, the Japanese government in Tokyo and many of the fief (*han*) governments employed several thousand foreigners (*yatoi*) to work as technicians and teachers and in other fields to help Japan develop as an industrial nation.[7]

Education is viewed by the Japanese as being essential for the individual, family, and country. Perseverance, hard work, diligence, but above all, persistence (*gambaru*), are considered important contributing factors to success in education and other areas of life. The Japanese assume that it will take many years of intensive training and study to master any worthwhile skill, and any shortcut is seen as harmful because it is the persistence needed to attain the goal which makes it worthwhile. They believe that true experience of life can be enjoyed only through mental training (*shūyō*). Helmut Morsbach explains "when someone is undergoing training in Japan, it is a commonly held belief that the body is greatly malleable as long as the will is strong enough."[8]

Confidence that an unlimited amount of energy can be derived from self (*hara*) is explained by Takie Sugiyama Lebra. She writes that, "Many a Japanese finds satisfaction in work deriving from energy expenditure, attaches moral significance to a steady flow of physical or mental energy, namely perseverance and endurance to the point of masochism and holds an optimistic belief in what one can accomplish through single-minded effort."[9] This practice of self-discipline has a recognized place in Japanese life. In the important matters of life, the Japanese feel that the demands on the body and mind are essential for achievement.

Educators in Japan believe that all students can achieve if they persevere (*gaman suru*) and endure hardship, especially in the preschool and elementary years. For example, William K. Cummings noted that one of the five major goals for one elementary school faculty in Japan was "to encourage the will to endure whatever is attempted."[10] The Japanese believe that effort and hard work are essential to task mastery. A 1986 study by Robert D. Hess and his colleagues confirms the importance placed on effort by the Japanese:

In Japan poor performance in mathematics was attributed to lack of effort; in the United States, explanations were more evenly divided among ability, effort, and training at school. Japanese mothers were less likely to blame training at school as a cause of low achievement in mathematics.... Their children generally shared this view of things.[11]

In Japan, the Japanese mother sees, as her main goal in life, the preparation of her children to get along in the various elements of society, such as school, neighborhood, and other groups. She provides the bridge from home to school; it is her responsibility to see that her children are well prepared for this most important transition. The Japanese mother's abilities in this area are measured by *seken* (the whole country), that is, neighborhood, school, family members, and others involved with her children. The importance of perseverance is continually imparted to the young child by the mother. Cummings suggests that these child-rearing practices in Japan instill a lasting behavior of perseverance.

The mother, through a close relationship with her child, strives to encourage him or her to study and to become familiar with letters and numbers even before the child enters elementary school. Phonetic games, activity books, and children's magazines are commonly used by Japanese mothers to encourage their children to recognize letters and numbers. As a result of this home learning environment provided by the mother, many Japanese children enter the first grade with the ability to read and write the forty-eight basic Japanese phonetic symbols.

Japanese teachers believe that all students can be motivated to learn, thus a desire to do one's best in mastering tasks is greatly influenced by teachers and the school environment. Group activities are used extensively to motivate students. Young Japanese students are motivated to work hard and to persist in the task at hand because the group depends on individual contribution for achievement, and, in turn, the individual as a contributor gains self-recognition and reward. In other words, the Japanese learn, at a very young age, that group loyalty, effort, and persistence are essential if one is to live a happy life. Loyalty of an individual to the group remains one of the most important attributes of the Japanese. This structural tendency, which has developed in the course of history, is one of the major cultural characteristics of the Japanese.

While conducting research in Japanese preschool and elementary school classrooms, the author has observed a variety of activities, both inside and outside the classroom. Students were observed participating in academic work, creative art projects, and sports activities. Nearly all of the activities, academic and others, were group oriented. During a first grade mathematics lesson, for example, classes often worked together while their teacher explained the steps needed to solve a measuring problem. After discussion and working together, the teacher suggested that the entire class move to the hallway outside the classroom and practice what they were learning. Using tapes, rulers, and various objects, the students used their newly acquired skills to test their measuring abilities. In these instances, students tried many different approaches to measurement. There was great enthusiasm and sharing among the class members. The students would try several different ways of measuring, always with great persistence in working it through to the final solution. They were intense and displayed complete concentration on the task at hand.

Recent studies of early childhood education in Japan stress the value placed on the maintenance of harmony in social relationships.[12] Japanese teachers of young children commonly assign the responsibility for many classroom activities to the pupils, including rule making, solving conflicts, and a variety of other classroom chores. Teachers can be observed encouraging children to manage and solve disagreements when they occur. Problems are seen as belonging to everyone, and, therefore, the entire group is part of the process of conflict resolution.

Shigaki describes the responses to the question of what kind of child Japanese and American teachers want to develop.[13] Japanese teachers responded with a *ningen-rashii kodomo* (a humanlike child). American early childhood educators questioned in the Shigaki study listed honesty, self-confidence, and independence as the most important values to transmit to their pupils. No mention was made of the value of harmony in social relationships by the American educators.

We have in this section examined the persistence element of Japanese behavior from historical and cultural perspectives. The important role of the Confucian tradition in the development of Japanese culture was described. The role of the mother, group reinforcement, and teacher influence have been discussed in relationship to the persistence element.

TASK PERSISTENCE COMPARISON BETWEEN JAPAN AND THE UNITED STATES

How well do Japanese elementary school children persist in a task, under noncompetitive conditions, in comparison to their peers in the United States? A noncompetitive condition refers to working at a task independently, isolated from other students, and without teacher influence. This section discusses the empirical comparative study of task persistence of elementary school children, under noncompetitive conditions, that the author conducted in Japan and the United States in 1984 and 1985.[14] That study also analyzed the relationship between teacher behavior and task persistence and the relationship between home and family attitudes and task persistence.

The Research Setting

The field work for the Japanese portion of the study was conducted in Fukuoka Prefecture, one of the largest prefectures, located on Kyūshū Island in southern Japan. The prefecture's population is over 4.7 million and occupies a land area of 1,915 square miles, smaller than the state of Delaware, which has 2,370 square miles in land area.

Fukuoka City and Kitakyūshū City are the largest cities in the prefecture and each has a population of over 1 million. These two cities serve as the crossroads of Fukuoka Prefecture and as the centers of culture, economy, and transportation for Kyūshū Island. Fukuoka Prefecture is the section of the Japanese Archipelago closest to the Korean Peninsula and the continent of Asia. It is of major historical significance to the Japanese people because it was the first area of Japan to be exposed to continental culture.

The field work for the U.S. portion of the study was conducted in the San Francisco Bay Area. The population of the nine counties included in the Bay Area is approximately 5.5 million. San Francisco, San Jose, and Oakland are the three largest cities in the area and have a combined population of over 1.9 million. The San Francisco Bay Area has a diversified economy, with service industries predominating.

The two regions, Fukuoka Prefecture and the San Francisco Bay Area, were selected for the study for their comparability in population, number of schools, and economic activity. In addition, the educational systems in the two regions are quite similar in organizational structure except for the strong central government control in Japan.

Table 6.1
Numerical Profile of Student Sample (N = 193)

	School Type											
	Private			Public Urban			Public Rural			Total		
	Boys	Girls	Total	Boys	Girls	Total	Boys	Girls	Total	Boys	Girls	Total
Japanese	10	10	20	30	24	54	14	19	33	54	53	107
American	7	12	19	21	24	45	11	11	22	39	47	86
Total	17	22	39	51	48	99	25	30	55	93	100	193

Sample

The study was conducted in four elementary schools in Fukuoka Prefecture and in four elementary schools in the Bay Area. During meetings with educational authorities in each country, schools that were judged to be a representative sample of elementary schools were selected. One private school, two urban public schools, and one rural public school were selected in each country, and pupils from one first grade class in each of the schools were chosen as the target group. This method of selection allowed for pupil representation from a variety of social, economic, and occupational groups.

Subjects for the Japanese segment of the study consisted of 107 first grade pupils, 54 boys and 53 girls, ranging in age from six years and four months to seven years and six months. A total of 86 first grade pupils, 39 boys and 47 girls, were chosen for the American portion of the study. The American pupils ranged in age from five years and ten months to eight years and four months. A numerical profile of the student sample for both countries is shown in Table 6.1.

Sampling Procedure

The sampling procedures and instrumentation were identical for both segments of the study, except that in Japan the research was conducted in Japanese. The task persistence part of the study was divided into two phases.

During phase one, the pupils selected for the study were individually taken out of the classroom into a separate, unoccupied room. Each child was given the first stage of a manipulative puzzlelike game (technic) which has a series of increasing stages of difficulty. The ultimate goal for the child was to master the task of correctly assembling each stage of the game. The pupil was given an example of how to assemble part of the game and instructed to tell the experimenter when he or she was finished or wanted to stop. When the first stage of difficulty was completed, the child was given the next segment of the game, one stage higher in difficulty. This procedure was continued until the child failed to complete a stage, requested assistance, or said he or she could not do any more. If the pupil continued to persist, but was not assembling the manipulative game correctly, he was allowed to continue for a total of fifteen minutes, at which time the session ended. The stage of difficulty at which the pupil stopped was recorded for use during phase two of the study.

During phase two, the pupils selected for the study were again individually taken out of the classroom and into a separate room. Each child was given the same manipulative puzzlelike game as before except that it was two stages higher in difficulty than the point where he or she had stopped during phase one. This made the task challenging and unsolvable for most of the pupils. The child was allowed a maximum of fifteen minutes to work on this task. The length of time that the pupil actually spent working at the task was recorded using a stop watch. If the child finished the stage of difficulty given to him or her, but it was not correct, the child was told that it was not correct and asked whether he or she wanted to keep trying or to stop. If the child completed the stage of difficulty correctly, he or she was given another segment of the game one step higher in difficulty. Timing ended when the pupil asked for help, asked to stop, or at the end of fifteen minutes.

Results of the Study

Japanese children persisted significantly longer than American children in all four schools (see Table 6.2). The two-way analysis of variance of culture by school type produced a very significant F ratio for culture main effect ($F = 54.77$, $df = 1/187$, $p < .001$). The school type main effect ($F < 1$, $df = 2/187$) and the interaction between culture and school type ($F < 1$, $df = 2/187$) were not significant.

The two-way analysis of variance was also computed utilizing culture and sex main effects. Again, culture main effect was extremely significant ($F = 69.86$, $df = 1/189$, $p < .001$). Sex main effect ($F < 1$, $df = 189$) and the interaction between culture and sex ($F < 1$, $df = 1/189$) were not significant. Thus, the analyses revealed that culture makes a significant difference in the degree of task persistence, but the type of school or sex of the pupil, by itself, or interacting with culture main effect, does not make any significant difference in the magnitude of task persistence.

In reviewing the raw data in Table 6.2, we find the Japanese raw time-on-task group mean of 13.93 minutes (SD 2.53) to be significantly higher than the American raw time-on-task group mean of 9.47 minutes (SD 4.44). Only twenty-three (26.7 percent) of the American pupils persisted as long as, or longer than, the Japanese average, and only eleven (10 percent) of the Japanese pupils persisted on the task for 9.47 minutes or less, the American mean time. The data

Table 6.2
Means and Standard Deviations of Raw Time-on-Task by Culture, School Type, and Sex

	School Type									Total
	Private			Public Urban			Public Rural			
	Boys	Girls	Total	Boys	Girls	Total	Boys	Girls	Total	
Japanese										
M	13.60	14.20	13.90	14.07	13.79	13.94	14.00	13.89	13.94	13.93
SD	2.80	2.53	2.61	2.65	2.52	2.57	2.32	2.69	2.50	2.53
N	10	10	20	30	24	54	14	19	33	107
American										
M	8.63	12.73	11.22	9.35	8.59	8.94	9.93	8.11	9.02	9.47
SD	4.59	3.32	4.23	4.70	3.93	4.28	4.73	4.79	4.73	4.44
N	7	12	19	21	24	45	11	11	22	86
Total										
M	11.53	13.41	12.59	12.12	11.19	11.67	12.20	11.77	11.96	11.94
SD	4.39	2.98	3.72	4.31	3.90	4.26	4.08	4.54	4.30	4.15
N	17	22	39	51	48	99	25	30	55	193

also revealed a substantially larger variance in the American time-on-task in comparison to the Japanese time-on-task. This indicates that the Japanese pupils are very homogeneous.

The raw data also indicated, although the data were not statistically significant, that the boys in the American private school persisted in the task 4.10 minutes less than the girls. In both Japanese and American private schools, the girls persisted in the task for a longer time and the boys persisted on the task for a shorter time than the pupils in the public schools within each culture.

Although this chapter examines in detail only that part of the original study that compared the time-on-task persistence of first grade pupils from four schools in Japan with time-on-task persistence of first-grade pupils from four schools in the United States, the research project also compared observed teachers' verbal and nonverbal behavior toward children in the first grade classrooms under study. Additionally, the larger study also compared parental reports of student home study habits and their encouragement of their children's academic efforts for all parents of the selected first grade pupils in the four schools in Japan and the four schools in the United States.

The findings of observed teachers' verbal and nonverbal behavior toward children in the four first grade classrooms in Japan compared to the four first grade classrooms in the United States revealed no significant differences between the Japanese and Americans in the proportions of positive and negative teacher behavior and reinforcement. The data also revealed that the type of school does not make any significant difference in the proportions of positive and negative teacher behavior toward their pupils.

A thirty-item questionnaire was developed for the home and family reinforcement segment of the research. The statistical analyses of the questionnaire scores indicated that culture and type of school had significant effects on the answers given by the parents. The two-way analysis of variance of culture by school type revealed culture main effect to be very significant ($F = 84.07$, $df = 1/168$, $p < .001$). School type main effect ($F = 5.82$, $df = 2/168$, $p < .01$) and culture by school type interaction ($F = 6.26$, $df = 2/168$, $p < .01$) were also significant.

The Spearman Rho rank-order correlation coefficient, using the time-on-task for each pupil and the total questionnaire score for the respective pupil's parents, was computed for each culture to test the relationship between time-on-task persistence and home/family encouragement and support. The results indicated that there is a positive correlation in both cultures between time-on-task for each pupil and the questionnaire score for the respective pupil's parents. The correlation in the American sample ($r_s = .467$, $t = 4.344$, $df = 72$, $p < .001$) and the Japanese sample ($r_s = .269$, $t = 2.760$, $df = 98$, $p < .01$) was significant.

Conclusions

Education in Japan is highly valued and diversified, and a continuous stream of students passes through the schools and into the nation's labor market. Educational standards are uniformly high throughout the country as a consequence of strong central government control and a reinforcing culture which supports such standards. The high level of educational support results not only from an admiration of intellectual accomplishment, but also from a very strong belief in the malleability of human beings.

One of the dominant contributing factors to Japan's economic success has been its educational system. There is a commonly held belief among the Japanese that the persistence element of behavior in young Japanese children and the instilling of such behavior is responsible for much of this economic success. On the other hand, there is a relative lack of persistence by young American children and a tendency to "give up" when performing tasks. Morsbach, for example, concluded that

It is finally not so much the flamboyant aspect of persistence which should concern us when trying to say something about the average Japanese personality. Rather it is its appearance in the many humdrum situations where Westerners are more likely to give up, or at least start getting bad-tempered and obstreperous. And it is due to the diligent execution of boring routines that the Japanese seem to have been able to prosper in everyday life.[15]

Approximately 30 percent of American students give up and drop out of high school in contrast to less than 3 percent in Japan.[16] The result is that many American pupils are not properly prepared for the modern work world. This lack of persistence has important implications in an age of rapid technological progress.

The data from the original comparative study, collected in 1984 and 1985, indicated a large difference in task persistence between Japanese and American first graders. The data did not, however, provide a direct explanation for this difference. There are several plausible explanations for the persistence element of behavior in young Japanese children, but the cultural aspect of training and educating to instill a behavior of perseverance seems to be the most likely explanation. The mother plays a major role, starting in infancy, in alerting the Japanese child to the importance of persistence in life. Through the socialization process, the Japanese mother creates a home learning environment and transmits to her child the importance of persistence and hard work.

American mothers are more likely to be satisfied with the progress of their children than Japanese mothers even though American children may be falling behind academically. This can be explained by the way the American and Japanese mothers view their role in helping children learn. Japanese mothers attribute their children's progress to hard work, persistence, and their own role in actively helping their children learn; American mothers see their role as one of encouraging and accepting. Unlike the Japanese, American mothers attribute ability as the main reason for their children doing well rather than effort.

Other possible explanations for the strong persistence behavior in Japanese children, although not supported empirically, include the amount of early nursery school and kindergarten training they receive. More than 90 percent of Japanese children receive preschool training.[17] Preschool education serves as the transition from the self-centered home life and training to the group-oriented formal education experience.

Several aspects of the data from the larger study, upon which this chapter is based, reveal some interesting results which might lend support to the importance of the role of the Japanese mother in transmitting persistence behavior to her child. The frequencies of teachers' interaction with pupils in American classrooms were 1.8 times more than the interaction in the Japanese classrooms. Task persistence is inculcated so early by the Japanese mother that teachers in Japan need not emphasize effort and persistence values as much as teachers in the United States. The data also revealed a substantially larger variance in the U.S. time-on-task in comparison to the Japanese time-on-task. This suggests that Japanese pupils are very homogeneous.

The study's results confirm that Japanese elementary school children persist longer and complete tasks more often, under noncompetitive conditions, than do their peers in the United States. Cultural differences in task persistence were not, however, attributable to teacher behavior or parental encouragement. Task persistence is inculcated so early and the transmission of effort and persistence values are done so well in Japan that mothers need not work on them so hard, nor do teachers need to emphasize them as much as one might expect.

NOTES

1. Priscilla N. Blinco, "Task Persistence of Young Children in Japan and the United States: A Comparative Study" (Ph.D. diss., Stanford University, 1987).
2. Charles R. Boxer, *The Christian Century in Japan* (Berkeley: University of California Press, 1951), pp. 190–98.
3. John Whitney Hall, *Japan: From Prehistory to Modern Times* (New York: Dell, 1970), p. 187.
4. A.L. Sadler, trans., *The Code of the Samurai*, a translation of Daidōji Yūzan, *Budō Shoshinshū* (Tokyo: Charles E. Tuttle, 1988), pp. 18–19.
5. Richard Rubinger, *Private Academies of Tokugawa Japan* (Princeton N.J.: Princeton University Press, 1982), p. 5.
6. Edward R. Beauchamp, *An American Teacher in Early Meiji Japan* (Honolulu: University of Hawaii Press, 1976), p. 1.
7. Ibid., p. 2.
8. Helmut Morsbach, "Socio-Psychological Aspects of Persistence in Japan," *Japan Times*, December 20, 1978, p. 7.
9. Takie Sugiyama Lebra, *Japanese Patterns of Behavior* (Honolulu: University of Hawaii Press, 1976), p. 163.
10. William K. Cummings, *Education and Equality in Japan* (Princeton N.J.: Princeton University Press, 1980), p. 13.
11. Robert D. Hess et al., "Family Influences on School Readiness and Achievement in Japan and the United States: An Overview of a Longitudinal Study," in Harold Stevenson, Azuma Hiroshi, and Hakuta Kenji, eds., *Child Development and Education in Japan* (New York: W.H. Freeman, 1986), p. 161.
12. For some of the recent studies of early childhood education in Japan see the following: Blinco, "Task Persistence of Young Children in Japan and the United States", Joy Hendry, *Becoming Japanese* (Honolulu: University of Hawaii Press, 1986); Catherine C. Lewis, "Cooperation and Control in Japanese Nursery Schools," *Comparative Education Review* 28 (1984), pp. 69–84; Catherine C. Lewis, "Children's Social Development in Japan: Research Directions," in Harold Stevenson, Azuma Hiroshi, and Hakuta Kenji, eds., *Child Development and Education in Japan* (New York: W.H. Freeman, 1986); Irene S. Shigaki, "Child Care Practices in Japan and the United States: How Do They Reflect Cultural Values in Young Children," *Young Children*, May 1983, pp. 13–24.
13. Shigaki, "Child Care Practices in Japan and the United States," pp. 15–16.
14. Blinco, "Task Persistence of Young Children in Japan and the United States."
15. Morsbach, "Socio-Psychological Aspects of Persistence," p. 7.
16. Norman Jonas, "No Pain, No Gain: How America Can Grow Again," *Business Week*, April 20, 1987, p. 68.
17. U.S. Department of Education, *Japanese Education Today* (Washington, D.C.: U.S. Government Printing Office, 1987), p. 22.

7

Teaching of Mathematics in Japanese Schools

Nancy C. Whitman

Curriculum and instruction are two important factors influencing mathematical achievement. This chapter traces the evolution of the present mathematics curriculum in Japan, its methods, and materials and analyzes its success.

THE MATHEMATICS CURRICULUM

The high achievement of Japanese students in mathematics is recognized worldwide. However, the achievement of the Japanese in mathematical studies is not a recent phenomenon. Prior to the Meiji Restoration, the Japanese had developed a mathematics based on the works of the Chinese with its own specialized methodology.[1] This indigenous mathematics (*wasan*) flourished during the seventeenth and eighteenth centuries. In the first half of the seventeenth century, use of the *soroban* (beads calculation) was common throughout the country. Mastery of the *soroban*, followed by an intensive study of algebra, led to the development of *yendan* (the method of explanations or analysis) and *tenzan* algebra (theory of equations, solution of indeterminate equations, algebraic treatment of geometrical relations, and so forth) by Seki Kowa, Japan's greatest mathematician. The method for measuring a circle by analytical means, called *yenri*, was also invented. Numerous other aspects of *wasan* were studied during this period. The general approach in *wasan* was practical, intuitive, and inductive rather than deductive. It is against this historical background of mathematics development that we should view the evolution of the mathematics curriculum to its present state.

Evolution of the Mathematics Curriculum

Soon after the Meiji Restoration of 1868, a choice had to be made between using the mathematics of the old Japanese school or Western mathematics in the nation's elementary schools. The words of Fujisawa Rikitaro reflects the choice made and the sentiment at that time:

> It was surely a wise policy on the part of the educational authorities that they, in organizing the new system of education, put this mathematics of the old Japanese school entirely out of sight, and were anxious to introduce free and unmolested mathematics which has no schools and whose universal language is intelligible to all the united nations.[2]

The nonprofessional use of the *soroban* had permeated the whole social structure. Nonetheless, it was rejected from the newly organized elementary education. As a consequence the tradesmen and merchants, for whom use of the *soroban* was indispensable, were obliged to learn its use elsewhere. Throughout Japan there arose small evening classes in *soroban* use with private instructors. Students from the elementary schools often attended these classes. Here we see traces of the early development of *juku*[3] in response to the failure of the official education program to meet the needs of a substantial group of students.

Okabe Susumu characterized Japanese mathematics education, from 1870 to 1900, as follows:

1. Its primary aim was to introduce and spread Western mathematics throughout Japan. Mathematics education was provided to everyone regardless of age.
2. Mathematics education was provided without taking into consideration the psychological development of students and was not based on their daily lives.
3. Western mathematics was taught deductively. Initial chapters of textbooks generally dealt with definitions and exercises using abstract numbers and calculations. Emphasis was placed on solving problems and doing calculations quickly and accurately.[4]

The introduction and spread of Western mathematics in Japan was a monumental task as various adjustments had to be made to incorporate Western mathematics into the Japanese context. For example, the use of Western symbolic expressions such as $a^2 + b^2$ and the use of Arabic numerals and alphabet had to be incorporated into the Japanese method of writing. Traditionally, Japanese sentences are written from the top to the bottom of the page and progress from the right side of the page to the left. Figures 7.1 and 7.2 show two ways that were used to incorporate Western mathematical symbols into the Japanese writing system. Figure 7.3 shows the method of writing that eventually was used by the Japanese.

After several decades, a Japanese solution to the problems posed by Western mathematics emerged. In 1905, the Ministry of Education issued the first arithmetic textbooks to be used on a national basis. Their contents reflected that of

Figure 7.1
A Treatise on Algebra (1889)

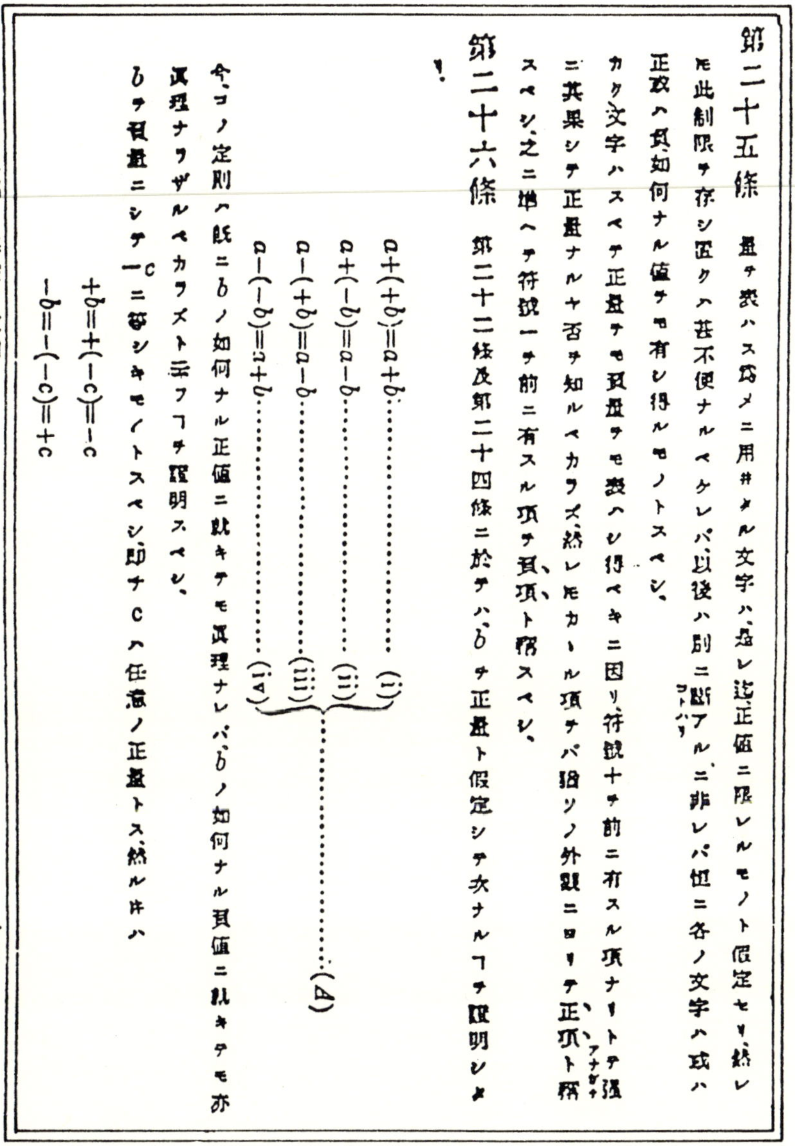

第二十五條 蓋シ數ハ廣キ意ニ用ヰメル文字ハ盡レ迄正値ニ限レルモノト假定セリ然レ
ニ此制限テ存シ置クハ甚不便ナルヘケレバ以後ハ別ニ斷アルニ非レバ恒ニ各ノ文字ハ或ハ
正或ハ其ノ如何ナル値テモ有リ得ルモノトスベシ
カク文字ハスベテ正盡テモ盡ハソリ得ベキニ因リ符號十テ前ニ有スル項ナリトテ必
ニ其果シテ正盡ナルヤ否テ知ルベカラズ然レモカカル項ナバ恆ソノ外觀ニ由テ正項ト稱
スベシ之ニ堆ヘテ符號一テ前ニ有スル項テ其ノ項ト務スベシ

第二十六條 第二十二條及第二十四條ニ於テハa, bテ正盡ト假定シテ次ナル丁テ證明シヨ

$a+(+b)=a+b$ ………………(i)
$a+(-b)=a-b$ ………………(ii)
$a-(+b)=a-b$ ………………(iii)
$a-(-b)=a+b$ ………………(iv)

今コノ定則ハ既ニbノ如何ナル正値ニ就キテモ真理ナレバbノ如何ナル其ノ値ニ就キテモ亦
真理ナラザルベカラズ即テ bテ證明スベシ
bテ其ノ盡ニシテ$-c$ニ等シキモノトスベシ即チcハ任意ノ正盡トス然ルトキハ
$+b=+(-c)=-c$
$-b=-(-c)=+c$

Figure 7.2
1877 Algebra Text

第二款 二號ハ其兩邊ニ在ル所ノ數相等レキヲ指スノ

相等號トナス

假例ハ
$a = 17$ トナセハ
$2a = 34$ ナリ
ノ義ニシテ∴號ハ如何トナ

第三款 ∴號ハ故ニ或ハ乃チノ義ヲ示ス

第四款 十號ハ加フ指スノ即チ其右邊ニ在ル數ト他數ト相加フヲ指スノ即チ其右邊ニ在ル數ヨリ他數ヲ減スヲ指スノ頁號ト爲ス

逆ニ在ル數ヲ他數ヨリ減スヲ指スノ又一號ハ減スヲ指スノ頁號ト爲ス

假例ハ

$5 + 3 = 8.$
$5 - 3 = 2.$

乃ナ
$a = 3$
及
$b = 4$
トナセハ

$a + b = 3 + 4 = 7.$
$a + b + 2 = 3 + 4.$
$+ 2 = 9.$
$10 - a = 10 - 3.$
$= 7.$
$10 - a - b = 10$
$- 3 - 4 = 7 - 4$
$= 3.$

Algebra text published in 1877. Author unknown. Note the horizontal method of writing equations. (Cited by Shimada Shigeru. "Problem-Solving - The Present State and Historical Development in Japan." In Proceedings of the U.S. - Japan Seminar on Mathematical Problem Solving, edited by Becker Jerry P. and Miwa Tatsuro (Carbondale: Southern Illinois University, 1987)

Figure 7.3
1889 Algebra Text

(4)

$x^2-\dfrac{3x}{4}$. 本例ニ在テハ x ノ係數ノ半ハ $-\dfrac{3}{8}$ +

リ、故ニ $\left(-\dfrac{3}{8}\right)^2$ 即チ $\left(\dfrac{3}{8}\right)^2$ ヲ加ヘ $x^2-\dfrac{3x}{4}+\left(\dfrac{3}{8}\right)^2$

即チ $\left(x-\dfrac{3}{8}\right)^2$ ヲ得、

以上例示シタル方ヲ稱シテ平方ヲ完全ニナス コト云フ、

(230) 茲ニ雜二次方程式解方ノ規則ヲ揭ク、諸項ヲ轉移シテ唯未知數ヲ有スルモノノミヲ一節ニ置キ、次ニ方程式ヲ約シテ x^2 ノ係數ヲ $+1$ トナシ、次ニ各節ニ x ノ係數ノ半ノ平方ヲ加ヘ、終リニ各節・平方根ヲ求ムヘシ、

上ノ規則ニ遵テ演算スルトキハ最後ニ至リテ未知數ノ兩價ヲ直ニ索出シ得ルノ點ニ到達スルコト、下ノ數様ニ揭クル例題ニ就テ、自ラ悟リ得ベシ、

(231)　　$x^2-10x+24=0$ ヲ解ケ、

項ヲ轉移シ　　　　$x^2-10x=-24$;

$\left(\dfrac{10}{2}\right)^2$ ヲ加ヘ　　$x^2-10x+5^2=-24+25=1$;

平方根ヲ取リ　　　$x-5=\pm 1$;

Algebra text translated by Omori Toshitugu and Yatabe Umekichi, published in 1889 by Chikobunsha. Kunmou Daisuugaku (Algebra for Beginners). Original text written by I. Todhunter of Cambridge University. Note the format uses the western style of writing from left to right. (Cited by Shimada Shigeru. "Problem-Solving - The Present State and Historical Development in Japan." In Proceedings of the U.S. - Japan Seminar on Mathematical Problem Solving, edited by Becker Jerry P. and Miwa Tatsuro (Carbondale: Southern Illinois University, 1987) the elementary school mathematics curriculum. By 1911, 98 percent of school age children were in school, and they studied this common arithmetic curriculum which is outlined below.

Grade One

Counting up to ten using two separate sets of names.
Arabic notation and Chinese ideographs up to one hundred.
Comparison of two numbers in terms of greater than, less than.
Addition and subtraction.
Multiplication.
Division as the inverse of multiplication and as partition into equal parts.
Mental calculations of numbers not exceeding twenty.

Grade Two

Numeration up to one thousand.
Mental calculation of numbers not exceeding one hundred.
Review and extension of addition and subtraction.
Multiplication tables.
Multiplication by multiples of ten and one hundred.
Division by single digits, ten, and one hundred.
Division with remainder.
Division so that quotient is a multiple of ten or one hundred.

Grade Three

Addition, subtraction, multiplication, and single-digit and two-digit division within the limits of numbers less than 10,000.
Mental calculations and applied problems for all four operations.

Grade Four

Practice of all four operations within the limits of numbers less than 100 million. Division by three or more digits is included.
Integers: numeration and notation, mental calculations, addition, subtraction, multiplication, and division.
Measurement: length, area, capacity, weight, money, and time.
Decimals: numeration and notation, mental calculations, addition, subtraction, multiplication, and division.

Grade Five

Integers and decimals: numeration and notation, calculations using the four basic operations, and applied problems.

Measurement: length, area, volume, capacity, weights, money, time, and applied problems. The metric system, along with selected foreign weights and measures, is introduced in the latter third of the year.

Grade Six

Fractions: addition, subtraction, multiplication, division, and applied problems. Expressing decimal fractions as common fractions and vice versa.

Ratio and percentage: Applied problems including land tax, income tax, and interest.

Extensive review of integers, decimals, measurement, fractions, ratio, and rate problems. *Soroban* calculation is optional.[5]

The elementary school mathematics curriculum was essentially an arithmetic curriculum with a focus on the use of arithmetic in measurement. Emphasis was also placed on simple mental computation. Completely lacking was the study of geometry and simple statistics. Multiplication, division, and decimal concepts were introduced early compared to current curricula in the United States.

Following elementary school, only boys were able to enter the five-year middle school. Although not compulsory, those wishing to be considered of the educated class felt obliged to attend; others attended other kinds of schools. In 1912, about 7 million boys and girls attended the six-year elementary school, but only 120,000 males continued on into the five-year middle school and only about 16,000 actually graduated.[6]

The mathematics curriculum of the middle school is outlined below.

Grade Seven

Integers and decimals, numbers associated with measurement, properties of integers, fractions, and ratio and proportion.

Grade Eight

Arithmetic: ratio and proportion, percentage, and power and roots.

Algebra: adding, subtracting, multiplying, and dividing integral expressions and linear equations with one unknown.

Grade Nine

Algebra: equations including simultaneous quadratic equations, integral expressions, and fractional expressions.

Geometry: lines and circles.

Grade Ten

Algebra: irrational expressions, ratio and proportion, progressions (arithmetic and geometric), permutation and combination, binomial theorem, and logarithms.

Geometry: circles, areas, proportions, and applications of proportion.

Grade Eleven

Geometry: applications of proportion, planes, and polyhedra, and solids with curved surfaces.

Trigonometry: measurement of angles, circular functions, solution of right-angled triangles, formulas for the sum of angles, relations between the sides and circular functions of the angles of a triangle, use of logarithmic tables, solution of triangles, measurements of heights and distances, and practical exercises.[7]

The seventh grade curriculum was essentially a review and, perhaps, an extension of arithmetic. The eighth grade was devoted primarily to algebra, the ninth grade covered both algebra and geometry, and the tenth grade extended the study of algebra and geometry. Finally, the eleventh grade continued the study of algebra and covered the study of trigonometry. In general, the middle-school mathematics program prepared students for university preparatory mathematics.

This curriculum, introduced at the turn of the century, remained essentially unaltered until 1925, four years after the government decided to adopt the metric system of measurement. By grades, we see the following changes:

Grade One. No change.

Grade Two. Meter, centimeter, and millimeter are introduced to measure length.

Grade Three. Kilometer, liter, deciliter, kilogram, and gram are introduced.

Grade Four. Time was saved by deleting instruction in the old *shakukan* (traditional units for measuring length and mass) system. Topics previously taught in the fifth grade are taught here. These included topics such as square, rectangle, cube, and rectangular parallelpiped and the area, volume, and angles of these figures.

Grade Five. Matters dealing with fractions formerly taught in the sixth grade are taught here.

Grade Six. Most of the materials on proportions previously taught after grade six are taught here.[8]

With the adoption of the metric system the Japanese were able to gain time for the study of additional mathematics topics. The curriculum no longer included instruction in the *shakukan* system and in the relationship between the metric system and *shakukan* system. In addition, less time was needed to teach the metric system since it was mathematically simpler than the *shakukan* system.

In 1931 the elementary mathematics textbooks underwent substantial revisions reflecting educational trends both in Japan and overseas. The laboratory technique of mathematics instruction expounded by John Perry in England and Eliakim Hastings Moore in the United States was incorporated into the textbooks. The principles by which the textbooks were compiled, the scope and nature of the teaching materials, and the arrangements and distribution of teaching materials had a profound influence on mathematics education which is still visible today.

Concrete matters were to be taught first, leading gradually to generalizations, and the teaching of new materials was to begin in a way which would enable the students to find solutions themselves. The content was to be taught, as much as possible, through the personal experiences of the students, and textbooks were to be available primarily for spontaneous study by the students. The works of Jean-Jacques Rousseau and John Dewey also influenced the 1931 revision, especially in regard to the role of the child in the learning process.

As did the 1931 revision of the elementary school mathematics program, the 1935 middle-school mathematics revisions reflected trends in education in Japan and abroad. The curriculum was divided into two categories: regular and optional studies. Regular studies were required of all students throughout middle school. At the ninth or tenth grade, however, students complemented their regular studies by taking courses needed to prepare them for business careers, or other courses to prepare them for further academic study. In addition to this division of mathematical studies, efforts were made to synthesize the contents of algebra, trigonometry, arithmetic, and geometry.

The next major change in the mathematics curricula occurred during the American Occupation of Japan (1945–1952). Compulsory education was extended to the ninth grade. This change terminated the differentiation of students by schools and mathematics curricula after elementary school. The junior high school now embraced students with a wide range of mathematics ability. The educational thought of John Dewey influenced the content of the new mathematics program. Emphasis was given to practical mathematics in daily living as compared to mathematics as an academic discipline. Major changes in the grade placement of mathematical concepts were made in the elementary school. For example, the multiplication and division of common and decimal fractions and some of the informal treatment of geometry were shifted from the elementary school to the junior high school. Multiplication and division on the *soroban* and mastery of mental computation by designated grade levels were omitted. The demonstrative treatment of geometry was eliminated from the high school curriculum. These changes resulted in the reduction of the amount of mathematics studied. For the first time in Japan's history, however, there was a required mathematics program for *all* junior high students.

Grade Seven

Concepts of the decimal number system and use of numbers not less than a trillion.

Use of integers, fractions, and decimal fractions and their four fundamental operations and estimations.

Concepts of ratio, rate, and percentage.

Use of graphs (bar, broken line, circular).

Knowledge of various systems of weights and measures.

Conversion within the metric system and measurements of length, area, and volume.

Knowledge of various plane and solid figures.

Reading maps and the concept of similar figures.

Practical business concerning buying and selling and saving.

Grade Eight

Review and supplement of the previous year.

Concepts of statistical rate and index.

Introduction to the use of letters in formulas and equations.

Solving linear equations with one unknown.

Understanding and use of proportional relations.

Concepts of congruence and similarity in geometry.

Reading area and direction in maps.

Concepts of errors and computation with approximate numbers.

Use of a slide rule.

Measuring areas and volumes by use of formula (triangle, parallelogram, circle, cylinder, cone, and figures composed of them).

Concept and use of signed numbers.

Use of histogram.

Grade Nine

Review and supplement of the previous year.

Use of signed numbers in abstract situations.

Use of proportional relations.

Use of linear equations with two unknowns.

Multiplication formulas and computation with simple algebraic expressions.

Concept of coordinate and graphical interpretation of linear relations.

Use of properties concerning simple geometric figures and geometric relations.

Pythagorean theorem and its application.

Meaning of square root and use of square root table.

Concept of trigonometric ratios and use of trigonomic tables.

Meaning and use of projection.

Application of mathematics to practical business.

With the changed structure of the postwar senior high school, a new mathematics program was required. Although high school education was not compulsory, an extremely high percentage of students attended, and all had to take at least one mathematics course to graduate. The four available courses were algebra-analysis I, algebra-analysis II, geometry, and general mathematics. Most students took algebra-analysis I and algebra-analysis II because geometry was an unpopular alternative. General mathematics was usually taken by commercial

Table 7.1
Teaching Hours per Week

Year of Revision	1	2	Grade 3	4	5	6	Total
1907	5	6	6	6	4	4	31
1919	5	5	6	6	4	4	30
1941	4	4	5	5	5	5	28
1947	3	4	4	4-5	4-5	4-5	23-26
1951	2.5**	2.5**	3**	3**	4**	4**	19
1960	3	4	5	6	6	6	30
1968	---	---	---	---	---	---	---
1980	4	5	5	5	5	5	29

*Based on Report on Mathematical Teaching in Educational System of School and Undergraduate Courses in Japan, by Wada Yoshinobu. (Faculty of Education, Tokyo University of Education, 1956), 28.

**Not explicitly stated in Course of Study.

students and girls. To improve the situation, these courses were replaced by mathematics I (mainly algebra and geometry), mathematics II (an extension of mathematics I), mathematics III (mainly calculus), and applied mathematics. Mathematics I was required of all students.

Following the American Occupation of Japan, often referred to as the "reverse-course" (1952–1956), major changes were again made to the elementary and junior high school mathematics programs. In general, the programs at both levels were strengthened. In terms of the time allocated to mathematics at the elementary school level, however, it was decreased substantially (see Table 7.1). Instead of the twenty-eight hours a week in 1941 and from twenty-three to twenty-six in 1947, by 1951 the recommended standard was only nineteen hours, but it rose again to thirty hours in 1960.

Instructional materials were organized into four major areas at the elementary level: (1) numbers and calculations, (2) quantity and measurement, (3) quantitative relationships, and (4) figures. The following contents were transferred from the junior high to elementary schools: multiplication and division of fractions and decimals, computation of percentages and rates, proportion, functional observation of formulas, measuration of simple diagrams, and simple concepts of rotation and symmetry. Multiplication and division on the *soroban* were to be offered according to local needs. In addition, the following items from the elementary mathematics program were transferred to other programs: Japanese weight measures, temperature and direction, and matters of business such as buying and selling.

At the junior high level, the minimum hours required for mathematics per week was four at grades seven and eight and three at grade nine. This compares with the prewar requirement of three hours at grades seven and eight and from four to five hours at grade nine in the middle schools. Major revisions included the elimination or reduction of business mathematics and approximate value and the elimination of decimal and common fractions. To be added were negative numbers and formulas, quadratic equations together with functional relations, demonstration of figures (proof), and the relation of the central angle to the circumference.

In the post-Occupation revisions, not only is there a strengthening of the mathematics curriculum but also a move away from the "daily living" approach to the study of mathematics and toward that of a systematic study.

The revisions of the 1970s resulted in the incorporation of "new" mathematics into the curriculum. This made the curriculum more abstract with the addition of more topics. Some of these topics included sets in grade four and abstract algebra in grade eight. In addition, logic, mapping and vectors, axiomatic construction of plane geometry, matrices, and probability and statistics were introduced at the high school level. Mathematics through grade nine continued to be required.

Aside from the incorporation of the new mathematics, the program remained essentially as it had been during the 1960s, and it continued to be required of all students. In the tenth grade students were required to take either mathematics I or general mathematics for a year, meeting a total of six hours per week. Although an elective, 98 percent of the grade eleven students took a mathematics course in the eleventh grade with the majority taking the more rigorous course. This is noteworthy in view of the fact that in the 1970s about 80 percent of this age group elected to attend high school.

The introduction of the new mathematics resulted in public criticism of the revised curriculum. Opponents cited what they viewed as the introduction of abstraction and of new terms and symbols at too early an age. Hence, in the 1980s, the curriculum retreated from the attempted incorporation of new mathematics to a more traditional approach. This is the curriculum currently being studied in Japanese schools.

The Current Curriculum

Japanese educators responded to the criticisms that the 1970 curriculum did not respond to the needs of the increasing number of underachievers in high

Teaching of Mathematics

school resulting from the increased rate of high school attendance. In 1950, for example, 42.5 percent continued on to high school, 57.7 percent in 1960, 82.1 percent in 1970, and 93.1 percent in 1977.[9] In addition high school courses did not take into account the pupil's antipathy to differentiation and his or her bias toward following an academic course. This attitude is reflected by 98 percent of high school students, who chose for the required academic course mathematics I, as compared to the nonacademic general mathematics during the 1970s.[10] Although the 1960 curriculum provided for "required" content and "elective" content to make it possible for some students to study only what was required, very few schools were prepared to provide such a course. Finally the content of the academic mathematics courses made extraordinary demands of the students.

To meet these criticisms the curriculum was changed as follows:

1. Reduction of instruction time: the seventh grade required one hour less per week and the tenth grade required two hours less per week.
2. The duplication of content from the elementary schools was discarded. A review of ideas previously taught was dropped; instead, these ideas were expanded upon or new concepts were introduced.
3. Several topics from junior high school were transferred to the high school years.
4. A general reduction in the amount of new math materials was made. For example, logic was no longer included.
5. Stress was placed on basic knowledge and development of the ability to think mathematically.

These changes in the 1970s curriculum are the basis of the current mathematics curriculum (see Table 7.2).

All elementary students study this set of contents regardless of the differences in their aptitudes. Mastery of the content is expected prior to entering junior high school (see Table 7.3).

The contents stated above are required for all students regardless of individual differences in aptitude or future career plans. Although the range of topics is the same for all students, the depth of treatment may be varied.

Figure 7.4 suggests the array of courses available to senior high school students. Mathematics I is required of all senior high school students, but after this course students may *elect* to study one of the following four courses: mathematics II, algebra and geometry, basic analysis, or probability and statistics. Students electing to study calculus must first study basic analysis. The following topics are covered in each of these courses:

Mathematics I

Numbers and algebraic expressions: numbers and sets; integral, rational, and real numbers; polynomial and rational expressions; quadratic equations and inequalities; and algebraic expressions and proof.

Table 7.2
Primary School Mathematics Curriculum, April 1980

Grade Level	Numbers & Calculations	Quantities & Measurement	Geometric Figures	Quantitative Relations
1	{0,1,...100} Addition Subtraction	Comparison of lengths, area, volumes Telling Time	Identification of shapes Position of objects: top and bottom, etc.	
2	{0,1,...1000} 2- & 3-digit addition 1-digit multiplication Equality and inequality Mental calculations	Units of length (mm, cm, m) and volume (dl, e) Time: day, hour, minute	Squares, rectangles - angled triangles Right angle	
3	{0,1,...10,000} & {0.1,0.2,...0.9} Addition & subtraction 2-digit multiplication 1-digit dimension Decimal fractions Soroban addition & subtraction	Units of length (km) & of weights (g, kg) Time	Drawing figures with ruler & compass Isosceles, equilateral triangles Circles, sphere Angles	Formulas using symbols Bar graphs
4	{0,1,...100,000,000} 2-digit division Addition, subtraction of decimals Simple multiplication & division of decimals Addition & subtraction of fractions	Units of area (cm^2, m^2, km^2) & of angles (°)	Parallelogram, trapezoids, rhombuses, cube, rectangular parallelopipeds	Algebraic expression of formulas Broken-line graphs

Table 7.2 (continued)

Grade Level	Numbers & Calculations	Quantities & Measurement	Geometric Figures	Quantitative Relations
5	Even & odd #s Multiples & divisors Multiplication & division of decimals Fractions Addition & subtraction of fractions Estimation using round #s	Units of volume (cm^3, m^3) Measurement of areas of polygons & circles & of volumes of cubes & rectangular parallelpiped Meaning of speed & mean (averages)	Congruence of plane figures Meaning of pi Regular polygons	Percentage Circle graphs Representing relationships using a, x in place of
6	Multiplication & division of fractions Integers, decimals & fractions	Proportion Metric system Units of area (a, ha) of volumes (ml, kl) & of weights (mg, t)	Line & point Similar figures Prisms, circular cylinders, pyramids, circular cones	Ratio Direct & inverse proportions Frequency tables and graphs

Based on <u>Course of Study for Elementary School in Japan</u>. (Tokyo: Ministry of Education, Science and Culture, 1983) 36-55.

Functions: quadratic functions, and rational and irrational functions.

Geometric figures: trigonometric ratios, and plane figures and their equations (line and circles).

Mathematics II

The content of this course consists of basic elements elaborated upon in algebra and geometry, basic analysis, and probability and statistics. Specifically, the contents are probability and statistics; vectors and their applications; differentiation and integration; geometric and arithmetic series; exponential, logarithmic, and trigonometric functions; and electronic computers and flowcharts.

Algebra and geometry

Second degree conics, vectors, and matrix and space figures (coordinates and vectors in space).

Basic analysis

Series (arithmetic, geometric, et cetera); mathematical induction; exponential, logarithmic, and trigonometric functions; derivatives and integrations and their applications.

Table 7.3
Lower Junior High School Mathematics Curriculum, April 1981

Grade	Numbers & Algebraic Expressions	Functions	Geometric Figures	Probability & Statistics
7	Prime factorization GCM and LCM Integers: +,-,x Monomials (x,-), & polynomials (+,-) Linear equations	Variables & domains Coordinates Tables & graphs Direct & inverse proportions	Incidence relations relations between straight lines & planes in space Construction of angle bisector, bisector of segment, etc. Measurement of arc length, area of sector, volume and surface area of cylinder, cones, spheres	
8	Solving linear inequalities Solving simultaneous linear equalities & (2 unknowns)	Functional relations Linear functions	Properties of parallel lines Conditions for congruence and similarity of triangles	Frequency distributions Histograms Relative & cumulative frequencies Mean value, range, variance
9	Square root Quadratic equations Irrational numbers Formulas like: $(a\pm b)^2 = a^2 \pm 2ab + b^2$ $(a+b)(a-b) = a^2 - b^2$	Sets & functions Domains & ranges	Circles & lines Pythagorean theorem Similarity Tangential lines Point of tangency	Probability Population and samples Mean value

Based on <u>Course of Study for Lower Secondary Schools in Japan</u>, 1983.

Figure 7.4
Required and Elective Mathematics Courses in Senior High School

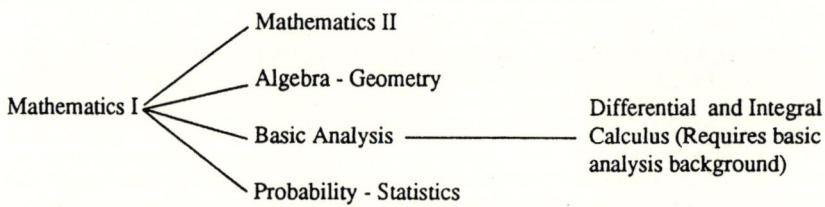

Differential and integral calculus

Limits, differential calculus, and applications, integral calculus and applications including equations as

$$\frac{dy}{dx} = ky.$$

Probability and statistics

Description of data distribution of variants; representative values and measures of dispersion; number of cases of possibilities (permutation and combinations, binomial theorem); probability (basic laws, independent trials, conditional probability); probability distributions (binomial and normal); and statistical inference.

What is presented above is an abbreviated version of the official mathematics curriculum for the schools in Japan as announced in the official 1983 Course of Study. Next to be described is the process by which the official curriculum is put into practice.

To implement the mathematics curriculum the required number of school hours to be used during the year is provided in the Enforcement Regulations of the School Law and in the Course of Study. For the program now in effect the required school hours in mathematics for grades one through nine and the mathematics courses are shown in Table 7.4.

The time spent on mathematical instruction is most intense in grades two through six; the intensity level in grade seven, and for senior high school electives, is much lower.

Although the course of study itemizes and outlines the aims and content of each subject, it is the individual schools which organize, extend, and enrich the content. For example, at Kitamachi Junior High School, in Tokyo, the mathematics teachers meet at the start of the school year to organize the mathematics curriculum. Kitamachi's mathematics curriculum, along with the other subject areas, is compiled in a book which is used not only by the teachers but also by various committees, including the board of education. This very detailed plan includes the months of instruction, the chapters of the text, the section of the text and the amount of days to be spent in instructing each section, and the descriptive content relative to each section. Table 7.5 illustrates the curriculum plan developed by the Kitamachi teachers for the seventh grade portion of the mathematics curriculum.

The mathematics curriculum plan is built around the organization of the mathematics textbook. Because of the central role played by textbooks in Japanese curriculum planning, it is necessary to provide a brief description of the nature of Japanese mathematics textbooks.

In Japan mathematics textbooks are soft covered, measure approximately six inches by eight inches, and average about 175 pages. They contain only the

Table 7.4
Required Number of School Hours in Grade and Mathematics Courses

Grade	Number of School Hours*
1	136
2	175
3	175
4	175
5	175
6	175
7	105
8	140
9	140

Course	
Mathematics I (required)	140
Mathematics II (elective)	105
Algebra and Geometry (elective)	105
Basic Analysis (elective)	105
Differential and Integral Calculus (elective)	105
Probability and Statistics (elective)	105

* One school hour is equal to 45 minutes in grades 1-6 and 50 minutes in grades 7-9 and in senior high school courses.

essential mathematical ideas and skills that the students are expected to learn. Drill and practice exercises are kept to a minimum. Because no attempt is made by teachers to provide for differentiated instruction, the variety of problems according to ability levels is limited.

In Japan textbooks are provided free of charge to students in public and private

Table 7.5
Organization of the Grade 7 Mathematics Curriculum by the Kitamachi Mathematics Teachers

MATH: THE FIRST GRADE IN KITAMACHI JUNIOR HIGH SCHOOL

MO	Chap	Sec	Hrs	Item	Description
April 9 hrs	1. Integers 10 hrs	1. Nature of Integers	3	1. Integers	- natural numbers, meaning of integers, relationships in division - meaning of divisors and multiples
				2. Prime numbers and prime factors	- meaning of primes, factors, and prime factors - meaning of factoring into prime factors and its usage - finding the divisors of prime factors thru factorization - 2-exponent, 3-exponent, and the involution and index
		2. Common divisors & Common multiples	5	1. Common divisors LCM	- meaning of common divisors and LCM - the method of seeking LCM and its application
				2. Common multiples GCM	- meaning of common multiples and GCM - the method of seeking GCM and its application
				Section Problems	
			1	Chapter Problems	
May 12 hrs	2. Positive & Negative Numbers 21 hrs		1	Research	- the method of finding multiples
		1. Positive & Negative Numbers	4	1. Numbers with signs	- introduction of negative numbers as seen on such things as thermometer gauges - using positive and negative numbers to show changes and measurements in things that have opposite features
				2. Greater and lesser numbers	- using inequalities to show the size relationships of positive and negative numbers - meaning of absolute values - the relationships between size of numbers and absolute value
				Section Problems	
		2. Addition & Subtraction	7	1. Addition	- meaning of adding positive and negative numbers - the method of adding like and unlike numbers - commutative addition. Law of associativity for addition - adding more than three terms
				2. Subtraction	- meaning of subtracting positive and negative numbers - changing subtraction to addition and computing
				3. Computation of both addition and subtraction	- computing both subtraction and addition - when $\pm$ sign used on numbers and when as a computing indicator

Table 7.5 (continued)

MO	Chap	Sec	Hrs	Item	Description
May				Section Problems	
June 12 hrs	Positive & Negative Numbers (continued)	Multiplication & Division	8	1. Multiplication	- meaning of multiplication of positive and negative numbers - methods of multiplication with same & different signs - commutative law of multiplication, Law of Associativity for multiplication - multiplying more than three terms
				2. Division	- meaning of division of positive & negative numbers - meaning of reciprocal numbers; changing division to multiplication using opposite (reciprocal) numbers - computation of both multiplication & division
				3. Computation using the four rules	- using the four rules with positive & negative numbers - law of distribution
				Section Problems	
			2	Chapter Problems	
July 8 hrs	3. Letters and Expressions 12 hrs	1. Using Literal Expressions	6	1. Numbers & letters	- using letters instead of numbers - using letters in an equation
				2. Rules of letter usage	- showing products in an equation using letter expressions - showing quotient in an equation using letter expressions
				3. Expression of quantities	- showing the relationships of quantities using literal expressions - the way of showing the sum of differing units
				Section Problems	
		2. Literal Expressions & computation	5	1. Substitution & value of expressions	- meaning of substitution & value of expressions - seeking the value of an expression thru substituting number values of an expression using letters
				2. Addition & subtraction of first degree linear expressions	- meaning of terms & coefficient - meaning of the first degree expression - multiplying numbers & first degree linear expressions - meaning of similar terms - addition & subtraction of first degree linear expressions
				Section Problems	
September 9 hrs			1	Chapter Problems	
	Equations	1. Equation	2	1. Equations	- meaning of equation - meaning of solving equations

Table 7.5 (continued)

MO	Chap	Sec	Hrs	Item	Description
September (continued)	4. Equations 13 hrs	2. Method of Solving Equations	9	1. Nature of equality	- meaning of equality - meaning of solving equations
				2. Nature of equality & method of solving equations	- meaning of solving equations - solving easy/simple equations using the nature of equality
				3. Method of solving first degree linear equations	- meaning of transposition (of terms) & its application to solving equations - clearing of fractions/taking away of denominators of & equation - summary of solving first degree linear equations
				4. Application of first degree linear equation	- application of first degree linear equations - summing up of common solution for applied problems - examples of various problems & their solutions
				Section Problems	
			2	Chapter Problems	
October 12 hrs	5. Functions & Proportions 13 hrs	1. Change & Functions	3	1. Variables	- letters are used as variables explaining changing size of quantities - using inequality sign showing the (changing) area
				2. Functions	- recognizing two values changing proportionately that come out of phenomina (events) - meaning of functions - expressing functions through various ways: equations, graphs, arrows, & words - when y is a function of x, seeking the value of y thru the value of x or seeking the (change) area of y thru the area of x
				Section Problems	
		1. Proportion & Inverse Proportion	4	1. Proportions	- finding two corresponding values & showing it by an equation - meaning of proportion & proportional constant/invariables - solving actual problems using proportional equations where the proportion given number (constant) is negative
				2. Inverse Proportion	- recognizing two inverse proportional values from events & showing it in an equation - meaning of inverse proportions & proportional constants - solving actual problems using inverse proportions equations
				Section Problems	
November 12 hrs		3. Coordinates & Graphs	5	1. Coordinates	- meaning of coordinates on a plane figure - seeking the symmetric coordinator & transposed points - characteristics of coordinates based on quadrant location

Table 7.5 (continued)

MO	Chap	Sec	Hrs	Item	Description
November 12 hrs (continued)	Functions & Proportions (continued)	Coordinates & Graphs (continued)		2. Graph of functions	- characteristics of graphs of y=ax - seeking such things as increased or changed area using the graph of y=ax - from the slope, determine such things as numberical values & equations - characteristics of graphs of $y = \frac{a}{x}$
			1	Section Problems	
December 8 hrs		1. Circle & Straight Lines	5	1. Angles & straight lines	- way of symbolizing lines, line segments, & half straight lines - angles & how to show them
				2. Circles & sectors	- how to symbolize circles, arcs & chords - the relationships among the length of the arc, the area & the central angle of a semi-circle - pi & approximations - circumference & the length of an arc - areas of circle & sectors
				Section Problems	
	6.	Construction & Set of Points	5	1. Basic construction	- meaning of construction - the way of drawing an angle bisector - the way of drawing a perpendicular line that passes a point on a straight line - construction of a perpendicular bisector line of a line segment
				2. Set of points & diagram	- construction of a perpendicular line from a point outside of the straight line - distance from a point & a straight line
				Section Problems	
			1	Chapter Problems	
January 9 hrs	7. Space Figure	1. Space Figure	9	1. Relation of position of straight line & plane	- parallel lines & planes - positional relationships of two lines in space - conditions that determine planes - perpendicularity of straight lines & planes; that of planes & planes - perpendicular lines & two planes that are parallel
				2. Polyhedron	- meaning of polyhedron - right polyhedron
				3. Various views	- function of solid that results from shifting plane - shape of cut edge of solid by a plane - showing a solid figure on a plane surface
				Section Problems	
		Surface Area & Volume of a Solid	4	1. Prism & cylinder	- volume of cylinder & prism - base area, side surface area & surface area of cylinder & prism

Table 7.5 (continued)

MO	Chap	Sec	Hrs	Item	Description
February 11 hrs	Space Figure (continued)	Surface Area & Volume of Solid	4	2. Pyramid, circular cone & sphere	- volume of pyramid & cone - side surface area of a cone - volume & surface area of sphere
				Section Problems	
			1	Chapter Problems	
March 3 hrs	Conclusion	(Summary)	11	Practice Problems	- computation practice - review for the year by review problems 1-7

Source: Kitamachi Junior High School, Kyo ka nen kan shi do kei kaku [Instructional Planning Guide (for the year 1983)].

schools in grades one through nine. The Ministry of Education authorizes the textbooks that may be selected. Six are authorized for elementary school mathematics, six for junior high school mathematics, and ten for senior high school mathematics. A ward (school district) determines which texts will be used by the entire ward based on the votes of the schools.

To meet curricular objectives, schools can require that students purchase supplementary materials and drill workbooks to supplement the textbook. However, most teachers find it necessary to develop *printo* (supplementary materials) to assist their students. These include glossaries, summaries of key concepts and generalizations, and problems for application. Teachers also write their own quizzes and examinations.

To further aid in the implementation of the curriculum various activities are conducted to aid the teacher. Among them are (1) national workshops sponsored by the Ministry of Education, (2) regional workshops conducted by various board of education or educational research centers, (3) school level meetings to communicate the results of research, (4) educational television programs, (5) guide materials prepared by the Ministry of Education, and (6) national and regional professional meetings on mathematics education.

What have been the results of these extensive efforts to implement the curriculum? The data from the Second International Study of Mathematics provides us with some evidence on the extent to which the curriculum has been successful in its goals. The mean index of appropriateness of the test items for the Japanese population was 0.93 for seventh graders and 0.90 for twelfth graders studying mathematics, that is, the test items reflected 93 percent and 90 percent of the mathematics curriculum of these students. To obtain a measure of the extent to which the curriculum (as reflected by the test items) is implemented, questionnaires were completed by classroom teachers. Teachers were asked, for example, whether they had provided instruction for each of the items on the achievement tests. For the seventh graders, the mean index of implementation was 0.77; for

Table 7.6
The Difference between Content Coverage and Student Achievement in Japan's Seventh Grade Mathematics Program

Topic Subtest	Number of Items	Implemented Curriculum Coverage (Mean % of Content)	Student Achievement (Mean % of Correct Responses)	Difference Between % of Content Coverage and of Correct Responses
Arithmetic	46	85	60	25
Algebra	30	83	60	23
Geometry	39	52	58	-06
Statistics	18	76	71	05
Measurement	24	95	69	26
Computation	53	79	66	13
Comprehension	51	70	57	13
Application	45	81	64	17
Analysis	08	71	60	11
Non-verbal	15	92	70	22
Verbal	16	97	66	21
TOTAL		77	62	15

* Based on "Comparisons of Achievement in Problem Solving on SIMS (Second International Mathematics Study) Between the United States and Japan," by Sawada Toshio. In <u>Proceeding of the U.S. - Japan Seminar on Mathematical Problem Solving</u>, edited by Becker, Jerry P. and Miwa Tatsuro (Carbondale: Southern Illinois University, 1987) 126, 128.

twelfth graders, it was 0.91. This means that approximately 72 percent (0.77 x 0.93) of the mathematics curriculum was taught at the seventh grade level, and 82 percent (0.91 x 0.90) at the twelfth grade level. The lower rate of implementation at the junior high level may be attributed to its broader range of students as compared to the ''mathematics specialist'' nature of the senior high school students as well as the relatively low (52 percent) implementation of the geometry curriculum. In comparison with the other nineteen countries in the International Association for the Evaluation of Educational Achievement (IEA) study, however, the degree of implementation of Japan's mathematics curriculum was the highest at both levels of instruction.

In terms of implementation we can now evaluate student achievement. At the seventh grade level (except in geometry), in no category did the student achievement equal or exceed the teacher's perception of the student's opportunity to learn that content category (see Table 7.6). The greatest disparity between the implemented curriculum and student achievement were in arithmetic, algebra, measurement, and nonverbal and verbal problems. The smallest disparity oc-

Table 7.7
The Difference between Content Coverage and Student Achievement in Japan's Senior High School Mathematics Program

Topic	Number of Items	Implemented Curriculum (Mean % of Content Coverage)	Student Achievement (Mean % of Correct Responses)	Difference Between Mean % of Content Coverage and of Correct Responses
Sets/Relations	07	93	80	13
Number Systems	16	78	72	06
Algebra	29	96	76	20
Geometry	29	85	58	27
Elementary Functions & Calculus	44	94	69	25
Probability & Statistics	07	85	72	13
Finite Mathematics	04	97	76	21
Other Items				

* Data from Eizo Nagasaki's "Sugaku No Rishujoleyo Nitsuiteno Saibunseki -- Dainikai IEA Kokusaisugaku Kyoikuchosa Kettsuka Yori -- Kenkyuhokoku No.9," (Reanalysis of Opportunity to Learn in Mathematics - Second IEA Mathematics Study, Research Report No.9), (National Institute for Educational Research, 1984)

curred in geometry and statistics. In the case of geometry, the teachers underestimated the student opportunity to learn geometry.

In comparison with other countries in the international study, Japan's scores were the highest average of any country at the junior high level. Furthermore, while other countries' samples consisted of eighth grade students, that in Japan consisted of seventh grade students.

At the senior high level, the difference between the content coverage and student achievement can be seen in Table 7.7.

In the Second International Study, Japan received the second highest average scores of any country on the senior high school mathematics tests.

In comparing Japan's mathematics achievement of 1980-1981 to that of 1964, a decline in arithmetic and verbal scores (Table 7.8) for seventh graders is found. These results may reflect the decreasing emphasis given to teaching arithmetic at that level.

Table 7.8
Changes in Achievement on the First International Mathematics Study (FIMS) and the Second International Mathematics Study (SIMS)

Topic Subtest	Number of Items	Average % of Correct Responses	
		FIMS	SIMS
Arithmetic	14	65	60
Algebra	09	55	61
Geometry	05	67	68
Statistics	05	73	74
Measurement	02	73	74
Non-Verbal	21	62	63
Verbal	14	70	66
TOTAL	35	65	64

* Based on "Comparisons of Achievement in Problem Solving on SIMS (Second International Mathematics Study) Between the United States and Japan," by Sawada Toshio. In <u>Proceeding of the U.S. - Japan Seminar on Mathematical Problem Solving</u>, edited by Becker, Jerry P. & Miwa Tatsuro (Carbondale: Southern Illinois University, 1987) 131.

Although the mathematics achievement of Japanese students is high relative to that of other countries, an analysis of the data relative to implementation efforts by educators and student achievement in 1960 leads to the conclusion that it may not be as impressive as it appears. Curriculum changes scheduled for 1990 (kindergarten), 1992 (junior high), and 1994 (senior high) should provide an indication of how Japan's achievement in mathematics is viewed in that country.

Summary of Highlights of Curriculum Changes

1872	Western mathematics was introduced and spread throughout Japan.
1905	First official elementary school textbook was issued; a reflection of Japan's adaptation of Western mathematics.
1925	Adoption of the metric system. By deleting the old *shakukan* system in grade 4, major topics from grades 5, 6, and 7 were advanced one year.

1931	Revisions were made in response to the influence of John Perry and Eliakim Hastings Moore. The method of teaching focused on experimental-exploratory activities.
1945–1952	Revisions under the American Occupation resulted in an emphasis on mathematics for daily living and a general reduction in the content taught.
1960	Revisions after the American Occupation resulted in the upgrading of the mathematics curriculum. Steps were taken to change from a daily-living approach to a systematic content approach.
1970	Aspects of new mathematics were incorporated into the mathematics program.
1980	Revisions reflect a retreat from the incorporation of new mathematics into the program. Requirements became less stringent.

MATHEMATICS INSTRUCTION

Inside the Classroom

Contrary to the Western image of Asian classes in which students spend much of their time responding in unison to the teacher's directions, a visitor to an elementary mathematics classroom in Japan will be struck by the amount of mathematical activity that is occurring. The teacher may be leading a discussion on a mathematical concept, and the students follow the teacher by watching, listening, and taking notes. The teacher addresses questions to the class as a whole rather than to individual students and imparts information by seeking answers, responses, and explanations from the students.[11] Students share their problem solutions and thinking by talking about them.

Students are eager to participate in classroom activities, and there is no shortage of students to engage in the various activities suggested by the teacher. The students are not intimidated into a response, regardless of whether their ideas or procedures are correct. The classroom provides a nonthreatening arena for students.

When not engaged in the activities prescribed by the teacher, students can be observed "socializing" with their peers. This occurs in about 10 percent of the class time.[12] At the same time the teacher will be working with the students as a class, as a subgroup, or as individuals more than 90 percent of the time.

The teaching method of most Japanese elementary mathematics teachers is embedded in mathematics textbooks. The textbooks allow students to learn by creating and discovering; for example, the students learn about various geometric shapes and their properties by activities that allow them to see how they fit into the environment and how they relate to each other.[13] The teaching methods that Japanese teachers use also reflect the emphasis that Japanese mathematics educators place on helping students to develop "flexibility in mathematical thinking." This flexibility is attained through the mastery of a multitude of mental representations of mathematical ideas. Such representations, Japanese teachers believe, are best developed by providing numerous opportunities for students to interact with concrete representations of the mathematics they are studying, and by helping students to discover manipulative strategies that are useful in different contexts throughout the mathematics curriculum.[14]

Junior high school mathematics teachers also instruct the class as a whole. They devote a great deal of time to explaining and demonstrating new concepts, generalizations, and skills, and they guide students in learning and practicing the ideas presented. Frequently this is done by walking around the room and observing whether students are progressing satisfactorily on work given by the teacher after the explanation or demonstration. This is also done by having groups of students work at the blackboard as well as at their seats or by having individual students come before the class to explain or demonstrate a proof, skill, or idea.

According to the IEA Survey of 1980, the average number of hours of homework assigned to Japanese seventh graders was 1.7 hours per week. This lack of emphasis on homework is also reflected by the fact that little or no class time is devoted to correcting or doing homework in class. In one school observed, the teacher placed the homework assignment on the bulletin board with its due date. The homework was assigned a week in advance, at which time it was collected and corrected by the teacher. At another school the homework was corrected, outside of class, by the students themselves since the answers were provided in the workbook. As a check on the student's progress with the homework a weekly quiz was given. Most teachers believe that there is no time in class to correct homework. This attitude toward doing homework in class reflects a commonly held belief among Japanese mathematics teachers that they should use the class time exclusively to present the subject matter. In a recent questionnaire,[15] 94 percent of the Japanese teachers surveyed rated this use of class time as of most or greatest importance. Also, there is a widespread belief that Japanese students learn more effectively by hearing the teacher's explanation rather than by reading the textbook.[16]

As a reflection of the typical belief of Japanese mathematics teachers, they spend more than half of their class time developing a lesson. On many days, more than three-fourths of the class time was used in this way. Essentially, this process consists of (1) briefly reviewing or identifying prerequisite knowledge, (2) focusing on the meaning and comprehension of concepts and generalizations by actively demonstrating and exploring with students, (3) assessing the student's comprehension by asking questions and closely supervising student's work, and (4) providing short practice opportunities in a meaningful context.[17]

In the mathematics class, students are encouraged and willingly display their mathematical knowledge. During one class observation, a student explained a solution that the teacher had not considered, and she applauded his response and suggested his classmates likewise applaud. On another occasion, as many as six students came before the class to demonstrate the supposed validity of their arguments. As they proceeded the first five realized, as did their classmates, the fallacy of their arguments. The class spontaneously cheered the student who finally presented a valid argument. In a classroom atmosphere where logical reasoning is stressed, students are willing to challenge the teacher's word although whenever a student does so his classmates tease him or her.

The number of students in the junior high school mathematics classroom not "on task" is generally about 10 percent. Some of the things students do when not on task include: looking out the windows, drawing pictures, reading comic books, hiding in the closet, and visiting with their peers. In general, this inappropriate behavior is ignored by the teacher and the other students unless it becomes truly disruptive.

Although the students in grades one to nine mathematics classes are not streamed (i.e., homogeneously grouped by one's ability and achievement), the teacher teaches the same content to all students. Seldom do the teachers make provisions for the individual differences in the ability or interest of the student.[18]

At the senior high level, the predominant approach is for the mathematics teacher to lecture to the class in which students are expected to be attentive and take notes. At times they are called on to respond orally or to go to the blackboard to provide an explanation. The latter is most likely when a drawing or graph is needed for the explanation. When given problems to work on at their desks, students frequently discuss them with neighboring students. However, students infrequently leave their seats except when called on to respond to a question or suggestion, and they appear to take their mathematics study seriously. They realize the importance of mathematical knowledge in successfully passing university entrance examinations. Indeed, in a fundamental sense, students taking advanced mathematics are self-selected. That is, taking mathematics courses at the senior high level is optional except for mathematics I which is required of all high school students. It is in the mathematics I classroom where a visitor is likely to see less than concerted effort on the part of students. The other classes have a relatively select group of students (about 12 percent of a given grade level), and visitors will notice that these classes are handled very much like university-level mathematics classes in the United States. In fact, the level of mathematics being taught is that found at the university level in the United States.

As noted earlier, absent from the high school mathematics classroom is an emphasis on homework—its correction, explanation, and work in class. Students, however, are given about three hours of homework per week to complete.[19]

Outside the Classroom

Instruction in mathematics occurs not only in school, but also in the home and at *juku*. Parental attitudes toward mathematics have a strong positive influence on student attitudes.[20] This is a major reason for the success of Japanese students in learning mathematics. (This is suggested by Sawada Toshio, director of the Science Education Research Center, National Institute for Education Re-

Table 7.9
Source of Mathematics Homework Help, 1984, N = 1811

	Grade			
Source*	5	6	7	8
Father	27%	19%	13%	08%
Mother	53	28	13	07
Older brother or sister	21	18	15	16
Juku teacher	29	36	40	47
Home tutor	03	05	04	06

* More than one source could be selected.

> Based on data in "An Analysis of the Effect of Arithmetic and Mathematics at Juku," Sawada Toshio and Kobayashi Sachino (National Institute for Educational Research, Tokyo, 1986)

search, Tokyo, Japan, in a private communication, on November 30, 1987.) Students not only discuss school with their parents[21] but also seek their help in doing homework. When asked who helps you with your mathematics homework, 60 percent of the fifth graders sampled responded that their parents helped. In addition to seeking help from their parents, students also seek the assistance of their older siblings and their *juku* teacher. As the grade level increased, the amount of help sought at home decreased and that sought from the *juku* teacher increased (Table 7.9).

In a survey conducted by the National Institute for Educational Research, it was found that the percentage of students attending supplementary mathematics lessons at *juku* increased by grade level.

Grade Five	Grade Six	Grade Seven	Grade Eight
31%	41%	44%	52%

The frequency with which these students attended *juku* and the number of hours spent at *juku* are shown in Tables 7.10 and 7.11. Irrespective of grade level, students most frequently attended *juku* twice a week for a period of two hours.

Higher achieving students appear to attend *juku* more often than do middle

Table 7.10
Frequency of *Juku* Attendance, 1984, N = 1811

Number of Hours	Percents of Students			
	Grade 5	Grade 6	Grade 7	Grade 8
1	21	19	30	38
2	61	56	49	44
3	14	14	14	15
4	04	06	06	01
Greater than 5	00	05	01	02

* Based on data in "An Analysis of the Effect of Arithmetic and Mathematics Education at Juku," Sawada Toshio and Kobayashi Sachino (National Institute for Educational Research, Tokyo, 1986)

or low achieving students. In particular, for grades seven and eight, more than half of the top achieving students attend *juku* (Table 7.12).

What type of supplementary instruction do students who attend mathematics classes in *juku* receive? According to the above mentioned study *juku* focus their teaching on numbers and formulas; they do not teach problems about thinking and geometry. Although *juku* may be expected to perform the role of review of regular schoolwork for the students of low achievement, this did not appear to always be the case.

In addition to studying mathematics in school, students are expected to learn a certain amount of mathematics outside of class. To this end they are assigned homework which may include problems to solve in the text, workbook problems, and *printo*. Although the amount of homework assigned varies among teachers, one recent survey found that the average number of hours of mathematics homework for grades five, six, seven, and eight were 2.0, 3.4, 1.6, and 2.0, respectively.[22] In the 1980 IEA Survey, the average number of hours assigned to seventh graders throughout Japan was 1.7 hours and for senior high students 3.0 hours. Another recent study suggests that the mean hours of homework per week expected of junior high students in Tokyo is 1.7.[23] In these three surveys, the number of hours of homework expected of junior high students was quite similar.

Table 7.11
Number of Hours at *Juku*, 1984, N = 1811

Number of Hours	Percents of Students			
	Grade 5	Grade 6	Grade 7	Grade 8
1	39	32	13	13
2	40	41	47	62
3	09	07	20	14
4	09	10	09	07
5	01	03	05	01
6	01	03	04	03
Greater than 7	01	04	02	00

* Based on data in "An Analysis of the Effect of Arithmetic and Mathematics Education at Juku," Sawada Toshio and Kobayashi Sachino (National Institute for Educational Research, Tokyo, 1986)

SUMMARY

Since 1905 when the first official elementary school textbook was issued, major mathematics curriculum changes have occurred about every ten years. Many of these changes were in recognition of the ideas expounded by leading Western educators. The use of the metric system and the method of teaching focused on experimental-exploratory activities are examples of adopted Western ideas that are still being practiced today. There is a much lessened emphasis on "mathematics for daily living" and "new" mathematics.

Although the Japanese mathematics curriculum and methods of instruction are basically those that Western educators have promoted, there have developed in Japan some differences in instruction due to cultural circumstances. For example, instruction is primarily led by the teacher due in part to the large number of students who are not grouped by ability. Furthermore, the importance of homework is deemphasized. No doubt the influence and help of siblings, parents, and *juku* teachers are contributing factors. The mathematics curriculum is extremely concise. Repetition or review of concepts is rare. It is here where Americans

Table 7.12
Mathematics Achievement and *Juku* Attendance, 1984, N = 1811

	Percent of Students Attending Juku		
Grade Level	Top Achievement	Middle Achievement	Low Achievement
5	41	31	19
6	46	39	34
7	52	38	34
8	55	46	47

* Based on data in "An Analysis of the Effect of Arithmetic and Mathematics Education at Juku," Sawada Toshio and Kobayashi Sachino. National Institute for Educational Research, Tokyo, 1986.

can best learn from the Japanese experience since, in the United States, the repetition of concepts is commonplace.[24]

CHANGES IN THE FUTURE

Shortly after the completion of this manuscript Japan announced the new curriculum guides for the primary, junior high, and high schools.[25] The primary guide will be implemented in 1990, the junior high school guide in 1992, and the high school guide in 1994. In effect this allows the primary grades one year to prepare for changes in the curriculum, the junior high schools three years, and the high schools five years. It also provides time for textbook publishers to prepare materials based on the new guides.

In mathematics education, major changes have been made in the junior high and senior high schools. In the junior high school the streaming of mathematics classes in grade nine will be allowed as a way of structuring the classes for instruction. The effects of this change should be carefully studied since Japan has been unique in not streaming mathematics classes.

The new high school mathematics program will in effect provide for greater flexibility in structuring the mathematics curriculum. Thus, while all schools are expected to teach the contents of the courses math 1, 2, and 3 they may choose and teach topics from math A, B, and C. For example, schools may offer the following curriculum:

Math 1 and math A
Math 2 and math B

Math 3 and math C

or

Math 1

Math 2 and math B

Math 3 and math A & C

This change recognizes the variability in students' ability and hence is providing greater flexibility to the schools in developing their curricula. It also recognizes the needs of an information-based society and is promoting the study and effective use of computers. This mathematics program also provides for more selected topics to promote "thinking skills." Applications and everyday life knowledge are stressed. The contents of the courses are as follows:

Mathematics 1: quadratic functions, geometry and measurement, counting methods of cases and probability.

Mathematics 2: functions and equations of figures, and changes in value of a function.

Mathematics 3: Functions and limits, and limits.

Mathematics A: Numbers and polynomials, two-dimensional geometry, sequence and series, and computer.

Mathematics B: Vectors, complex numbers, probability distribution, and computing algorithms.

Mathematics C: Matrix and linear equations, curves, numerical computing, and statistics.

Mathematics 1 is required of all students. If mathematics A is studied, it must be studied in the same grade as mathematics 1. If mathematics 2 and mathematics 3 are adopted for the school curriculum, the sequence must be mathematics 1, 2, and 3. More than one course may be studied in the same grade; however, the contents and materials must be organized.

NOTES

1. David Eugene Smith and Mikami Yoshio, *A History of Japanese Mathematics* (Chicago: Open Court, 1914); Mikami Yoshio, *The Development of Mathematics in China and Japan* (New York: G.E. Stechert, 1913).

2. Fujisawa Rikitaro, *Summary Report of the Teaching of Mathematics in Japan* (Tokyo: Japanese Subcommittee of the International Commission on the Teaching of Mathematics, 1912), p. 23.

3. *Juku*, privately established schools which teach academic and nonacademic subjects. Academic *juku* offer tutorial, enrichment, remedial, and examination-preparatory classes which supplement regular schoolwork. Most classes are held after school and on weekends.

4. Okabe Susumu, "The Prototype of Mathematics Education in Japan—The Introduction and Spread of European Mathematics in 1870–1900," *Proceedings of the Fourth Japan-China Conference on Mathematics Education*, ed. Machida Shoichiro (Yamanashi,

Japan: Organizing Committee of the Fourth Japan-China Conference on Mathematics Education, 1986), p. 120.

5. Fujisawa, *Summary Report*, pp. 66–74.

6. Ibid., pp. 3, 91.

7. Ibid., pp. 96–100.

8. Japanese National Commission on the Teaching of Mathematics, *Divisional Reports on Present Tendencies in the Development of Mathematical Teaching in Japan* (Tokyo: Tokyo University of Literature and Science, 1936), p. 38.

9. Kawaguchi Tadsu, "Secondary School Mathematics in Japan," *Studies in Mathematics Education*, ed. Morris Robert (Paris: UNESCO, 1980), 1:48.

10. Ibid., 1:49.

11. James W. Stigler, Lee Shin-Ying, and Harold W. Stevenson, "Mathematics Classrooms in Japan, Taiwan, and the United States," *Child Development* 58 (October 1987), pp. 1272–85.

12. Ibid., p. 1274

13. Diane Komenaka and Nancy Whitman, "A Comparison of the Textbook Curriculum of Geometry in the Elementary Schools of Japan and Hawaii," *Pacific Educational Research Journal* 5 (January 1989), p. 23.

14. Diane Lambdin Kroll and Yabe Toshiake, "A Japanese Educator's Perspective on Teaching Mathematics in the Elementary School," *Arithmetic Teacher* 35 (October 1987), pp. 36–43.

15. Nancy Whitman, Lai Morris, Sawada Toshio, Nagasaki Eizo, Hanako Senuma, Hashimoto Yoshihiko, and Makino Masahiro, *Mathematics Instruction in Tokyo's and Hawaii's Junior High Schools* (Honolulu: University of Hawaii, College of Education, 1986), p. 17.

16. Sugiyama Yoshishige, "A Comparison of Word Problems in American and Japanese Textbooks," *Proceedings of the U.S.–Japan Seminar on Mathematical Problem Solving* (Carbondale: Southern Illinois University, 1987), p. 228.

17. Nancy C. Whitman, "The Japanese Lower Secondary School." Typescript. Honolulu: University of Hawaii. Department of Curriculum and Instruction.

18. Whitman et al., *Mathematics Instruction*, pp. 19–21.

19. *Chugaku kokosei no sugaku seiseki to shojoken, dai-ni-kai kokusai sugaku kyoiku chosa kokunai hokoku* [Mathematics Achievement and Associated Factors of Secondary School Students]. Second International Mathematics Study, National Report of Japan, Volume 11. (Tokyo: National Institute for Educational Research, 1982), p. 147

20. Imai Toshihiro, "Variables of Parents and Teachers as Related to Students' Attitude toward Mathematics," *Proceedings of ICME-JSME Regional Conference on Mathematical Education* (Tokyo: Society of Mathematical Education, 1984), pp. 417–23.

21. Delwyn L. Harnisch and Sato Takahiro, "Differences in Educational Influences and Achievement in Mathematics for Secondary Students in Japan and the United States," *Proceedings of ICME-JSME Regional Conference on Mathematical Education* (Tokyo: Society of Mathematical Education, 1984), p. 179.

22. Sawada Toshio and Kobayashi Sachino, *An Analysis of the Effect of Arithmetic and Mathematics Education at Juku*, trans. Patricia J. Horvath (Tokyo: National Institute for Educational Research, 1986), p. 179.

23. Whitman et al., *Mathematics Instruction*, p. 16.

24. James R. Flanders, "How Much of the Content in Mathematics Textbooks is New?" *Arithmetic Teacher* 35 (September 1989), pp. 18–23; Komenaka and Whitman,

"A Comparison of the Textbook Curriculum of Geometry in the Elementary Schools of Japan and Hawaii," p. 18.

25. Japanese Government, Ministry of Education, Science and Culture, *Koto gakko gakushu shido yoryo* [Curriculum Guide for High Schools] (Tokyo: Ministry of Education, Science and Culture, March 1989); *Chugakko gakushu shido yoryo* [Curriculum Guide for Junior High Schools] (Tokyo: Ministry of Education, Science and Culture, March 1989; *Shoggaku gakushu shido yoryo* [Curriculum Guide for Elementary Schools] (Tokyo: Ministry of Education, Science and Culture, March 1989).

8

Japan's Science and Engineering Pipeline: Structure, Policies, and Trends

William K. Cummings

The U.S. Science Policy community has, in recent years, developed a new awareness of the scale and capabilities of the Japanese science and engineering work force. Though the Japanese population is less that half the size of the American, Japanese higher education graduates as many engineers annually as the United States and about half as many scientists. In selecting their students, Japan's universities and colleges can draw from an exceptionally well-prepared crop of high school graduates. Comparative studies of mathematics and science achievement indicate that the overall academic quality of Japanese education through high school is superior to American education, and that much larger proportions of the Japanese school and university-age cohorts pursue studies in subjects conducive to an understanding of scientific and technical matters. It may be that these characteristics of the Japanese work force are important parts of the explanation for contemporary Japan's competitiveness in high-technology innovation, production, and marketing.

The apparent edge of the Japanese work force is an emerging trend, based on major structural reforms in the education system that took place after World War II followed by steady implementation and modification of these reforms. This chapter highlights the principal differences between the structures of American and Japanese education that account for Japan's work force edge.

The Japanese system has its weaknesses, many of which are readily acknowledged by Japan's leaders.[1] Education at the school level is too monolithic and competitive, so that young people learn what they must to compete in the exams but lack the leisure to pursue unique interests and to develop their creative powers. Higher education is not as challenging as it might be, at least to the average student. Both graduate and postgraduate education require more support and organization. Many of these problems are being addressed by a current wave of educational reform, which also will be reviewed.

THE ORIGINS OF JAPANESE WORK FORCE POLICIES

The foundations of Japanese work force policies go back over one hundred years to that fertile period when a youthful group of aristocrats led the revolution of 1868 that deposed the old Tokugawa shogunate and established the Meiji state. Although the members of this group were firmly committed to Eastern morality they also recognized Japan's backward state in Western technology. Accordingly, they introduced a wide-ranging set of policies designed to enable Japan to catch up with the West.

Missions were sent abroad to examine Western institutions, and within a few years a new mass educational system was launched which included courses in Western science and mathematics from the first grades of primary school. Western scholars were invited to Japan to help establish secondary schools and universities and to teach the most promising youth, who within a decade were sufficiently knowledgeable to take the places of their mentors. Drawing largely on indigenous talent, in 1886 the Japanese government established the first Imperial University. This institution was modeled on continental universities with the traditional faculties of law, philosophy (*bungakubu*), science, and medicine; but, reflecting the practical disposition of the Japanese leaders, faculties of engineering and agriculture were also included.

Attendance at the Imperial University was accorded tremendous prestige, and it was a sure ticket to an elite career either in government or in the emerging business sector. Hence the desire to enter the Imperial University was widespread. In 1897 a second Imperial University was established in Kyoto, followed by several more in succeeding years.

In the decades that followed, the government proceeded to fill out the system with a diverse array of secondary and tertiary institutions. Government policy was aimed at fulfilling perceived manpower needs while achieving regional balance and maintaining quality. At the secondary level, a number of different tracks were structured: a narrow academic track through middle schools and higher schools to university entrance, a side track off of the above starting with middle school graduation to technical colleges and teacher's education colleges, another track beginning with primary school graduation into vocational or domestic training, and yet other tracks leading to teacher education, military training, and other options. Most of the secondary schools were segregated by sex, and girls were not eligible for admission to universities.

EDUCATION AND THE DUALISTIC EMPLOYMENT SYSTEM

Prior to Japan's modernization drive, agriculture was the dominant economic pursuit in Japan. The small class of samurai (about 5 percent of the labor force) occupied positions in feudal bureaucracies as tax collectors, civil works administrators, legalists, and scribes. Hereditary status and performance in fief schools were the basis for the feudal appointments.

To effect development, it is sometimes said that the Japanese planners approached their task in reverse order, building their schools first and then their factories. Indeed it was certainly the case that the early universities and technical institutes were established before any significant industrial development occurred. More commonly, those specialized institutions receiving government funds were established to support emerging industrial efforts. Partly because of the close ties between educational and industrial planning, success in the educational sector came to be recognized as a precondition for recruitment to key positions in the emerging industrial sector. From early on, graduation from the law school of the Imperial Universities of Tokyo or Kyoto was recognized as a prerequisite for employment in the higher civil service. Over time other such linkages were established.

During the first decades of development, light industries and small retail establishments were the major employers, and their demands for specialized skills were modest. But from the early twentieth century, the number of medium and large establishments rapidly increased, and the demand for skilled and technically competent manpower picked up. Initially, employers recruited from the full pool of capable manpower, but following World War I key industrial leaders began to articulate a familistic ideology of labor relations wherein managers and workers would enter into a contract of mutual commitments.

As this ideology took hold, employers became more disposed to seek new recruits fresh out of school and to eschew recruiting employees from the ranks of their competitors. Over the ensuing years, the details of the lifetime employment system practiced by most large Japanese organizations were elaborated. Two features that have an important bearing on science and technology work force policies are (1) the condition that employment begin right after school and (2) the recruitment of employees to work in all parts of their organization rather than on a particular task. Partly due to this second feature, employers prefer broadly trained recruits (liberal arts majors with some understanding of science and technology and vice versa). Following from this second condition also are the essentially identical beginning salaries offered to all recruits, regardless of academic specialization, and the caution employers exhibit in recruiting highly specialized graduates with advanced professional skills; employers would prefer to see their staff acquire such expertise on the job rather than at a university.

With the lifetime approach to employment, employer concern for avoiding recruitment mistakes increased. To ensure high-quality recruits, each employer sought to establish close and favored relations with a small number of feeder schools. The first preference of employers was for the most highly regarded schools. For university-level recruits, this meant that most employers hoped to obtain their recruits from the Imperial Universities and the top private institutions. In the face of so many anxious employers, these universities tended to ration out their graduates (through faculty recommendations) in order to satisfy as many employers as possible.

Employer emphasis on educational qualifications also had a profound impact on the approach of young people to career preparation. Both the need to do well in school and to gain admission to a well-placed terminal institution (collegiate or otherwise) became more salient. The close links of education with employment in the expanding modern sector of large- and medium-scale organizations became a spur both to seriousness in school work and to the rapid expansion of educational institutions.

EDUCATIONAL EXPANSION

Initially, the national government exercised restraint in the establishment of universities, and through 1918 only eight had been established, each accorded funds and prestige in the order of its founding. In response to the post–World War I economic boom and the keen popular demand for higher education, additional public institutions were established.

Within the framework of government regulations on educational standards, private schools were allowed to be established. Over time, large numbers were founded, often to complement the offerings of public institutions; for example, at the postsecondary level, while government schools tended to stress technical specialties, many private schools offered courses in foreign languages, literature, office skills, and other subjects that were of interest to the growing middle class. Because of limited funds and a disadvantageous position in placing graduates in prestigious government jobs, most private institutions were not as highly regarded as the public institutions. By the time of World War II, approximately 40 percent of the secondary-level age cohort and 10 percent of the tertiary-level age cohort were enrolled in some type of institution. About half at each level were in private institutions.[2]

Over time, the successful pursuit of formal education came to be viewed as the means to a secure job in a large organization of either the public or private sector. Top universities sent their graduates to elite positions in government and business. Middle-rank universities supplied the next echelon, and so on down the hierarchy. During the depressed economic circumstances of the 1930s, these education employment linkages were somewhat disturbed; nevertheless, the myth prevailed that success in education guaranteed success in a career.

In sum, the central government exercised strong leadership in the establishment of the "old system." The result was a complex system with multiple layers or tracks and multiple sectors of sponsorship (hence sometimes described as a "multilayer multisector" or ML-MS system).[3] Three noteworthy features influenced the science and technology pipeline:

1. The hierarchy in institutional prestige
2. Several nodes of terminal education beyond which the individual had to leave the formal educational system
3. Segregation of tracks for males and females.

Postwar reforms led to changes in these features.

THE NEW SYSTEM

Following World War II, Japan was occupied by the Allied forces who, under the leadership of General Douglas MacArthur of the United States, promoted various reforms to "democratize and demilitarize" the nation. Education was a key area of reform, and here the overall thrust was to simplify and Americanize the system through expanding opportunities and eliminating terminal tracks. Also, the Occupation proposed decentralization of control. In terms of structure, the old ML-MS system was to be transformed into a "new 6-3-3-4 coeducational system" with nine years of compulsory schooling (six at elementary and three at lower secondary), with further opportunity for three years of upper secondary and a variety of postsecondary educational opportunities.

These proposals implied major restructuring and expansion at a time when Japan was only slowly recovering from the ravages of a long and exhausting war. The process of implementation stretched into the mid-1950s. The following sections summarize several of the resultant changes, highlighting both the contrast of Japan's new system with its old system and the main outlines of the American system.

Centralization

A key proposal of the Occupation was to shift control and support of the educational system from the central Ministry of Education to prefectural (forty-seven in Japan) and district levels. For the governance of public universities, boards of trustees were proposed but soon ruled out; in the absence of other proposals, the public universities became self-governing bodies, although they were dependent on the national and (in some instances) local governments for financial and administrative support. For the governance of schools, locally elected school boards were actually tried for several years, and then due to "excess" politicization the electoral principle was replaced by appointed bodies. The change from the electoral to an appointment principle has effectively shifted the locus of school politics to the prefectural level; one consequence has been to reduce the complications in consolidating local districts as the size of school-aged cohorts have changed.

Currently Japan has fifty prefectural-level school boards (forty-seven prefectures plus one each for the urban areas of Tokyo, Kyoto, and Osaka) and about 500 local school boards; all members are appointed. In contrast, in the United States a few states have state-level school boards, but the majority place control of public education in the hands of local school boards, many of which are elected. Currently, there are some 16,000 school boards in the United States.

Finance

Similarly, decentralized financing of education was proposed by the Occupation, but in view of the general postwar condition of destitution this concept was essentially abandoned. At the tertiary level, the central government assumed responsibility for most of the public institutions, and private institutions were left to obtain their revenues in whatever manner possible. At the school level, new tax laws provided local and prefectural governments with new revenue sources sufficient to cover part of the cost of public education. The postwar constitution's assertion that the national government should guarantee equal education for all through the ninth grade resulted in special budget-equalizing regulations requiring the central government to supplement the educational budgets of the poorer prefectures up to that level sufficient to realize a minimal common educational standard. Included in the regulations are provisions for supplementary benefits to schools in isolated areas (islands, mountainous areas) or areas with large minority populations.[4]

Recent analyses of compulsory-level educational expenditures in Japan indicate no more than a 60-percent variation in the average per pupil expenditure across prefectures, and some inner-city schools, which receive large numbers of *burakumin* (a Japanese minority), are funded well above the national average.[5] The U.S. Constitution asserts that education is a local responsibility. The variation across states is in excess of 200 percent,[6] and between school districts there is even greater disparity; inner-city schools are often disadvantaged.

Teachers

Equality of educational finance has had an important impact on the status and welfare of Japan's teachers. In response to the rapid postwar emergence of a militant Japan Teachers Union (Nikkyoso), which participated in general strikes and sought to enter into collective bargaining with the central government over salaries and working conditions, a law was passed making teachers the employees of local governments. Nevertheless, in order for the central government to realize equal education across prefectures, it relies on a uniform salary schedule for determining the amount of subsidy it should provide to local educational budgets. This salary schedule is similar to those for most public employees in Japan with a modest entry-level salary and steady annual seniority increments and substantial retirement benefits. Differences in educational attainment and level of teaching (compulsory versus high school) are rewarded with small increments. The annual increments, designed to reward loyal service and increasing personal needs as the teacher acquires a family, mean that teachers with twenty years of service receive nearly three times the real income of entering teachers.

Due to this uniform schedule (once adjustments are made for age and school level), teachers throughout Japan can look forward to an essentially identical lifetime income cycle. For most of the postwar period, the level of teacher pay was fixed at a level correspondent with that for local officials, and since 1975 it has actually been raised above that level. Thus from an economic standpoint, teaching in Japan is an attractive job. Japanese school authorities report a surplus of qualified candidates for openings, even for mathematics and science teaching positions. Surveys indicate that nearly 100 percent of Japan's teachers have the proper qualifications for the subject areas and levels they teach.[7]

In contrast, teacher pay in the United States varies widely by location. A recent study indicates that average teacher pay in the United States is about 70 percent of the pay received by other professionals with comparable education and tenure. In Japan, average teacher pay is equal to that of comparable professionals.[8] In absolute terms and taking into account the national differences in purchasing power, teachers in Japan receive at least as much in salary as American teachers but can look forward to far more substantial fringe benefits and retirement income.

Curriculum and Texts

In the old system the central government planned a fixed curriculum for each type of school and supervised the writing and printing of texts for each subject. The Occupation, believing this resulted in excessive uniformity even to the extreme of indoctrination, proposed the relaxation of central authority. Initially, only general curricular goals were authorized leaving to individual school boards and the private sector the task of specifying detailed curricula and preparing texts. However, in the immediate austere condition of postwar Japan where even paper was scarce, this liberalization led to excessive waste and duplication, so some tightening up followed.

The central Ministry of Education (Mombusho) took the initiative to develop detailed courses of study for each school type, allowing generous provision for electives so that each school board could tailor a curriculum suitable to its local needs. In addition, to ensure that texts conformed with the courses of study, the ministry established special review committees to inspect and authorize the drafts prepared by commercial publishers.

The outcome of these changes is subject to debate. For most subjects, at least five "quality" texts are approved annually by the ministry's committees allowing local school boards a range of choice; however, those groups who do not share the ministry's educational viewpoint often challenge the fairness of the process. Moreover, while local school boards have considerable room to diversify their curriculum, in fact far less occurs than critics feel necessary. Thus, while formal control of curriculum and texts was relaxed, the ministry exercises considerable influence so that schools across the country teach pretty much the same things.

In the United States there are no equivalent central means for developing curriculum or preparing texts; these decisions are left to local school boards and private publishers. However, some would maintain that, due to the influence of accreditation boards and the preferences of key states such as California and Texas, a surprisingly high level of uniformity is achieved in actual offerings across the country. Perhaps the major U.S.–Japanese differences lie in what is offered, and who takes advantage of those offerings. As discussed below, the Japanese mathematics and science curricula are more demanding at an earlier stage in the schooling cycle, and Japanese children are far more likely to respond to the challenge than are the American children.

Primary Education

The new system of Japanese primary schools acquired many of the features of the American elementary school. Primary schools were expected to receive pupils from their immediate neighborhood and to place them in coeducational classes without distinction by ability or other characteristics.

As in the United States, the curriculum was to extend over six years, though in Japan each school year was longer (currently 240-plus days in Japan compared with the 180 days typical in the United States). The major difference is that the Japanese primary school curriculum offers more than the typical American elementary school, and considerably more time is devoted to art, music, physical education, and language.[9]

The number of hours over a school year devoted to mathematics is virtually the same in Japan as it is in American primary schools; however, the Japanese curriculum is more demanding and is uniformly taught to all students in contrast with the United States where different levels are taught to different ability groups. Despite or perhaps because of the greater demands placed on Japanese students, they apparently are more successful in mastering elementary-level mathematics. Japanese primary-level students routinely outperform Americans on international tests of mathematics achievement.[10] The Japanese science curriculum is structured more systematically, begins at an earlier age, and is offered separately from social science rather than integrated as is the case in many American elementary schools.

Lower Secondary

A major departure of the new postwar system was the extension of compulsory education through the ninth grade, through the vehicle of the lower secondary school. An immediate concern of postwar educational administrators was the location of buildings and teachers for this essentially new institution. While the Japanese lower secondary school had some resemblance to the form of the American junior high, there are several differences of interest. Whereas the American junior high usually initiates young people into electives and the selection of teachers, the Japanese lower secondary school is organized much like a primary school, except that the number of students in the same grade level tends to be greater. Admission is based on the neighborhood principle. Entering students are assigned homerooms in such a manner as to mix rather than stratify ability groups, and it is with this homeroom group that a student takes all of his or her classes. While homeroom assignments may shift in the second and third years, all students of a common grade level pursue essentially the same curriculum, except for home economics and industrial arts options that are available, respectively, to girls and boys.

By American standards, this common curriculum is demanding. It includes elementary algebra in the seventh grade and some exposure to geometry, trigonometry, and more advanced algebra topics over the next two years. Many American high schools avoid these subjects, and Americans can graduate with very little mathematics or science. The Japanese lower secondary school provides three years of science, social science, Japanese language, and English as a foreign language and offers instruction in fine arts, music, and physical education. Teachers move between homerooms over the course of the school day teaching their specialty.

The Structure of Upper Secondary Education

The intent of the American Occupation was, following the American model, to foster neighborhood comprehensive high schools which would receive all of the children from a given geographic area, provide them with a wide choice of elective subjects from both vocational and academic curricula, and thereby allow young people to develop over the course of high school an education suited to each one's individualized needs.[11] The Japanese who were responsible for implementing the Occupation guidelines did simplify the former diverse array of upper secondary institutions, but the final outcome (which has continued to evolve over the postwar period) departed from the Occupations's plans, and hence differs from the "typical" American high school in several respects.

Neighborhood Principle. Because school districts in Japan usually contain a larger population in the school-age cohort, many have sufficient numbers to support several public upper secondary schools. The Occupation encouraged local districts to implement the neighborhood principle by establishing subdistrict boundaries and requiring all youth within the respective areas to attend the high school specified for that area. Many districts attempted this artificial reform, but their commitment was not strong.

Courses and Curriculum Types rather than Electives. Rather than institute comprehensive high schools, the Japanese authorities decided to define several distinct three-year courses and leave to the respective governing bodies (mainly local governments or private sponsors) the decision as to which among these they wished to include in particular high schools. In contrast with the American system, a student at the point of entry to high school takes up one or the other of these courses, after which time it is difficult to shift to a different course. In a given school, all students taking a particular course will pursue essentially the same sequence of subjects over the three-year course. Thus, in Japan, student choice is available when selecting the course to study rather than the particular subject to study. The two broad groups of courses are the academic-general and the vocational-specialized; within each group there are further distinctions.

Academic-General Courses. In the academic-general group are those courses geared for college preparation and those of a more general nature ostensibly intended to prepare individuals for immediate entry to the labor force; within the academic course, a further important distinction is the curricular branching (often beginning in the second year) between the set of subjects for those preparing for a science or engineering college major and for those preparing for a liberal arts major.

Table 8.1 illustrates the differences in the content of these two branches following the curricular reforms of 1979. Clearly, the students in the science curricular branch receive a more thorough grounding in mathematics and science, but even those specializing in the arts branch receive substantial exposure to mathematics and science; a minority actually make use of that exposure to compete for admission to university faculties specializing in science and engineering.

Vocational-Specialized Courses. Vocational-specialized courses combine a core of general education subjects with a concentration of specialized courses designed to prepare students for a particular line of work. The general education core at a technical high school includes mathematics I (intermediate algebra with some geometry and trigonometry), basic analysis, and calculus as well as science I, physics, and chemistry (Table 8.2). The core is rather demanding, and not a few who complete a vocational school find they have sufficient background to compete for entrance to one of the lesser universities.

While there is considerable diversity in the occupational objectives of the specialized group, the courses are commonly grouped into those designed to prepare students for work in agriculture, industry, commerce, fisheries, nursing, and home economics. Iwaki Hideo observes that the popularity of most of these courses peaked in the mid-1960s, after which time the enrollments have declined, most dramatically in agriculture and home economics, least in business; nursing is the exception with a peak in the 1970s.[12]

Private Upper Secondary Education

Given the burden of establishing a large number of lower secondary schools and the absence of a strong immediate social demand for upper secondary school grad-

Table 8.1
Senior High School Course Time Tables

a. Credit requirements for students who wish to advance to arts departments of universities.

Subject Areas	Subjects	10th	Grade 11th	12th	Total Credits
Japanese Language	Japanese Language I	5			5
	Japanese Language II		5		5
	Modern Japanese Language			3	3
	Classics			3	3
Social Studies	Contemporary Society	4			4
	Japanese History		6*	4**	10
	Geography		(3x2)	(2x2)	
	Politics and Economy			2	2
Mathematics	Mathematics I	5			5
	Algebra & Geometry		3	2	5
	Basic Analysis		2	2	4
Science	Science I	4			4
	Science II			2	2
	Chemistry				
	Biology		3	2	5
Health and Physical Education	Physical Education	2	2	3	7
	Health	1	1		2
Art	Music I				
	Fine Arts I	2	1		3
	Calligraphy I				
Foreign Language	English I	5			5
	English II		2	3	5
	English II B		3		3
	English II C			4	4
Home Economics	General Home Economics	2	2		4
	Additional credits	2	2	2	6
	Total for all subjects	32	32	32	96
	Homeroom activities	1	1	1	3
	Club activities	1	1	1	3
	GRAND TOTAL	34	34	34	102

*Six credits from two subjects from among Japanese History, World History, and Geography (three credits for each subject).
**Four credits in two subjects from among Japanese History, World History, and Geography (two credits for each subject).

(continued)

Table 8.1 (continued)

b. Credit requirements for students who wish to advance to science departments of universities

Subject Areas	Subjects	Grade 10th	11th	12th	Total Credits
Japanese Language	Japanese Language I	5			5
	Japanese Language II		4		4
	Modern Japanese Language			4	4
Social Studies	Contemporary Society	4			4
	Japanese History				
	Geography		3	2	5
	Politics and Economy			2	2
Mathematics	Mathematics I	5			5
	Algebra & Geometry		3	2	5
	Basic Analysis		3	2	5
	Differential and Integral Calculus			3	3
Science	Science I	4			4
	Physics		3	3	6
	Chemistry		3	3	6
Health and Physical Education	Physical Education	2	2	3	7
	Health	1	1		2
Art	Music I				
	Fine Arts I	2	1		3
	Calligraphy				
Foreign Language	English I	5			5
	English II		2	3	5
	English IIB		3		3
	English IIC			3	3
Home Economics	General Home Economics	2	2		4
Additional credits		2	2	2	6
Total for all subjects		32	32	32	96
Homeroom activities		1	1	1	3
Club activities		1	1	1	3
GRAND TOTAL		34	34	34	102

Source: National Institute of Education Research, *Basic Facts and Figures about the Educational System in Japan, Dec. 1983.*

Table 8.2
Curriculum at a Technical High School (Unit: credit = 35 [50-minute] hours)

Subject Area	Subject	Year 1	Year 2	Year 3	Total
Japanese Language	Japanese Language I	4			4
			2	3	5
Social Studies	Contemporary Society	2	2		4
	World History			3	3
	Geography			2	2
Mathematics	Mathematics I	4			4
	Basic analysis		3		3
	Differentiation and integration			2	2
Science	Science I	4			4
	Physics		2		2
	Chemistry		2		2
P.E.	Physical Education	2	2	3	7
	Health	1	1		2
Art	Music I/Art I	2			2
English	English I	3			3
	English II		3		3
GENERAL SUBJECTS: TOTAL		22	17	13	52

Subject	Vocational Subjects							
	Engineering Course				Electrical Course			
	Year 1	Year 2	Year 3	Total	Year 1	Year 2	Year 3	Total
Fundamentals of Industry	4			4	3			3
Practice		4	4	8		4	6	10
Drawing	3	3	4	10		2	2	4
Industrial Mathematics	2			2	2			2
Machine Engineering Work		2	2	4				
Machine Design	1	2	3	6				
Prime Movers		2	2	4				
Basic Electricity		2		2	5	3		8
Electrical Technology I						3	4	7
Electrical Technology II						3	3	6
VOCATIONAL TOTALS				40				40

<u>Note</u>: Up to 4 optional credits may be taken from either the general or the vocational menu.

uates, public authorities initially established places for less than half of the eligible age cohort. Complementing the public institutions were private institutions, often attached to private universities or other private institutions. Because the public authorities were unwilling to provide sufficient places to accommodate all of the graduates of the lower secondary schools, a demand quickly developed for the expansion of the private sector. Private educators were quick to respond, and by 1960 their institutions provided half of the places for upper secondary education.

Private schools are required to follow the same course of study as public institutions. The great majority of private institutions are located in urban areas and offer the academic-general courses. Some have a reputation for high quality (that is, large numbers of their graduates get into top universities), but the majority tend to attract students whose records were too low to qualify them for the limited number of places in the public sector.

Tertiary Education

Another dramatic proposal of the Occupation era was the expansion of public higher education by establishing a public university in every prefecture, thereby hopefully eliminating the elitist dominance of the old Imperial Universities. As with other reforms requiring personnel and building budgets, this proposal encountered difficulties. Most prefectural governments were reluctant to support a university along with their other new burdens. Thus, the central government assumed responsibility for establishing most of the institutions. Through the consolidation of existing upper secondary and tertiary institutions, some semblance of conformity was realized as early as 1949.

Several of the "new" public universities offered instruction in a wide variety of academic areas, mainly because they were based on the old Imperial Universities or existing arts and science faculties. Most, however, were based on combinations of former specialized institutes, as in agriculture or teacher education, and assumed an initial form equal to the sum of these parts. The government's initial policy was to limit the full development of these lesser universities, rather than restricting their expansion to fields felt to have high priority in national development. Engineering was one such field and thus assumed a very prominent place in the new national universities. By 1960, thirty-seven of the seventy-four national universities had engineering faculties (and thirty-one had science faculties).[13]

The new laws on university establishment made it much easier for private bodies to found higher educational institutions. A number of long-established private schools sought recognition as universities; others sought permission to create short-term (*tanki*) universities with two-year courses, similar to American junior colleges. Because of government restrictions in establishing places for higher education and the increasing private demand, over time the private sector of private higher education rapidly expanded. In general, the private sector complemented the public sector, emphasizing the humanities and social sciences. Many of the new private institutions were junior colleges.

Exams and the Elite Path

The postwar reformers hoped, through expanding higher education, to create greater competition for the elite universities and thereby to weaken the link between attendance at particular universities and the quality of career prospects. However, given the insecurities of postwar Japan and the doubtful quality of many of the new institutions, both students and employers saw little reason to alter the prewar pattern. The brightest and most ambitious students continued to seek entry to the most highly regarded institutions, which now seemed even more prominent when contrasted with the much larger number of universities, and employers continued to prefer recruits from these top institutions.

The focus of the new system, even more than the old, was the competition to gain entry to the handful of elite universities that enjoyed the confidence of prestigious employers in government and business. The new system, by radically expanding the upper secondary level, provided much larger numbers of young people with the qualifications to seek entry to these elite institutions. To sort out the applicants, the institution of entrance exams was strengthened.

Most of the top institutions of both the public and private sector designed their own unique exam format. Usually, the constituent faculties of the respective institutions became the examining bodies, but at a given institution a prospective student was restricted to taking the exam of only one faculty.

The emphasis on academic content in the university entrance exams, combined with the keen ambition of young people, has influenced the lower levels of the system. For example, whereas in the old system upper secondary schools once graduated approximately as many students as there were university places, now there was a surplus. Thus upper secondary schools that aspired to send students upward encountered the need of carefully selecting their students and then offering a challenging academic program. Similarly, middle schools felt pressure.

One important outcome has been the development of comprehensive (multisubject) entrance exams at each major passage in the schooling hierarchy. These exams tend to induce student application across all subject areas. Supplementing the entrance exams are several different kinds of aptitude exams administered by private bodies to enable interested students to assay their relative ability. The increasing availability of these various exams combined with the publication of results by schools has sharpened public perceptions concerning which schools do the best job in academic preparation. These perceptions have in turn influenced educational policy.

Tight Education-Work Link

The pressure on students to do well in studies means that other youthful activities receive lower priority. Athletics and social activities are progressively curtailed as young people approach the stage of university entrance; in this context of singular dedication to academic progress, it is socially taboo to drop out for a period of months or a year to explore other alternatives. Employers organize to recruit those students who decide, at the end of their studies, to seek work. Thus employers seek graduates of the lower secondary, upper secondary, junior college, and university courses. As economic conditions strengthened, the job prospects at each of these points of passage improved. By the early 1960s, virtually all who graduated could expect jobs.

In sum, a tight link was established between education and work in Japan. Security and full employment were the reward for foregoing freedom and youthful exploration of alternate life-styles. Whereas the unemployment rate of American adolescents often ranges above 20 percent, in Japan, since the early 1960s, it has been virtually nil.

The Pipeline in 1961

The Occupation reforms had been largely consolidated by 1961, and subsequent policy has been directed to new ends. 1961 represents a kind of turning point in American education as well, for it was roughly from that time that the post-Sputnik drive for quality began to take root. Hence 1960 is a good baseline point for examining Japan's science and engineering pipeline, and a summary of the enrollment ratios for the different school levels in 1960 is a good indicator of the situation. The pipeline experience by actual cohorts would differ somewhat owing to demographic fluctuations and shifts in educational opportunities.

As illustrated in Figure 8.1, virtually all of the eligible youth completed primary and lower secondary education in 1961; 62.3 percent attended upper secondary, of which 58.3 percent were in the academic-general course (sex differences are insignificant for both statistics). Although data are not available on the science-arts choice, it is safe to assume that about half were in the science course. Also, 15.9 percent of the males and 5.6 percent of the females attend some form of tertiary educational institution. Most males attended four-year colleges; the females are divided between two- and four-year colleges (about 9 percent attend four-year colleges). About 90 percent graduate from their program (nearly all within the expected four-to-five-year time period). One-third of these specialize in science and engineering, so 30 percent of the cohort moves into the science and engineering pipeline.

THE ERA OF MIRACLE GROWTH AND EDUCATIONAL EXPANSION AND UPGRADING

From 1961, Japan's economic leaders under the leadership of Prime Minister Ikeda embarked on an ambitious plan of export-oriented growth to double the per capita income in a single decade. At the time the goal seemed unattainable, but in fact it proved an easy task. The rapid economic growth of the 1960s was sustained well into the 1970s, and even today the Japanese economy continues to expand at least 25 percent more rapidly than the economies of other industrial nations. The rapid economic expansion led to full employment and a rapid increase in the number of jobs in medium- and large-scale organizations.

Coincidental with the push for rapid economic growth was a sudden increase in the number of young people eligible for work. From 1962 the first cohort of

Figure 8.1
Progression Rates in the Japanese Educational System, 1961

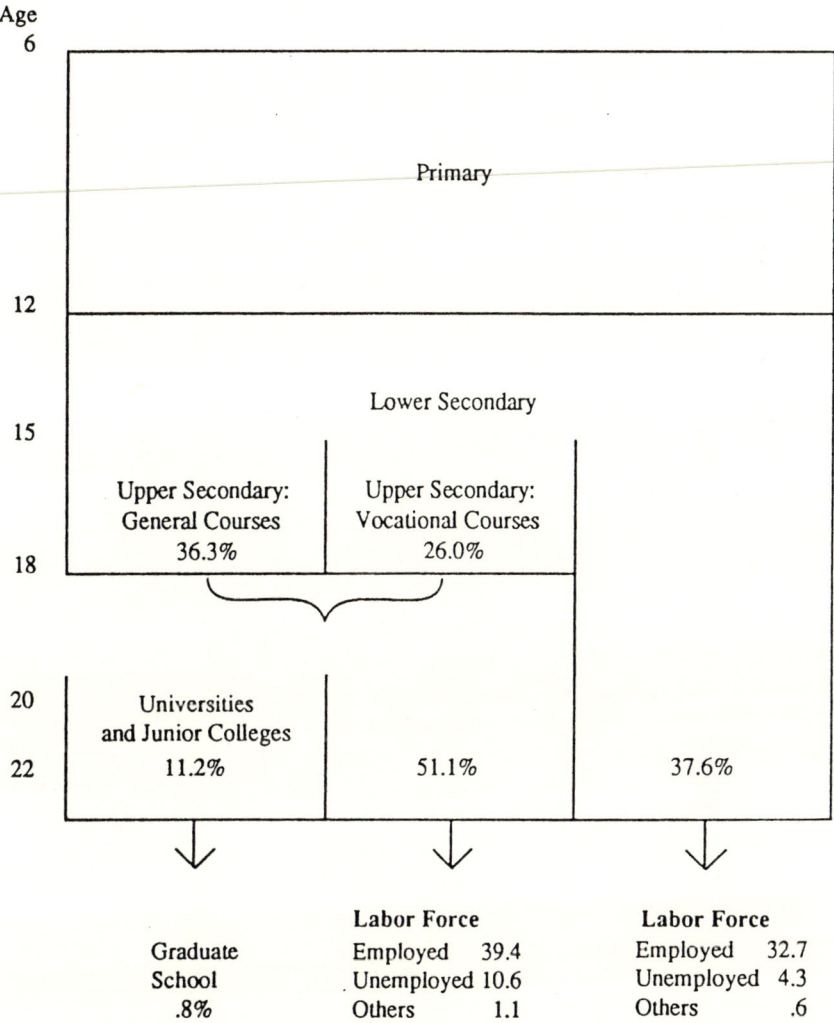

the postwar baby boom began to enter high school. The public responded to these employment opportunities by encouraging more of their children to consider upper secondary and tertiary education.

Already by 1960, Japan had an impressive educational system at least in terms of quantitative indicators. The science and engineering pipeline was preparing as large a proportion of the cohort for engineers as the American pipeline, and somewhat less than half the American proportion for scientists. In both respects, Japan was already ahead of the major industrial nations of Western Europe.

The dual factors of rapid economic growth and the baby boom interacted with the baseline structure to achieve rapid expansion and upgrading of the science and engineering pipeline.[14]

Compulsory Level

In 1961 a new curriculum was introduced which modestly elevated the expected standards for primary and lower secondary education. New schools and classrooms had been established over the 1950s to accommodate the baby boom. In 1958, a new law was enacted which required local governments to provide a science laboratory in each primary and lower secondary school, and related regulations guaranteed a minimum provision of equipment for the laboratories.

Upper Secondary

During the 1950s only modest expansion was allowed in the number of places for entrants to public schools, but in response to the new demographic and economic developments of the 1960s steps were taken to expand the industrial and business courses of public upper secondary schools. From 1962 a new publicly sponsored higher technical college was established which combined the three upper secondary years with two additional years of practical education. While public sector expansion focused on the vocational courses, private schools recognizing the popular demand for academic course education rapidly expanded academic course offerings. Eventually, the public sector followed the private lead, modestly increasing its number of academic track places. Curricular reforms implemented in 1963 and 1973 increased the expected standards of performance.

Figure 8.2 illustrates the trends in the number of places by course. School expansion, which mainly involved the academic track, was much in excess of the growth in cohort size; thus over the 1960–1980 period, the upper secondary enrollment rate increased from 54.9 percent to 92.9 percent. With Japan's custom of automatic promotion, virtually all who are enrolled graduate. Japan's 90-percent level for high school graduates compares favorably with the United States where only six-tenths of the cohort graduate on schedule, and no more than 85 percent of the cohort eventually obtain a high school diploma.

Increasing the Size of School Districts

As in the United States, the majority of public upper secondary schools are managed by local authorities, but relative to the United States, Japan's local authorities tend to be responsible for larger areas, at least if measured by population. Thus it is common in Japan for a local authority to be responsible for several upper secondary schools.

Figure 8.2
Number of Students in General and Vocational Courses

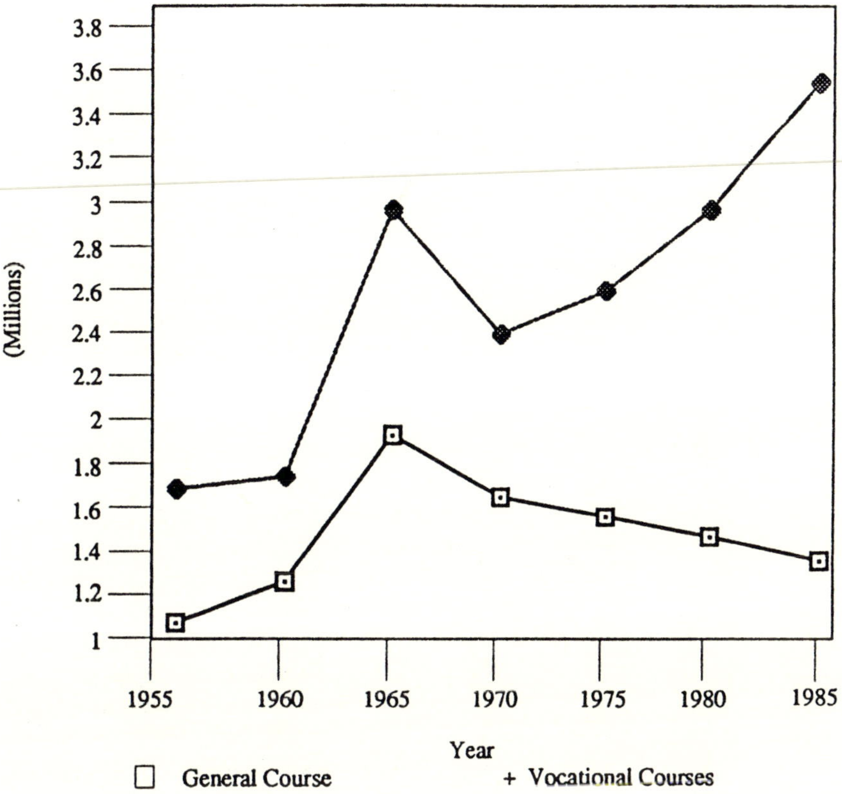

Initially, local authorities established geographic divisions to realize the neighborhood principle; however, in many instances, this change eliminated the possibility of parents sending their children to nearby schools that had been renowned in the old system for their success in grooming candidates for the top universities. Parents objected, and when public authorities would not compromise, many of these parents elected to send their children to reputable private upper secondary schools rather than risk the education offered by the neighborhood school. Gradually, a counterreform evolved, one which combined all of the high schools of a district in a hierarchical system and assigned lower secondary graduates into the upper secondary schools according to their ability. This approach, which has obvious parallels to the magnet schools established in certain United States urban areas, tended to appease the Japanese public. One obvious outcome was to intensify the effort among lower secondary level students to study hard to qualify for entry to the top public upper secondary school in their district. On the other hand, the stratification of student placement by ability probably has contributed to a greater overall dispersion in the ability of secondary-level students.

U.S.–Japan Comparisons of Secondary-Level Education

Given the complexity and diversity in high school offerings in both Japan and the United States, cross-national comparisons are difficult to make. Victor Kobayashi attempted a comprehensive analysis of the minimum amount of class time (in clock hours) required to graduate from high school in the two systems.[15] His computations for the Japanese system, which hold true for all students in both the academic-general and vocational courses, were calculated by combining the requirements for the last year of lower secondary school (ninth grade which, in the American system, is usually part of high school) and the three upper secondary years. Focusing only on the minimum requirement, the contrast is 3,150 hours in Japan compared with the U.S. average across the states of 2,100 hours; the Japanese minimum requirements are significantly greater in mathematics, science, physical education and health, and art and music.

For a different perspective on the U.S. experience, Kobayashi next drew on U.S. surveys of the units actually earned. He found that "the *average* number of units earned by U.S. high school graduates in 1982 was 2,616 clock hours, as compared with the 3,150 classroom hours that are *minimally* required of all Japanese high school students: a difference of 534 clock hours."[16] A further computation indicated that the average U.S. college-bound youth also spent less time in class than is minimally required in Japan. Of course, most Japanese high school students spend far more time in class than is minimally required. Thus Kobayashi concluded that Japanese students spend more time in class than their American counterparts. He further argued that classroom time is used more efficiently in Japan, and hence Japanese students learn more. How much more?

Thomas Rohlen[17] has suggested that the difference is of such a magnitude that the college-bound Japanese high school graduate already knows more than the average U.S. college graduate. This may be an overstatement. One objective indication of the difference comes from the IEA surveys. The mathematics surveys, which have now been fully released, indicate for 1980 that 12 percent of Japanese high school seniors studied calculus compared with slightly over 1 percent in the United States. The IEA achievement tests administered to these two elite groups (12 percent of Japanese seniors and 1 percent of American seniors) indicate that the Japanese average is considerably ahead of the American, sixty-seven out of a hundred compared with forty-eight for the United States. Similar differentials have been revealed in preliminary reports from the IEA science surveys.[18]

Many of the questions in the 1980 mathematics achievement test had also been given to equivalent school populations in 1964. For these common questions, the average score for Japanese 12th grades in 1980 was 12 percent greater than in 1964. The improvement in the U.S. case was 5 percent.[19]

Japanese superiority in international achievement tests has been so consistently demonstrated that there can be little doubt that more is learned there. A key component in the high average scores of Japanese young people is the relatively small number who receive low scores, at least through the lower secondary level. In other words, Japanese education appears to convey mathematical and science concepts to a larger proportion of the cohort than does American education.

Tertiary Education

Expansion of tertiary education in Japan has tended to follow the pattern of secondary education. Public authorities have been reluctant to acknowledge the value of mass higher education, believing that the state's responsibility should be limited to expansion in specific areas essential for economic development, primarily engineering and related specialties. Thus, public sector expansion has proceeded at a moderate pace and overwhelmingly in science and engineering fields. In contrast, the private sector has readily acknowledged the value of higher education and has rapidly expanded to meet the popular demand. Initial private expansion was fastest at the junior college level but subsequently shifted to four-year institutions.

To cover the costs of expansion, private institutions steadily increased their tuition charges until they were besieged by occasionally violent student protests and lockouts in the late 1960s. In response to this situation, the national government decided to recognize the public value of private education and established a Private School Promotion Foundation to provide substantial subsidies to private institutions. The foundation, which receives nearly all of its revenues from the national government, awards subsidies based primarily on an estimate of the personnel costs of individual institutions; this approach was chosen to reward those private institutions with low student-teacher ratios (which coincidentally are the institutions with stronger science and engineering commitments). The foundation's subsidies currently constitute about 30 percent of the revenues of private institutions.[20]

Despite the subsidies, the financial state of private institutions is inferior to that of the public institutions. Table 8.3 presents several comparative indicators. Private institutions are sometimes said to have one-third of the resources of public institutions.

Through the combination of public and private sector expansion, Japanese higher education has steadily increased enrollments, as illustrated in Figure 8.3. Kaneko Motohisa observes that Japanese expansion has been of greater magnitude than that in Europe or the United States and, moreover, has endured longer; whereas the enrollment ratios of the other leading industrial societies peaked in the mid-1970s, Japanese expansion continued through the early 1980s.

Relative to the size of its college-age population, Japan's system of undergraduate education is among the largest in the world. As illustrated in Table 8.4, the Japanese ratio of first university degrees as a proportion of the twenty-

Table 8.3
Educational Conditions in National, Public, and Private Universities (Recent Years)

Condition	National-Public Universities	Private Universities
Expenditures per student (1000 yen)	220.3	87.9
Building area per student (square meters)	31.3	13.0
Campus area per student (square meters)	111.8	68.8
Students per full-time teaching staff member	8.1	25.4

Source: Nippon Shiritsu Daigaku Renmei (1984, p. 16).

two-year-old population exceeds that of every other country except the United States, which has an identical ratio.

Relative to the United States, Japanese higher education, as shown in Figure 8.4, graduates similar proportions in the physical and life sciences, a smaller proportion in the mathematical sciences, over twice as many in the agricultural sciences, and about three times as many in engineering. Especially notable is the large proportion of Japanese students graduating in engineering.

Japan, with about half the U.S. population, began to exceed the United States in the granting of first-degree engineering degrees in 1976 and retained the lead through 1982. While figures on engineering degrees by detailed field are not available, it is possible to compare enrollments. As indicated in Table 8.5, a substantially larger proportion of Japanese engineering undergraduates are enrolled in the fields of electrical and computing engineering and civil engineering and architecture. U.S. enrollments are slightly larger in the fields of aeronautic, nuclear, mining, and "other" (mainly general) engineering. The two countries have essentially identical proportions in the fields of mechanical, chemical and textile, industrial, and materials engineering.

The overall size of undergraduate enrollments began to stabilize in the mid-1970s, and, largely due to a decrease in the size of the college-age cohort, enrollments are expected to decline. In the context of slow growth in enrollments, the shifts in admissions reported in Table 8.6 provide a useful indicator of future directions for Japanese higher education. Life science fields are most evident among the high-growth fields at both the first-degree and master's levels. More traditional engineering fields (e.g., marine, textile, and mechanical) and core social science fields have been losing enrollments.

Figure 8.3
Cohort Enrollment Rates in Japan, 1951–1981

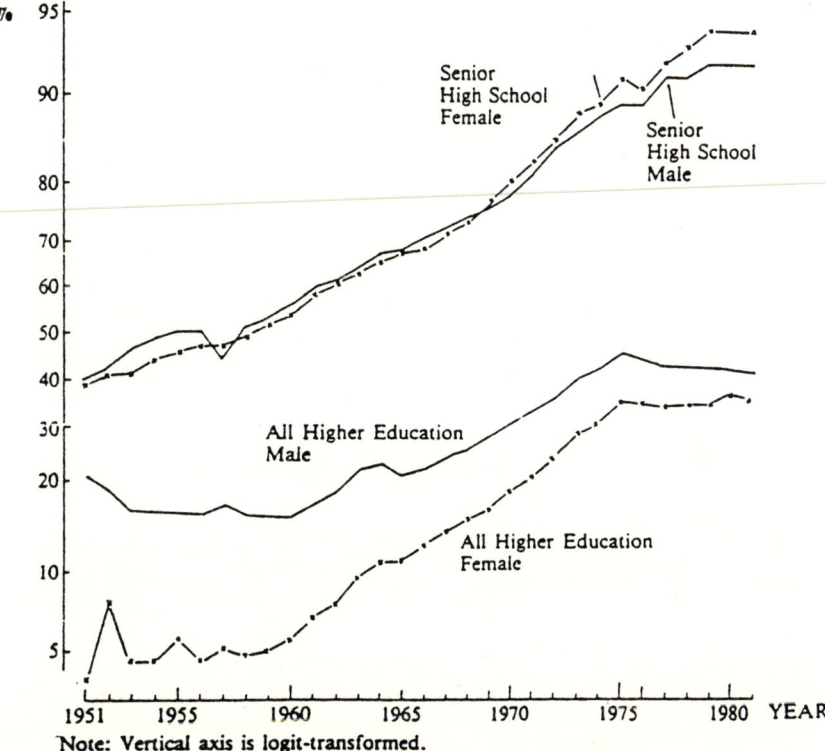

Note: Vertical axis is logit-transformed.

Source: M. Kaneko, Enrollment Expansion in Postwar Japan, p. 2.

Parallel to these changes at the first-degree level is a transformation in the nature of the courses offered by junior colleges and other postsecondary institutions (*kakusho gakko* and *senshu gakko,* which offer shorter cycle courses). The most popular new specialties are in such fields as information processing, laboratory technician, electronics, and international relations.

Education beyond the bachelor's level in Japan, which is usually viewed as preparation for an academic career, is organized somewhat along European lines. Prospective graduate students, even though they may take entrance exams to graduate programs, usually first seek the encouragement of a particular professor whom they admire and hope to work with. Once admitted, the graduate student tends to look on this professor as his guardian. Given the narrow purpose of graduate education and the particularistic mode of relations, there are not as many postgraduate students in Japan in comparison with the United States and

Table 8.4
First University Degrees as a Proportion of the Twenty-two-Year-Old Population

	Number of Degrees	Percent of 22-Year-Olds
United States (1983)		
Total	1,054,200	23.4
Natural Sciences	104,800	2.3
Engineering	72,900	1.2
Agriculture	19,200	0.4
Other	857,300	19.0
Japan (1983)		
Total	369,100	23.6
Natural Sciences	11,700	0.7
Engineering	69,600	4.5
Agriculture	13,300	0.9
Other	274,500	17.6
West Germany (1983)		
Total	54,800	5.3
Natural Sciences	8,900	0.9
Engineering	7,700	0.7
Agriculture	2,100	0.2
Other	36,100	3.5
United Kingdom (1983)		
Total	74,100	8.1
Natural Sciences	17,400	1.9
Engineering	10,600	1.2
Agriculture	1,400	0.2
Other	274,500	30.0
France (1983)		
Total	44,600	5.2
Natural Sciences	8,700	1.0
Engineering	12,600	1.5
Agriculture		
Other	23,300	2.7
Soviet Union (1983)		
Total	849,500	17.0
Natural Sciences	52,000	1.0
Engineering	331,500	6.6
Agriculture	69,200	1.4
Other	396,800	7.9

Note: French agricultural degrees are included with natural sciences.
Sources: National Science Foundation, U.S. Bureau of the Census and national sources listed in first degree table.

Figure 8.4
First University Degrees by Major Field of Study

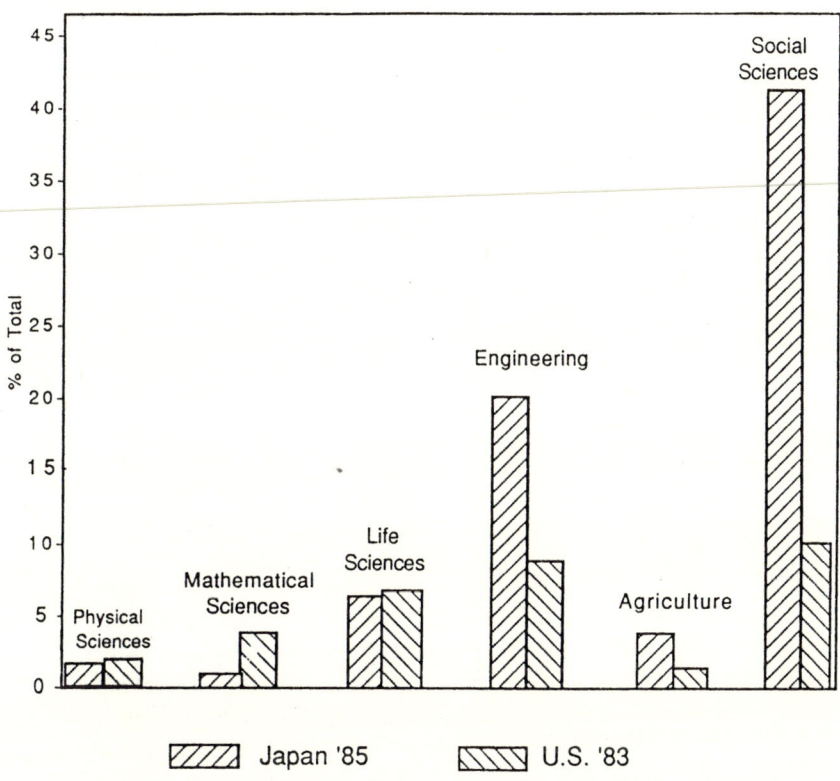

Source: NSF, Ministry of Education.
Note: U.S. data for 1983; 81.3% in other fields not shown. Japanese data for 1985; 28.3% in other fields not shown.

most European countries. Japan's ratio of master's enrollments to undergraduate enrollments is one-third that of the United States and one-half that of the major European countries. Similar differences can be observed in doctoral course enrollments.[21]

However, these statistics may not fully reflect the number of Japanese researchers who receive some form of graduate education. Many of Japan's scientists and engineers leave the university for industry or other employment immediately upon completion of their first degree. While pursuing a career at a new location, the former student usually maintains contact with his or her former professors. If and when he or she completes a research project that meets with the professor's approval, he or she may submit a report as a basis for obtaining

Table 8.5
Japan–U.S. Comparison of Enrollment in First-Degree Engineering Programs

	Japan 1984		U.S. 1983	
	Number	Percent	Number	Percent
Mechanical	73674	21.5	71459	19.9
Electrical and computing	100105	29.2	85513	23.8
Civil engineering, architecture	76986	22.5	41234	11.5
Chemical and textile	41876	12.2	36992	10.3
Nuclear	1542	0.5	2071	0.6
Mining	1569	0.5	4004	1.1
Metalurgical and materials	7243	2.1	4811	1.3
Marine	1015	0.3	2847	0.8
Aeronautic	2319	0.7	14115	3.9
Industrial	19928	5.8	22549	6.3
Other	16199	4.7	73769	20.5
Total	342456	100.0	359364	100.0

Source: Mombusho, Gakko Kihon Chosa 1984 (note only full-time studies; Engineering Manpower Commission of the American Association of Engineering Societies, Inc. Engineering and Technology Enrollments Fall 1983, Part 1 Engineering Total Full-time Studies (note some are in two-year programs).

a thesis degree (*ronbun hakase*). Sixty percent of the science and engineering doctorates granted in 1984 were granted on this basis.[22]

The major constraint on graduate enrollment is the lack of associated employment opportunities. For example, in 1983, 51 percent of science and 44.9 percent of agricultural doctoral course graduates could not obtain jobs.[23] However, this situation is expected to change. Over the past two decades, the employment opportunities for master's level engineers have improved, and engineering students have become a virtual majority of all master's students. At the doctoral level, the most popular fields are medicine and dentistry. The Japanese Ministry of Education would like to see more students enrolled in graduate education and has announced a plan that would lead to a threefold increase in master's level enrollments and a fourfold increase in doctoral enrollments by the year 2000.[24]

Consideration of graduate education is not complete without an appreciation of the rapidity with which Japanese expenditures on research and development have grown over the past decade and of their future prospects. Between 1965

Table 8.6
Science and Engineering Fields with 10 Percent or Greater Shift in Number Admitted between 1975 and 1983

All Universities	Admissions to First-Degree Programs	Admissions to Master's Programs
Geology	+57%	
Biology	+51%	
Mathematics	+29%	
Chemistry	+16%	
Nursing	+14%	
Physics	+13%	
Pharmacy	+12%	
Dentistry	+11%	
Commerce and economics	-12%	
Law and political science	-14%	
Agricultural economics	-16%	
Textile engineering	-35%	
Marine engineering	-50%	
Veterinary Science		380%
Pharmacy		78%
Nuclear Physics		70%
Electrical engineering		57%
Aeronautical engineering		45%
Forestry products		38%
Chemistry		39%
Civil engineering and architecture		34%
Irrigation engineering		34%
Applied physics		34%
Physics		33%
Geology		30%
Applied chemistry		28%
Mathematics		25%
Agricultural chemistry		20%
Biology		19%
Mechanical engineering		18%
Law and political science		-15%
Sociology		-20%

and 1984, Japanese research and development expenditures—converted with Organization for Economic Cooperation and Development (OECD) deflators and purchasing power parities into U.S. dollars—increased at an average annual rate of 9.3 percent compared to the United States' 2.5 percent. As a percent of the gross national product, Japanese expenditures increased from less than 1 percent to 2.6 percent in 1984, or about the U.S. level. Japanese planners propose a further expansion to 3.3 percent by 1995.[25] These trends in research and development expenditure are the grounds for anticipating expanding employment opportunities for the products of graduate education.

Traditionally, foreign students have constituted an exceptionally small proportion of Japanese enrollments at all degree levels. In 1982, foreign students accounted for only 0.5 percent of all students in Japanese higher education compared with 3 percent in the United States and between 4 and 10 percent in the major European countries. At the graduate level, foreign students in Japan constitute approximately 7 percent of the enrollment. In 1984 the Ministry of Education announced a plan to increase the number of foreign students tenfold by the year 2000.[26] If this were to take place, foreign students would constitute approximately 5 percent of all students in Japanese higher education, and possibly 25 percent of all graduate students. Currently, foreign students of Western origin are most likely to specialize in the humanities and social sciences; those from Asia and the Third World are most likely to specialize in the sciences and engineering. In the absence of new policies, these trends of regional specialization will most probably continue.

THE PIPELINE IN 1985

The past quarter century has resulted in a much broader science and engineering pipeline, which can be appreciated by comparing Figure 8.5 with Figure 8.1. Virtually the entire age cohort completes high school, with over two-thirds in academic high schools; about one-half of these students are enrolled in science courses. Over one-fifth of the cohort attends four-year universities, with about three of every ten specializing in science or engineering. In 1985, about 6 percent of the cohort was prepared for a career in science or engineering compared with 3 percent in 1960. Over the twenty-five-year period from 1960 to 1985, the U.S. pipeline had fluctuated around a 3 percent level. Thus, over the past quarter century, Japan has doubled its level of preparation while the United States has evidenced no significant change.

THE JAPANESE POLICY MECHANISM AND THE FUTURE

Science and technology policy is coming to be viewed with increasing importance in Japanese society as the economy comes to depend more on high-technology production and enters into direct competition with other advanced societies. Moreover, for the sake of national pride, Japan, which has long looked

Figure 8.5
Progression Rates in the Japanese Educational System, 1985

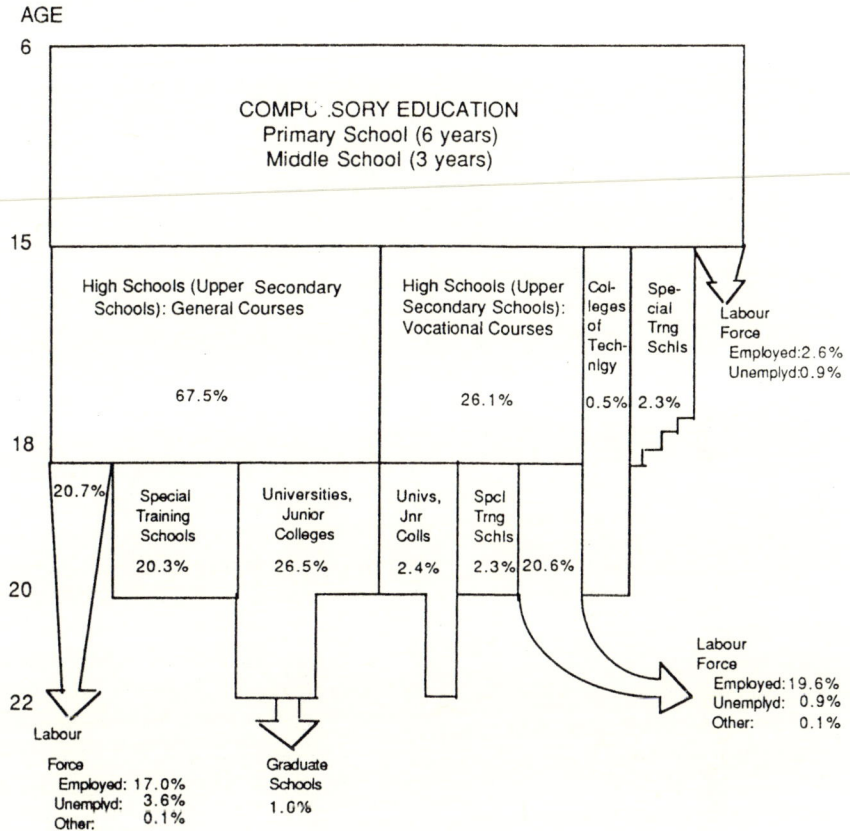

Source: Ministry of Education, Science and Culture, *Mombu Tokei Yoran*, 1986.

to the West for scientific leadership and technical innovation, now wishes to reverse this trend and gain international recognition.

These sentiments are echoed by a variety of sources. Business leaders are devoting ever larger sums of money to their corporate research and development budgets and are increasing their pressure on government for new initiatives. Politicians are so caught up in the new vision that they supported the launching of the Science and Technology Expo at Tsukaba Science City in 1984–1985.

Concerning national science and technology policy, there are several contenders seeking to advance special initiatives. The Prime Minister's Science and Technology Council has emerged as the most prominent among them. In 1986, the council published its 11th Recommendation, which called for increased emphasis on fundamental research:

> Japan will no longer have any model in the world to lead her future. Therefore, it is absolutely necessary for Japan to make efforts, trials, and even errors. That means Japan will have no way to ensure the development of the nation, without plentiful stocks of fundamental basic research activities.[27]

The report goes on to stress the importance of "promoting creativeness in science and technology" through placing greater emphasis on fundamental research and through strengthening interaction with scientists from other nations.

Although some of the council's aims can be realized by depending on the current stock of scientists and engineers, Japan's leaders are keenly aware that the current science and engineering work force was educated in a system that stressed conformity, and moreover, that the current work force is aging, especially in the sciences. Hence, they see an urgent need to look ahead. But, as one turns to the new generation, one can discern a number of other problems. First, the size of the cohorts is decreasing; second, the will to work is waning; and third, above all, the education system stifles the very creative qualities needed for fundamental research.

Hence, contemporaneous with the Science and Technology Council's recommendation was the prime minister's decision to form a high-level National Council on Educational Reform (Rinkyso). This council held scores of meetings between 1984 and 1987 and in 1987 issued its final report. The broad outlines of this report are already evident.[28] As in the Science and Technology Council's 11th Recommendation, a paramount concern is to introduce greater diversity in the school system and thereby hopefully to stimulate more creativity among gifted students. More attention to ability grouping is urged, and, at the secondary level, it is suggested that some local councils consider combining lower and upper secondary schools into single institutions to pursue a more integrated program of study which will shield young people from the distractions of exam preparation.

Other proposals of the National Council are as follows:

1. Add a year of supervised teaching to teacher training. The council believes that more guidance should be given to new teachers, and more care should be exercised before job security as a teacher is guaranteed.
2. Strengthen undergraduate education. The council subscribes to the view that the undergraduate educational system is unstimulating at best, often an outright waste of time.
3. Establish more structure in graduate education, and significantly expand graduate education. Here the council seems to advocate a systematic program of education along U.S. lines; it anticipates a growing demand for individuals with advanced scientific, technical, and analytical skills.

4. Establish more opportunities for postdoctoral research fellowships. A small program has been under way for several years, and the council feels this should be expanded. To the extent possible, the council advocates that postdoctoral fellows be given broad freedom to pursue sustained research of their own choosing so as to fully realize their creative potential.
5. Improve the research environment in universities. The council points to many factors including the shortage of funds, the hierarchical relations among university staff caused by the antiquated chair system, excessive inbreeding (at several of the top universities, over 80 percent of the staff are former students), and the scarcity of colleagues because of the small size of many departments.
6. Facilitate university-industry ties in research and training. The council is aware that industry has vast resources to support research as well as much outstanding talent and thus proposes that new avenues be established to enable university research teams to draw on these resources and reciprocally for industry to make use of the fine brains and facilities found in the universities. Since World War II, owing both to the horrors associated with wartime collaboration with industry and out of a firm belief that Japanese society needs an autonomous university sector for the preservation of democratic values, Japanese academics have resisted formal cooperation with both government and business.
7. Internationalize Japanese education and research by increasing the number of foreign students on Japanese university campuses and by supporting an increased level of interaction between Japanese and foreign scientists. Among other reasons, the council recognizes that new points of view will stimulate Japanese research into new creative heights.

One thing is certain—the Japanese system will undergo substantial change over the coming years.

REFLECTIONS

The Japanese system, if viewed in terms of comparative quantitative indicators, appears to be well prepared for the coming decades when economic strength will depend, above all, on those who are able both to develop new scientific and technical insights and to translate them into practical solutions. Processes have been set into motion to provide the Japanese work force with a plentiful supply of such people.

1. *Postwar reforms.* At the core of the Japanese story are those reforms introduced immediately after World War II which eliminated the numerous tracks and established a uniform system of education for all through the ninth grade. Some of these changes had been sought by Japanese educators long before the Occupation, but they would not have been possible without this unprecedented interruption of normal government.
2. *Firm national leadership.* Much of the postwar story involves a steady pursuit of long-standing commitments through strong central government. The faith in science and engineering has been realized through steady annual budgetary increments and modest changes in former practices, rarely through radical leaps forward.

3. *Science and engineering as a core commitment.* Since the Meiji Restoration, Japan's leaders have demonstrated an unswerving belief that development depends on creating industrial strength, which in turn requires an extensive science and engineering work force. Policies of educational expansion and curriculum change have consistently reflected this commitment.

4. *Practice of anticipating science and engineering demand.* The Japanese faith in science and engineering has led policymakers to push the expansion of programs and disciplines in the absence of clear demand. The expansion of engineering in the 1960s was based on the assumption of the importance of engineers rather than on a strong market demand. Similarly, the current expansion of graduate and postgraduate education is based on a vision of a preferred future society, rather than on current indicators. This futuristic view has usually proved prescient, thanks to the coordination of different sectors and the continuing forward thrust of the Japanese economy.

5. *Creating science and engineering demand.* In the early stages of these forward thrusts, demand is sometimes created for the new graduates. For example, currently, the government is establishing a number of new university-industry collaborative research programs, requiring postgraduate researchers, in an apparent effort to stimulate industrial demand for research personnel with advanced training.

6. *Essentialist curriculum.* Japanese educational philosophy stresses the importance of mastering key subjects, rather than responding to innate idiosyncracies of individuals. Only with mastery of fundamentals can the individual expect to realize creativity. Thus the curriculum requires all young people to study the essentials of math, science, and foreign languages with few electives. Entrance exams to each successive level are based on what students know rather than on aptitude, thus rewarding hard study and achievement over innate intelligence.

7. *Hierarchical educational system.* The Japanese policymakers seem to prefer a system where differential value is attached to respective secondary and tertiary institutions. In this hierarchical system, going to college is not enough. Rather, young people know that which college they attend makes a significant difference. Hence, they feel pressure to study hard and strive to do their best, recognizing that most others in their cohort are also making the same effort.

8. *Reliance on private sector.* For secondary initiatives, the government has shown a willingness to tolerate and even encourage the private sector through subsidies when it serves a public purpose. Currently, the private sector is establishing a number of training schools which will assist the established labor force as well as enable new recruits to obtain proficiency in computer-related skills which, the government believes, are not adequately taught in the essentialist-oriented formal educational system.

Underlying the steady expansion of Japanese education is a strong public faith that success in schooling leads to a secure adult career. Employers confirm this faith through their recruitment of graduates straight from school and by their commitment to continue employing these recruits until they either resign or retire. The Japanese work contract, which emphasizes stability and security, pervades all walks of life including universities and research laboratories. This strength of the Japanese system is also its major weakness. It induces a penchant toward conformity and uniformity that sometimes conflicts with the creativity and initiative required in the best scientific and technical work. Thus, a major concern in the present reform effort is to bring greater flexibility and less instability to a system that is premised on limited choice and stability. Japan's challenge is to identify the structural reforms required to reverse the traditional pattern of education. The current interests in expanding graduate education, breaking down the traditional chair system, expanding university-industry-government collaboration, and increasing the number of foreign researchers in Japanese laboratories are all part of the thrust for a new, more stimulating educational process.

NOTES

1. National Council on Educational Reform, *First Report on Educational Reform* (Tokyo, June 26, 1985); *Second Report on Educational Reform* (Tokyo, April 23, 1986); *Third Report on Educational Reform* (Tokyo, April 1, 1987). Also see Amano Ikuo, "The Dilemma of Japanese Education Today," *The Japan Foundation Newsletter* 8, 5 (March 1986), pp. 1–9.

2. Ronald S. Anderson, *Education in Japan: A Century of Modern Development* (Washington, D.C.: Government Printing Office, 1975); Ministry of Education, *Japan's Modern Educational System* (Tokyo: Ministry of Education, 1980).

3. Amano Ikuo, "Continuity and Change in the Structure of Japanese Higher Education," in William K. Cummings et al., eds., *Changes in the Japanese University* (New York: Praeger, 1979), pp. 10–39.

4. Ministry of Education, *Higher Education in Japan with Particular Reference to the Role and Functions of Universities*. Submitted to OECD, October 1984. (Tokyo: Ministry of Education, 1984).

5. Ministry of Education, *Education Annual* (Tokyo: Ministry of Education, 1986).

6. Center for Educational Statistics, *Digest of Educational Statistics, 1985–86* (Washington, D.C.: 1986).

7. Department of Education, *Japanese Education Today* (Washington, D.C.: 1987), pp. 15ff.

8. Stephen M. Barro, "International Comparison of Teachers' Salaries." Unpublished draft memo (August 1987).

9. Victor N. Kobayashi, "Japanese and U.S. Curricula Compared," in William K. Cummings et al., eds., *Educational Policies in Crisis: Japanese and American Perspectives* (New York: Praeger, 1986), pp. 61–95.

10. Curtis C. McKnight et al., *The Underachieving Curriculum: Assessing U.S. School Mathematics from an International Perspective* (Champaign, Ill.: University of Illinois Press, 1987).

11. Anderson, *Education in Japan*.

12. Iwaki Hideo, "Current Issues/Problems and Policy Trends about Japanese Upper Secondary Education." Unpublished memo (1985).

13. Seki Masao, "Nihon ni okeru rikokei daigaku seido no hatten—1950–1980" ["The Process of Transition in Japanese Universities of Natural Sciences and Engineering between 1950 and 1980"], *Daigaku Ronshu* 10 (March 1981), pp. 39–64.

14. Kaneko Motohisa, *Enrollment Expansion in Postwar Japan* (Hiroshima: Research Institute for Higher Education, Hiroshima University, 1987).

15. Kobayashi, "Japanese and U.S. Curricula Compared," pp. 83–85.

16. Ibid., p. 86.

17. Thomas P. Rohlen, *Japan's High Schools* (Berkeley: University of California Press, 1983).

18. Larry E. Sutter, "An Examination of Country Differences in Mathematics Achievement" (Paper presented at the annual meeting of the American Sociological Association, August 20, 1987.)

19. William K. Cummings, "Patterns of Academic Achievement in Japan and the United States," in William K. Cummings et al., eds., *Educational Policies in Crisis,* p. 118.

20. William K. Cummings, "The Japanese Private University," *Minerva* 1, no. 3 (July 1973), pp. 348–71.

21. Ministry of Education, *Education in Japan, 1982: A Graphic Presentation* (Tokyo: Ministry of Education 1984).

22. Kagaku Gijutsucho, *Indicators of Science and Technology* (Tokyo: Ministry of Education, 1986), p. 119.

23. Kobayashi Shunichi et al., "Daigaku ni okeru kenkyusha no ryudoka ni kan-suru kenkyu" ["A Study of the Mobility of University Researchers"], *Daigaku Ronsho* 14 (1985), pp. 71–93.

24. Ministry of Education, *The Systematic Planning and Administration of Higher Education in Japan after 1986* (Tokyo: Ministry of Education, 1984).

25. William K. Cummings, "Statistical Profile of Japanese Scientific and Technical Research and Development" (Washington, D.C.: U.S. Department of Education, October 10, 1986, Mimeographed).

26. Ministry of Education, *Systematic Planning and Administration.*

27. "Prime Minister's Science and Technology Recommendations" (Tokyo: Prime Minister's Office, 1984), p. 2.

28. National Council on Educational Reform, *First Report on Educational Reform; Second Report on Educational Reform; Third Report on Educational Reform.*

9

The Contribution of Education to Japan's Economic Growth

Robert Evans, Jr.

For many individuals, and certainly for most economists, one of the major economic events of modern times has been Japan's transformation from a semifeudal, underdeveloped country to a modern world power during the years from the middle of the nineteenth century to the last quarter of the twentieth century. A number of explanations have been offered to explain these rapid and significant changes. This chapter examines the role and place of education in this transformation. Was educational change and development central to the transformation? Is it true, as is argued by Benjamin Duke,[1] that much of Japan's success can be directly traced to her schools? Or does the truth lie closer to the traditional economic explanations with their almost complete wall of silence concerning education as a major factor? The answer is a complex one, and a proper conclusion depends on definitions and judgments concerning the influence of different factors.

This chapter is divided into four sections. The first sets out and investigates the major forms by which education has been said to play a major role in economic transformations. The second section describes the development of education and, more briefly, the economy of Japan since the Meiji Restoration in 1868. Its purpose will be to show the extent to which the magnitude and pace of educational change have been linked in time to the economic transformation. The third section discusses the interrelationships and the interactions between education and economy. The fourth section is a summary and a conclusion.

Economic growth as a process consists of three things: One is to produce more and more products with, relatively speaking, fewer and fewer inputs. The second is to increase the availability of inputs through savings and subsequent investment in physical capital and land development. Increased labor inputs follow from natural population growth and changes in hours of work and labor force participation. The third is to provide an increased quality of input. Superior capital is achieved through the incorporation of inventions and innovations into physical capital. An improved or higher quality labor force is achieved through formal education and on-the-job training. This chapter describes how education, broadly defined, has the potential to make contributions to these three processes.

THE POTENTIAL CONTRIBUTION OF EDUCATION TO ECONOMIC GROWTH

The economic value of education has been perceived by economists in different ways. The great English economist Alfred Marshall concluded that the wisdom of expending funds on education was not measured by its direct fruits, which he suggested might not be that great. The greater value to Marshall was that education opened up new opportunities to individuals. Out of these opportunities would come the new Beethovens, Pasteurs, and Shakespeares of the new ages. He went on to say that the most valuable capital of all was that invested in human beings and that the most precious part came from the care and influence of mothers.[2]

Economists who followed Marshall gave little formal consideration to education as a form of capital and to education as it might contribute to economic growth. It was not until the early 1960s, beginning at the University of Chicago under the intellectual leadership of Theodore Schultz and Gary S. Becker, that there came a reinvigoration of the analysis of human capital and of education's role in the production of human capital. Most economists welcomed the redevelopment of the human capital analysis, but others felt that it degraded human beings to analyze their working lives as if people were machines. To paraphrase one of them, people are not bags of cement.

In recent years economists have devoted less time and attention to the role of education in the development of human capital and to education's contribution to the economic growth and development of nations. This may reflect agreement with Professor Mark Blaug who believes that human capital as a conceptual idea has been developed as far as it can be.[3] Or it may only be that new intellectual fashions have now taken center stage.

Education has the potential for making a number of different contributions to economic growth in any country. The first and most obvious one is that it directly contributes to a better quality labor force. It is reasonable to suppose that a more literate worker will be a more productive worker than a worker who has not had the advantage of such an education. Many economists believe that the more significant portions of increased labor quality are the result of formal on-the-job training and/or the knowledge that comes from experience on a job. Still, it is reasonable to believe that increases in worker quality from on-the-job training and from experience will be greater for those individuals with a higher and more formal education.

Second, education contributes to growth by increasing the stock of scientific and technical knowledge and by encouraging the dissemination of that knowledge among enterprises and within the work force. For most countries, and certainly for Japan at least until the early 1970s, the source of new technology lies beyond their borders. Yet even where new technology is not homegrown, it may be important to have a strong domestic educational industry in order for workers to be mindful of the opportunities available from foreign sources and to be able to exploit those which are applicable to their own country.

Third, education opens a student's mind to new vistas and opportunities. Such an expansion of the student's mental processes should encourage new entrepreneurial talent. It may also encourage consumer interest in new and varied products, thus adding to the demand side of growth as well as the supply side. Educated individuals also may be more receptive to changes in the social and economic barriers which must fall if growth is to succeed. A whole host of noneconomic contributions could also be suggested. These would include impacts, for example, on child rearing, health practices, and wise political judgments, many of which Robert H. Haveman and Barbara L. Wolfe list and discuss.[4]

Last, there is the issue of high-level workers, doctors, engineers, teachers, and so on. Economic growth clearly requires an expansion in a country's supply of high-level talent. The importance of well-educated industrial leaders in Japan was recognized by the Meiji government in its drive to emulate, economically, the West. Along with the eradication of illiteracy, the achievement of an adequate number of individuals educated at the highest level was one of the two constants during a period of educational experimentation in the 1870s.[5] The importance of highly trained manpower may be seen in the proportion of presidents of corporations who were college graduates. In the 1880s, 17 percent of business leaders had higher level educations. This proportion rose to 63 percent by 1920 and 91 percent by 1960.[6] For elites in general 28 percent had completed college in 1903. This number rose to 37 percent in 1928 and 94 percent by 1964.[7] These results suggest that during the prewar period of growth higher education played a more important role in the business sector than in other sectors of the economy. Growth in the number of persons in certain high-level occupations is shown in Table 9.1.

A dramatic increase in the proportion of the labor force engaged in professional and technical occupations also characterized the years of rapid postwar growth. In 1957 at the beginning of the growth spurt 4.6 percent of workers were professional and technical workers. In 1975 this proportion had grown by 50 percent to 6.7 percent. The proportion has continued to grow to 9.26 percent in 1985.[8] The latter growth probably reflects the slow restructuring of the Japanese economy toward a more service-based economy.

The association between high levels of education and success as company

Table 9.1
Number of Persons per 10,000 Population in Selected High-Level Occupations

Year	Teachers	Scientists and Engineers	Physicians and Dentists	Nurses	Licensed Pharmacists
1880	5.5	0.0	9.6	....	....
1885	8.3	0.1	10.6	....	....
1890	7.1	0.3	10.1	....	0.7
1895	14.4	0.8	9.5	....	0.7
1900	17.5	1.5	11.2	....	0.8
1905	21.2	1.7	7.8	....	0.7
1910	25.8	2.0	8.0	2.0	1.0
1915	28.8	2.6	8.9	3.6	1.1
1920	31.2	4.1	9.3	6.3	1.3
1925	35.4	5.9	9.6	2.6	3.3
1930	38.5	8.4	10.8	11.9	3.0
1935	38.6	10.7	11.3	15.7	3.6
1940	39.6	14.2	12.4	19.2	4.4
1945	40.8	27.6	2.5	4.4	1.0
1950	71.8	30.9	12.4	15.6	5.5
1955	72.6	34.9	14.1	14.4	5.9
1960	74.5	42.3	14.6	19.9	6.5
1965	79.0	56.6	14.8	25.0	7.0
1970	76.9	80.1	15.2	26.5	7.7
1975	87.6	113.3	17.6	35.5	9.4
1980	100.3	....	21.0	47.6	11.6
1984	....	....	20.4	49.6	10.8

Sources: Solomon B. Levine and Kawada Hisashi, Human Resources in Japanese Industrial Development (Princeton, N.J.: Princeton University Press, 1980), p. 70; Japan Statistical Yearbook, 1987, p. 638.

officers raises several significant issues: the roles of intelligence, motivation, signals, and credentialism. Analysis done in the early 1960s of the contribution of education to human capital involved calculations of discounted additional earnings received by individuals with college educations relative to those who had only a high school education. It was soon evident that many other things in addition to four years of education separated college and high school educated members of the labor force. Was education merely associated with the measured differences in income? If not, to what extent had four years of formal education contributed to the differences?

The average college educated individual had a higher level of conventionally measured intelligence than the average high school educated individual. Perhaps it was the level of intelligence rather than the level of education that had led to the large increases in income. Completion of four years of college education demonstrated a degree of motivation that the high school graduate might or might not possess. The importance which major Japanese firms place on attracting employees from the "right" colleges is in large part a reflection of the presumed intelligence and motivation of those graduates. Esaka Akira noted that, in the mid-1980s among presidents of corporations listed on the Tokyo Stock Exchange, 27 percent of the department and section chief were graduates of only four top public and private universities. Among presidents, one institution, Tokyo University, stood out with twice as many graduates as each of its two close rivals, Kyoto University and Keio University.[9] Firms probably were more interested in the fact that these individuals had graduated from those specific universities than what these graduates may have learned in Tokyo University or Keio University that was not learned by those who graduated from lesser universities. It is believed that the Japanese educational system with its many examinations assures that the most able students attend the first ranked universities. Tokyo and Keio Universities with their long histories and many distinguished graduates are perceived to be these top ranked universities for business. The student who wishes to be a government cabinet minister, however, should attend only Tokyo University. A belief that the value of a college education lies less in what the graduate may have learned and more in what such an education promises to the prospective employer in terms of the potential employee's level of intelligence and motivation is the key point in the argument that what education provides is essentially a signal to the prospective employer. Professor Yoshino and Lifson in their study of trading companies have written that core staff employees are recruited by using the very best colleges as screening devices.[10] As Ronald Dore recently wrote, "Academic achievement is seen as a good predictor of the capacity to develop occupational competence through on the job learning."[11] Initially a college education assures the employer of well above average levels of intelligence and motivation. Subsequent wage differentials for these college graduates relative to high school graduates within a single firm reflect the contribution of intelligence and motivation. This view is a particularly attractive argument for Japan where firms place such an emphasis upon the generally trained worker as opposed to one with specific job skills. Unfortunately there is no simple way to separate the contributions to growth of education as knowledge and as a signal to allocate the best employees to the most demanding tasks.

Credentialism argues that, when the supply of labor with a given level of education rises, job requirements will also rise. This need not necessarily reflect that the jobs now require a greater level of specific knowledge. Rather it reflects the fact that there are a limited number of "good" jobs in any economy and that levels of education are an excellent rationing device. Thus higher income for the more educated worker reflects the opportunities given to those with such an education rather than the direct contribution of education to economic success.

GROWTH IN EDUCATION AND IN THE ECONOMY

At the time of the Meiji Restoration (1868) Japan had, for a country of her standard of living, a well-developed educational sector but one which was quite diverse in its nature and diverse in the opportunity for a child to participate in it. It was a country which, in the words of Bertrand Russell, was "economically but not culturally backward."[12] There were 50 prefectural schools, some 744 local schools, and 6,691 *terakoya* (temple) schools. The *terakoya* once had a religious connection but by the mid-nineteenth century this was no longer true.[13] For the most part much of this education was unsystematic, and initiatives rested with the consumers rather than the producers of education. There was wide divergence in the extent of education by region and by social class that was available to the average male. The oldest and most comprehensive of the local schools was in Kyoto and was in operation by 1869. With many schools being dependent upon one or a few key individuals rather than on well-developed and rooted institutions there also was discontinuity as schools came into existence for a while and then closed or moved. Still, the system provided facilities and personnel for the Meiji period, and Western learning had been added to the classical curriculum.[14]

In the early Meiji period there was a strong interest and concern with education. Mori Arinori in 1872 corresponded with prominent Americans asking them about the effect of education on material prosperity, commerce, manufacturing, and so on. The replies suggested that education would awaken the farmers to new possibilities, tie Japan into the world economy, and lay the basis for prosperity and prestige. Surely this was an accurate prediction.[15] Initially the new government's concern was largely with the provision of university education, a recognition by the government of the importance of highly skilled and educated workers.[16] In 1872 the Fundamental Code of Education [*Gakusei*] was promulgated, and the basic education law was passed in 1879. Under these regulations, as Richard Rubinger has pointed out, there were three fundamental shifts from Tokugawa patterns. One change was from widespread geographical variation in the provision and the quality of education toward national standardization. There was movement from schools with strong class distinctions to those which sponsored mobility based upon talent and ability. And, finally, there was movement from a loose system based largely on private initiative to a compulsory system with clear goals and structure. As an example, lists of textbooks from which schools could choose their books were issued in 1881, and twenty-two years later identical texts in every school were required.[17] This high degree of structure is not always seen as being positive. This can be seen in the Japanese

Table 9.2
Number of Students (1,000)

1885	Primary	Secondary	Post-Secondary
1883	3,238	16	15
1893	3,338	25	21
1903	5,084	216	53
1913	7,096	681	84
1923	9,137	1,691	145
1933	11,035	2,287	218
1943	12,848	5,222	398
1953	11,225	7,715	536
1960	12,591	9,126	712
1970	9,493	8,948	1,714
1980	11,287	9,716	2,253
1985	11,095	11,168	2,268
1986	10,665	11,365	2,325

Sources: Ministry of Education Sources as quoted in Education in 1968-70, Part II on "Historical Statistics," pp. 102-107.

1980 Data from Mombusho, 1981, pp. 3, 15, 18 as quoted in Estelle Janes and Gail Benjamin, Institution for Social and Policy Studies, Yale, Working Paper 2081, May 1984, and for 1985 and 1986; Japan Statistical Yearbook, 1987, pp. 649, 664.

public's enthusiastic response to a description of Tomoe Gakue, Kobayashi Sosaku's school which emphasized independent study. The school was described in a book by Kuroyanagi Tetsuko, which sold 4.5 million copies the first year.[18] The move toward compulsory education was slow. There was opposition to the public schools, and this opposition by rural households was linked with elements of opposition to military conscription and to the solar calendar. The culmination of this opposition came in 1877 with the Saigo Revolt.[19] The proportion of eligible students enrolled in elementary education increased slowly. This may be seen in the modest number of students shown in Table 9.2. The enrollment ratio in Tokyo was 57.8 percent in 1874. In the next twenty years it only increased to 62.1 percent. More impressive gains were found in areas with sparse education under the Tokugawa. For example, the enrollment ratio in Kagoshima rose from 7 percent to 52 percent over these same years.[20] Enrollment ratios for the three levels of education for the century from 1885 to 1985 are shown in Table 9.3. Too much should not be made of enrollment ratios in the early years, for classroom attendance was often much lower than the enrollment.[21]

Table 9.3
Enrollment Ratios

Year	1st Level[a]	2nd Level[b]	3rd Level[c]
1885	39.2	0.2	0.4
1890	35.2	0.3	0.5
1895	41.6	2.8	0.4
1898	45.6	3.6	0.5
1903	53.1	8.1	0.8
1908	50.5	27.7	1.2
1913	56.5	36.4	1.3
1920	60.2	48.9	1.8
1925	59.3	57.9	2.7
1930	61.1	73.0	3.3
1935	60.9	74.5	3.1
1940	60.2	90.0	4.0
1945	61.6	93.1	7.1
1947	58.7	87.9	6.4
1950	61.5	90.3	5.2
1955	61.2	109.9	7.3
1960	62.3	111.5	8.5
1965	57.4	114.6	12.0
1970	59.5	114.1	15.5
1975	60.2	130.3	23.0
1980	62.2	117.5	28.7
1985	59.7	126.5	27.7

[a]Percentage of age group 5-14 inclusive.
[b]Percentage of age group 15-19 inclusive.
[c]Percentage of age group 20-24 inclusive.

Sources: Solomon B. Levine and Kawada Hisashi, Human Resources in Japanese Industrial Development (Princeton, N.J.: Princeton University Press, 1980), p. 64, and Japan Statistical Yearbook, 1987, pp. 38, 649, 664.

One factor in the slow expansion of education was the continued need for families to pay school fees. Tuition could be as high as 50 sen per month when the annual income of an employed worker might average 21 yen.[22] Tuition requirements for elementary schools were not abolished until 1900. Five years later, in 1905, almost all Japanese children received a primary education. In that same year, however, less than 5 percent of eligible students attended secondary school and less than 1 percent went beyond high school. Just before Japan turned seriously toward war, in 1935, about 40 percent of students received a secondary education and 3 percent a higher education. By 1955 when the Japanese per capita real income had reached prewar levels (1934–1936), almost 80 percent of the eligible children attended secondary schools and 8.8 percent went on to college.[23]

In the immediate postwar years, the Occupation, the Japanese people, and the Japanese government believed that education was the essential element. For the Occupation, education was to be the backbone of its social reforms. The average citizen regarded schools as the only secure source for his or her child's future. For Japanese government officials there were three motivations: They had a concern for the cognitive development of young people, an interest in the role of education in progress and modernization, and a belief that industry and commerce would depend upon patterns of loyalty and motivation for excellence which they associated with the outcomes of education.[24]

A month after the end of the Occupation, the Industrial Promotion Law was passed and companies urged schools to provide more scientific and mathematical education.[25] During the following years of rapid economic growth following reconstruction, the proportion of the relevant population in secondary schools moved above 90 percent. In 1986, 94.2 percent of all middle school graduates went on to high school. Of high school graduates, 26.4 percent of the males and 34.1 percent of the females went on to higher education. In the case of women, the majority attended junior colleges rather than four-year colleges and universities. In 1975 the rates for men and women had been essentially equal, but the male proportion declined in subsequent years.[26] This has reflected relatively decreased job opportunities during these years of slower growth, a factor discussed in the section on rates of return to a college education.

Table 9.4 shows the Japanese levels of educational attainment, per capita national income, and public expenditures as a proportion of national income for selected years since the Meiji era compared to similar measures developed for seventy-five countries in the middle 1950s.[27]

By looking at Table 9.4 it can be seen that in 1890 Japan's educational levels and national income per capita were equivalent to similarly underdeveloped countries in the 1950s. Only in the proportion of public expenditures did Japan appear more similar to more developed countries. In the twentieth century Japan's educational levels outpaced her economic growth. Japan more than achieved the educational level of partially developed countries by 1908 but did not achieve the equivalent level of economic output until just after the great Kanto earthquake

Table 9.4
International Human Resource Development

Country Type [1950s]	Median Composite Educational Attainment	Per Capita Income 1960 Dollars	Public Expenditures on Education as Percent of National Income
Underdeveloped	3.0	$71	3.2
Partially developed	23.0	173	2.0
Semi advanced	48.0	357	3.1
Advanced	105.0	1,000	4.0
Japan			
1890	2.7	70	1.3
1908	29.8	93	2.5
1925	60.8	181	3.4
1935	74.1	225	3.3
1955	140.8	319	4.7
1970	184.2	1,154	4.9
1985	254.4	2,620	5.8

Sources: Frederick H. Harbison and Charles A. Myers, Education Manpower and Economic Growth (New York: McGraw-Hill, 1964), pp. 45-48; Solomon B. Levine and Kawada Hisashi, Human Resources in Japanese Industrial Development (Princeton, N.J.: Princeton University Press, 1980), p. 82; Japan Statistical Yearbook, 1987, pp. 553-666.

of 1923. Compared to semiadvanced countries in the 1950s (Chile, Portugal), Japan had reached her median educational level in 1920 but did not achieve a comparable level of economic output until 1956. Japan had the educational level of an advanced country in 1945, but it was almost fifteen years after she had recovered from World War II before her per capita national income reached the median of the advanced countries.

A comparison of these ratios suggests that Japanese educational levels have run consistently ahead of her economic output. There had been the base for growth, but it could be argued that the direct relationship between changes in the level of education and the rate of economic growth was lacking. Education would seem to have facilitated growth by providing a pool from which employers could draw rather than directly leading to growth. This is quite consistent with Alfred Marshall's views which were cited earlier.

Alternatively one could argue that school enrollment rations measure entrants to the labor force and that there should be some respectable number of years' lag between the addition of more highly educated workers and the achievement of higher levels of gross national product. On this basis, the long reported lags reported for Japan would be consistent with expectations.

A more positive assessment has been provided by Ito Ryoji, who has shown a close correspondence between the rates of growth in the number of students with a secondary education and the index of manufacturing output for the years from 1890 to 1920.[28] In addition Professor Gary Saxonhouse has shown that increased primary education for workers in the cotton spinning industry directly increased productivity. He suggested, "Within the primary school. . . . [t]he demands of constant attention and regular attendance, the necessity of confronting new situations and skills and mastering them . . . [were] similar to the Japanese mill compound."[29] Arno Pearse in his 1929 report on the Japanese and Chinese cotton textile industries stated, "One notices everywhere the result of a good general education . . . every mill girl reads and writes and possesses a general education on a par with that of European Countries. . . ."[30] This argument has a modern counterpart as well. Benjamin Duke has recently argued that Japanese schools play a primary role in instilling a sense of perseverance or work ethic in Japanese children and young people.[31]

The role of increases in factors of production in addition to additional units of physical capital and hours of labor in increased economic output has long been studied, but questions still remain. A major researcher in this area Edward Denison has studied the contribution of additional education to increased output. For ten advanced countries he estimated that between 1950 and 1962 about 7 percent of their growth was related to additional education. For the United States between 1948 and 1969 he estimated 10.4 percent. For Japan between 1953 and 1971, when her growth was double that of all of the other nine advanced nations put together, the contribution of education was only 3.9 percent, about 60 percent of the average for the other nine and less than 40 percent of the United States' experience.[32] The seemingly small contribution of education in Japan's early postwar growth has been perceived as perplexing. Watanabe Tsunehiko suggested that it might reflect the already high level of education in Japan. In 1950 the average years of schooling for males exceeded that of eight of the European countries studied by Denison and was only slightly lower than that in the United States,[33] a point noted by Denison and Chung.[34] Edward Lincoln suggested that the surplus of education relative to the economic needs in the 1950s masked the contribution,[35] a statement which echoed Ohkawa Kazushi and Henry Rosovsky's earlier comment that a fuller utilization of highly qualified labor was an important consideration.[36]

INTERRELATIONSHIPS: EDUCATION AND THE ECONOMY

A country's educational system and its labor economy are closely linked. Decisions made in one interact and dictate decisions made for the other sector.

This was clearly the case in Japan. An educational emphasis in the early Meiji period upon a generally literate population with a small number of highly educated workers left the labor market and individual firms within that market to devise a system that would provide the required skilled trades and a middle-management-level education. The development of extensive training within industry led to a desire by employers to attract only the best employees and that "best" came to be defined in large part as graduation from the "right" school or college. This tended to reinforce the equity standard that lay behind the early insistence upon general literacy even when the direct economic returns from that literacy were probably limited. These interactions between the educational system and the labor economy are examined in three subsections: vocational education, training within firms, and the rates of return to education.

Vocational Education

During the Meiji period initial efforts toward vocational education were directed toward the establishment of higher technical schools to turn out the engineers required by expanding industries. Today's Tokyo Institute of Technology began in 1881 as the Tokyo Worker Training School. At that time it was associated with the Technical Normal School which provided a number of early vocational school principals. In 1899 the Vocational Education Act, modeled deliberately upon German practices, was passed. Lower vocational schools in large numbers were established after 1894. In 1903 there were two types of vocational schools in addition to vocational continuation schools and apprentice schools. These apprentice schools provided an excellent education, but it was as independent businessmen—the career for more than half of the graduates— rather than as technical employees that the apprentice schools' graduates played a major role in the economy. As a supplier of skilled workmen to the new factories, these schools played less of a role.[37] Generally speaking, attempts to provide formal public education for craftsmen before 1940 were not successful.

The Vocational Training Law, an attempt to provide Japan with a unified vocational education system, was passed in 1958. At the prefectural level general vocational training centers were established; the Labor Welfare Corporation was established to provide higher level training in comprehensive vocational centers. After 1945 school vocational education became a program after the ninth year of required schooling. It was not set up to be strictly terminal but was also intended to prepare students for higher education. In addition, many special schools outside the formal public system provided specific vocational education. The largest proportion of students in such schools in 1985 were students in paramedical occupations including nursing.[38] During the rapid growth of the 1960s the comprehensive vocational centers were unable to keep pace with the rapid changes, and once again firms themselves took up the slack. I clearly remember visiting on the same day in 1973 a public vocational school and, within sight of the school, the vocational school of a Nissan automobile plant.

The Nissan plant was clean, bright, and well stocked with the most modern machines; the public school had none of these attributes. As a consequence most graduates of the public center went to work for small businesses.

The oil shock in 1973-1974 and the slowdown in the rate of economic growth that dates from that time and has continued into the 1980s has opened new challenges for the vocational education system. Amendments to the basic law in 1978 formally recognized the historical pattern of training within enterprises by stressing the primary responsibility which employers had for the adequate training of their employees. It reserved to the government the responsibility of assisting employers and taking care of workers with special situations.

In a society like Japan's where the limited options for power and future economic rewards are largely found within the government and large enterprises, and where within these institutions opportunity rests heavily upon the university from which an employee graduated, it is not surprising that vocationally oriented high schools, even those which send a reasonable proportion of graduates on to higher education, will be seen as less than ideal by parents. This was clearly shown in Thomas Rohlen's study of high schools when he discussed the commercial high school and the night vocational high school in his small sample. These schools attracted students from the lower social classes. The commercial high school's students came from families in which only 6 percent of the fathers were university educated. At the night vocational school only 2 percent fit this category. At the most academic high school in the sample the proportion was 60 percent. At the commercial high school about 30 percent and at the night school about 34 percent of the students' mothers were employed. Only 15 percent of mothers of students in the best academic high school were employed. Between 13 and 15 percent of the vocational students had less than two parents present in their home, but only 1 percent of the students at the best academic high school had only a single parent.[39]

Training within Firms

It was within the factories themselves, especially among the largest employers, that training was provided. As early as 1899 the Mitsubishi Nagasaki Shipyard had established a school for its own workers; the National Police had established an officers' academy even earlier, in 1885.[40] Other firms also had in-house schools, while some like Shibaura, in addition to their own training, sent workers to outside schools. Shibaura sent 950 workers to a one-year program at the Tokyo Workers' School between 1905 and 1938. Some 700 workers graduated, but in the early years many of the workers upon graduation went to work for other companies or for themselves. Companies increased their training efforts in the 1920s though interfirm mobility of the trained workers remained high.[41] There was considerable variation in the degree of within-firm training. This reflected different conditions within an industry, the level and pace of technological change, and the general level of education in the society. In the area of finance, the rising level of general education within the society meant that the major banks could, and did, give up their formal programs. In general there was less within-enterprise training in textiles, mining, and banking compared to telecommunications, steel, and shipbuilding; some of the most systematic training was to be found in the more technologically advanced firms in heavy machinery, electrical equipment, and chemicals.[42]

According to the 1984 Ministry of Labor's survey on employment management, 82.2 percent of all firms provided their employees with some training, mostly within the firm.[43] The proportion of firms which provided training varied from 100 percent for firms employing 5,000 or more to 78.4 percent for firms employing from 30 to 99 employees. The most important reasons given for training were to improve current operations and to facilitate the introduction of new products or systems of production. Not surprisingly a significant proportion of training was provided to new employees, both those hired upon graduation from school and those employed in mid-career. The one group of employees for whom little training was provided was clerical employees.[44]

On-the-job training plays a major role in skill acquisition and development, especially in large firms. This means, according to Professor Koike Kazuo, that a sequence of job progression is established in each shop. In a steel mill, after ten years of training, job progression, and job rotation, an employee would have experience in more than thirty positions including maintenance positions and working with each of the major blast furnaces within the mill.[45] Professor Koshiro Kazutoshi also has pointed out that continuing education and training are an integral part of the Japanese employment system. In 1977, 574 different courses were offered in a single steel company.[46] This technological background for blue-collar workers and the wide development of different skills have enabled extensive productivity improvements, and they have made it easier for firms to introduce technological changes.

There are significant differences between the practices in small and large firms. The larger the firm, the greater the training, as cited above. This means that the larger firms offer workers a wider range of skills and the opportunity to acquire them over a longer time period.[47] This would explain both the difference in wages by size of firm and also the fact that the divergence increases as the workers become older. In 1981, male high school graduates aged from 25 to 29 with continuous employment in firms of from 10 to 99 employees earned, in wages plus bonus payments, 92 percent as much as did similar male workers in firms of 1,000 and more workers. At the ages of from 35 to 39 the ratio was less, 81 percent, and at the ages of from 50 to 54 it was only 69 percent.[48]

Returns to Education

If education is useful to employers, either directly or as a screening device, it would be expected that individuals investing in additional education for themselves would earn an economic return based on the total of direct expenses plus foregone earnings which would equal that obtained had the individual made an investment in regular financial instruments. This premise was the foundation for much of the early human capital literature and remains an article of faith to those who still champion the cause of human capital. For a society there may be returns from the additional education of individuals which do not rebound to the individual. In such cases the public return from education will exceed the private. In such a situation the state would have a strong incentive to subsidize the education of some or all of its citizens. Typically the estimation for many of the public externalities will be difficult or impossible to make. Consequently, with the public subsidies included as costs, but many of the public benefits not included, the usual empirical estimates of social returns lie below private returns.

Rates of return calculations for the period from 1966 to 1980 were done by the Ministry of Labor and have been reported by Taira Koji and Solomon Levine.[49] For male university graduates employed by large firms (1,000 or more employees) in manufacturing, the rate of return on costs associated with a university education was 9.0 percent in 1966. This was well above the rate of 5.7 percent on one-year bank time deposits. For those employed by smaller firms (from ten to ninety-nine employees), the rate was only 4.5 percent. This occurred during the heart of the era of rapid growth and it should not be surprising that a university education was such a bargain. Since 1966 the rates of return have moved downward and closer together. In 1980 these rates were 5.0 percent and 3.9 percent. Both were below the one-year time deposit rate. The decline in private rates of return since 1966 is part of a longer trend. In 1954, at the beginning of the postwar growth phase in the Japanese economy, the private rate of return before taxes was 13.4 percent with an after tax rate of 9.0 percent.[50] Other scholars report similar downward movements. One recent study calculated internal rates of return which declined from 11.0 percent in 1959 to 6.5 percent in 1980.[51]

The downward shift and the relatively low absolute value of the rates of return for a college education are inconsistent with the experience of many other countries. In Great Britain there was little change in the rate of return for a college education between 1971 and 1978. In the United States the rate was 15.4 percent in 1969. It then fell in the 1970s, to about 10 percent, but it appears to have risen in recent years. For a sample of nine advanced industrial countries, the private rate of return in the late 1970s and early 1980s ranged from a high of 23.0 percent for Great Britain in 1978 to a low of 4.2 percent for Austria in 1981. The median rate was 10.3 percent.[52]

Other investigators have reported more optimistic results for Japan. For 1978 Yano Masakazu found that national university graduates enjoyed a 9 percent return and private school graduates a 7.0 to 7.5 percent return depending upon the students' area of study. The most favored were those who were graduates of the old imperial universities, for they received 9.5 percent. Those who graduated from the new private universities were worst off, achieving only a 6.9 percent return.[53] These differences reflect the lower tuition rates at the national universities and the more attractive opportunities that faced their graduates upon graduation. For example, a little more than one-third of the national university graduates were employed in major companies, those with 5,000 and more employees. For old imperial university graduates, the ratio was almost 60 percent. About 10 percent of all national and 4.5 percent of old imperial university graduates were employed in firms of less than 500 employees. For private universities, the same ratios were 11.0 percent of graduates going to large firms and almost half, 47.7 percent, to the smaller firms. Given the differentials in compensation, wages, bonuses, and benefits between the various sizes of firm, it is not surprising that the rates of return favor the national university graduates.

Evaluated strictly within a private economic context, an individual would have been better off to go to work after high school and bank his college expenses. Since the greatest portion of the downward shift in rates of return occurred while rapid growth continued, it suggests that the need for college-trained manpower did not expand as rapidly as did the supply of new graduates. This meant that there were fewer opportunities for white-collar jobs and for significant career advancement following employment. This can be seen in the movement of compensation, wages plus bonuses for college-educated workers compared to high-school-educated workers. In 1965 white-collar college-educated males ages 25 to 29 earned 14 percent more than blue-collar high school graduates of the same age. At ages 40 to 49 the differential was 110 percent. By 1980 these two percentages had declined to 4 percent and 63 percent.[54] As Amano Ikuo noted, "Already there is a growing number of very well-educated college graduates who will not receive promotion to managerial positions or can not even find white collar jobs."[55] For example, in 1979, a university graduate had a probability of being a department manager at between the age of 40 and 59 that was four times that for a high school graduate in the same age range. To be a section chief between the age of 30 and 39 in 1979, however, the college-educated probability was just greater than twice that of the high-school-educated graduate.[56]

The lessened opportunities would, if followed, lead to a lower proportion of Japanese males attending college, exactly what has occurred, with the proportion of male high school graduates going on to college declining from 33.8 percent in 1975 to 26.4 percent in 1986.[57] These advancement ratios vary by region: Tokyo's 61.5 percent for 1975 fell to 53.0 percent in 1979; in the lowest ranked prefectures, there was a modest increase from 20 percent in 1975 to 22 percent in 1979.[58] Such decisions would particularly affect prospective graduates of the high cost but low-valued private colleges rather than graduates of first rank private universities such as Keio and Wasada Universities or the much cheaper public universities.

Nonetheless, education is both a productive investment and a consumption good. With rising incomes, families and individuals can choose to buy more of the consumption value of higher education. Real disposable family income more than doubled from 1959 to 1980 and increased another 15 percent in 1985. The male college application rate rose directly with disposable income until 1966 and again moved upward with disposable income from 1970 to 1975.[59] From 1975 to 1985 the proportion of male high school graduates going on to college fell by 6.8 percentage points and has declined slightly in 1986 and 1987.[60] A high income elasticity of demand for higher education would seem to be the primary explanation for the continued increase in the proportion of Japanese women who are going on to higher education, more often junior colleges, for clearly the economic opportunities in the labor market would not justify the expense of a four-year school. However, opportunities in the marriage market may justify the expenditures.

SUMMARY AND CONCLUSION

The key to understanding the Japanese experience is to understand two dominant themes. One is the degree to which the education system during the Meiji years and in the immediate postwar years has been explicitly designed to encourage and promote the economic growth of Japan. A second is the close interplay between the nature of the educational system and the operation of the labor market.

In the early period there was an emphasis upon the widespread provision of general education, but a significant portion of the cost was paid by parents, in addition to their taxes. At the same time, there was a recognition that a more limited number of highly trained and educated workers would be needed by Japanese industry and government. By stressing academic merit as the key to obtaining the high level of education, the Japanese were able to provide channels of upward mobility on an equitable basis and to assure themselves that the very best talents would be available.

What was left out was the middle. Firms which needed trained blue-collar workers and middle managers had to turn inward upon their own resources through the provision of internal training. In most democratic countries, the problem with extensive company-sponsored training is that the costs are incurred at the time of the training while the benefits of the training accrue to the firm over a long period of years. During these years the employee may be bid away by other firms or leave for other reasons. Success for such an approach requires a system of forgiven loans or aspects of an employment system which encourages long tenure for the trained worker. It is just such a system which slowly, and for many other reasons besides the dependency upon on-the-job training, evolved in Japan between the two wars. Wartime policies, postwar Occupation policies, the rise of unions, and calculated management decisions greatly strengthened the training-within-industry approach to the provision of many industrial skills.

No society can create educational resources at exactly the rate needed by the economic growth of the country. In Japan there has generally been overproduction of formal education. This was noted by Harry Oshima for the Meiji period and by Solomon Levine and Kawada Hisashi for the 1920s. Similarly the decline in the rates of return to male college educations especially in the last ten years would appear to reflect a similar surplus in our own era.

An excess supply, defined by the needs of the economy, of education in Japan over most of the last century has meant a number of things. First, it meant that Japan always had an adequate supply of trained manpower so that she was able to exploit whatever economic opportunities presented themselves. Second, it provided the basis for an equitable advancement opportunity for all citizens, or at least for male citizens. Third, the universal nature of education provided Japan with an institution which could transmit traditional values to each new generation. Finally, it has meant that no simple measurement of economic growth and educational levels or changes could capture the very real contributions which educational excellence in Japan has made to her economic growth over the past one hundred years.

NOTES

1. Benjamin Duke, *Lessons for Industrial America: The Japanese School* (New York: Praeger, 1986), p. 20.
2. Alfred Marshall, *Principls of Economics* (New York: Harper, 1952), pp. 211, 216, 564.
3. Mark Blaug, "Human Capital Theory: A Slightly Jaundiced View," *Journal of Economic Literature* 14 (September 1976), p. 850.
4. Robert B. Haveman and Barbara L. Wolfe, "Education, Productivity and Well-Being," in Edwin Dean, ed., *Education and Economic Productivity* (Cambridge, Eng.: Cambridge University Press, 1984), p. 37.
5. Solomon B. Levine and Kawada Hisashi, *Human Resources in Japanese Industrial Development* (Princeton, N.J.: Princeton University Press, 1980), p. 49.
6. Mannari Hiroshi, *Bijinesu-erito* [The Business Elite] (Tokyo: Tokyo University Press, 1965), p. 124.
7. William K. Cummings, *Education and Equality in Japan* (Princeton, N.J.: Princeton University Press, 1980), p. 27.
8. *Japan Statistical Yearbook, 1987* (Tokyo, 1987), p. 27.
9. *Japanese Education Today* (Washington, D.C.: U.S. Department of Education, 1987), p. 56.
10. Michael Y. Yoshino and Thomas B. Lifson, *The Invisible Link* (Cambridge, Mass.: MIT Press, 1986), p. 139.
11. Ronald P. Dore, *Taking Japan Seriously* (Stanford, Calif.: Stanford University Press, 1987), p. 69.
12. Herbert Passin, *Society and Education in Japan* (New York: Teachers College Press, Columbia University, 1965), p. 11.
13. Ibid., pp. 11–21.
14. Richard Rubinger, "Education from One Room to One System," in Marius B. Jansen and Gilbert Rozman, eds., *Japan in Transition: From Tokugawa to Meiji* (Princeton, N.J.: Princeton University Press, 1986), pp. 200–218.
15. Passin, *Society and Education in Japan*, pp. 3–5.

16. Ronald P. Dore, *The Diploma Disease* (Berkeley: University of California, 1976), p. 36.
17. Rubinger, "Education from One Room to One System," p. 195.
18. Kuroyanagi Tetsuko, *Totto-chan: The Little Girl by the Window* (Tokyo: Kodanshu, 1982).
19. Passin, *Society and Education in Japan*, p. 80.
20. Rubinger, "Education from One Room to One System," p. 219.
21. Taira Koji, "Education and Literacy in Meiji Japan: An Interpretation," *Explorations in Economic History* 8 (Summer 1971), p. 374.
22. Harry T. Oshima, "Meiji Fiscal Policy and Agricultural Progress," in William W. Lockwood, ed., *The State and Economic Enterprise in Japan* (Princeton, N.J.: Princeton University Press, 1965), p. 378. Also note that the yen, at that time, was worth about 50 cents and monthly wages for farm laborers ranged from $12 to $14 a month, plus board. Sources for these data are Lockwood, *The State and Economic Enterprise in Japan*, p. 313; and Stanley Lebergott, "Wage Trends, 1800–1900," in National Bureau of Economic Research, *Trends in the American Economy in the Nineteenth Century*, volume 24 in *Studies in Income and Wealth* (Princeton, N.J. 1966), p. 462.
23. Ministry of Education, *Japan's Growth and Education* (Tokyo: Minister of Education, 1963), p. 161.
24. Merry White, *The Japanese Educational Challenge* (New York: Macmillan, 1987), pp. 64–65.
25. "Schooling in Japan," *Education Week*, February 20, 1985, p. 18.
26. *Japan Statistical Yearbook, 1987*.
27. Frederick Harbison and Charles A. Meyers, *Educational Manpower and Economic Growth* (New York: McGraw-Hill, 1964), pp. 45–48.
28. Ito Ryoji, "Education as a Basic Factor in Japan's Economic Growth," *The Developing Economies* 1 (January-June 1963), p. 39.
29. Gary Saxenhouse, "Productivity Change and Labor Absorption in Japanese Cotton Spinning, 1891–1935,"*Quarterly Journal of Economics* (May 1977), p. 217.
30. Otsuka Keijiro, Gustav Ranis, and Gary Saxenhouse, *Comparative Technology Choice in Development* (New York, 1988), p. 30.
31. Duke, *Lessons for Industrial America*, pp. 126, 147.
32. Edward F. Denison and William K. Chung, *How Japan's Economy Grew So Fast* (Washington, D.C., 1976), pp. 42–43.
33. Watanabe Tsunehiko, "Improvement of Labor Quality and Economic Growth: Postwar Japan's Experience," *Economic Development and Cultural Change* 21 (October 1972), p. 37.
34. Denison and Chung, *How Japan's Economy Grew So Fast*, p. 59.
35. Edward J. Lincoln, *Japan: Facing Economic Maturity* (Washington, D.C., 1988), p. 18.
36. Ohkawa Kazushi and Henry Rosovsky, *Japanese Economic Growth* (Stanford, Calif. 1973), p. 210.
37. Toyoda Toshio, "From Apprentice to Worker," *Enterpreneurship* (April 1982), p. 16.
38. Ishikawa Toshio, *Vocational Training* (Tokyo: Tokyo University Press, 1987), p. 9.
39. Thomas P. Rohlen, *Japan's High Schools* (Berkeley: University of California Press, 1983), p. 130.

40. Eleanor D. Westney, *Imitation and Innovation* (Cambridge, Mass.: Harvard University Press, 1987), p. 76.
41. Andrew Gordon, *The Evolution of Labor Relations in Japan, 1853–1955* (Cambridge, Mass.: Harvard University Press, 1985), pp. 74, 132.
42. Levine and Kawada, *Human Resources in Japanese Industrial Development*, pp. 206, 220, 255, 258.
43. Ishikawa, *Vocational Training*, p. 20.
44. Ibid., pp. 20–23.
45. Koike Kazuo, "Internal Labor Markets: Workers in Large Firms," in Shirai Taishiro, ed., *Contemporary Japanese Labor Markets* (Madison, Wisc.: University of Wisconsin Press, 1983), pp. 42–44.
46. Koshiro Kazutoshi, "The Quality of Working Life in Japanese Factories," in Shirai Taishiro, ed., *Contemporary Japanese Labor Markets*, pp. 75–76.
47. Koike Kazuo, "Workers in Small Firms and Women in Industry," in Shirai Taishiro, ed., *Contemporary Japanese Labor Markets*, pp. 100–102.
48. Robert Evans, Jr., "Pay Differentials: The Case of Japan," *Monthly Labor Review* 107 (October 1984), p. 25.
49. Taira Koji and Solomon B. Levine, "Education and Labor Force Skills in Postwar Japan" (Paper prepared for U.S. Study of Education in Japan Project, 1985), p. 35.
50. Umetani Shunichiro, *Vocational Training in Japan* (Hamburg: Mitteilungen des Instituts für Asienkunde. 1980), p. 31.
51. Nakata Yoshi-fumi and Carl Mosk, "The Demand for College Education in Postwar Japan," *Journal of Human Resources* 22 (Summer 1987), p. 382
52. George Psacharopoulous, "Returns to Education: A Further International Update and Implications," *Journal of Human Resources* 20 (Fall 1985), pp. 599–600.
53. Yano Masakazu, "Rates of Return from Education and Resource Allocation," in Ichikawa Shogo, *Allocation of Educational Resources in Japan* (Tokyo: National Institute for Educational Research, 1978), p. 141, as cited in Estelle James and Gail Benjamin, "Public vs Private Education: The Japanese Experiment" (Program on Non-Profit Organization, working paper 81, May 1984).
54. Robert Evans, Jr., "Lifetime Earnings in Japan," *Monthly Labor Review* 107 (April 1984), p. 35.
55. Amano Ikuo, "The Dilemma of Japanese Education Today," *The Japan Foundation Newsletter* 13 (March 1986), p. 8.
56. Economic Planning Agency, *Annual Report on National Life* (Tokyo, 1981), p. 160.
57. Japan Institute of Labor, *Employment and Employment Policy* (Tokyo, 1988), p. 10.
58. Economic Planning Agency, *Annual Report on National Life*, p. 163.
59. Nakata and Mosk, "The Demand for College Education," p. 381.
60. *Japan Statistical Yearbook, 1988* (Tokyo, 1988), p. 664.

10

The Education of Women in Japan

Kumiko Fujimura-Fanselow and Anne E. Imamura

INTRODUCTION

This chapter examines the education of women in Japan. The first section focuses on gender differences in participation at various levels within the educational system. The relationship between women's education and women's roles, both within the family and in other institutions of society, is then examined. What has been the impact of education on women's role in the home, the community, and the work place? At the same time, how are women's choices and decisions regarding education and their ability to utilize their education through involvement in various activities outside the home, including work force participation, affected by the changes occurring in women's familial roles in contemporary Japanese society?

GENDER INEQUALITIES IN EDUCATIONAL ACCESS AND PARTICIPATION

Despite the recent proliferation of English language literature on Japanese education, surprisingly little has been written on issues pertaining to women's education. It is also true that recent discussions of educational reform in Japan have consistently failed to address the issue of women's education. A close examination of the situation reveals that, in spite of the postwar educational reforms that abolished legal barriers to educational access for females at all levels and thereby offered greater opportunities for women to pursue education on an equal basis with males, significant gender differences in patterns of educational participation persist. The level of education attained by women as a whole continues to be lower than that among men; many women continue to pursue their studies in sex-segregated institutions, particularly at the high school level and beyond; and gender differentiation is further evident in terms of the content of study pursued. Fujimura-Fanselow has noted that a variety of contemporary social and cultural variables, as well as factors having to do with the educational system and the labor market, are responsible for existing gender differentials in educational participation and achievement.[1] At the same time, the current situation may be seen as representing a continuation of a pattern of gender inequalities in educational access and participation dating back to prewar Japanese society and the system of education that had its inception in the Meiji period (1868–1912).[2]

WOMEN'S EDUCATION IN PREWAR JAPAN

When the Meiji government began to establish Japan's first modern, comprehensive system of education, in its quest to create a new social order, it recognized the importance of educating women as well as men and made provisions for their education at least at the elementary level. During the course of the Meiji era, however, the goal of education for women was increasingly perceived as less important than educating men, and the structure and content of education came increasingly to reflect this essentially philosophical decision.

At the elementary level there was relative equality in access for males and females. The Fundamental Code of Education, promulgated in 1872 by the newly established Ministry of Education, called for four years of compulsory education for both boys and girls. The content assigned was the same for both sexes: reading, writing, and arithmetic. Initially, attendance rates among females lagged considerably behind that of males (30 versus 63 percent in 1888), as most parents felt that it was both unnecessary and unfeminine for their daughters to receive academic training, rather than training in household skills. Others objected to having their daughters taught in a coeducational setting. As a result of the rapidly industrializing economy's expanding need for female workers following the Sino-Japanese War (1894–1895), female rates of elementary school attendance rose to 90 percent by 1904.[3] In 1907 compulsory education was extended to six years, followed by two years of noncompulsory higher elementary school. By the end of the Meiji era in 1912, compulsory school attendance was nearly universal among both females and males.

Secondary education, however, was gender differentiated in both structure and content. The Fundamental Code of Education had provided for the establishment of secondary or middle schools and universities, and, although no specific mention was made as to whether these schools were meant for just males or for both sexes, the general understanding was that they were exclusively for males. Initially, however, some middle schools did enroll women, but following the Education Act of 1880, which called for the abolishment of coeducation beyond elementary school, women were formally excluded from public middle schools. In 1880, 307 women were enrolled in public middle schools and 2,440 in private ones, but thereafter their numbers dwindled, and by 1884 there were no women enrolled in middle schools.[4]

Secondary as well as higher education for women developed primarily through private, rather than government, efforts. Christian mission schools, such as the Ferris Seminary in Yokohama established in 1870 and Kobe Jogakuin established in 1875 in Kobe, were the first to provide secondary-level education for women (see Robins-Mowry, 1983, for a discussion of the role played by Christians as well as by various Western-rooted organizations in advancing women's education during this period). The government began to establish normal schools for women in 1875, enrolling higher elementary school graduates (eighth grade). The impetus for the establishment of these institutions was the need to recruit more teachers and the hope that more parents would be willing to send their daughters to school if they could be taught by women. There was also a financial consideration, that is, three female teachers could be hired for the price of two male teachers,[5] and by 1877 there were five normal schools.

The years 1879 and 1880 marked a turning away from a Western-influenced, liberal school system to a more conservative one based on Confucianism and emphasizing moral education (especially loyalty to the emperor and nationalism). At the same time the Ministry of Education began to assume greater direction and control over all aspects of education. In terms of the impact of these developments on women's education, greater attention was now paid to it, but education became increasingly gender differentiated in both structure and content. Following the 1880 decision to abolish coeducation at the secondary level, coeducation was further restricted to the first three years of elementary school in 1892. Simultaneously, sewing was made a required part of the curriculum for girls in elementary school.

In its 1882 annual report, the Ministry of Education criticized the education pursued in most of the existing secondary schools for girls:

Girls' high school education should not have the same curriculum as that of the boys. The most important aspect of education for girls is moral education. . . . In addition to teaching the principles of correct behavior, household economy, the nursing of infants, sewing and handicrafts should be part of the curriculum.[6]

This made clear the official view that education beyond the elementary level should be differentiated for males and females and that the purpose of female education should be to impart such knowledge as would be helpful to a woman in her destined role as wife and mother. This was a concept of female education that came to be known as *ryosai kembo no kyoiku*, or education for the training of good wives and wise mothers.

Also in 1882 the government began to provide secondary education for females with the establishment of a girls' high school attached to the Tokyo Women's Normal School. Secondary schools for females, however, only slowly made their appearance in other parts of the country. As late as 1894 there were only eight public girls' high schools throughout Japan with a total enrollment of just 1,500 (in contrast to twenty privately operated girls' high schools enrolling about the same number of students).[7] The same forces that operated to promote female attendance in elementary school following the Sino-Japanese War also created an increased demand for secondary education among females, and the national government began actively to encourage the development of these schools. The 1899 Higher Girls' School Law called on local governments to establish at least one such institution in each prefecture with a four-year course of study, and in 1920 five-year secondary schools for girls opened. In 1910, when the Higher Girls' School Law was revised, a practical course was established to be offered either at the existing girls' high schools or in separate girls' high schools for practical arts. In the 1920s and 1930s both the number of girls' high schools and their enrollment caught up with and surpassed the number of boys' middle schools and their enrollment.

The percentage of female elementary school graduates attending these schools was very small—about 2 percent in 1915, under 5 percent in 1924, and 10 percent in 1935. The young women who attended these schools came mostly from middle- and upper-class city and town families or wealthier farm families, and their formal education usually ended upon graduation.

Given the belief that the purpose of higher education was to provide students with professional training in order to pursue careers, higher education for women was considered to be fundamentally unnecessary. The very fact that the secondary schools for women were designated as "higher schools," whereas the secondary schools for men were called "middle schools," reflected the general view that, in the case of women, a secondary-level education was indeed of a sufficiently high level. As in the case of secondary schools, institutions of higher education for women were initially established by the private sector. The first such institution was the Joshi Eigaku Juku (now called Tsuda College), established in 1900 by Tsuda Umeko, a Christian woman who had studied at Bryn Mawr College in the United States from 1889 to 1892. In the same year a women's medical school, Tokyo Joshi Igakko (today called Tokyo Women's Medical College) was opened in Tokyo, followed by a school of fine arts, Joshi Bijutsu Gakkō (Tokyo Women's College of Fine Arts) and Nihon Joshi Daigakko (now known as Japan Women's University) in 1901. The late 1910s and 1920s witnessed the establishment of numerous private women's colleges, many of them Christian sponsored. By 1937 forty-two private women's colleges offered three-year courses. The majority of these institutions were, however, in Tokyo and a handful of other large cities, notably Kyoto and Osaka; women residing in rural areas had little access to them.

The only provision made by the national government for the postsecondary education of women was in the form of the two national women's higher normal schools, the first of which opened in Tokyo in 1890 (now called Ochanomizu Women's University) and the other which appeared in Nara in 1908 (today called Nara Women's University). The purpose in establishing these schools was to train teachers for girls' high schools and women's normal schools. The first public or prefectural college for women appeared in Fukuoka in 1922; however, only five more such institutions were established in the prewar period. Even though many of the institutions of higher education for women carried the title "university," none was accredited as such. Rather, they stood on a lower level than the universities and had the status of *senmongakkō*, or special schools. As such, they could not award a recognized degree, merely a certificate of achievement. Some of the men's universities, both national and private, opened their campuses to women on a limited basis, but only as auditors. Tohoku Imperial University's faculty of science was the first of the Imperial universities to do so in 1913; however, admission to the most prestigious imperial universities, namely Tokyo and Kyoto Imperial University, was denied to women. It was not until after World War II that university education became available for women on the same basis as men.

On the eve of World War II, about 10 percent of the girls graduating from elementary school went on to girls' high school (Hall 1949: 243). Of those graduating from high school, fewer than one out of ten went on to attend some type of postsecondary institution (Hara 1971: 87, table 3). These women tended to come from rather affluent families.[8] Prevailing social opinion strongly disapproved of women acquiring higher education; a common argument was that academic study would make a young woman *namaiki* (conceited, impertinent, forward) and therefore would make it difficult for her to find a husband; if she married, she would be disliked by her husband for her pride and conceit. Thus, many of those women who pursued higher education did so in the face of opposition from parents and others around them. By the eve of World War II, however, upper-class families had gradually come to look with favor upon higher education as a means of providing their daughters with general cultural enrichment, which would enhance their position when it came to marriage. Higher education that led to a clear occupational objective, such as training for the teaching profession, continued to be frowned on by many. This reflected the general norm that a woman's place was in the home and a disapproval of women going out into the world and working, regardless of the type of occupation. This prejudice against practical or vocational training for women continues to have a strong influence and important implications in terms of occupational participation on the part of women graduates today.

GENDER INEQUALITIES IN EDUCATIONAL PARTICIPATION TODAY

The postwar reform of Japanese education undertaken following World War II theoretically allowed women to pursue education on an equal basis with men.

The various sex-segregated tracks that had existed beyond elementary school were consolidated at each level resulting in a single-track structure, each level qualifying students for the next higher level. University status was granted to various existing institutions, including women's colleges and normal schools. Compulsory education was extended from six to nine years, and a 6-3-3-4 structure was adopted (six years of elementary school beginning at age six, three years of lower secondary school, three years of upper secondary school, and four years of university). Coeducation was extended to all levels including university, and a common curriculum was instituted in all schools. These reforms were embodied in both the School Education Law and the Fundamental Law of Education of 1947.

Since then, women's access to education at all levels has considerably expanded, but the pattern of gender differentiation in educational participation and attainment has persisted. The differences are most readily apparent at the postsecondary level where women continue to be underrepresented among student bodies at four-year universities but constitute a very high majority in junior colleges. Much of the research on women's education in Japan has focused on this level.[9] In fact, though, differences found at this level represent the culmination of a process that begins much earlier in the educational process—in lower secondary school and high school. Only recently have researchers become aware of the related issues of precollege gender differentiation and the nature of the education system, that is, its structure, curriculum, the guidance given to students, the expectations conveyed to students by teachers, and so on, which help to perpetuate sex differences in educational outcomes, including choices regarding college.[10]

Gender Differences at the Secondary Level

On the other hand, there appears to be little gender differentiation at the compulsory elementary and lower secondary levels, where a common, uniform curriculum and program of study are pursued by all students, mostly in coeducational classrooms. By the time students apply for upper secondary school, however, gender-related differences became apparent. The percentage of girls graduating from lower secondary school and continuing their studies in upper secondary school has increased from 37 percent in 1950, to 56 percent in 1960, 83 percent in 1970, and 95 percent in 1979.[11] In 1986, 95.3 percent of female lower secondary school graduates entered upper secondary school; this rate exceeded that for boys, which was 93.1 percent.[12] Significant differences appear, however, when we examine the types of high schools female and male students attend and the curricula they pursue, which reflect in turn differing aspirations and expectations regarding postsecondary education.

First of all, despite the fact that the postwar educational reforms called for the adoption of the principle of coeducation at all levels, many students are still found in single-sex high schools. Private high schools account for about 24 percent of all high schools and enroll 28 percent of all high school students.[13] More than 60 percent are single-sex schools, and the very best private schools are exclusively male. As for public high schools, in major urban centers such as Tokyo and Kyoto, these schools are coeducational. In many other areas of the country, notably the northern Kanto and Tohoku regions, however, a significant number of public high schools are still single-sex institutions. High schools newly established after the war are invariably coeducational, but many prewar boys' middle schools or girls' high schools have remained single-sex institutions (Kokusai fujinnen o kikkake to shite kōdō o okosu onnatachi no kai 1982: 39).

Second, although more girls than boys (74 versus 71 percent in 1986) are enrolled in the general academic program in high school,[14] fewer are found in the most competitive and prestigious academic high schools. Thomas Rohlen, for example, notes that the best public academic high schools regularly enroll a ratio of fifty-five males to forty-five females.[15] At the top public high schools in Tokyo that were formerly boys' middle schools, such as Hibiya, more than two-thirds of the students are male. Of those who choose a vocational program in high school, girls are apt to take home economics or commercial studies in preparation for taking clerical jobs after graduation, whereas boys tend to study technical subjects. The proportion of students going on to four-year universities is much higher among technical students than commercial or home economics graduates.

Admission to high school is determined on the basis of entrance examinations, and high schools are ranked on the basis of their success rate in preparing students for admission to the nation's most prestigious universities. Students aiming for admission into one of the top academic high schools begin preparing for the entrance examinations in lower secondary school by attending special extra-study schools known as *juku* or by hiring a private tutor. It appears that by the time girls reach the second or third year of lower secondary school many of them have lowered their ambitions and have decided to attend a junior college rather than a four-year university. They are, therefore, less likely to seek admission to top-ranking high schools. A recent survey conducted with third, fifth, and eighth graders and their mothers in Tokyo found that the percentage of students aspiring to a four-year university was about the same among boys and girls (39 percent and 41 percent) in the third grade, somewhat higher among boys than girls in the fifth grade (45 percent vs. 33 percent), and more than twice as high among boys as compared to girls at the eighth grade level (71 percent vs. 32 percent). On the other hand, the percentage of girls aspiring to junior college was found to be much higher among eighth graders (29 percent) as compared to third and fifth graders (8 percent and 13 percent).[16] Girls are also more likely than boys to enter a private high school and, in many cases, a high school that is attached to a women's junior college or university which graduates can usually enter without undergoing an entrance examination.

Parental attitudes and expectations also play an important role in creating and sustaining these patterns. Many parents seem to feel that the rigorous preparation and competition—as well as the cost—entailed in gaining admission to one of the top high schools and later to a prestigious university are unavoidable in the case of their sons, but they are unnecessary for their daughters.

Nationwide public opinion surveys conducted over the past several years reveal that, although there has been a general rise in the levels of education that Japanese desire for children of both sexes, parents continue to assign higher priority to the education of sons. Most parents want their daughters to receive at least a high school education, but beyond that they are likey to think in terms of a junior college for their daughters and a four-year university for their sons. In a 1984 national opinion poll conducted by the Office of the Prime Minister, 21 percent of female and 17 percent of male respondents indicated that they thought girls should receive a four-year university education, in contrast to 54 percent and 48 percent in the case of boys.[17] In the previously cited survey of Tokyo students and their mothers, 68 percent of the mothers indicated that they wanted a four-year university education for their sons, as compared to just 37 percent in the case of their daughters.[18] Those parents with more education and a higher socioeconomic level who resided in large urban centers, however, are more likely to want a university education for their daughters. It remains true, however, that, at every level, Japanese parents exhibit lower aspirations for their daughters than their sons.

There is also some evidence to suggest that teachers and guidance counselors may steer young women to less competitive high schools and colleges but encourage male students to aim for the prize institutions. In addition, evidence of discriminatory practices in admission procedures at public high schools have come to light in recent years. In Tokyo, for example, it has been revealed that the top public high schools, which were formerly boys' middle schools (e.g., Hibiya, Shinjuku, Nishiko, and Tachikawa) require a higher score on the entrance examinations for girls and maintain a quota for admitting women.[19] In addition, there have been reports from other parts of Japan of administrators at coeducational high schools urging their counterparts in lower secondary schools to discourage female students from applying to their schools and to send more boys.[20] While the scope of such discriminatory practices has yet to be ascertained, at the basis of such practices very frequently is the notion that, although girls may score high on high school entrance examinations, once they are admitted they do not work as hard to get into the top universities as boys do, which reduces the number of successful applicants to such universities and causes the reputation of the high school to decline.

Finally, within high school academic programs there is often sex-linked streaming. In the second and third years, students have the choice of specializing either in literature or science; literature majors take more courses in English and in Japanese literature, whereas science majors take more mathematics and science courses. The majority of male students opt for the science course; most females go into literature. Parents and teachers are apt to encourage girls to go into literature, partly because that is considered to be a more appropriate field of study for girls and partly because job opportunities for women graduating from the scientific fields are very limited.[21] There may be further differentiation based on whether a student plans to apply to a national university or to a private one and, within the two types of universities, whether he or she plans to apply to a science-related faculty or a literary faculty. Students are then given intensive preparation for the entrance examinations in the subject areas required by the institutions and faculties to which they plan to apply. (In Japan students apply to a particular faculty within a university, and entrance examinations are prepared by each faculty.) For those who plan to attend a junior college, the preparation is much less rigorous. Most junior colleges do not require entrance exams, merely recommendations, and those that do have examinations require applicants to sit in just two or three subjects.

Young women on the whole are less likely to enter the top academic high schools and once admitted elect to pursue programs that prepare them to enter the literature, education, or social science faculties at universities rather than the scientific or technological fields; or they decide to forego the rigorous and competitive preparation for university admission altogether and instead aim for a junior college. Not surprisingly, females constitute a minority among high school students enrolled in *yobikō*, which are privately operated schools (numbering more than 200 nationwide) that offer classes designed exclusively for entrance exam preparation. Those applying for university admission tend to be a much more select group than their male counterparts in terms of social class.[22] They are also likely to be academically superior. For example, a study which examined college aspirations among high school students found that among males with below-average grades in academically middle-rank high schools, more than 70 percent aspired to a four-year university. In the case of female students, however, only the top students in the best high schools had a similarly high aspiration level.[23]

Gender Inequalities in Participation in Higher Education

The gender differences found at the secondary level are manifested even more strikingly at the postsecondary level. Between 1960 and 1986 there was a fourfold increase in the proportion of girls entering institutions of higher education (as compared with about a twofold increase in the case of males). The proportion of female eighteen-year-olds entering college rose from just 5.5 percent in 1960 to 18 percent in 1970; since the mid-1970s, the figure has exceeded 32 percent (Mombusho annual). However, in the case of women, a substantial part of the enrollment increase has occurred at the junior college (*tanki daigaku* or short-term universities) level, whereas in the case of males it has taken place almost entirely at the four-year university level. Although it is possible for graduates from junior colleges to transfer to four-year universities, very few in fact do so. Of the roughly 300,000 young women who entered higher education in 1986, fewer than four out of ten women attended a four-year university; the remainder entered junior colleges. In contrast, nearly all—95 percent—of the 340,000 males entering college went to four-year universities.[24] Women overwhelmingly dominate the student population in junior colleges (90 percent), yet at four-year universities they account for only 24 percent.[25] Female university enrollments have increased slightly over the last five years; nevertheless, the proportion lags behind that in most industrialized societies.

Junior colleges are attractive to parents who want their daughters to receive general cultural enrichment through some type of higher education—as a mark of middle-class status and as a sort of marriage credential—yet at the same time are unable or unwilling to meet the cost of a four-year university education. The average cost (tuition, fees, and living expenses) per year at private universities (which account for 72 percent of all universities and enroll 73 percent of all university students) in 1982 amounted to ¥1.4 million or roughly 30 percent of the average family income. Tuition at private junior colleges is comparable to that at private four-year universities, but the payments need to be made for just two years instead of four, so the cost is one-half of that required for a four-year university. Additionally, junior colleges are somewhat more widely distributed throughout the country and less concentrated in a handful of large metropolitan centers so that they are more likely to be within commuting distance of their students. This is important not only in terms of costs but also in view of the reluctance that many parents feel about allowing their daughters to attend school away from home and parental supervision. Another relevant factor is that up until just a few years ago employment opportunities for women graduating from junior colleges had been much better than those available to university graduates, a point that is discussed in greater detail later.

Of those women attending four-year universities, one out of four is enrolled at an institution with an exclusively female student population, which numbered 85 out of a total of 460 in 1985 (Amano 1986: 141, table 5–1). Women make up only a very small percentage at the most prestigious coeducational universities such as Tokyo University and Kyoto University, where they represented only 7 and 8 percent, respectively, of all students admitted in 1980.[26] This is attributable in part to the fact that in any given year a large percentage of the successful applicants to these highly competitive universities are those who have spent a year or two as a *rōnin* following unsuccessful attempts (*rōnin*, named for the masterless samurai of the Tokugawa period, are students who, having failed to pass the entrance examinations for the top-rank school of their choice, spend a year or more preparing for a retake rather than enter a lower ranking institution). Most parents are unwilling to spend the resources to support a *rōnin* daughter, so that few women even try for these schools. Another factor is that, at an institution such as Tokyo University, the admission quota in faculties such as education, literature, and pharmaceutical studies, which tend to be most popular among women, is small in contrast to the faculties that tend to attract relatively few women, such as engineering and law.[27] Women who spend a year or two as a *rōnin* are at a disadvantage in terms of obtaining employment at the point of graduation from university. Companies hiring university graduates frequently set a lower age limit for women than men, usually twenty-two or twenty-three, which means that a woman who has spent time as a *rōnin* is automatically excluded.

The comparatively low rate of female enrollment at four-year universities means that women continue to be a small minority of graduate students, although in terms of both absolute numbers and relative proportions, women's representation has increased over the past twenty-five years. In 1986, women made up about 14 percent of all students enrolled in master's degree programs and about 12 percent of those in doctoral degree programs (compared to 9 and 5 percent, respectively, in 1960).[28]

Sex segregation in higher education is also evident in the programs of study that women pursue. In recent years university women have made inroads into traditionally male-dominated faculties such as social science, including law, politics, economics, and industrial management (up from 7 percent of all women students in 1960 to 16 percent in 1986); engineering (from 0.5 to 2.3 percent); and agriculture (from 0.5 to 2.1 percent). In turn, there has been a decline in the relative proportion enrolled in education (from 28 to 17 percent) and home economics (from 28 to 8 percent). Nevertheless, 60 percent of all women enrolled in universities in 1986 were clustered in the traditionally female fields of literature, education, and home economics. The largest proportion of men (46 percent) were majoring in the social sciences and another 25 percent in engineering. Relatively few women receive training for business and professional careers, except in fields such as teaching or pharmacy. At the junior colleges, there has been a considerable increase in the proportion of women majoring in teacher education in preparation for teaching in preschools (up from 11 percent in 1960 to 29 percent in 1986), as well as in health-related fields. On the other hand, there has been a decrease in those majoring in home economics although that is still the most popular major (29 percent), followed by literature (26 percent).[29]

At the graduate level, too, we find similar differences: one-half of all male students in master's degree programs are enrolled in engineering, and the remainder are almost evenly distributed in the fields of science, agriculture, social sciences, and humanities. Among females, the largest percentage are enrolled in literature, followed by education, and then the social sciences. At the doctoral level, medicine and dentistry are the most popular fields among males, followed by engineering, humanities, science, and the social sciences. In the case of females, humanities enrolls the highest percentage, followed by medicine, dentistry, and the social sciences.[30]

Women's overrepresentation in such fields as literature, home economics, and education and their underrepresentation in science, engineering, law, and economics partly result from the limited range of study options at most private women's universities and junior colleges. At most women's universities the faculties of literature and home economics are the only ones available. This narrow range of curricula offerings is even more pronounced at private junior colleges. In addition, less than a third of the women's colleges (28 out of the 85) have graduate programs, as compared to 61 percent of all universities; only 12 of the women's colleges have doctoral programs.[31] Thus, women's colleges are generally not equipped to provide training for highly specialized professions.

Reminiscent of prewar days, higher education in Japan is to a large degree still gender differentiated both in structure and content. Men pursue higher education with the purpose of preparing for business and professional careers in university settings; a majority of women continue to pursue a general, cultural-enrichment education in single-sex, nonuniversity settings. At the same time, though, signs of change are evident. For example, the proportion of women entering coeducational rather than women's universities is gradually increasing, as is the proportion of women choosing nontraditional study options such as law, politics, economics, and engineering. Junior college women are majoring in home economics in fewer numbers and moving into teacher training and the health-related fields. Simultaneously, many women's universities and junior colleges have diversified their program offerings in response to these changes in demand. Finally, many colleges and universities, both single-sex and coeducational, have begun to offer courses in women's studies. As of 1987 128 junior colleges and universities offered such courses, representing 12.4 percent of all colleges and universities in Japan.[32]

Gender Inequalities within the Teaching Profession

Another aspect of gender inequality in education concerns the inequalities that exist within the teaching profession. In prewar days, teaching at the elementary or secondary level was the most common profession among women. There were very few women professors, except for those teaching at women's higher normal schools or at women's colleges. Teaching is still the most popular profession among women, but, as in the past, the proportion of women is smaller as one moves up the educational ladder, and women are likely to be found teaching subjects traditionally considered feminine, such as home economics, literature, and art, and few women are found in administrative positions.

Kindergartens (*yochien*) are staffed almost exclusively by women (94 percent); yet women head only 48 percent of all kindergartens (Mombusho 1987: 41). At the elementary schools, women account for 56 percent of the teachers but just 2.4 percent of the principals (Mombusho 1987: 44). Women constitute 34 percent of the teachers and just 0.4 percent of the principals in lower secondary schools (Mombusho 1987: 48); the corresponding figures at the upper secondary schools are 19 and 2.4 percent.[33]

At the college level, more women teach in junior colleges than in universities. Women make up 39 percent of all faculty members in junior colleges; 8.5 percent of four-year university faculty, and less than 4 percent of graduate level faculties. The higher the professional rank, the smaller is the representation of females:

women account for just 4 percent of full professors at universities and 24 percent of those at junior colleges and 4 percent of university and 14 percent of junior college presidents.[34] Within universities, women's representation is higher at private than at national universities, at all-female than at coeducational universities, and at more recently established ones than at the older, more prestigious universities. As of 1982, women represented a mere 1.1 percent of the faculty at the former imperial universities, which include Tokyo and Kyoto Universities.[35]

If teachers are potential role models for students, it is readily apparent that such models become fewer and fewer for girls as they progress through the educational system. The women teachers and professors they do come in contact with tend to reinforce traditional images.

Women's underrepresentation in college and university faculties results from the fact that faculty and researchers are recruited primarily through a patronage system, and women are generally excluded from that system except at women's junior colleges and universities, although even those institutions tend to recruit mostly males. Positions are rarely announced publicly, so that women do not have an opportunity to compete openly for a university teaching or research position. As a consequence, fewer women than men are able to obtain employment following completion of master's and doctoral degree programs. The various forms of discrimination that exist in academia are likely to prove much more difficult to attack than those found in business and industry.[36]

WOMEN'S PARTICIPATION IN SOCIAL EDUCATION

In addition to formal schooling, Japanese society provides opportunities for adult (or in Japanese terms "social") education. Broadly defined, social education may be divided into two categories. The first is academic courses arranged in a format conducive to adult participation (e.g., radio programs). The second is broader and includes a whole range of self-improvement activities from consumer education to learning a sport, art, or craft. Social education in the formal sense began in the 1920s and was geared to broaden the student rather than prepare him or her for some particular job. In the postwar period, social education took on a new meaning. "Social education would act as a means whereby people could learn about democracy, and by involvement in the organizations of social education would have a chance to practice the subtle skills of self rule."[37] In 1949, social education was made a legal right and it became mandatory for the several levels of government to provide it. Hence, we see today a wide range of classes at local government facilities.

In 1977, a National Women's Education Center in Saitama was opened "to train leaders on women's education, as well as to conduct specialized research in the field of women's education." Correspondence courses began in 1979 and the University of the Air (founded in 1981 as a corporation with special juridical status) began to admit students in 1985. Since 1977, 128 women's education centers have been established throughout Japan. It is interesting to note that the focus of these centers is to build up the educational role of the family (i.e., mother) rather than to raise the consciousness of women.

Women are also deeply involved in social education in the broader sense of self-improvement, obtained through participation in classes at cultural centers, which have been established by major Japanese businesses, and in cultural activities such as theater performance and visits to museums. The Asahi Cultural Center, established by one of Japan's major newspapers in 1974, was the first to be established. Over the last decade, both the number of such centers' classes and the number of students has increased incrementally, but 80 percent of the students are women.[38]

Very few of these classes are related to some practical end. Rather, they provide cultural "finishing" and ways for women to broaden their perspectives. Women's participation is seen to reflect such things as the legitimacy of educating oneself, the need to plan for a long widowhood, and the fact that the number of employed women exceeds the number of full-time housewives, which gives women money to spend on such activities.[39]

The significance of women's cultural involvement is reflected in the recent dominance of women recipients of major literary prizes in Japan, in the leisure industry's investment in programs and facilities (e.g., "children's rooms" in theaters) which attract women patrons, and in the growth of courses for women.

GENDER ROLES, THE FAMILY, AND EDUCATION

Issues pertaining to women's education are intricately tied to consideration of women's roles both within the family and in other institutions of society.[40] Thus, for example, the tendency on the part of most Japanese to assign lower priority to the education of women than men is a reflection in large part of conceptions of gender roles such as the assumption that women will marry and have children and not take up careers following completion of their education. This is not to say that gender roles today are a mere continuation of the traditional. Rather, the content of gender roles is indeed changing, and these changes impact on women's educational choices for themselves and for their daughters. In this context it is important to give some attention to the "traditional" women's role and recent changes.

Although Japanese women have long contributed to the economy either through participation in the family farm or business or by earning wages through piecework or employment outside the home, their primary roles have been as wives and mothers. Education, employment, and other activities were acceptable insofar as they contributed to or at least did not detract from their ability to manage the family with virtually no male assistance other than financial support.

The traditional model for the Japanese woman was to marry into her husband's family where she was subservient to her in-laws and served to bear new family members and to contribute to the family economically through housewifery and participation in the family enterprise or farm. Her central focus, virtually her entire day, was within the household.

In the last forty years, many changes have taken place in the housewife's role: longer life span, fewer children, better education, and a change from a family business to a husband breadwinner employed outside the home, all of which have contributed to women's increasing social participation.[41] This participation may take a variety of forms including social education, community activism, employment, and activities related to children or for leisure or self-enrichment. One result of these changes in the 1970s was the provision of a variety of role models for Japanese women which do not contradict the primacy of the domestic role, but allow for a great deal of behavioral flexibility within it. These new forms of social participation have, on the one hand, helped to legitimate housewives' activities in the eyes of society and, on the other, offered younger women more options than their mothers enjoyed.

These changes in Japanese women's lives are similar to those occurring in many other societies. Yet, it would be incorrect to assume that change will occur in exactly the same manner as in, say, the United States. For example, the social participation of the American woman may be curtailed by the presence of small children but expand as the children grow. The Japanese housewife's social participation may also follow a pattern of expansion and contraction. She may participate more outside the home when her children are in elementary school and return home when they are studying for high school and college entrance examinations. She may participate more when they are safely in college and return home when her husband retires or when she has elderly parents (in-laws) to care for.

These periods of greater and lesser involvement outside the home highlight three major forces operative on Japanese women's lives today. The first is the importance of the mother's involvement in her children's education. The strong social pressure to be available to care for children's needs and to provide emotional support as the children work their way through the school/examination system and the very real consequences of children failing the examinations influence the mother's outside-the-home activity. Women tend to choose jobs or other involvements that permit them to be home when the children are at home and to be free to attend school functions.

The importance of children's education is directly related to the second somewhat contradictory force. The cost of living, in particular the cost of educating children and of buying a home, bring increasing numbers of married women back to the labor force. As we shall see, increased education and the labor market itself are also important variables affecting this trend. Basically, it becomes more and more difficult financially for women to stay out of the labor force just as their desire to use their education and previous work experience makes staying home more difficult psychologically. A woman's dilemma then is to balance these "push" forces with the "pull" to be home to supervise the children's study.

The third major force is the elderly of Japanese society. This impacts on women in two contradictory ways. Women are the caretakers of the aged, and anticipating this responsibility provides another limitation to women's labor force participation. Recognizing that they soon may be caring for aged parents may lead women to view career building as a waste of time. It may make more sense to engage in a combination of part-time work and personal interest activities while they are free to do so. On the other hand, since women outlive men, aging is primarily a woman's problem. A search for meaningful acitivities for one's old age can lead women to develop outside interests, take up a job, or join a study group. The level of a woman's education can influence both her propensity to form such attachments and the kinds of activities she chooses.

Japanese women today are poised between the "pull" toward home and the "push" outside. Somewhere women will strike a balance which will reflect and affect education. (For example, mothers today want their daughters to be educated so they can work if they must.)

Women's role in the family is changing, and so is the role of the family for women. Whereas traditionally women's happiness was perceived to be in marriage, some 40 percent of women now feel that "if one can get by alone, there is no need to marry."[42] However, the vast majority do marry and have children. The divorce rate has leveled off at less than a quarter of that of the United States. On the one hand, the institution of marriage is strong. On the other hand, one might well ask if it is as strong as it was ten years ago.

The answer is clearly that many changes have been occurring within the family itself. From the standpoint of women's roles, we find first of all that the interest in outside-the-home involvement which developed so strongly in the 1970s has increased. On the one hand, this is reflected in the women's educational centers and the classes mentioned earlier. On the other, it is reflected in the percentages of wives who have interests beyond the home. Some 39.5 percent are interested in arts and crafts, 20.2 percent in sports and fitness, 16.1 percent in community activities (including PTA), 10.5 percent in study, 10.1 percent in consumer groups, and 6.5 percent in obtaining an educational license or certificate.[43] This compares with 15.9 percent of housewives in 1974 who would have liked to engage in handicrafts, 15.3 percent in travel, another 15.3 percent in education related to daily life, 10.1 percent who wished more reading time, and 9 percent who desired to spend more time on music, art, calligraphy, and the like.[44] Housewives of the 1980s show more interest in outside-the-home pursuits and indicate a desire to obtain a license or certificate which may have some practical value.

There is also clear-cut continuity with the past. As in the 1970s, mothers of small children tend not to get out much (58.3 percent), whereas those with grown children get out from one to four times a week. As in the past, children provide the purpose in life to roughly half the women versus slightly more than a quarter who say that helping their husbands is their purpose in life. In addition, these wives are, for the most part, home in the evening. (Three-quarters of them said that they almost never go out at night.)

The continuity with and development from the 1970s are evident. Outside-the-home activity is acceptable and desired. Women with higher education are more likely to participate in cultural activities. Yet, regardless of education and interest, women's schedules revolve around the needs of home and family, and they go out (as did the wives of the 1970s) during the time that the children are in school and their husbands are at work. In contrast to the United States, where the individual is expected to find a babysitter, a small but increasing number of Japanese leisure facilities are providing "children's rooms." This takes the burden away from the family in a way that, to our knowledge, is paralleled only by churches in the United States (though of course some ski lodges and hotels provide programs for children or babysitters at the individual parent's expense). As the level of women's education increases, it appears that they will demand more and more opportunities outside the home.

A different but related role of the Japanese housewife is that of holder of the family purse. This responsibility has been both symbolic and real. In the past, the mother-in-law controlled household (domestic) resources until her death or retirement, and gaining this control was one of the symbols of becoming a *shufu* (housewife) rather than a *yome* (bride). The situation in the past was that of power of control and responsibility of allocation. To control the purse did not mean to control the male head of the family but to allocate family resources for survival—to be sure that there was enough rice and other food for the year, clothing for the family, and savings. As families moved toward a salary-based income, housewives managed the husband's income. He received an "allowance" to spend as he willed. She had to make sure that the rest stretched. This left her with virtually no money of her own; it was all family money.

In recent years two things have happened to change this situation. The wife is increasingly likely to have a job and money of her own, and children are also increasingly likely to earn something. According to Sugawara Mariko, this loosens the housewife's control of what the children and husband eat (they are frequently not home for meals) and what they buy to wear or use for leisure.[45] There is, she argues, increased individualism within the family in terms of both tastes and in consumption power. This, in turn, impacts on wives and the work place. Whereas it was common to leave employment at marriage, now the percentage of women who do so (20.3 percent) is below that of those who continue in their jobs after marriage but resign because of pregnancy (37.8 percent). The vast majority (89.5 percent) of housewives have worked outside the home before marriage, and the majority (64.4 percent) of full-time housewives wish to work outside the home when family duties permit.[46] This indicates a rising acceptability of outside work for women.

Why do they wish to return to the labor force? Women give two reasons in addition to the push created by the need to supplement the family budget and to pay for the high cost of housing and children's education: to have some discretionary money and to broaden their circle of interpersonal relationships. These reasons reflect the educational level of women in two ways. First, women with higher education (whose husbands probably have higher incomes) are more likely to give the second reason than the first. Second, university graduate women have a slightly lower rate of wishing to return to employment (56.7 percent) than high school graduates (68.5 percent). This reflects the university graduates' belief that suitable work will not be available.[47] This is similar to the situation in the 1970s and, as then, also reflects the university graduates' broader cultural interests which offer them a variety of attractive alternative ways to spend their time. (Imamura 1987).

Hidden behind those statistics is another kind of work—the behind-the-scenes domestic support a wife gives her husband (*naijo no kō*). In traditional society, women worked on the farm or in the business, or they managed a household that required full-time attention. With the advent of the salaried family, the women's contribution became handling the household and child-rearing tasks and sending their husbands out to work properly fed and rested. There was no other way for them to be involved directly in their husbands' careers (with the exception of delivering seasonal gifts and making New Year's calls) because they had no business entertainment responsibilities as did American wives. Recently, a new form of *naijo no kō* has apppeared.[48] The advent of computers and word processing as a female skill means that women have skills that can be useful to husbands' careers after marriage. Husbands become too busy to keep up with all that they need to write, and wives help by writing manuscripts and editing them at home. Yet another example of the new *naijo no kō*, albeit most likely a rarer occurrence, is the wife who is trained in language and can interpret for her husband.

This phenomenon is directly linked to women's education. Education provides them with the skills in the first place. In the long run, husbands placing value on such skills will encourage more women to obtain further education. Thus, there is a push and pull effect, and one can hypothesize that mothers will want their daughters to get useful training.

In terms of women's lives and roles, these opportunities give wives a chance to work with their husbands and to be more involved in their lives. On the other hand, helping one's husband places the Japanese wife in a position similar to that of many Western wives in the past—uncredited coauthors of their husbands' work. Furthermore, the pressure to help their husbands without pay may keep educated and marketable women out of the labor force.

Another role of the woman in the family is related to aging. Two aspects of aging directly impact on women and education. The first is that care for the aged is in Japan clearly a family function. Traditionally, it was the role of the bride to care for the parents of her husband. Since Japan is the fastest aging society today, with the longest life span, and since couples are having fewer (1.7) children, it is increasingly likely that a woman will have to look after the elderly. In particular, it is likely that her mother-in-law will require care for a long time. This impacts on the housewife in at least two ways.

First, the Japanese government clearly regards the care of the aged as a family-based endeavor.[49] This creates great social pressure on the wife who is employed to quit work in her forties or fifties when her in-laws need her.[50] The social pressure comes from peers, neighbors, and, of course, from the elderly themselves.

The current generation of elderly expected that the family would provide for them as they provided for the previous generation. Also, this generation is less likely than the future elderly to have interests outside of family or work and are more likely to have health problems stemming from poor nutrition and difficult circumstances during and after World War II. Such elderly may refuse help from the public sector out of shame that their "bride" is not looking after them properly.[51]

The second way in which the aging of Japanese society impacts on women and education relates to the fact that Japanese women have the longest life expectancy in the world today and can expect to outlive their husbands. Women are encouraged to participate in social education while they are young so that they can have interests to pursue when they are older because they probably will be unable to participate in such classes when their husbands retire and are at home.

WOMEN, EDUCATION, AND EMPLOYMENT

The previous discussion of the evolution of gender roles in Japanese society and their impact on women's education has touched on aspects of the relationship between education and women's labor force participation. This section focuses specifically on this question, particularly on the issues concerning employment among university-educated women.

Increasing numbers of Japanese women have joined the employed labor force. Women now make up 36 percent of the employed labor force,[52] and since 1984 the number of employed women has outnumbered full-time housewives. In addition, the average length of women's employment has increased to seven years (full-time workers only), and the educational level of those workers has dramatically risen. At the same time, however, a substantial portion of the increase in numbers of women working has been due to an increase in part-timers, who now represent one-third of all employed women. Women in the labor force continue to combine home and job rather than follow a career path. Moreover, women's advancement into traditionally male-dominated professions and into managerial and administrative positions has been noticeably slow. Thus, in 1986, women accounted for 4.6 percent of technicians and engineers, 7.5 percent of scientists, and 7.2 percent of those in administrative or managerial positions.[53]

Various factors have restricted occupational advancement on the part of college-educated women. One of these factors is the influence of traditional social attitudes pertaining to sex roles. Another inhibiting factor has been the various forms of sexual discrimination in employment that all women—especially highly educated women—have been subjected to. These two factors have prevented women from utilizing their education to the fullest in the occupational sphere.

In prewar Japanese society, it was uncommon for women graduates from higher institutions to take up employment following graduation. This was due in part to the dominant attitude that young women should not work but rather should stay home and master the womanly arts and crafts. There was also little demand within society for the talents of educated women, and the range of occupations open to such women was limited to just a few, such as teaching and the health and medical fields. Thus, on the average, less than half of all college graduates (with the exception of those graduating from higher normal schools who were obligated to teach for a certain number of years following graduation) entered employment following graduation. If a young woman did take a job after graduation, she abandoned it upon marriage and devoted herself thereafter to her husband and children and the home. The small number of women who deviated from this socially accepted norm and became career women, or *shokugyō fujin*, frequently remained single.

In contrast, in recent years, it has become a common and socially accepted practice for women to work following college graduation. Ninety percent of college women exhibit a desire to work for at least some time following graduation, and over 80 percent of women graduating from junior colleges and 70 percent of those graduating from four-year universities do in fact take up employment following graduation.[54] Most parents are likely to look with favor on their daughters working as a way of broadening their horizons and giving them some experience in the larger society. In fact, some work experience, in addition to a college education, has come to be regarded as an important marriage credential for today's young woman. The implication is that with such a background a wife will have a better understanding of her husband's work and perhaps even be of some help to him in his career. The knowledge and experience she has gained will also be valuable when it comes to planning for and helping her children in their educational careers.

Not only are today's college graduates more likely to work, but also the range of occupations open to them is much broader. Among prewar graduates who took up employment, about half went into teaching, and the remainder went into health and medical fields and clerical work; very few took up other types of work. In contrast, among 1986 graduates from four-year universities, 39 percent went into clerical work, 24 percent went into teaching, another 12 percent became technical workers, 9 percent went into sales, and 6 percent went into the health and medical fields. Among junior college graduates, nearly 60 percent took up clerical work, another 11 percent became teachers, 8 percent went into health-related fields, another 9 percent went into the professional and technical fields, and about 7 percent went into sales.[55]

Although most women graduates now take up some type of employment, only a minority pursue work on a career basis. As was noted earlier, the average length of continuous employment in a single job has been rising over the recent years among all women (from 4 years in 1966, to 5.8 years in 1975, and 7.0 years in 1986), yet the length of time continues to be shorter among women who have graduated from college than among those with less education.[56] Among women in their twenties, those with higher education are more likely to be working than those with less education, partly because they tend to marry and bear children at a later age. However, among women who are in the early child-rearing years thirty to thirty-four, there is little difference in rates of employment according to level of education. College-educated women are just as likely as those with less education—if not slightly more so—to refrain from working during this stage, although of those who do work, more are likely to do so on a full-time basis. The percentage of college-educated women in their later thirties and forties who reenter the labor market after their children have become older is smaller than that of less-educated women, partly because such women are generally unwilling to take the kind of low-paying production or service industry jobs that are most commonly available to women their age and partly because they are less likely to be in a position of having to work from financial necessity.

Attitudes and norms pertaining to the role of women have been major factors in sustaining this pattern. Even among highly educated women, the majority subscribe to some of the traditional values and norms regarding the role of women. In a 1984 national public opinion survey, only 20 percent of all women and 24 percent of college-educated women expressed support for women continuing to work after they have children. Relatively few women today feel that women should stop working when they get married. A majority, including those with college degrees, think that women should not work while their children are still young. In the same survey, 45 percent of all women and 52 percent of college-educated women endorsed the view that women should stop work when they have children and return to work only after the children are grown.[57] Thus, while over 90 percent of college women today express a desire to work following graduation, the majority seem to view work as a temporary pursuit to be taken up until they get married or until they have children; only a minority have thought in terms of a career.

Cultural and attitudinal factors alone do not account for gender disparities in occupational achievement; equally significant is the fact of differential opportunities available to women and men in the Japanese labor market. One reason, in fact, why women's enrollment in four-year universities has been so much lower than men's is that, except in a few professions where women have long been visible, employment opportunities for women university graduates have been extremely limited, in comparison both to male graduates and to female graduates from junior colleges, so that most young women and their parents have found it not worthwhile to invest in a four-year university degree.

In Japan young women straight out of school are hired for jobs based on the assumption that they will work until they get married or, at most, until they have a child. Women are generally excluded from the traditional system of lifetime employment and the system of promotion and wages based on length of consecutive years of service within a particular company. Many employers have a policy—either official or unofficial—that requires women to retire at the time of marriage, pregnancy, or childbirth. Companies hire high school or junior college graduates as "office ladies" (OLs) to perform routine clerical work; however, graduates from four-year universities are not hired for such positions because they are more expensive and presumably will have fewer years before they will leave their jobs. At the same time, most employers have been reluctant to hire these female graduates to perform tasks comparable to those assigned to male university graduates. For this reason, until just a few years ago, employment rates among female university graduates had been lower than rates among junior college graduates.

Many companies have had a policy of not recruiting female university graduates. The Labor Standards Law of 1947 prohibits sex discrimination only in the area of pay where the type of work performed is the same or of equal value; it does not prohibit discrimination on the basis of sex in hiring, work assignment, promotion, welfare, benefits, and retirement. Until just a few years ago, it was common practice for employers seeking to hire university graduates to advertise separately for men and women. In addition, employers often set an age limit for women applicants—one that is lower than the age limit for males: "must be no older than or twenty-three" or "cannot have spent time as a *rōnin*" (another way of saying that an applicant cannot be older than twenty-three). They may also specify that prospective female applicants "must live at home" or "must live within a ninety-minute commuting distance." Employers stipulate these conditions when companies do not want to have to provide dormitory facilities for women workers; furthermore, many employers feel safer about employing young women who are living under the supervision of their parents. Even when women university graduates are hired, they are often subjected to further differential treatment in terms of on-the-job training, remuneration, and opportunities for promotion to administrative and managerial positions.[58] Until just a few years ago, the differential in starting pay for men and women was greater among university graduates than among high school and junior college graduates.[59]

Recently, legal and social changes have impacted on women in the work force. The major legal step has been the passage of the Equal Employment Opportunity Act in 1985. One major shortcoming of the legislation is that it actually "forbids" only certain discriminatory practices (e.g., with respect to retirement, benefits, and certain types of on-the-job training); in regard to many other forms of discrimination, such as recruitment, hiring, job placement, and promotion, it demands only that employers "make an effort" to end those practices. Another very serious shortcoming is that enforcement provisions seem to be inadequate.

Although the legislation has no real "teeth," its provision that recruitment not be sex specific has had some impact in terms of getting companies to open their doors to women university graduates. A Ministry of Labor survey found that the percentage of companies listed on the Tokyo Stock Exchange that planned to recruit both women and men scheduled to graduate from university the following March rose from 32 percent in 1985 to 72 percent in 1986.[60] One factor that has contributed to this trend is a shortage in recent years in the university-educated male labor force. As a result, more companies are being forced to turn to a hitherto untapped source of talent and skills—university-educated women— to fill positions formerly reserved for male graduates. This has been particularly noticeable among businesses catering to female clientele, such as supermarkets, department stores, retail specialty shops, manufacturers of office and home electrical and electronic equipment, banks, and brokerage firms.

Many major companies, most notably financial institutions and trading companies, now offer university-educated women a choice between traditional women's work (office lady, i.e., support-level clerical) and the career path or *sōgō shoku* traditionally reserved for male university graduates. Women hired for management-track positions are paid the same salary and assigned the same responsibilities as their male colleagues, which means also that they are called upon to perform overtime work, including after work drinking with colleagues and entertaining clients, and to accept job transfers within the country as well as assignments overseas. Since this new system is only two years old, no conclusions can be drawn about employment patterns or about the longevity of these women in the company. However, interesting comments have appeared in the media. For example, the vast majority of women appear to choose the traditional women's path. Among the possible reasons for this, one might hypothesize, are social pressure, fear of becoming unmarriageable, the lack of female role models to convince women that the extra effort will indeed result in promotion, and uncertainties about their ability to combine a demanding career with marriage and family. At the same time, it has been reported that even though companies may allow women to apply for management-track positions, they in fact often have a separate, much lower hiring quota for women than men. Very frequently a company will go through the motion of interviewing women when it fact many of the available positions have already been filled by men through an "old boy" network. Thus far the number of women who have actually been hired for such positions has been few, and the ones who have been hired have been exceptionally well qualified. To cite a few examples, Sumitomo Bank hired fifty-five women in the spring of 1988, of whom nineteen were hired for *sōgō shoku*; at Fuji Bank, the figures were 230 and 30; and at Mitsubishi Shoji, 44 and 2.[61] Moreover, women graduating from the literature, education, or home economic faculties (i.e., the very ones in which the majority of females are enrolled) are not, as a rule, hired for *sōgō shoku* unless, for example, they are exceptionally skilled in foreign languages.

According to the Japanese press, career path women are not necessarily welcomed by other women in the company. If, for example, there was only one woman in a particular field before, it was easy for her to keep clients because she was unique. With many women competitors, the pioneer woman may feel threatened. Another barrier between women is the stratification that may exist among women in the same workplace. Status-based conflicts of interest develop between part-time or temporary women (on the bottom), full-time "general office work" women (in the middle), and (resented) "regular line" women. Among the comments indicating resentment of regular line women is, "Male employees only eat lunch with the line women employees and only go out for a drink after hours with them, so their (men's) relations with office women have broken down."[62]

While it is too early to try to evaluate the impact that this legislation will have on women's occupational advancement, other positive developments are also occurring. A growing number of college women today are expressing a desire to pursue careers even after they have children, and toward that end they are looking to college to provide them with specialized, job-related knowledge and training. In the Japan Recruit Center's 1982 survey of college-bound high school seniors, nearly 56 percent of the the female respondents chose "to obtain qualifications or certificates" as one of the their top three motives for wanting to attend college, and 29 percent chose this as the single most significant motive.[63] Simultaneously, we find more women looking beyond the occupations traditionally favored by women and branching out into such diverse areas as advertising, banking and finance, retail sales, architecture, broadcasting, real estate, and computers. These changes have, in turn, been reflected by a gradual increase in the proportion of college women choosing nontraditional study options such as law, politics, economics, and engineering. These changes in the values and attitudes of a young generation of women may be viewed as a consequence of the rise in the levels of education attained by women over the postwar years. Most young women in college today have been raised by mothers who, in most instances, represented the first generation of women in their families to have ever had the opportunity to receive higher education. While those mothers on the whole did not elect life-styles that departed radically from those of lesser educated women, they nonetheless have passed on a different set of attitudes, values, and expectations to their daughters. In a sense, they have laid a foundation on which their daughters may build. College-educated women have been found to be more likely than other women and men to have educational aspirations as high for their daughters as for their sons;[64] they also tend to hold more progressive and egalitarian views on other matters related to education, for example, that "it is necessary for girls (as well as boys) to receive the type of education that will enable them to have an occupation and be independent in the future."[65]

In the mid-1970s, the *Nihon Keizai Shimbun* did a series of articles on married career women. In general, the career woman was depicted as first going to great lengths to get her house in order arranging everything so as not to place any burden on her family before she went to work. This image still appears in press reports, but another image is appearing alongside this one. A number of recent feature stories highlight both women's changing participation (e.g., the increase of female-owned small businesses in nontraditional sectors) and the accommodations companies are making to retain qualified women. Among the latter are flextime, a system in which mothers can switch to part-time while they have young children and are guaranteed a return to full-time work when the children are grown; a system of two-hour child care leave each day until the child is three years old; and a telephone "hot line" offering information on day care and child-rearing problems.[66] These changes all reflect women's improved education: Education leads women to continue in the labor force, and their skills increase their employers' desire to keep them even if only part time. In other words, skilled women have an increasing variety of options, and companies are willing to do more to keep them.

THE FUTURE: THE CHANGING IMAGE OF HOUSEWIVES—SELF-INDULGENT WOMEN

From a variety of standpoints, women's lives offer increased individual choices. However, individual-centered motives have not been among the most socially acceptable in Japan. It is not surprising to note that, as women's life choices become more individual, women are labeled "selfish." This label is applied to women who quit work at the slightest excuse, to women who suffer symptoms of menopause,[67] and to women who focus entirely on themselves and their families rather than on cooperating to deal with social problems.

The underlying issue seems to be one of contribution, which brings us back to the issue of education. In the United States, we ask what good is learning something. In Japan, one can also ask this question, but, because the answers differ, "legitimate" motives for education also vary. In the United States, education is "good for" increasing earning power, self-improvement, and the pursuit of personal interests. In Japan, education is also linked to status in terms of future employment. Studying something as a hobby is also acceptable. However, there is another overriding reason for which education is "good"—to improve the contribution a person can make to family, work, or other larger group. In one sense this distinction is like splitting hairs. In another sense, however, this deemphasis on the individual both stands in the way of and facilitates women's education. The former occurs when women leave their jobs or classes to concentrate on home and family. The latter occurs when skillful women rationalize their study because it helps them to be better housewives, to contribute more to the family, and to be better prepared for motherhood.

The future will continue to reflect the "pull" of the home and the "push" to the outside world. It is likely that women will continue to participate more in educational activities than men, and may continue to outshine men in the field of literary awards. It is also likely that Japanese women will continue to participate in the labor force in a variety of patterns consistent with family roles and life-style choices. As new job opportunities develop for women, women will demand better education for their daughters. Education and labor force participation will go hand in hand. This will occur not only for individual-based reasons (e.g., the desire to maximize their talents or to use their education) but also because the income of a dual-earner household is higher than that of a single-earner household. Yet this does not necessarily imply that the domestic role will lose its primacy.

As increasing job opportunities for women develop—to the extent that women's cultural opportunities outstrip men's—women will run the risk of being labeled selfish. The way to avoid this criticism is to channel new skills into social contributions. If and how this will occur, however, remains to be seen. The most likely scenario is that the increasing acceptance of a variety of roles for women and the needs of the labor market will engender a small, but increasing, number of career women, but the vast majority of women will combine family and employment. Regardless of career versus family choices, women will have an increasing variety of cultural opportunities available to them. The vicious circle will become one of combining all these "acceptable and desirable" alternatives into a package that neither is criticized as selfish nor creates overload.

NOTES

1. Kumiko Fujimura-Fanselow, "Women's Participation in Higher Education in Japan," *Comparative Education Review* 29, no. 4 (November 1985), pp. 471–89.
2. For a discussion of female education in prewar Japan see Shibukawa Hisako, *Kindai nihon josei-shi* [Women's History in Modern Japan], Vol. 1 (Tokyo: Kashima Kenkyū Shuppan-kai, 1970); Nihon Joshi Daigaku Joshi Kyōiku Kenkyūjo [Japan's Women's University Research Center on Women's Education], ed. *Taishō no joshi kyōiku* [Women's Education in the Taisho Period] (Tokyo: Kokudosha, 1975); and idem, *Meiji no joshi kyōiku* [Women's Education in the Meiji Period] (Tokyo: Kokudosha, 1967).
3. Nihon Joshi Daigaku, *Meiji no joshi kyōiku*, 1967, p. 200, table 1.
4. Ibid., p. 201, table 2.
5. Murakami Nobuhiko, *Meiji josei-shi* [A History of Women in the Meiji Period], Vol. 3 (Tokyo: Kōdansha, 1977), p. 236.
6. Nihon Joshi Daigaku, *Meiji no joshi kyōiku*, 1967, p. 25.
7. Ibid., p. 201, table 2.
8. Chi'iki shakai kenkyūjo [Center for Research on Local Communities], "Ochanomizu de gojunen" [Fifty Years after Graduation from Ochanomizu Women's University], *Kōnenrei o ikiru* [Living in One's Later Years] 7 (1975), pp. 67–69.
9. See Amano Masako, *Joshi kōtō kyōiku no zahyō* [The Coordinates of Women's Higher Education] (Tokyo: Kakiuchi Shuppan, 1986); Kumiko Fujimura-Fanselow, "Women's Participation in Higher Education in Japan"; Fujii Harue, *Nihon no joshi kōtō kyōiku* [Women's Higher Education in Japan] (Tokyo: Domesu, 1973); Ichibangase Yasuko, *Gendai joshi kyōiku hihan* [A Critique of Contemporary Women's Education] (Tokyo: Meiji Tosho, 1971); Hara Kimi, "Joshi kōtō kyōiku no shakaigakuteki ikkōsatsu" [A Sociological Examination of Women's Higher Education], *Kyōiku shakaigaku kenkyū* [Research in the Sociology of Education] 26 (October 1971).
10. Takeuchi Kiyoshi, "Joshi no seito bunka no tokushitsu" [Special Characteristics of Female Student Culture], *Kyōiku shakaigaku kenkyū* [Research in the Sociology of Education] 40 (1985); Kyōto Daigaku Kyōikugakubu, Kyōiku Shakaigaku Kenkyūshitsu

[Kyoto University, Faculty of Education, Seminar in Sociology of Education], "Gakushu fūdo" to "kakureta karikyuramu" ni kansuru shakaigakuteki kenkyū—"chishiki no haibun" no kanten kara [A Sociological Study of 'Learning Climates' and 'Hidden Curricula'—from the Standpoint of the 'Distribution of Knowledge'] no. 1 (October 1982); Fukaya Kazuko and Yokoi Tomiko, "Joshi chūgakusei" [Female Junior High Students], *Monograph: Chugakusei no sekai* [Monograph: The World of Junior High School Students] 8 (Tokyo: Fukutake Shoten, 1981); Takeuchi Kiyoshi, "Kōkōsei no seito bunka" [High School Student Culture], *Monograph: Kōkōsei 80* [Monograph: High School Students 1980], Vol. 2 (Tokyo: Fukutake Shoten, 1980).

11. Mombusho, *Gakkō kihon chōsa hōkokusho* [Report on Basic School Data] (Tokyo: Ministry of Education, annual).

12. Mombusho, *Mombu tokei yoran* [Summary of Educational Statistics] (Tokyo: Ministry of Education, 1987).

13. Ibid.

14. Ibid.

15. Thomas P. Rohlen, *Japan's High Schools* (Berkeley: University of California, 1983), p. 124.

16. Takeuchi, "Joshi no seito bunka no tokushitsu," p. 26, figure 2.

17. Tanaka Kimiko and Higashi Yoshinobu, *Shin-gendai fujin no ishiki* [The New Consciousness of Contemporary Women] (Tokyo: Gyōsei, 1985), pp. 40–42, table 2-3; pp. 45–47, table 2-4.

18. Ibid., p. 25.

19. "Danjo byōdō e undo—toritsukō no boshū tei'in" [Movement for Gender Equality—Quotas on Admission at Tokyo Metropolitan High Schools], *Asahi shimbun* [Asahi Newspaper], May 20, 1988.

20. Ibid., March 20, 1987.

21. "Rikei erabanu joshi gakusei: Nōryoku-sa, iie kankyo no mondai" [Girls Choosing Not to Go into Science: A Question of Environment Rather than Ability], *Nihon keizai shimbun* [Japan Economic News], November 24, 1987.

22. Tomoda Yasumasa, "Educational and Occupational Aspirations of Female Senior High School Students," *Bulletin of the Hiroshima Agricultural College* 4 (December 1972), pp. 247–62.

23. Kyōtō Daigaku Kyōikugakubu, p.37, figure V-2.

24. Mombusho, *Mombu tokei yoran*, p. 60.

25. Ibid., p. 72.

26. "Sokuho '80 daigaku gōkakusha shusshin kōkōbetsu ichiran" [Announcement: A Listing of Successful College Applicants by High Schools, 1980], *Shukan asahi* [Asahi Weekly], April 4, 1980, pp. 22–29, 179, 189.

27. Bando Kumiko, "Deeta kara mita joshi no kōtō kyōiku" [Women's Higher Education as Seen from the Data], *IDE* 288 (December 1987), p. 40.

28. Mombusho, *Mombu tokei yoran*, p. 76.

29. Ibid., pp. 74–75.

30. Ibid., pp. 76–77.

31. Bando, "Deeta kara mita joshi no kōtō kyōiku," pp. 44–45.

32. Kokuritsu fujin kyōiku kaikan [National Women's Education Center], *Shōwa 62-nendo kōtō kyōiku ni okeru joseigaku kanren koza kaisetsu jōkyo chōsa kekka hōkoku* [1987 Report of a Survey on the Establishment of Women's Studies Courses in Institutions of Higher Education] (Tokyo: Kokuritsu Fujin Kyōiku Kaikan, August 1987), p. 1.

33. Mombusho, *Mombu tokei yoran*, pp. 44, 48, 56.
34. Ibid., pp. 80–81.
35. Kano Yoshimasa, "Daigaku Kyoin ichiba no hendo—josei kenkyusha o chushin ni" [Changes in the Market for College Faculty—With Special Reference to Academic Women], *Kagawa daigaku kyōiku gakubu kenkyu hōkoku* [Research Report of the Education Faculty at Kagawa University] no. 57 (1983), p. 194, table 7.
36. Saruhashi Katsuko and Shobei Shiota, *Josei kenkyūsha* [Women Researchers] (Tokyo: Domesu Shuppan, 1985); Kano Yoshimasa, "Nihon no josei kenkyūsha—Sono genjō to rekishiteki hendō" [Women Researchers in Japan—Current Status and Historical Changes], in Shimbori Michiya, ed., *Daigaku kyōjushoku no sōgōteki kenkyū—academic profession no shakaigaku* [A Comprehensive Study of the College Academic Profession—Sociology of the Academic Professiona] (Tokyo: Oga Shuppan, 1984); Michii Takako, "The Chosen Few: Women Academics in Japan" (Ph.D. diss., State University of New York at Buffalo, 1982); Bando Masako, Noguchi Michika, and Shinyama Yoko, eds., *Josei to gakumon to seikatsu—fujin kenkyūsha no raifu saikuru* [Women: Study and Life—The Life Cycle of Women Researchers] (Tokyo: Keiso Shobo, 1981).
37. J.E. Thomas, *Learning Democracy in Japan: The Social Education of Japanese Adults* (Beverly Hills, Calif.: Sage Publications, 1985), p. 39.
38. Iwao Sumiko, "How Japan Is Providing a Soft Landing for Women in a Post Industrial Society," *Worldwide Education for Women: Progress, Prospects and Agenda for the Future* (Paper presented at Mount Holyoke College, South Hadley, Mass., November 4–8, 1987), p. 5.
39. "Everyday Facts of Life: Cultural Mothers, 'The Movable Nursery,' " *Look Japan* (August 1988), p. 34.
40. Kumiko Fujimura-Fanselow, "Women's Education in Japan," in Gail P. Kelly, ed., *International Handbook on Women's Education* (Westport, Conn.: Greenwood Press, 1989).
41. Anne E. Imamura, *Urban Japanese Housewives: At Home and in the Community* (Honolulu: University of Hawaii Press, 1987).
42. Iwao Sumiko, "The Japanese: Portrait of Change," *Japan Echo* XV (1988), p. 4.
43. "Honsha chōsa—kawaru sengyō shufu: oshiyoseru yoka jidai no nami" [Survey of Changing Full-Time Housewives: The Surging Wave of the Leisure Era], *Nihon keizai shimbun* [Japan Economic News], June 15, 1988.
44. Fujin ni kansuru shomondai chōsa kaigi [Research Group on Women's Issues], *Gendai nihon josei no ishiki to kōdō: fujin ni kansuru shomondai no sōgō chōsa hōkokusho* [The Mentality and Behavior of Contemporary Japanese Women: Report of a Comprehensive Survey on Various Women's Issues] (Tokyo: Okurasho insatsukyoku [Ministry of Finance Printing Office], 1974), p. 316.
45. Sugawara Mariko, "Shoku...kakei...jū...kojinka susumu kazoku: Musubitsuki yuruyakani" [Food...Family Finances...Housing...Increasing Individualism in the Family: Gentle Ties], *Nihon keizai shimbun* [Japan Economic News], March 4, 1988.
46. "Honsha chōsa—kawaru sengyō shufu: Usureru daidokoro no bannin no imēji" [Survey on Changing Full-time Housewives: The Fading Image of the 'Guardian of the Kitchen,'] *Nihon keizai shimbun* [Japan Economic News], June 12, 1988.
47. "Honsha chōsa—kawaru sengyō shufu: shokuba fukki e iyoku jūbun" [Survey of Changing Full-Time Housewives: Full of Confidence about Returning to Work], *Nihon keizai shimbun* [Japan Economic News], June 14, 1988.

48. "Wāpuro, pasokon, gogaku... naijo no kō no yogawari" [Word Processors, Home Computers, Language Ability... the Wife's behind the Scenes Help of Her Husband Is Undergoing Many Changes], *Nihon keizai shimbun* [Japan Economic News], April 13, 1988.

49. Kinjo Kyoko, *Kazoku to iu kankei* [The Family Relationship] (Tokyo: Iwanami Shinsho 305, Iwanami Shoten, 1985), pp. 165ff.

50. Frank K. Upham, *Law and Social Change in Postwar Japan* (Cambridge, Mass.: Harvard University Press, 1987), p. 144.

51. Kokuritsu fujin kyōiku kaikan [National Women's Education Center], "Zadankai: Kōreika ni mukete—fujin no gakushū to jissen" [Discussion: Women's Study and Actual Practice—Facing an Aging Society], *Fujin kyōiku joho (Tokushu) Kōreika shakai to seikatsu sekkei—gakushū to jissen* [Women's Education News (Special Issue), An Aging Society and Life Planning—Study and Practice] 14, 9 (1986), p. 16.

52. Rōdōsho fujin shōnen kyoku [Ministry of Labor, Women and Minors' Bureau], *Fujin rōdō no jitsujō* [Actual Condition of Women and Labor] (Tokyo: Ministry of Labor, 1987), appendix 12, table 11.

53. Ibid., appendix 15, table 12; appendix 26-7, table 21.

54. Mombusho, *Mombu tokei yoran*, pp. 88–91.

55. Ibid.

56. Rōdōsho fujin shōnen kyoku, *Fujin rōdō no jitsujō*, appendix 67, table 60.

57. Tanaka and Higashi, *Shin-gendai fujin no ishiki*, pp. 88–91, table 3, 4.

58. See Rōdōsho fujin shōnen kyoku, *Joshi rōdōsha ni kansuru chōsa hōkokusho* [Report of a Survey Concerning Women Workers] (Tokyo: Ministry of Labor, 1981).

59. Rōdōsho fujin shōnen kyoku, *Fujin rōdō no jitsujō*, appendix pp. 14–15, appendix table 12.

60. "Daisotsu josei 'saiyō no mon' hirogaru" [The 'Recruitment Gate' for Women University Graduate Widens], *Yomiuri shimbun* [Yomiuri Newspaper], December 28, 1986.

61. "Sansai ni shite shikō sakugo" [Trial and Error upon Reaching Age Three], *Nihon keizai shimbun* [Japan Economic News], June 26, 1988.

62. "Onna no hatarakikata—tayōka no kage ni mujin" [Women's Work Styles: Inconsistency in the Shadow of Diversity], *Nihon keizai shimbun* [Japan Economic News], March 7, 1988.

63. Nihon rikurūto sentā [Japan Recruit Center], "Shingaku dōki chōsa" [Survey of Motivations for Going on to Higher Education] (Tokyo: Japan Recruit Center, 1982), pp. 54–55.

64. Tanaka and Higashi, *Shin-gendai fujin no ishiki*, pp. 45–47, table 2-4.

65. Ibid., pp. 219–21, table 6-3; pp. 224–25, table 6-4; pp. 227–28, table 6-5.

66. "Waakingu mazaa: ureshii seido zokuzoku" [Increasing Systems to Make Mothers Happy], *Nihon keizai shimbun* [Japan Economic News], May 16, 1988.

67. Margaret Locke, "The Selfish Housewife and Menopausal Syndrome in Japan" (Working papers on Women in International Development, no. 154, East Lansing, Mich.: Michigan State University, 1987).

REFERENCES

Hall, Robert King. *Education for a New Japan*. New Haven, Conn.: Yale University Press, 1949.

Hara Kimi. "Joshi koto kyōiku no shakaigakuteki ikkosatu" [A Sociological Examination of Women's Higher Education]. *Kyoiku shakaigaku kenkyu* [Research in the Sociology of Education] 26 (October 1971).

Kokusai fujinnen o kikkake to shite kōdō o okosu onnatachi no kai, kyōiku bunka kai [Association of Women for Action Arising from the International Women's Year, Committee on Education]. *Danjo byodo no kyōiku o kangaeru series*, no.3— *Tsubasa o mogareta onnanoko: kyoshitsu no naka no seisabetsu [Series on Thinking about Gender Equality in Education, no. 3—Girls Whose Wings have been Clipped: Sex Discrimination in the Classroom,* March, 1982.

Mombusho annual. *Gakkō kihon chōsa hōkōkusho* [Report on School Basic Data]. Tokyo: Ministry of Education.

Robins-Mowry, Dorothy. *The Hidden Sun: Women of Modern Japan.* Boulder, Colo.: Westview Press, 1983.

11

Teacher Education in Japan

Nobuo Shimahara

INTRODUCTION

Traditionally, Japanese society has relied on formal education to develop character, to cultivate moral and cultural sensitivity, and, indeed, to advance industrialization and modernization. The Japanese belief that teachers should inclusively enhance the instrumental, moral, and expressive aspects of their children's formation has become so deeply entrenched in that tradition that it has become a virtual cultural expectation—one that has shaped the evolution of teacher training itself.

Before 1945, teacher training progressed according to various successive influences: The Western orientation of the early Meiji period later gave way to the Confucian ideology, which, itself, subsequently yielded to the nationalistic pressures of militarism. After 1945, teacher education was guided by the first United States Education Mission's recommendations on educational reform. In this chapter I discuss the education of Japanese teachers, their roles in the schools, and proposed reforms in their education. I focus on teachers' roles to allow the reader to appreciate better how reformers want to improve them in the 1980s.

TEACHERS ON TRIAL: PROLOGUE

Today teachers hold respectable positions in Japanese society. Although teaching has long been a comparatively attractive profession, its appeal has heightened during the past decade, and entry has become more competitive. Every year more than 200,000 applicants compete for fewer than 40,000 positions in the public school system. In 1985 graduates fresh from colleges and universities filled 59 percent of the available positions. The remaining 41 percent were filled by applicants switching to new careers and by *shushoku rōnin*, the previous year's graduates who had failed the appointment examination on their first attempt. This unprecedented competition for teaching jobs has grown somewhat analogous to the now familiar competition for admission to colleges and universities. And one need not seek far for the reasons. Teachers earn significantly more than other public employees, and their salaries compare favorably with salaries in the private sector. Furthermore, their employment is assured for a lifetime.

On the debit side, teachers receive considerable criticism from the public for their inadequacies. That the public view of teachers is predominantly critical is clearly reflected in the extensive debate on teacher education that has occurred throughout the postwar period. Teachers are frequently held responsible for the increasing incidents of violence and bullying in schools; these social and political matters are extensively reported in the mass media. Some reformers in the 1980s even believe that most social problems in the schools could be eliminated if teachers were to receive better preservice education.[1] Teachers' inability to deal effectively with those problems often leads to fatigue, depression, and even suicide. From 1978 to 1981, for example, 387 teachers committed suicide.[2]

Today society's reliance upon teachers is obviously as high as it was in the past. This reflects the group-oriented Japanese culture, in which teachers are assumed to play culturally compatible and inclusive roles. First of all, teachers are responsible for developing students' personalities. Hence teachers make a great effort to instill what are usually identified as "fundamental living habits" into their students at all levels. Second, the Japanese teacher is expected to be the primary agent not only for transmitting culture, but also for developing student motivation to do school work. Third, society's broad reliance upon teachers flows from the fact that schooling in Japan is intense and central to the lives of both primary and secondary students. The centrality of schooling in students' lives finds its expression in the public view of the school as a moral community. Each school is expected to maintain a high moral standard, and this standard is subject to public scrutiny. The centrality of schooling also manifests itself in the school's critical responsibility for promoting high academic standards. High academic attainment is essential for success in the high school and university entrance examinations, a functional centerpiece of the school system.

In brief, Japanese society's predominant dependence on its teachers contributes to their respected cultural image but simultaneously subjects them to constant criticism.

TEACHER EDUCATION PRIOR TO 1945: BACKGROUND

The history of teacher education in Japan parallels the evolution of that society as a nation-state from its inception in the Meiji Restoration of 1868. Teacher education began as part of the Japanese modernization early in the Meiji period.

The first comprehensive plan for establishing a national school system was laid out in 1872. It was in that year that the first normal school was founded in Tokyo by the Department of Education, the precursor of the Ministry of Education.

Marion M. Scott, an American teacher who was initially invited to Japan to teach English, was appointed as instructor of the school for three years.[3] Using instructional methods and materials then current in the United States, he was responsible for teaching twenty-four teacher trainees chosen from various prefectures. He divided the twenty-four students into six groups, each of which was responsible for instructing a group of fifteen pupils during the practice session; these pupils were enrolled in a school attached to the normal school.[4] Although the teacher trainees received their instruction in English, they practiced teaching in Japanese. Admission to the school required that applicants be at least twenty years of age and that they pass the entrance examination. This inception of teacher education in early Meiji Japan typifies the initial educational development—drawing upon Western experience while searching for advanced models of schooling. It goes without saying that the Western influence on Japanese teacher education continued to be significant during the 1870s.

By 1876, just four years after the Tokyo normal school had been established, ninety-four other normal schools were founded throughout the nation by the Department of Education. Among them were women's normal schools, the first of which was operating as early as 1874. Students were required to enroll in normal schools for two years where they studied such subjects as Japanese history, composition, geography, physical education, physics, arithmetic, and calligraphy. Normal school was considered "the place" where students were trained to become *shihan*, an exemplar for elementary pupils.[5] Interestingly, moral education was never part of the normal school curriculum during the early Meiji period.

In 1880 when the nation's second modern school reform occurred, Confucian influence began to supersede the Western orientation of the early Meiji era.[6] Confucianism rose in response to what was thought to be the excessive Westernization of Japan; that is, indiscriminate exposure to Western thought and civilization was considered to have deteriorated the moral fabric of Japanese society. Confucian ideology in education was enhanced first by Motoda Nagazane, the imperial lecturer who drafted Kyogaku Seishi, the Imperial Will on the Great Principles of Education, to build the moral basis of the imperial system. It stressed the concepts of loyalty to the imperial state and filial piety as the moral foundation of education. Kyogaku Seishi underscored the urgency of instilling Confucian ethics in the minds of elementary school children.[7] As a result, the government adopted it as a guiding framework for educational policy. Thus, the Department of Education rushed to print the first moral education textbooks composed of famous adages from traditional Eastern classics illustrative of Confucian thought. In 1881 it also issued an ethical guide for elementary school teachers which defined the teacher's role in promoting *sonno aikoku*, reverence for the emperor and patriotism through moral education. To promote moral education further, the government distributed to local schools copies of *Essentials of Primary Instruction*, a textbook edited by Motoda outlining twenty moral principles.[8]

In 1883 the national standards for training teachers were established, and they placed greater emphasis on Confucian ideology. In 1886 Mori Arinori, the first education minister, issued the normal school order that created the foundations of pre–World War II teacher education in Japan.[9] He viewed education as an instrument of nation building that would contribute to the enhancement of what was regarded as his obsession, Japan's international status. Mori underscored the importance of teacher education because he believed that teachers would play a central role in training the human resources required by the nation.[10] The training of character and the uniform development of cognitive and motivational orientation toward the state were brought into prominence in teacher education under his policy. "Attention," the normal school order stressed, "ought to be paid to ensuring that the students are those possessing a good and obedient, faithful, and respectful character."[11] All teacher trainees were housed in dormitories for the entire period of training so that they might achieve uniformity in their character development and might be supervised closely. This character training became a major characteristic of teacher education thereafter, part of the ethos of Japanese normal schools.

In 1897 the Ministry of Education issued the teacher education order that created three types of teacher training: normal schools, women's normal schools, and higher normal schools. Both normal schools and women's normal schools required four years of training for higher elementary school graduates. Entrance into higher normal schools, on the other hand, required graduation from normal school, and the training lasted for three years. The primary goal of the normal school was to train elementary school teachers; the higher normal school was designed to provide teachers for normal schools and middle schools. Teacher education was further reformed in 1919, 1924, and 1932. In 1929 Tokyo and Hiroshima Bunrika Colleges (teachers' colleges) were established to offer advanced studies in education for graduates of higher normal schools.[12] Training at the normal school level was expanded to five years for higher elementary graduates and from one to two years for students who graduated from middle school. In 1938 the Education Council recommended the further upgrading of the normal school to the level of professional school, which required graduation from middle school and training for three years. The recommendation was implemented in 1943.

Under growing militarism, in 1941, the government promulgated the national school order based on the Education Council's recommendation to emphasize training for the imperial subjects. The order clearly reflected the underlying nationalistic ideology of education under militarism. The aims of schooling were defined as follows: "The aims of the National School are to carry out elementary general education in accordance with the Imperial Way and to provide our people with the basic training required of Imperial Subjects."[13] Schooling had changed to an inclusive process of behavioristic and motivational training and acquisition of the practical knowledge requisite for the promotion of the imperial state. Group training was the method employed to implement the process. In contrast, individual freedom in schooling was judged to be inimical to the goals of the national school and was rejected. Under this order, teacher education was designed to train future teachers who could promote the imperial way through schooling.

To summarize, in the pre–World War II period, the development of teacher education was dictated by the succession of three ideological forces: Western thought which impacted on early Meiji reforms, Confucianism, and nationalism. The character training of future teachers was of the utmost importance and militaristic, and it took precedence over the intellectual development of teacher trainees.

TEACHER EDUCATION SINCE 1945

There is an interesting parallel between Meiji and postwar education reforms: Both reforms were considerably influenced by Western educational systems. On the other hand, the Meiji reforms were carried out under the initiatives of Meiji leaders, whereas the postwar reforms were imposed and implemented under the close supervision of the Occupation authorities.[14] Like teacher training in the early Meiji period, postwar teacher education was based on an American model. The United States Education Mission invited to Japan in 1946 by the Occupation authorities presented a framework for educational reforms which profoundly influenced the development of education for teachers. The mission's recommendations read: "The reorganized normal schools, all more nearly at the level of the higher normal schools, should become four-year institutions; they would continue general education and provide adequate professional training for teachers in elementary and secondary schools."[15] The recommendations became the basis for the development of a general principle of postwar teacher education, which includes three basic components: general education, studies in specialized fields, and professional education.[16] The Education Reform Committee, established by the Japanese government in 1946, was charged with formulating proposals for comprehensive educational reforms on the basis of the mission's recommendations.

The Education Reform Committee recommended that teacher education be placed within the university system, unlike prewar teacher training, which was conducted in a separate system, and that independent teacher colleges be developed to prepare teachers at the elementary and lower secondary levels.[17] This recommendation led to the Ministry of Education's policy of establishing at least one national university in each prefecture with a faculty or department responsible for teacher education. The purpose of teacher education at a university is to provide students with a broad liberal arts education, as well as specialized preparation, which was lacking in the programs at normal schools. Another significant difference between prewar and postwar teacher education is what the Japanese characterize as an "open system of licensing," whereby anyone who completes specialized study and a professional program at a postwar university is eligible for teacher certification. This policy is liberal and "open" in contrast to the closed, prewar system of licensing. In the prewar period, teacher certification was largely limited to those trained at normal schools operated under the direct control of the Ministry of Education. In 1949, teacher training at the normal school was replaced by broadly oriented teacher education programs offered first at forty-five universities with schools of education and seven teachers' colleges that included liberal arts programs.

As a consequence, teacher education became more liberal enabling not only colleges of education, but also a good many other institutions to establish programs to prepare teachers.[18] By 1979 nearly 85 percent of the 444 colleges and universities and 84 percent of the 518 junior colleges were participating in teacher education.[19] There are currently sixty-five colleges of education, fifty-eight of which are affiliated with national universities and seven with private institutions. Every year more than 800 institutions are graduating nearly 175,000 students with teaching certificates, accounting for 32 percent of the total college and university graduates in the nation.[20] Obviously, those institutions are oversupplying certified applicants for a profession that can employ only about 40,000 of them each year. Graduates of schools of education do not fare well in the face of this enlarged competition. In 1985 only 46 percent of the 31,000 graduates of schools of education could find jobs in the public schools and only 9 percent in private schools. Overall in 1985, graduates of other institutions filled one-third of the openings at the elementary level, two-thirds at the lower secondary level, and nearly nine-tenths at the upper secondary level.

Let us now examine the programs of teacher preparation. As developed by the Education Reform Committee, the paradigm of teacher preparation has three components: general education, specialized study, and professional education.[21] It is quite similar to the predominant model of teacher education in the United States. Specific requirements for teacher certification are defined in detail in the Educational Certification Law, which is enforced throughout the nation by the Ministry of Education.

Graduates of education programs may apply for a regular or a temporary certificate, depending upon their qualifications. Regular certificates are either first class or second class. Regular first-class certificates require the completion of course work at a four-year college or graduate work, depending upon the level of teaching for which the applicant seeks certification. Minimum legal requirements for teacher certification at four-year colleges are 124 credits earned in the requisite areas of course work (one credit consists of fifteen lecture sessions per semester, each running from forty-five to fifty minutes). Second-class certificates, for kindergarten, elementary, and lower secondary teachers, require sixty-two credits, or two years of course work.

In reality, the national colleges of education require for graduation minimum course work ranging from 124 to 159 credits for both elementary and lower secondary education majors. Research indicates that students at those colleges usually take even more credits, averaging between 160 and 180 and even more than 200 credits in extreme cases, to obtain more than one certificate.[22]

A typical four-year program for an elementary education major in a national college of education consists of from forty-eight to fifty-two credits in general education—at least a fourth in the humanities, a fourth in the social sciences, and a fourth in the natural sciences; from eight to twelve credits in foreign languages; and four credits in physical education. The requirements in general education for elementary majors apply to lower secondary majors as well.

A significant difference between elementary and lower secondary programs lies in the area of concentration: The lower secondary programs emphasize the field of specialty, whereas the elementary program lacks such concentration. Instead, the elementary program stresses professional studies, consisting of such areas as social and philosophical foundations of education, psychology of education, child psychology, moral education, practice teaching, and teaching methods. From thirty to thirty-six credits in professional studies are requisite for elementary majors. In addition, two credits are required in each elementary teaching subject. In contrast, the lower secondary program typically requires from forty to fifty credits in the field of concentration and only fourteen credits in professional studies, although most programs at the national colleges of education do demand between eighteen and twenty-six credits.

A typical kindergarten program is similar to the elementary program, but it demands heavy concentration on kindergarten education as the field of specialty.

Majors in the upper secondary program also need only fourteen credits in professional studies, but they must have a greater concentration in specialized study. First-class teaching certificates at the high school level require a master's degree or thirty credits of graduate education. To obtain second-class certificates, students must meet the same course work requirements as applicants for first-class certificates at the lower secondary level. Minimum requirements for student teaching are only two credits, equivalent to two weeks of practice in both secondary programs and four credits in the elementary program. National colleges of education, however, require that students engage in slightly more student teaching, an average of four or five credits in the lower secondary program.

SHORTCOMINGS OF TEACHER EDUCATION

The teacher education programs just described are typical at the national institutions whose primary commitment is in part to prepare teachers. Although the model of teacher education mentioned earlier has guided teacher education since 1949, actual programs vary considerably. Particularly since 1954, requirements in specialized subject areas have increased, while requirements in the professional component have decreased, causing many to ask whether the teacher education currently offered is adequate professional preparation.[23]

As already pointed out, the minimum requirement for certifying lower and upper secondary teachers is only fourteen credits in professional studies, including two credits for student teaching. Students seeking teacher certification at the institutions whose primary mission is not teacher education tend to meet only that minimum requirement, which accounts for less than 10 percent of their course work. Recall that these are the same students who, of late, fill two-thirds of the lower secondary jobs and nine-tenths of the secondary jobs in the public school system. Undoubtedly, such graduates have much greater depth in their special subject areas than the graduates of the colleges of education, but the adequacy of their professional program is questionable. Indeed, it has been questioned persistently by the Ministry of Education, its advisory organizations, and other professional educational organizations.

As early as 1958 the Central Council of Education, an influential policy-recommending body advisory to the minister of education, having broad representation from various occupational fields, raised that crucial question in its report on policies for enhancing teacher education. The report itself sprang from the ministry's concern with what it feared to be deteriorating teacher education in the nation. The council was unambiguously critical of the postwar liberalization of teacher education, which, in its opinion, had downgraded certification standards. But the council did support and has continued to support the fundamental principles of liberalization of teacher education at the university level. It saw a generally growing practice of meeting only the minimum certification requirements and of meeting them only nominally and argued that the purpose of teacher education programs even at national universities was unclear. It pointed out that only perfunctory attention was given to student teaching and urged that those problems be immediately remedied. Further, it stressed the pivotal importance of promoting a teacher's sense of mission—a pronounced orientation toward teaching, ubiquitously emphasized by school administrators in Japan. It urged the government to improve both preservice and in-service education, so that "teachers may enhance teaching with a sense of mission and high motivation."[24] In the council's view, the teachers in training at the time lacked this kind of devotion.

To answer those problems, the council proposed the creation of institutions whose purpose would be to prepare only teachers: a concept of teacher education analogous to the preservice training conducted at the normal schools.[25] As expected, the council's proposals met tenacious opposition by progressive forces, such as the Japan Pedagogical Society and the Japan Teachers Union (Nikkyoso), which deemed the proposals regressive. They insisted on the liberal model of teacher education.[26] As a result, the proposals did not materialize; nevertheless, they served as a benchmark for other proposals for teacher education reform in the 1960s.

Thirteen years later, in 1971, the council articulated its concern with teacher education in a most extensive report on educational reform. That report delineated critical issues and a broad scope of recommendations.[27] The council identified teacher education as one of the critical areas to be addressed in what it viewed as the third great educational reform, preceded only by the Meiji and Occupation reforms. It forcefully pointed out the urgent need for improving teacher preparation, in-service education, and reeducation. This recommendation included the creation of education universities at the undergraduate and graduate levels. In 1978, after several years of heated debate, it led to the enactment of a legislative measure, with strong support of the conservative majority party, that established those universities.

It also recommended that, in order to attract competent applicants to the teaching profession, starting salaries for elementary and secondary teachers be raised by from 30 to 40 percent above the starting salaries of other public employees. Although this specific recommendation for raising teacher salaries was legislated in a modified form in 1974, when the so-called Human Resource Procurement bill passed the National Diet, the teacher education curriculum remained basically unchanged in the 1970s. That legislation has significantly improved the economic status of teachers and made entry to teaching highly competitive. In view of that situation, the council issued another report in 1978 which reiterated the critical need for a campaign to promote more rigorous teacher preparation.[28]

Likewise, the Teacher Education Council, a standing advisory council in the Ministry of Education, issued reports in 1962, 1965, 1966, and 1972 which recommended reforms of the teacher education curriculum and certification criteria. Those reports by and large reflected the views expressed by the Central Council of Education, including the proposals for the creation of institutions for professional preparation in teaching and internship programs.

In 1983, the Teacher Education Council made another recommendation that became the basis of the latest bill, presented by the government to the Diet to improve teacher certification standards. The scope of changes recommended, which was relatively broad, aimed at upgrading teacher qualifications at all levels.[29] In essence, the council proposed more rigorous requirements in both the specialized subject and the professional education components at all levels. It introduced three classes of teaching certificates to encourage graduate training for teachers: a special certificate obtainable upon the completion of course work at the master's level, a standard certificate requiring a bachelor's degree, and a temporary certificate. Although the bill was the culmination of sustained attempts by the Ministry of Education to make professional preparation in teaching more rigorous, it was defeated in the Diet in 1984. Nevertheless, as we shall see later, teacher education was again a central issue under consideration by the National Council on Education Reform since its formation in the fall of 1984.

Other organizations also reviewed teacher education and its policies. Among them, the most notable were the Japanese Association of Colleges of Teacher Education; the Association of National Universities, which has a standing committee which monitors teacher preparation; and the Japan Pedagogical Association. They all address the central issues of teacher education, such as those discussed here, but, as academic organizations, the Association of National Universities and the Japan Pedagogical Association often differ with the Ministry of Education and its advisory councils. These academic organizations strongly support liberal teacher education free from direct control of the Ministry of Education and the postwar policy that teacher education be broadly based in university education.[30] Both the Japan Pedagogical Association and the Association of National Universities, for example, expressed strong reservations regarding the establishment of specialized education universities, which might advance political control of teacher education by the Ministry of Education.[31] Partly because such organizations, private university associations, and the Japan Teachers Union are opposed to state control of teacher education, as practiced in the prewar period, they have been critical of the policies advanced by the ministry.

Besides curriculum and standards for professional training, which have been controversial throughout the postwar era, Japanese teacher education has other problems. Noticeable among them is the observation of Japanese scholars that a well-integrated sequence of teacher education course work is lacking.[32] These observations suggest that teacher education is fragmented because the three components of the teacher education curriculum are not cogently integrated. Moreover, in trying to obtain more than one certificate, students are inclined to take too many courses at the cost of depth and rigor in the area of specialization. Another problem, perhaps more fundamental, is related to a debate among Japanese scholars regarding education as a discipline. According to them, education has not yet developed into a discipline, as the natural and social sciences have—a familiar observation also made in the United States. College educators and researchers have not yet coherently defined the field of study unique to education. This is in part a source of what is seen as fragmentation in teacher education.

ENTRY INTO TEACHING

In 1985, 37.4 percent of the 38,239 available positions in the nation's public schools were filled by applicants who had bachelor's degrees from colleges of education, and another 53.4 percent were won by applicants with the same degree from academically based universities. Only 3.3 percent were filled by master's degree holders, and 5.9 percent were taken by junior college graduates. These statistics reveal a pattern of employment that has developed over the past decade. Notable in this pattern is that nine out of ten new entrants are four-year-college graduates and that replacements in the teaching profession are dominated by noneducation university graduates.

This pattern suggests several characteristics of Japan's teaching profession. First, Japan has a broad array of human resources to meet education's demands. Second, entrants with graduate degrees still constitute a small fraction in Japan's system. Third, employment opportunities as elementary and secondary teachers have diminished for junior college graduates with second-class certificates; better qualified applicants overshadow them in the competition for the limited numbers of positions. Despite those recent changes, the public schools still have significant numbers of older teachers who have had two or fewer years of college-level preparation. In 1983–1984, for example, approximately 41 percent of the elementary school teachers, 24 percent of the lower secondary teachers, and 11 percent of the upper secondary teachers had not obtained bachelor's degrees. In contrast, in the United States, in 1980, 99.6 percent of all teachers had at least a bachelor's degree; 56, 47, and 45 percent of high school, junior high and middle school, and elementary teachers, respectively, held at least a master's degree.[33]

Competition for entry into the teaching profession intensified as early as 1974, when the Human Resource Procurement bill became law, and reached its peak in 1979. That legislative measure, coupled with the depressing effects of the oil crisis of 1973 upon industry, led to a dramatic rise in the number of applicants for teaching positions. For example, the total number of applicants who actually took appointment examinations nearly doubled, from 128,000 in 1974 to 245,000 in 1979, although the number of positions increased by only 13.5 percent. The competition has slightly declined since 1979, but the prefectural boards of education still enjoy a fivefold oversupply of teacher applicants.

The relative quality of teacher applicants, however, is very hard to determine in Japan. Because they graduate from broadly diversified schools, significant variations in their intellectual quality are to be expected. Recall again that most recent entrants to the profession at both the lower and upper secondary levels earned their degrees in specializations other than education. Japan has no established criteria with which to compare their intellectual and technical competence to that of those who enter different occupations. What can be generalized, however, is that the quality of teacher applicants cannot be judged in terms of the intellectual quality of the students at the colleges of education and vice versa.

Prospective teachers cannot gain entry to the teaching profession unless they pass competitive appointment examinations given once a year by each of the forty-seven prefectures and ten largest municipalities. Graduation from a university with a teaching certificate is not sufficient for appointment, no matter how good one's academic course work may have been. Japan's meritocracy operates in determining entry to the profession. Once applicants gain entry, they enjoy lifetime employment and are promoted on the basis of seniority, as in all other parts of the public sector and in private industry. Dismissals are very few; teachers can be dismissed only for extraordinarily unethical conduct.

However, as in industry, individual-centered meritocratic principles no longer operate after entry into the professional group. Partly because of its commitment to the practice of lifetime employment, each board of education of the fifty-seven prefectures and municipalities carefully selects teacher applicants.

Given the intense competition in appointment examinations, passing them has become a primary goal of aspiring teachers, just as passing university entrance examinations is the overriding concern of high school students. Applicants need to concentrate on preparing for the examinations before taking them. Appointment examinations provide opportunities for all applicants—education majors and others—to compete universally and equally. The aim of the examinations is to select the best qualified applicants from the competitive pool where achievement is a major criterion. The examinations are given in two stages. The first stage consists of written tests in general education and in specialized fields and skill tests in such areas as physical education, music, art, and English conversation. All teacher applicants for lower secondary jobs are required to take a test of physical fitness. The second stage consists of interviews. In those cities and prefectures that have a concentration of *burakumin*, a Japanese minority, *dowa* education,[34] literally translated as assimilation education, is a required examination subject.

It is relevant to point out that age is one criterion in Japan that determines an applicant's qualification for appointment examinations. More than half of the forty-seven prefectures require that applicants be under the age of thirty; only two prefectures have no age limit. Although this practice is much more liberal than that of industry, there is similarity between the two. Large corporations in Japan recruit new university and high school graduates almost exclusively.

IN-SERVICE EDUCATION

More than two-thirds of the teachers who responded to a 1978 survey indicated that their professional preparation was inadequate.[35] The survey probably reflects the shortcomings of teacher education pointed out earlier. Moreover, prefectural and local boards of education are all dissatisfied with today's teacher education.[36] In view of these problems of teacher education, the importance of in-service education looms large.

There are five types of in-service education in Japan.[37] The first is the program given at an education center; the second, the in-house workshop *konai kenshu* conducted under the guidance of *shido shuji*, an instructional supervisor appointed by the superintendent of schools; the third, the program given to administrators by the Ministry of Education at a national training center, such as Tsukuba; the fourth, the informal in-service workshop promoted by teachers themselves through participating in district-wide study groups regularly organized to improve teaching competence. Although the fifth type of activity tends to be limited to active teachers, it is widespread and popular in Japan. In addition, beginning in 1978, two-year full-time advanced education has been given to teachers selected from all over the country at three nationally funded institutions (Hyogo, Joetsu, and Naruto Education Universities), earlier referred to as education universities, to provide graduate professional education to active teachers. These graduate institutions were created because the graduate schools in Japan failed to offer advanced professional studies to working teachers. The teachers who complete this program receive a master's degree and return to teach school.

These three institutions, however, graduate only several hundred students each year and have a very limited effect at present upon the teaching profession. The most widespread in-service education in Japan combines the first and second types and coordinates them to complement each other.

Hiroshima Municipal Center, a typical education center, is financed by the municipal board of education and is staffed by twenty-eight full-time specialists, including five administrators. These specialists are recruited primarily from a pool of the city's experienced, competent teachers, who take leave of absences from their schools and are appointed as *shido shuji*. The center offers 159 separate sessions in twenty-one different categories, each of which lasts from one to five days. These categories include subject areas from kindergarten through high school, teaching methodology, school administration, educational technology, student guidance, class management, and so on. Instructors include *shido shuji* at the center and corporate managers as guest speakers.

The Ministry of Education requires first-year teachers to receive in-service education for a minimum of twenty days. They undergo training for three days at the center and participate in a three-day, intensive retreat elsewhere. They also participate in an in-house workshop for fourteen days, under the supervision of municipal *shido shuji*. For example, participants regularly conduct demonstration classes before their colleagues and a *shido shuji*, followed by feedback sessions. Teachers, including the first-year teachers, also participate in citywide study group meetings organized to discuss a variety of concerns, including teaching methods and curriculum. Sixth-year teachers spend three days at the center for professional enrichment. There is also a program for administrators, including department chairpersons, assistant principals, and principals, but the emphasis is on first-year principals. Administrators are expected to participate in in-service workshops for from four to eight days a year. A typical training session consists of lectures, discussion, and case studies.

In addition to these programs, the center offers a six-month program for six selected teachers, who work full time on special projects which they choose, and a three-month program for twenty-two additional teachers. The latter are granted released time from their respective schools to work on their projects.

In-service education in Hiroshima City is typical, although some variations exist. Some prefectural centers provide in-service education to tenth, fifteenth, and twentieth year teachers as well.

It is relevant to note that the staff members who provide in-service programs are mainly *shido shuji*, experienced teachers and principals as well as a few university professors. Research suggests that neither educational administrators nor teachers consider the university professors to be particularly useful in in-service education because the professors are unfamiliar with teaching and administrative practices.[38] For their part, education professors question the approach of experienced teachers and administrators in retraining practitioners, which creates a separation between the practitioners and the professors who taught them. A deep mutual distrust appears to sustain the perennial question of the proper role of institutions of teacher education in the professional development of teachers.

It is also relevant to point out that the prefectural boards of education urge teachers to use their in-service enrichment programs to comprehend fully and to master the holistic role of a teacher, so that they may develop a sense of mission, or *shimeikan*. The boards' concern lies in the Japanese cultural notion that schooling is not merely a process of cognitive transmission, but also a process of developing morality and character.

All in all, in-service education programs at education centers and individual schools are actively promoted, and they are producing successful results. The same survey cited above suggests that two-thirds of first-year participants consider their in-service education to be useful.[39] In the view of the administrators of in-service education, however, the programs are far from adequate. According to its director, the Education Center for Hiroshima, for example, needs more funding to offer better programs, and teachers, especially first-year teachers, need more released time at the center.[40]

Under the active guidance of the Ministry of Education, prefectural and municipal boards of education offer in-service education for public school teachers at all levels. Programs for these teachers are offered mainly at the education center, which promotes, besides in-service education, educational research and counseling and guidance services. Each of the forty-seven prefectures and ten municipalities has an education center which offers in-service workshops, at various stages of a teacher's career, throughout the year.

TEACHER ROLES: CULTURAL EXPECTATION

To appreciate the need for reforming teacher education as articulated by reformers in the 1980s, we must discuss the cultural expectations of teacher roles in Japan. Teachers' roles are shaped by the society's cultural expectations of teachers. They differ from the roles of American teachers, just as Japanese and American cultures display notably contrasting features. Although Japanese education has been significantly influenced by American education since the Meiji Restoration, the roles of teachers in Japan remain distinctive to the present day. That simply reveals the powerful influence of Japanese culture upon the premises and patterns of educational practices.

Culture provides a general design for life, a covert rationale that guides human behavior. Members of a culture are usually not conscious of its force, although it gives a direction to their actions and shapes their behavioral and attitudinal patterns. Culture can be compared to the grammar that members of a group follow unconsciously to communicate with each other. It exerts a powerful and ubiquitous influence on the ways in which individual members act to solve their problems. The importance of culture needs to be highlighted here so that we can better appreciate Japanese teachers' roles.

Viewed from this perspective, schooling in Japan is a unique cultural process in which moral and expressive activities are universally enunciated from preschool through high school, and teachers are expected to enhance them actively regardless of age grades.[41] These activities include character development, moral sensitivity, and habit formation promoted through ritualism and collective activities in the context of *shudan seikatsu*, the Japanese term referring to group life or group activities.[42]

As alluded to at the outset, unlike American teachers, Japanese teachers are generally expected to play diffuse roles rather than role-specific functions narrowly defined within a structure of specializations, so that they may inclusively enhance moral, expressive, and instrumental aspects of student activities in the school setting. That expectation emphasizes the convergence of the public and private domains of student life. Teachers' roles in Japan are commonly defined in this framework of expectations relative to all levels of schooling, although there is a greater degree of specialization at the higher levels, which reduces the extent to which teachers inclusively give attention to various aspects of student life.

The centrality of moral education and the emphasis on forming sound habits define the scope of teachers' responsibilities. The courses of study for both elementary and lower secondary schools state identically:

It should be a basic principle that moral education in the school be provided throughout all the educational activities of the school. Therefore, proper instruction for moral development should be given not only in the hours for Moral Education, but also in the hours for each Subject and Special Activities, in conformity with their respective characteristics. In carrying out moral education at school, due consideration should be given to establishing closer human relationships between teachers and students and among students themselves, and to guiding thoroughly the practice of moral codes in the basic behavior of everyday life in cooperation with the home and the local community concerned.[43]

The same purpose of moral education is stated in the high school course of study, although moral education in the high school is not a formal instructional area as such.

Moral education is one of only three prominent areas in the course of study at the compulsory level; the others are curriculum and special activities. It is offered as an independent area of instruction and is also diffusely and less formally promoted throughout such diverse aspects of schooling as class management, student guidance, and other dimensions of special activities. In this sense, moral education and the teachers' efforts to promote sound habits are closely related aspects of schooling.

As mentioned earlier, central to moral education in Japanese schools is character development, which is assumed to accompany the acquisition of proper habits concerning such attitudinal and behavioral characteristics as regularity, orderliness, cooperation, self-discipline, persistence, and respectfulness. Research reveals that acquiring such habits is accomplished through *shudan seikatsu*, as group activities, and it begins at the preschool level, where teachers start to stress the conscious development of group activities.[44] Teachers deliberately and energetically guide children to internalize the pronounced cultural premise in schooling that each person is a member of a group. What is often referred to as "group consciousness" in Japan is consistently stressed through the high school years.[45]

Development of proper habits is also a primary concern in class management and student guidance, and it engages teachers extensively at the elementary and lower secondary levels. Class management, as practiced in the Japanese school, refers to the managerial efforts of a teacher to establish a class environment conducive to effective learning and teaching. Such an environment is characterized by the patterning of attitudes and behavior contributing to order, cooperation, and concentration in the learning process.

Student guidance, however, as the term is used in Japan, refers to the inclusive guidance provided to students that encompasses a gamut of problems, including student habits and academic, social, and personal problems. In the Japanese school system, there are no guidance and counseling specialists, as in the United States. Student guidance is ordinarily provided by a *tannin*, a teacher assigned to a particular class at a particular level. The teacher is responsible for teaching, class management, and student guidance. As *tannins* are expected to deal with the academic and extra-academic problems of their classes, they are able to see students in a holistic frame of reference and can serve as active agents for motivating students to academic work.[46]

Student guidance and part of class management are vital elements of special activities, which also include student activities, such as classroom assembly and club activities; school events, including ceremonial events, cultural performances, sports events, excursions, camping, events related to health and safety, and activities involving work and production; and "class guidance," a primary function of student guidance. Japanese teachers are expected to involve themselves in these activities energetically.

Every school bulletin carefully describes in detail student activities, plans for school events, and student guidance. Moreover, under the guidance of the Ministry of Education, local school districts promote a campaign to build "fundamental habits" conducive to school work and active student life. The student-guidance-related efforts that teachers promote in the elementary and lower secondary schools include a variety of ritualized activities, such as morning and afternoon meetings of students conducted in every classroom, daily cleaning, excursions, camping, teachers' home visitations, and athletic meetings. Similar activities go on at the upper secondary level, but generally high school teachers tend to consider student guidance less important; their central concern is academic instruction.[47]

Yet high schools in Japan by no means ignore student guidance, which, in their view, is still vital to establish order and to foster an orientation conducive to effective *shudan seikatsu*. For example, a high school in Hiroshima organizes a camping trip for nearly 500 sophomores every year as a way to induct them into the culture of the school. This camping program, which lasts for three full days, involves many students, many teachers, and some community volunteers and requires careful preparation. The principal suggests that the sophomores' camping experience is their most important orientation to the school. According to him, it provides an opportunity for students to learn the basic premises and rules underlying disciplined behavior and the attitudes needed for group life and work at the school. This type of extracurricular program is common from the fifth grade on, and one can readily see that its success depends on the active participation of dedicated teachers.[48]

The emphasis on character development, moral sensitivity, and habit building displays a ubiquitous cultural quality not unique to the school environment, but rather common in other institutional settings, such as industrial training.[49] In Japan, teachers regard disciplined habits as a foundation for diligent school work. The uniqueness of Japanese teachers lies in their approach to the basic social structure of student life upon which teaching and learning are based.

PROPOSALS TO REFORM TEACHER EDUCATION

At the outset of this chapter it was noted that Japanese teachers are subject to frequent criticism as a result of the deep-seated cultural expectations of society toward teachers. Even the latest educational reform proposals address teachers' shortcomings. The National Council on Educational Reform (NCER) was charged with the task of recommending a comprehensive educational reform. NCER had a three-year mandate to study major problems in education and to complete recommendations, which it presented in four separate reports submitted to the prime minister in 1985, 1986, and 1987. Unlike the Central Council of Education, which received little political support for its proposals for educational reform in 1971, the recent national council received unparalleled backing from the prime minister, who made educational reform a political priority,[50] and from the majority Liberal Democratic Party. It should be noted, however, that there are a number of similar recommendations in the reports of the NCER and the Central Council. Both bodies addressed a broad range of problems, including the quality of teachers and teacher education. In fact, the basic conceptual framework of NCER's recommendations had already been anticipated and delineated by the Central Council of Education in 1971.

Reviewing the pertinent literature suggests that two factors are most significant in the current reform movement. One is economic, the other social, but both are integral to the political concerns of the Japanese government.[51] From the Meiji period through the 1960s, the West had served as a paradigm for Japanese modernization for nearly a century, but now Japan's achievements are outstripping those of its models. Japan's long-standing fixation with the West as the source of all things modern has been changed in the past decade or so. Japan is seeking a new development paradigm to advance its economy and technology. Reforming education is, in significant part, governed by this consideration.

With respect to social factors, NCER points out pathological conditions in society, characterized by the weakening of the traditional moral structure and values and the rise of deviant behavior.[52] The council is keenly aware that Japanese education suffers from uniformity and rigidity, which was created when schooling was considered a central instrument for development dictated by the "catch-up ideology."[53] Thus, "most important in the educational reform to come," declares the council, "is to do away with the uniformity, rigidity, closedness and lack of internationalism, all of which are deep-rooted defects of our educational system."[54] In the reformers' view, the uniformity and rigidity of Japanese education have, in an important measure, contributed to the present undesirable state of schooling.

In its first report, NCER describes the conditions of schooling as "extremely critical and grievous."[55] Those pathological conditions are characterized by excessive competition in entrance examinations, bullying, school violence, juvenile delinquency, and refusal to attend school. Japanese education is said to suffer of late from a "grave state of desolation" illustrated by those conditions in society and schools.[56] NCER's emotionally charged indictment of education is directed in part toward what it regards to be mediocre teachers who lack "a sense of mission" and the "ability to guide" students and who are insensitive to parental and community needs.[57] NCER also attributes those conditions to an inadequacy in teaching moral education.[58] As a result, "there has been increasing public criticism expressing distrust of our school, teachers and the education sector as a whole."[59] "Irresponsible attitudes among teachers," the council argues, have contributed to the rapid decrease in public confidence in schools and teachers.[60] Such a critical commentary on teachers points to the perception that Japanese teachers have failed to meet the deep-seated cultural expectations of the teaching profession discussed earlier.

To redress those shortcomings, NCER proposes reforms in teacher preservice and in-service education, the teacher appointment system, teacher evaluation, teacher certification, and student teaching. Those proposals are outlined largely in NCER's second report. The fourth and final report merely summarized them, and the third report made no reference to teacher education. The centerpiece of NCER's proposal to improve professional education for teachers is an internship program for all neophyte teachers across the nation. According to this proposal, all beginning teachers will be appointed conditionally and will serve in schools under the guidance of supervising teachers for one year before being considered for permanent employment. The purpose of internship is to "gain the practical ability to teach and sense of mission."[61]

This internship program, the council says, will give prefectural boards of education, which appoint public school teachers, the opportunity to evaluate teacher trainees during the trial year. This kind of selection mechanism does not exist in the present system, under which, incidentally, neophyte teachers receive conditional appointments for a half-year and then gain permanent appointments. Customarily, once applicants gain entry into the teaching profession, they are assured of lifetime employment. Dismissals are very rare and occur only for unethical conduct. Similar proposals have surfaced repeatedly in the past but, for lack of popular and legislative support, have failed. It has been proposed that neophyte teachers' internship involve participation in in-service education programs and research projects at education centers. The report further points out the need for improving other types of in-service education discussed earlier, as well as graduate study in education. It proposes that opportunities for much more systematic professional development be given on a cyclical basis than currently exist in present in-service education. To enrich every teacher's career will require greater coordination and commitment among schools, education centers, and boards of education. Relative to graduate study, NCER recommends that existing master's programs be reconceptualized so as to meet more effectively the needs of in-service education. It also calls for much more active utilization of the new education universities for long-term in-service education.

Further, the council wants to relax the present rigid teacher certification requirements to attract competent individuals from other fields and occupations. Accordingly, it has proposed modifications in both the certification process and the appointment examinations. In addition, it has urged that teacher education curricula be restructured to meet more effectively the emerging needs and problems of children and society. NCER fails, however, to delineate the new teacher education curriculum that it advocates, although it does insist that student teaching be made a more rigorous preparation for teaching.

Other NCER recommendations lack the specificity needed to be able to render a sound judgment of their merits. It is, however, quite clear that NCER places great importance on internship and more liberalized certification requirements.

It is significant to note that the NCER's emphasis on internships reflects Japanese industry's view of training human resources. It is also interesting to contrast Japanese and U.S. reform efforts designed to improve teacher quality. The central thrust of American reform proposal is to upgrade preservice education as illustrated by the rhetoric of both the Holmes Group and the Carnegie Task Force on Teaching as a Profession.[62] In contrast, Japanese reformers are focusing on internships and better in-service education to improve teacher competence. To summarize, Japanese teachers are expected to play more inclusive roles than American teachers. It is that cultural expectation that defines teacher competence, and the proposal for internships is grounded in that cultural expectation. This internship program has already been introduced on a small scale and probably will be implemented nationwide.

Reformers are attempting to enlarge the pool of applicants for teaching by broadening current certification regulations to attract talented individuals from the entire spectrum of academic and occupational fields. This is their approach to meeting the diversified needs of the future and preparing Japanese education for the twenty-first century.

NOTES

1. Newspaper account, *Asahi shimbun*, November 13, 1985.
2. Hayakawa Misao, "The Quality and Socioeconomic Status of Teachers in Japan" (Paper prepared for the U.S. Department of Education, 1986), p. 130.
3. Shinoda Hiroshi, "Training of Elementary School Teachers" (*Shoto kyoin no yosei*), in Shinoda Hiroshi and Tezuka Takehiko, eds., *History of Schools (Gakko no rekishi)* (Tokyo: Daiichi Hoki, 1979), pp. 16–17.
4. Shinoda Hiroshi, "Education System Order and Teacher Education" (*Gakusei to kyoin yosei*), in Kokuritsu Kyōiku Kenkyujo, ed., *Japanese Modern Education: A History of the First Hundred Years (Nippon kindai kyoiku hyakunen shi)*, 4 vols. (Tokyo: Kokuritsu Kyoiku Kenkyujo, 1974), 3: 864–75.
5. Tsuchiya Motonori, *Postwar Education and Teacher Training* (Sengo kyōiku to kyoin yosei) (Tokyo: Shin Nippon Shinsho, 1984).
6. Sato Hideo, "Transformation of Policy on Teachers and Teacher Training System" (Kyoin seisaku no tenkan to kyoin yosei seido), in Kokuritsu Kyōiku Kenkyujo, ed., *Japanese Modern Education* 3: 1281–95.
7. Ministry of Education, *Japan's Modern Educational System: A History of the First Hundred Years* (Tokyo: Mombusho, 1980), p. 77.
8. Ibid., p. 79.
9. Sato Hideo, "Normal School Order and the Establishment of Teacher Training Policy" (Shihangakko rei to kyoin sei seisaku no kakuritsu), in Kokuritsu Kyoiku Kenkyujo, ed., *Japanese Modern Education* 4: 681–703. For details of Mori's role as minister of education, see Ivan Hall, *Mori Arinori* (Cambridge, Mass.: Harvard University Press, 1973).
10. Tsuchiya, *Postwar Education and Teacher Training*, p. 131.
11. Ministry of Education, *Japan's Modern Educational System*, p. 131.
12. Shinoda, "Training of Elementary School Teachers," pp. 109–14.
13. Ministry of Education, *Japan's Modern Educational System*, p. 203.
14. Edward Beauchamp, "The Development of Japanese Educational Policy, 1945–1985," *History of Education Quarterly* 27, no. 3 (Fall 1987): 302–5.
15. Ministry of Education, *Japan's Modern Educational System*, pp. 234–35.
16. Shinoda, "Training of Elementary School Teachers," p. 182; Hayashi Sanpei, "Reform of the Ideal and System of Teacher Training" (Kyoin yosei no rinen to seido no kakushin) in Kokuritsu Kyoiku Kenkyujo, ed., *Japanese Modern Education* 6: 487–515.
17. Ministry of Education, *Japan's Modern Educational System*, p. 251.
18. U.S. Department of Education, *Japanese Education Today* (Washington, D.C.: Government Printing Office, 1987), pp. 15–16.
19. Hayakawa, "The Quality and Socioeconomic Status of Teachers," p. 47
20. Ministry of Education, *Japan's Modern Educational System*, p. 68.
21. U.S. Department of Education, *Japanese Education Today*, p. 16.
22. Japan Pedagogical Association, *Collected Materials on Teacher Education* (Kyoshi kyoiku ni kansuru shiryoshi) (Tokyo: Nippon Kyōiku Gakkai, 1980), p. 201.
23. Association of National Universities, Special Committee on the Teacher Education System, *Teacher Education in the University* (Daigaku ni okeru kyoin yosei) (Tokyo: Kokudaikyo, 1984), p. 17.

24. Central Council of Education, *Basic Plan Concerning the Comprehensive Expansion and Improvement of School Education in the Future* (Kongo ni okeru gakko kyōiku no sogoteki kakuju seibi no tameno kihonteki shisaku ni tsuite) (Tokyo: Mombusho, 1971), p. 54.

25. Central Council of Education, "Basic Policies for Improving the Teacher Education System" (Kyoin yosei seido kaizen hosaku ni tsuite), the council's recommendation submitted to the minister of education, 1958, in Research Institute for Modern Education, Yokohama National University, ed., *Central Council of Education and Educational Reform* (Chukyoshin to kyōiku kaikaku) (Tokyo: Sanitsu Shobo, 1983), pp. 49–50.

26. Tsuchiya, *Postwar Education and Teacher Training*, p. 26.

27. See Central Council of Education, *Basic Plan Concerning the Comprehensive Expansion and Improvement of School Education*.

28. See Central Council of Education, "On the Improvement of Teacher Competence" (Kyoin no shishitsu noryoku no kojo ni tsuite), the council's recommendation submitted to the minister of education, 1978, in Research Institute for Modern Education, Yokohama National University, ed., *Central Council of Education and Educational Reform* (Chukyoshin to kyōiku kaikaku) (Tokyo: Sanitsu Shobo, 1983).

29. See Teacher Education Council, *On the Improvement of Teacher Education and the Certification System* (Tokyo: Mombusho, 1983).

30. Association of National Universities, *Teacher Education*, pp. 80–108.

31. Tsuchiya, *Postwar Education and Teacher Training*, pp. 96–97.

32. Okamoto Yoichi, "The Purpose and Character of Colleges of Education" (Kyoikukei daigaku gakubu no mokuteki seikaku), in Suda Isamu and Kobayashi Tetsuya, eds., *On Teacher Education* (Kyoin yosei o kangaeru) (Tokyo: Gosei, 1982), pp. 71–87.

33. See National Education Association, *Status of the American Public School Teachers 1980–81* (Washington, D.C.: NEA, 1982).

34. Shimahara Nobuo, "Toward the Equality of a Japanese Minority: the Case of Burakumin," *Comparative Education* 20 (1984), pp. 339–53.

35. Ichikawa Shogo, ed., *Encyclopedia of Inservice Education* (Kyōiku kenkyu jiten) (Tokyo: Kyoiku Kaihatsu Kenkyujo, 1983), p. 41.

36. Hayakawa, "The Quality and Socioeconomic Status of Teachers," p. 87.

37. U.S. Department of Education, *Japanese Education Today*, pp. 17–18.

38. Hayakawa, "The Quality and Socioeconomic Status of Teachers," p. 81.

39. Ibid., p. 83.

40. Shimahara Nobuo, field notes, 1985.

41. Shimahara Nobuo, "The Cultural Basis of Student Achievement in Japan," *Comparative Education* 22 (1986), pp. 19–25.

42. U.S. Department of Education, *Japanese Education Today*, pp. 27–36.

43. Ministry of Education, *Course of Study for Elementary Schools in Japan* (Tokyo: Ministry of Education, 1983), p. 1.

44. Louis Peak, "Classroom Discipline and Management in Japanese Elementary School Classrooms" (Paper prepared for the U.S. Department of Education, 1986), pp. 16–27.

45. Robert LeVine and Merry White, *Human Conditions: The Cultural Basis of Human Development* (London: Routledge & Kegan Paul, 1986), pp. 93–127.

46. Shimahara, "The Cultural Basis of Student Achievement," pp. 12–25.

47. Kataoka Tokuo, "The Influence of Class Management and Student Guidance upon

Academic Achievement at the Elementary and Lower Secondary Education Level'' (Paper prepared for the U.S. Department of Education, 1986), p. 3.

48. Shimahara, field notes.

49. See Shimahara, "The Cultural Basis of Student Achievement."

50. Shimahara Nobuo, "Japanese Education Reforms in the 1980s," *Issues in Education* 4 (1987), pp. 89–90.

51. Ibid., pp. 86–89.

52. See National Council on Educational Reform, *Second Report on Educational Reform* (Kyōiku kaikaku ni kansuru dainiji toshin), *Bulletin of the Ministry of Education* (Monbu Jiho) 1327 (1987).

53. See National Council on Educational Reform, *First Report on Educational Reform* (Tokyo: Government of Japan, 1985) (in English); Shimahara, "Japanese Education Reforms."

54. National Council on Educational Reform, First Report (English), p. 26.

55. National Council on Educational Reform, *First Report on Educational Reform* (Kyoiku kaikaku ni kansuru daiichiji toshin), *Bulletin of the Ministry of Education* (Monbu Jiho) 1327 (1987), p. 53.

56. National Council on Educational Reform, *Summary of Second Report on Educational Reform* (Tokyo: Government of Japan, 1986) (in English), pp. 1–2.

57. National Council on Educational Reform, *First Report* (in Japanese), p. 53.

58. Ibid.

59. National Council on Educational Reform, *First Report* (in English), p. 4.

60. Ibid., p. 6.

61. National Council on Educational Reform, *Second Report*, p. 127.

62. See Holmes Group, *Tomorrow's Teacher: A Report of the Holmes Group* (East Lansing, Mich.: Holmes Group, 1986); The Carnegie Forum on Education and the Economy, *A Nation Prepared: Teachers for the 21st Century* (New York: Carnegie Forum on Education and the Economy, 1986).

12

The Role of Education in Preserving the Ethnic Identity of Korean Residents in Japan

Umakoshi Toru

BACKGROUND

The catchphrase, internationalization, has become increasingly popular throughout the Japanese educational world. Evidence of this trend is found in the work of the prestigious Ad Hoc Council on Education Reform, which employed internationalization as a major element in its overall reform strategy. Indeed, the internationalization of Japanese education was one of the major issues analyzed in the council's final report of August 1987.

The term "internationalization" of education is wide ranging and difficult to define to the satisfaction of all. In this chapter, however, it is used in the broader context of an educational movement designed to reform Japanese education to better fit an international framework and to gain international equivalency.

An overview of current trends in the internationalization of Japanese education suggests that the major areas of concern of both the government and the general public are the education of foreign students in Japan, the education and readjustment of children of Japanese parents returning from overseas, and the employment of foreign teachers. It is clear that these are serious issues that deserve the attention and action of the government, but there is another equally important issue that has, thus far, been virtually ignored—the problem of educating Japan's resident Korean population. Although the council's several reports mention international schools in Japan, they fail to acknowledge the problems associated with the nation's more than 150 *minzoku gakko* (ethnic schools) and the problems of resident Koreans. Despite the fact that they account for less than 10 percent of the number of resident Korean children, the government has placed a much greater emphasis on the problems associated with the education of Japanese youngsters living abroad and their reintegration into Japanese society when they return home.

Korean families resident in Japan face the serious prospect of the gradual disappearance of their ethnic identity. Recognition of this situation, or positive government assistance to the Korean minority to preserve its ethnic heritage is not now, nor has it ever been, a priority of the Japanese authorities. Indeed, in this regard, Japan lags far behind many advanced nations in protecting the identity of its minorities. Administratively, virtually no support has been given to ethnic education in Japanese public schools where the policy is that there should be no differences in the treatment of Japanese and resident Koreans. There are, however, a number of isolated cases in which a group of concerned teachers provide special classes and a few "progressive" schools which offer some form of ethnic education programs, but these are still quite unusual.

THE CHANGING SITUATION OF RESIDENT KOREAN CHILDREN

In 1987 the population of resident Koreans in Japan numbered approximately 680,000. Rapidly increasing numbers of short-term visitors, mostly from nearby South Korea, account for about 80,000 of this group; the remainder are classified as permanent residents. Most of these residents are second and third generation, but educational problems are now beginning to appear within third- and even fourth-generation youngsters. An analysis of the situation suggests that four major changes are occurring among resident Koreans in Japan.

First, Ministry of Health and Welfare statistics indicate that the rate of intermarriage between resident Koreans and Japanese increased more than 50 percent in 1976, and by 1985 this figure had climbed to 71.6 percent.

Second, the Ministry of Justice reports that the number of naturalized Koreans increased by approximately 5,000 per year between 1952 and 1986 and that the total for this period numbers almost 136,000. The passage of the Revised Japanese Nationality Act of 1984 amended the previous patrilineal system to a more equitable system under which children can choose the nationality of either of their parents. As a result, the number of Koreans becoming naturalized Japanese has increased.

Third, there has been a significant decrease in Korean language fluency among second-, third-, and fourth-generation resident Koreans. A survey, conducted by the Association of Korean Residents in Japan (Mindan), indicates that more than 90 percent of the third generation have little or no command of their mother tongue.[1]

Fourth, there is the problem of a choice of names for resident Koreans. Almost 90 percent of Korean residents have two names, one of which is their original Korean family name, which is registered in their family register in Korea. The second is a Japanese name which is used in daily activities, which often masks their Korean origins. Japanese names were forced on all Koreans during the period of Japanese colonization of Korea (1910–1945), and even today 62 percent feel compelled to use their Japanese name for "convenience" as shown in the above mentioned survey.[2] To use or not to use one's Korean name in public is a source of great difficulty to many resident Koreans.

These things are causing severe conflict among Korean residents in Japan, and it may be said that many residents are rapidly approaching a crossroads in their ethnic identity. One scholar, Chun Jeon, argues that the changes outlined above were inevitable because of the heavy pressures exerted by Japan's monolithic and conformist society which forced Koreans in Japan to choose one of two paths: to becoming a Japanese national of Korean descent or to retain Korean nationality as a permanent resident in Japan.[3] Clearly, the formation of ethnic identity depends greatly on which of these paths is chosen.

EDUCATION AND THE FORMATION OF ETHNIC IDENTITY

In general, the main elements of ethnic identity consist of physical traits and names. In the case of Koreans, however, affiliations with political groups influence the degree of ethnic identity felt by resident Koreans. Koreans in Japan have a choice of possible homelands with which to identify; one is South Korea (Republic of Korea, ROK) and the other is North Korea (Democratic People's Republic of Korea, DPRK).

To further complicate matters, the two "homelands" have both been changing dramatically since "liberation" at the end of World War II, and so has the Japanese society in which they have been living. Thus, ethnic identity is not merely a simple matter of cultural preference, but it relates to the homeland's political ideology and a rejection of assimilation into Japanese society.

Accordingly, socialization for the younger generation becomes an extremely complex problem. With what and to whom will they identify? What language and name will they use? Answers to these questions are greatly influenced not only by family and the larger resident community, but also by one's school education.

EDUCATIONAL PROBLEMS OF KOREAN CHILDREN IN JAPAN

As of April 1988, the number of school-age resident Korean children in Japan was 164,000; 86.4 percent of them were attending Japanese (national, municipal, and private) schools. The remaining 13.6 percent were enrolled in ethnic schools managed by Korean residents in Japan. The great majority of the latter (92.2 percent) are enrolled in ethnic schools operated by the North Korean–affiliated Chosoren, or the Federation of Korean Residents in Japan. Only a very small minority (7.8 percent) of Korean children in Japan attend ethnic schools conducted by the South Korean–affiliated Mindan, or Association of Korean Residents in Japan.[4] Perhaps most significantly, however, a clear shift from ethnic schools to Japanese schools has occurred, which has cut deeply into the enrollment figures of both ethnic schools.

MINDAN ETHNIC SCHOOLS

Although the vast majority of Korean residents, 62 percent in January 1988, align themselves with the Mindan, the actual number of schools operated by this organization are very few. In fact, in the entire nation, there are only three elementary, four junior high, and four senior high schools with a total enrollment of 1,745 pupils. In addition, these schools are found in only three major cities: Tokyo, Osaka, and Kyoto. Indeed, only six of these schools found in Osaka have been granted legal status as private school corporations under the terms of the School Education law. The remaining five schools in Tokyo and Osaka are classified under the rubric of "miscellaneous" schools; that is, they are not legally considered to be institutions of formal education. Mindan is eager to upgrade to an equivalent status of Japanese schools. The curriculum of these schools is designed in accordance with the national course of study prescribed by the Ministry of Education. In addition there are courses in Korean language and history as well as various cultural activities. The language of instruction, however, is Japanese.

Judging from the shrinking number of ethnic Korean schools, it appears as if there is little impetus within the Korean community to expand ethnic-based schooling for its children. Indeed, it might be said that there is an increasing trend toward educating resident Korean children in mainstream Japanese schools. Some South Korean government officials, who support Mindan, have noted generational differences among resident Koreans and have even suggested that separate ethnic schools might be more of a "sentimental, wishful thinking on the part of the first generation rather than a practical answer to the educational needs of the present generation."[5]

From the perspective of the South Korean government, the problem of educating the children of Korean businessmen, who have been assigned to Japan by their companies, is the most pressing issue. For example, some 76 percent of the children attending Tokyo Kankoku Gakuen (a Mindan-managed ethnic school) are the children of these relatively short-term residents. This school, which was originally established for the children of permanent Korean residents, is one of those schools that Mindan would like to upgrade from its miscellaneous school status. The South Korean government, however, recognizing the needs of short-term Korean businessmen, is hesitant about making any changes which would affect the school's ability to meet the needs of short-term resident children.

Through Mindan, the Korean government established so-called Korean Education Centers in many local areas, but the number of such centers has declined from forty-one in 1987 to only twenty-seven in 1988. It is planned to replace the current twenty-seven with six large Comprehensive Education Centers, located in major cities, in the near future. Thus, an overall slowing and thinning out of Mindan-sponsored ethnic education is apparent. The education of resident Korean children in mainstream Japanese schools is proceeding apace.

CHOSOREN ETHNIC SCHOOLS

Having discussed the situation and problems of Mindan ethnic schools, let us now turn to the North Korean Chosoren ethnic schools. Most agree that the Chosoren schools have a stronger commitment to ethnic education in general, and to language education in particular, than their Mindan counterparts. A fundamental principle of the Chosoren, embedded in Article 4 of its regulations, is that "democratic ethnic education should be carried out in the mother tongue." Chosoren also operates a much greater number of schools, 152 in twenty-nine prefectures. If one includes kindergartens, the number of schools jumps to 218. These schools educate approximately 20,000 children.

These figures suggest that Chosoren schools, in terms of their number and the comprehensive education they offer, are quite impressive. On the other hand, however, they too seem to be on a downward trajectory with the number of pupils attending declining by 58 percent since 1967. Clearly the four changes occurring in Mindan communities are also taking their toll in Chosoren counterparts.

The legal status of Chosoren schools is "miscellaneous," and they have been established under Article 83 of Japan's School Education Law. The Chosoren school system is the same as the Japanese public system, with a 6-3-3 school ladder, and the curricular structure is essentially in accordance with the Japanese Course of Study. The major differences between Chosoren schools and Japanese schools are as follows: (1) the Chosoren's basic philosophy of education is based on North Korean educational guidelines; (2) the language of instruction is Korean and all textbooks are written in Korean (Japanese is taught only as a foreign language); (3) social studies content deals with the history, geography, and culture of both North Korea and Japan. Other notable differences related to ethnicity are that Chosoren students use only their Korean names in class, and girls wear uniforms in the style of the traditional *chima chogori* national costume.

In the education of their children, Chosorens place primary emphasis on preserving Korean national identity. However, the expectations of third- and fourth-generation parents are becoming more diversified, and the Chosoren schools are having to consider the need for curriculum reform while at the same time striving to maintain ethnic preservation. Recently, the number of required hours for teaching English and Japanese have been greatly increased in secondary schools; now Chosoren secondary schools require more hours of English and Japanese than do Japanese secondary schools.

Three major problems currently confront the Chosoren schools: (1) financial problems exacerbated by declining enrollments, (2) miscellaneous school status which prevents their graduates from sitting for entrance examinations to higher level schools and institutions of higher education, and (3) parental expectations of significant curricular reforms.

In the case of financing education, one half of the funds for running Chosoren schools are reputed to come from the government of North Korea, and that country's current economic problems make it difficult for it to provide additional support. Furthermore, declining enrollments make financial management even more difficult. As to the miscellaneous school status, no national university allows graduates of such schools to take its entrance examination at the normal time; that is, in order to be eligible to take these entrance examinations, these students must first pass a special qualification examination or reenter and graduate from an evening course at an accredited Japanese high school. Since 1985, however, seventy-three municipal and private colleges and universities have allowed Chosoren graduates to take their entrance examinations despite the opposition of the Ministry of Education. Many believe that the time has come for national universities to modify their admission policies toward resident Koreans since special provisions have recently been made to accommodate the needs of Japanese students returning from overseas, adult and foreign students. Finally, the idea of linking ethnic identity with repatriation to North Korea is rapidly losing popularity among third- and fourth-generation students. Many students do not wish to be repatriated and prefer to live in Japan; many believe that the school curriculum should reflect the wishes and needs of these students who will live and work in Japanese society.

ETHNIC EDUCATION IN THE JAPANESE PUBLIC SCHOOL SYSTEM

The Japanese public school system enrolls 86.4 percent of resident Korean children and should be considered as the single most important institution in the development of the ethnic identity of resident Korean children. This important reality, however, has been ignored by both national and local educational authorities. This laissez-faire attitude on their part appears to be quite contradictory to recent trends toward promoting the internationalization of Japanese education. As mentioned earlier, special consideration is being given to a range of special interest groups—Japanese returnees and overseas children and foreign students wishing to attend Japanese universities. At the same time, the real problems of resident Korean children and their struggle for an identity remain unattended by Japanese officials. It must be emphasized here that, since the majority of resident Koreans are not attending ethnic schools, they are missing an important source of support and information that could help them solve their search for ethnic identity.

Several important historical events form the context of the problems of ethnic education in Japan. In accordance with the 1965 Normalization Treaty between Japan and the Republic of Korea, an agreement was reached regarding the education of Korean children in Japan. A Ministry of Education directive to local educational authorities provided the following guidelines for their education.[6]

First, permission to enter will be granted to resident Korean children when they apply to Japanese public elementary and lower secondary schools. Second, graduates of these schools will be admitted to upper secondary schools and institutions of higher education in Japan. Third, curriculum content and instruction shall be exactly the same as for Japanese children; that is, no special provisions shall be made for ethnic-related education.

In other words, compulsory educational attendance does not apply to non-Japanese residents, and they are not required to attend school. Foreign residents are, however, allowed admittance to public schools only if they apply to the local board of education. This is in striking contrast to Japanese citizens who are automatically notified that it is time for their school-age children to begin school. Also, according to Article 1 of the School Education law, ethnic schools are excluded from the Japanese school system. As a result, graduates of these ethnic schools cannot obtain the entrance qualifications necessary to be admitted to upper level schools. Finally, the principle of equality in education for resident Korean children attending Japanese public schools means that they are deprived of an opportunity for ethnic education within the Japanese system.

In the year following the Normalization Treaty, the Japanese government submitted a bill to the Diet concerning the regulation of schools managed by foreigners, but this (and other) attempts were met by strong opposition from both the Mindan and Chosoren as well as concerned Japanese citizens. Attempts at assimilation policies by the government were naturally criticized by resident Koreans and, in fact, are in conflict with any definition of the internationalization of Japanese education that would teach respect for diverse cultures and reflect a degree of sensitivity toward the maintenance of Korean national identity.

Despite government apathy toward ethnic education in public schools, steady efforts have been made to keep a modest ethnic education movement alive. For example, in 1977 three cities—Osaka, Nagoya, and Fukuoka—with large numbers of Korean residents established ethnic classes in their public schools. At that time, twenty-eight public elementary schools had established ethnic education classes which 1,300 resident Korean children attended.[7] These classes consisted of between two and four hours of instruction per week in such subjects as Korean history, language, and music. Although governmental regulations did not allow the establishment of formal classes of this sort, they were established through the action of local educational authorities who were sympathetic to the needs of resident Koreans. Another kind of effort promoting ethnic education is found in some lower and upper secondary schools. In the vocational high schools of Osaka, Lobe, and Hiroshima, Korean culture study groups and circles have been established as extracurricular activities.

One of the most complex problems within Japanese schools with Korean residents is how to deal with the so-called name dilemma. Resident Korean students usually use their Japanese names in daily life so that they can avoid the stigma of being different, a considerable obstacle in Japanese culture. Most students find it more comfortable to pass as Japanese rather than be labeled Korean. The roots of this problem lie in Japan's occupation of Korea (1910–1945) when all Koreans were forced to change their names from Korean to Japanese ones. Today, some Japanese teachers in cities with a large Korean population, such as Osaka, Kobe, Nagoya, and Kanagawa, have attempted to find ways to reduce the stigma attached to being Korean. A central theme raised by these teachers was the use of Korean names. The idea is to encourage teachers to address Korean students by their Korean names as well as encourage students to use their Korean names both in class and in social situations. The purpose of this approach is to foster pride in being Korean and to encourage students to stand up against discrimination. Another reason for encouraging the use of Korean names is to heighten awareness among Japanese students about Korean culture and history and to remind them of the presence and importance of Korean residents in Japan. It is hoped that these measures will help to reduce prejudice against Korean residents.

Regardless of the good intentions underlying these activities, it is no simple matter to ask, or indeed force, resident Korean youngsters to use their Korean names. In fact, about 90 percent of resident Koreans use their Japanese names socially. In addition, among children of the third and fourth generation a growing number are not informed of their Korean backgrounds until they are adults. For these children, it is a great shock to suddenly find out at school that they are not Japanese but Korean. Although the name dilemma is not inherently an educational problem, it is functionally one of the most complex and explosive issues in ethnic education in Japanese public schools.

FUTURE OF ETHNIC EDUCATION IN JAPAN

Judging from the current situation, a bright future for ethnic education in Japan appears unlikely. In light of the increased support for ethnic or multicultural education in several other advanced industrial nations, and the gradual emergence of a sense that ethnic education is an important indicator of the degree of internationalization in a society, there is some reason for cautious optimism. There is no doubt that greater efforts must be made by Japan to improve the existing situation.

As was mentioned earlier, the number of Koreans being granted Japanese citizenship is increasing, thanks to the revision of the Japanese Nationality Act. Thus there will be a continuing increase in the number of Japanese citizens of Korean descent. How will these new citizens deal with their ethnicity? Will they reject the use of their Korean names in favor of Japanese ones? Will they encourage their children to take ethnic education classes? Recently, there has been some movement among resident Koreans to recover their Korean names.[8] Several legal cases have been won by Koreans wishing to retain their Korean names. Japanese society must not, in the future, attempt to suppress resident Korean attempts to protect their ethnic identity.

Resident Koreans wishing to maintain their Korean nationality need to be granted the same social and educational rights as Japanese citizens, while being allowed to preserve their unique cultural heritage. Two objectives—social equality and respect for cultural differences—should be pursued simultaneously. Issues of ethnicity and ethnic education cannot be taken lightly in the education of children; schools play a vital role both in maintaining culture and values and in transmitting them to new generations. Schools, however, cannot help in this task without adequate planning and the active involvement of the resident Korean community. If Korean residents in Japan wish to preserve their ethnic heritage, they must present their needs, goals, and strategies for doing so in a unified, logical, and clearly organized manner. If this is not done, neither Japanese society nor the schools can be expected to respond in a positive manner.

Once the ethnic education needs of resident Koreans are made clear, it is of utmost importance that Japanese education authorities make creative and sincere efforts to accommodate them. If Japanese educational authorities do so, it will not only benefit the resident Korean community, but it will add needed diversity and flexibility to an overly rigid Japanese public school system, thereby benefiting Japanese children as well.

Japanese public schools also must find a solution to the name dilemma facing Korean youngsters; indeed, the school should be the starting point for the reform of this regrettable remnant of Japan's colonial assimilation policy in the years prior to World War II. While respecting the wishes of individual Korean students, the school has the responsibility of providing an atmosphere free of prejudice, in which Korean children can use their names without fear of being stigmatized by doing so.

Finally, judging from the current situation, there is a pressing need for the reform of ethnic education in Japan. Immediate attention to the following issues is needed:

1. Korean culture, history, and language should be taught within the framework of the history, social studies, and language curricula in Japanese public schools.

2. Exchange programs between Japanese public schools and Korean ethnic schools should be encouraged, particularly in extracurricular activities, in order to promote mutual understanding.

3. At the local administrative level, Korean ethnic schools should be upgraded from the miscellaneous school category to the status of normal, accredited schools.

4. Resident Korean teachers should be aggressively recruited as full-time teachers in Japanese public schools.

5. Japanese firms and industries must cease employment discrimination against resident Korean high school and college graduates.

These efforts will produce positive benefits, not only for internationalizing Japanese education but also for the larger society. The positive promotion of ethnic education will produce a win-win situation in which important benefits will accrue to both resident Korean and Japanese children.

NOTES

1. Mindan [Association of Korean Residents in Japan], *Zainichi kankokujin no ishiki chosa* [Survey of the Consciousness of Korean Residents in Japan] (1987), pp. 6–7.
2. Ibid., pp. 33–34.
3. Jeon Chun, "Zainichi kankokujin no ima to daisandaime igono ten tenbou" [The Present Situation of Korean Residents and Future Prospects of the Third Generation], *Hoteki chii ni kansuru ronbunshu* [A Study of the Legal Status of Resident Koreans] (1987), p. 3.
4. These statistical data were collected from the Mindan and Chosoren by the author.
5. Interview by the author, October 1988.
6. Tanaka Hiroshi, "Kokusaika no gyakkousuru nihon no kyōiku" [Japanese Education Going against Internationalization], *Ekonomisuto* [Economics] (1987), pp. 76–81.
7. Chang Shik Kim, "Zainichi doho no minzoku kyōiku" [Ethnic Education of Korean Residents in Japan], *Zainichi doha* [Korean Residents in Japan] (1980), p. 58.
8. Minzokumai wo torimodosu kai [Group for Recovering Ethnic Names], *Nihonseki chosenjin no tatakai no kiseki* [The Record of the Struggle of Koreans with Japanese Nationality] (1988), p. 98.

13

"Examination Hell"

Peter Frost

> Which of the following cannot be changed into a word ending in 'ion': decide, destroy, depend, intent or describe?[1]

Students seeking to enter the literature faculty (*gakubu*) of Tokyo University were required to answer this question, as well as a host of others equally difficult. To prepare for this ordeal, students and their parents schemed to get into the best primary and secondary schools, enrolled by age twelve in elite cram schools (*yobiko* and *juku*), and, often, spent at least one extra year as *rōnins,* a term that literally means masterless samurai, but in this case simply describes anyone who spends an extra year or more studying for the university entrance examinations. This general phenomenon is popularly known as "examination hell." This term refers not only to the fact that over 30 percent of the age cohort is applying for admission to Japan's universities under a system that seems a great deal more tense than does university admissions in the United States, but also to the idea that admissions decisions are almost solely made upon the basis of written achievement (vs. aptitude) tests administered by the university faculty themselves. Most of these questions are in the form of multiple choice requiring an encyclopedia-like knowledge of information that most Americans would consider quite trivial.

Compounding the problems that Americans face in understanding this particular kind of university admissions system is the fact that the Japanese themselves do not appear to like it. At least since the 1920s there have been repeated complaints in the Japanese press that examination hell has prevented Japanese students from having a healthy childhood, has blunted intellectual curiosity, has discouraged females from applying to universities, has overlooked less academic leadership skills, and has encouraged those students who finally do get admitted to do almost no academic work while in college.[2] "The typical prospective examinee has come to be close-minded, selfish and lonely," wrote Tokyo University Professor Shimizu Yoshihiro in 1963. "Even his parents tend to become nervous and be on edge."[3] Stress upon memorized facts, added Shimizu's colleague Orihara Hiroshi in 1967, does not encourage Japanese children to "hold a lantern to the unknown."[4] It is necessary "to correct excessive competition in entrance examinations" intones an otherwise extraordinarily bland preliminary report by a blue ribbon commission studying Japanese education in 1985.[5] "Medicinal reading for those of you who are desperate to get into Tokyo University!" trumpets the dust jacket of the current best-seller *Bye-Bye Tokyo U. (Sayonara todai).*[6] Why, then, an American may well ask, do Japanese have as a central part of their educational life a system of university entrance examinations that they themselves call "hell"?

Part of the answer, suggests American sociologist Ezra Vogel, lies in the fact that the strong Japanese value of "particularism" or loyalty to the group needs to be balanced periodically by the value of "performance" or quite rigid and objective testing. As a society that stresses the close personal ties of students in a particular homeroom, Vogel says, Japanese educators prefer not to separate students out into honors or nonhonors tracks or even to hold back marginal students, but rather to condense any possible competition into a brief examination period which has the further advantage of being distant from the school and hence well outside the normal relations of the group. A system of short but brutally effective tests thus separates primary school classmates into secondary schools on the basis of ability, refines the groups again for university admissions, and does the same before elite males begin lifetime employment.[7] The system thrives despite "horror stories" that are "small in number," writes Vogel in his deliberately provocative book *Japan as Number One,* because it is fair, supports those who work hard, and encourages the basic education that most Japanese think is needed for Japan's survival.[8]

Psychologist Christie Kiefer agrees with Vogel's claim that examinations help to minimize competition within the classroom, but he notes that plenty of competitive tension still exists within the Japanese community. This tension is actually rather helpful to the traditional Japanese family structure, he asserts, because it allows Japanese mothers to maintain a considerable amount of control over what happens to their children's education. Help with homework, late night snacks, and a sharing of the joys and sorrows of examination results also keep Japan's mothers closely tied to their male, and, in rarer cases, female offspring. At the same time, continues Kiefer, the fact that the child's teacher—also usually a male—serves as a coach for the examinations rather than as a harsh judge of progress permits a warm relationship to develop between teacher and student.

This makes it far easier for the Japanese male student to move psychologically from the mother-centered world of the child to the male-centered world of bureaucracy. Since Kiefer also claims that this phenomenon helps to explain the "displaced anger" the university student feels toward the outside world, his theory is obviously broadly drawn, extremely difficult to prove, and clearly more provocative than conclusive. Kiefer's analysis does alert us, however, to the idea that examination hell may well be a good deal more useful socially than most Japanese appear ready to admit.[9]

Ronald Dore, by contrast, draws our attention to the international implications of examination hell. It is a characteristic of later developing countries, he states, for there to be a very noticeable gap between a relatively small elite, who enjoy top jobs in the bureaucracy or modern sectors of the economy, and the great mass of the populace, who are likely to remain in agriculture or other traditional sectors of the economy and hence to have less income, less prestige, and a good deal less security. In such cases, continues Dore, there is naturally tremendous pressure put upon the government to guarantee that access to this limited elite will be decided in the fairest possible way. This need for fairness, in turn, creates a tendency for access to be decided by formal tests in which there are very objective "right or wrong" answers for which a widely enrolled school system can prepare. To put this another way, there is less pressure to get into a good university in the United States because there is, or at least has been, a wider variety of reasonably prestigious jobs and graduate training available to American university graduates. Dore's work thus has the particular advantage of comparing the Japanese situation to countries as diverse as China, Cuba, and Sri Lanka. His work reminds us that in many respects it is the American attitude toward learning that needs explanation rather than the presence of tough entrance examinations in Japan.[10]

These three schools of interpretation are clearly pointing toward the heart of the entrance examination problem, and it is necessary to expand upon this framework by adding a considerable amount of historical detail. Vogel and Kiefer, for example, are certainly correct in suggesting that examination hell fits certain particular Japanese psychological needs, yet both works tend to describe an existing situation rather than to seek to find the historical roots of the problem. Similarly, Dore's "late developer" thesis is immensely useful in reminding us of seemingly similar situations in other countries, and yet there are many areas of the problem in which—as Dore's keen mind is the first to recognize—the unique aspects of the Japanese university admissions process ought to be underscored.[11] For a variety of reasons, then, this chapter traces the development of examinations from the earliest, rather Chinese-inspired, educational system, through the nineteenth- and early twentieth-century European-inspired models, to the postwar university system as developed under the American Occupation of Japan (1945–1952). The aim is not so much to choose among the admittedly different and even contradictory Vogel, Kiefer, and Dore analyses, but rather to add crucial details, particularly in the construction of a state ideology, which might help to make clear why the Japanese have maintained a system that they themselves have professed to dislike.

CLASSICAL INFLUENCES

To journey into classical Japanese history in order to find the roots of present-day examination hell might at first glance appear to be a singularly odd decision. Certainly, the Japanese never seemed to accept the Chinese idea that civil service positions should be open to any male, regardless of social rank, who could pass formal written exminations or difficult Confucian classics. As Edwin Reischauer puts it in his popular text *The Japanese,* this educational ideal was "probably too foreign to their highly aristocratic society to be readily acceptable." "Both rank and position in the Japanese bureaucracy," Reischauer continues, "quickly became determined by inherited status rather than individual merit."[12] Surely too the Japanese in this period opted not so much for Confucian scholarship with its tremendous, even pedantic, emphasis upon talmudic memorization as a Zen or, perhaps, Bushido-like emphasis upon nonverbal action by a warrior class ready to die on the spot for their superiors. If traditional Japan consisted largely of a peasant mass dominated first by the courtly aristocrats of the Nara (710–794) and Heian (794–1185) periods and then by the "centralized feudalism" of the Tokugawa (1600–1868), why look here for the source of a modern educational dilemma?

Part of the reason to look back lies in the scholarly reverence that has been given to some of Japan's oldest heroes. The great Imperial Prince Shotoku Taishi (574–622), for example, has traditionally been credited not only with writing the "Constitution" of 604, but also with creating a twelve cap (or level) system of bureaucracy, being one of the few Japanese to master the very intricate Buddhist *sutra,* and founding the Hōryū-ji temple near Nara, a magnificent structure whose full name has often been translated as the Temple for the Study of the Circulating Law (Hōryū Gakumon-ji).[13] "Few men are utterly bad. They may be taught," wrote the prince in his constitution, a document that is actually more a set of moral maxims than a legal document. "When wise men are entrusted with office," he continues, "the sound of praise arises . . . .therefore did the wise sovereigns of antiquity seek the man to fill the office, and not the office for the sake of the man."[14] In the myths and accomplishments of Shotoku Taishi's life, in sum, we can see a very clear link between the idea that academic study is important for religious enlightenment and the idea that bureaucracy or the state should be organized around the best people. Study, religion, and state duty are symbolized both by Shotoku Taishi's own life and by the institutions that he created.

Sugawara no Michizane (845–903) provides another example of the ways in which the traditional Japanese court valued scholarship more than we might think. Descended from a very old aristocratic family, both Michizane's father and grandfather had been active in the adaption of Chinese culture to Japan. At the age of seventeen, Michizane entered the official Confucian university (*daigakuryo*) which, contrary to Reischauer's broad generalization, had been established by the Omi Codes (c.670) and the more famous Taiho Code (701) as part of a system whereby aristocrats of the fifth rank or above—and by Michizane's time a few commoners as well—could study the traditional Confucian classics in preparation for Chinese-style civil service examinations. After studying at the university for eight years, Michizane passed the apparently rigorous examinations and was promoted to very high posts within the imperial court government at Kyoto. Sugawara no Michizane thus, first of all, reflects an educational ideal that his biographer Robert Borgen at one point claims was "[i]n a few aspects . . . actually more egalitarian than its T'ang model." Borgen supports this startling statement in part by quoting a Japanese professor at the university who in 827 protested loudly that "great talent is not limited to the aristocracy."[15] Strong words indeed!

More important, Sugawara no Michizane's fame as a noble scholar has way outlived these initial attempts at civil service examinations. Apparently ousted most unfairly from the capital city in Kyoto in 901 and forced to die in exile in 903, Michizane's unsatisfied spirit was said to have been responsible for a series of plagues and other disasters that soon swept over the city. Frightened, the emperor overcame opposition from the Fujiwara family who dominated court politics at the time, and promoted Michizane posthumously to a high rank in the government. Since then, the so-called Temmangu Shinto shrines to Michizane and the sacred bull who is said to have saved his life in 901 have served as rallying points where a supposedly nonreligious current Japanese populace can regularly be found hanging up votive offerings (*ema*) asking for success on examinations.[16] A fine example of what the late Ivan Morris called "the nobility of failure," Sugawara no Michizane has stood for centuries as the model of a dedicated patriot whose sense of scholarship as the true criteria for public office stood out in a period when the traditional court was all but overwhelmed by the grubby world of politics.[17] The link, to repeat, was once again among scholarship, ethics, and state power. This was a link that would survive even in the most militaristic periods of Japan's feudal experience.

Indeed, the rise of a warrior society and the accompanying emphasis upon the Zen religion should not be thought completely antithetical to the concepts behind the modern examination system. Certainly Zen's well-known verbal riddles (*kōan* and *mondo*) and many of its most famous ink paintings asserted that a truly moral person could not rely upon conventional academic study. Yet Buddhist temples in general and Zen temples in particular regularly taught both those commoners who wanted to read the holy books and those who wished merely to have an education. The Tokugawa period (1600–1868) also saw the establishment of the Shoheiko or official Confucian univerity (*daigaku*) and of various schools for the samurai in the various parts of Japan not directly administered by the Tokugawa. As the Western world began to threaten Japan's autonomy in the middle nineteenth century, the Tokugawa authorities quickly established schools for the investigation of barbarian culture (Bansho Torishirabe-sho, 1856), military science (Kobujo, 1856), and medicine (Igakusho, 1858).[18] Like the earlier government universities, these schools had an importance that went well beyond their small size and limited number of influential graduates. They were rather yet another statement that the central government should establish schools of higher education which could prepare bright and moral young men for careers in civil government.

The training that these bright young men received was heavily slanted toward memorization and repetition. Aptitude was not really recognized, nor was creative individualist thinking. Rather Zen stressed the absolute subordination of a terribly hardworking student to a strict but ultimately loving teacher. "Draw bamboos for ten years, become a bamboo, then forget all about bamboos when you are drawing," notes George Duthuit in a passage quoted approvingly by the classic Zen writer D.T. Suzuki. "In the possession of an infallible technique, the individual places himself at the mercy of inspiration."[19] This concept, adds Ronald Dore in his definitive English-language study of Tokugawa education, was also helpful in bridging the gap between the Tokugawa political practice of assigning young men jobs by social rank and more egalitarian theories of education; if effort counted, then anyone, however stupid at birth, could by hard work live up to the obligations of the job assigned to him. Theory and practicality combined to stress effort rather than originality, teacher dominance, memorization skills, and a level of detail that Americans might find trivial. Diligence was what was being tested, just as surely as moral discipline was the ultimate aim of the education.

Ninomiya Sontoku (1787–1856) thus stands out as a third cultural hero of the premodern period. Apparently an orphan boy who was raised in poverty and also suffered, Cinderella-like, from wicked stepparents, Ninomiya studied hard, taught and published on the need for an agrarian-based morality, and eventually became one of the very few Japanese admitted to honorary samurai status despite his peasant birth.[20] By the nineteenth and early twentieth centuries, Ninomiya was rather commonly depicted in school yard statues as a small boy of obviously humble birth who steadies a large bundle of sticks on his back with one hand while he holds a book in the other. Ninomiya hence symbolizes the kinds of mental abilities that come more from hard work than from the natural gifts of aptitude. He also represents the rather radical notion that anyone who wants to ought to be able to get an education. Finally, Ninomiya stands once again for the notion that the purpose of study ought to be the training of people who would be of practical value to the state. While it is certainly true that civil service examinations never took hold in Japan as they did in China, in sum, a quick look at both the educational institutions and the cultural heroes of early Japan repeatedly suggests the close link between pre-1868 education and the post-1868 development of a formal examination system.

EUROPEAN INFLUENCES

The traditional link among personal morality, education, and national security became even stronger after the Meiji Restoration of 1868. Basing government policy upon the emperor's promise that "All classes high and low shall unite in vigorously carrying out the administration of affairs of state" and that "knowledge shall be sought throughout the world so as to strengthen the foundations of Imperial rule," the new government attempted to establish a system of national education as early as 1872.[21] Four years of required primary education were planned in 1872, required in 1886, reaffirmed after some slippage in 1900, and extended to six years after 1907. Students then went on to middle school (*chūgakkō*) which by the twentieth century taught students from the seventh to eleventh grades (ages 12 to 17), and from there, if they were college bound and hence male, to higher school (*kōtōgakkō*) which went from grades twelve to fourteen (ages 17 to 20), and finally the university (*daigaku*) which educated students for three years (ages 20 to 23).[22] The first, and best-endowed, such university sprang from an amalgamation of various institutions which was officially called Tokyo University in 1877, Imperial University in 1888, and Tokyo Imperial University in 1897. Imperial universities at Kyoto (1897), Tohoku (1907), Kyushu (1910), and Hokkaido (1918) soon followed; private universities, many of which had started earlier, were permitted to use the *daigaku* name after 1918.[23]

Enrollments steadily increased in the primary and middle school level not only because the population itself was in the process of doubling, but also because Japan's increasing urbanization and prosperity made it possible for a greater percentage of parents to consider sending their children to school; products of an age that talked openly of raising their social status (*risshin shusse*), who devoured books such as Samuel Smile's *Self-Help* and enshrined an American educator's apparently casual remark, "Boys be ambitious!," it was not surprising that Japanese children increasingly filled the schools. Estimates of primary school attendance are hard to come by, but apparently the number rose from perhaps 40 percent for men and 20 percent for women in the early Meiji period, to 60 percent for men and 25 percent for women in the 1880s, and practically to 100 percent for both sexes by the start of the twentieth century.[24] Middle schools expanded rapidly to keep pace with this demand, increasing their spaces from 27,758 in 1900 to 142,957 in 1943; this rapid growth actually increased the acceptance rate for the first level after compulsory education from 60 percent in 1900 to 73 percent in 1943.[25] This tremendous growth both in absolute and in percentage terms was obviously the first reason why Japan began to face a problem in school admissions by the beginning of the twentieth century.

Prior to 1945, however, the chief bottleneck for admissions was not at the university level, but rather at the higher school level. The main cause of the problem was that despite a sixfold increase in available spaces from 1,210 in

1896 to 6,454 in 1943, the number of applicants swelled so dramatically that the acceptance rate for all higher schools, Masuda Koichi tells us, dropped in this same period from 56 percent to a mere 9 percent.[26] Compounding the crisis was the fact that the greater age, endowment, and prestige of the imperial universities—particularly Tokyo Imperial University—their legions of famous graduates, and their surefire connections for the most rewarding public and private sector jobs made entrance into these institutions, and hence into the five nationally sponsored higher schools—again, particularly Higher School Number One in Tokyo—absolutely essential. Using a slightly different set of figures, therefore, Herbert Passin has suggested that only one out of thirteen middle school graduates could attend higher schools, and only one out of twenty-five could expect to make it to the nationally run higher schools.[27] "You students of First Higher," intoned the famous educator Kinoshita Hiroji upon his arrival at the Tokyo school in 1888, "will someday stand in the upper crust of society."[28]

In such circumstances, it is not surprising that the government was unable to stop the various higher schools from administering very difficult written entrance examinations. In 1927, for example, the government suggested that written examinations for the middle and higher schools be made optional, with greater attention being paid to the school record, the principal's report, and an oral interview. Wartime regulations also urged greater emphasis upon the physical examination and tried to force students to go to school in their own district, the idea here being that a residency requirement might flatten the hierarchy of schools by spreading the ablest students around. Unfortunately, the various admissions officers found it hard to make decisions based simply on school records limited to one particular school. Principals' reports were regarded as untrustworthy, as they would usually praise a student without much discrimination. Oral interviews thus often became simply another form of entrance examination, and many schools simply exercised their option to have a written examination if they so desired.[29] Clearly what was at stake here was, as Dore has already suggested, a deeply perceived need to use written, factual examinations that could be graded right or wrong as a means of making completely objective admissions decisions. Given the high stakes, anything else would have been sheer disaster for higher school authorities.

Underlying the prewar examination system, in sum, lay a number of complex factors, the first and most obvious of which was that there was only a limited number of spaces in a clearly defined educational hierarchy for the increasing number of Japanese men who wished to get ahead. The idea of judging these students by written examinations, Masuda Koichi tells us, was not only a concept dating back to early Japanese traditions, but also an educational practice in vogue in those European school systems that the Japanese were using as models in their own nation building.[30] With so much at stake, short, factual, or "right or wrong" answers seemed to be the most objective and hence both the fairest and the most discriminating way to distinguish between students who probably did not differ all that much in their training and ability. Most important of all, the rising notions of progress, social mobility, and the right of the individual to serve the state if able were still in conflict with a society bound by obligations and a sense of place. "Probably no Meiji leader thought about matters in quite this way," notes Thomas Rohlen, "but the fact remains that outside of education, particularism retained its extraordinary power, and the Meiji leadership was anxious to assure that the nation would benefit from the secure flow of talent to the top. The sacredness of exams in Japan, even today, seems proportional to the power of particularistic forces it holds at bay."[31]

AMERICAN INFLUENCES

Japan began a third major period of educational reform when the Allied Occupation of Japan (1945–1952) saw American officials working with their Japanese counterparts to rebuild completely the prewar school system. Inspired largely by a report written by Dr. George Stoddard, soon to be the president of the University of Illinois, in March 1946 after consultation with the counterpart Education Reform Council (Kyōiku Sasshin Iinkai), Occupation officials extended compulsory education from six to nine years, required coeducation at basic levels, and changed the traditional multitrack system of various schools for men and women to a largely single-track 6-3-3-4 system of elementary, junior high, senior high, and four-year undergraduate universities operating at the standard American age levels. Two-year junior colleges were quickly added, most of which catered to women seeking to terminate their education at that level. Other reforms sought to simplify the written language, to decentralize some of the power of the Ministry of Education, to hold elections for local school boards, and to encourage adult education. These reforms were vigorously pushed through in the Occupation period despite the fact that Japan was still impoverished from the war. They had, it should be emphasized, the support of at least a strong minority of liberal educators.[32]

Rereading the Stoddard report today, it is easy to see why the Occupation would be opposed to the prewar examination system. Arguing that "there has been too great a gap between the world of higher learning occupied by scholars, and the unidentified millions of the Japanese people," the report proposed instead to build new universities which would have as their "three great functions" guarding "as a treasure beyond price the tradition of intellectual liberty," preparing "young men and women of talent for positions of leadership," and training these same citizens "for technical proficiency in both old and new professions."[33] Given this stress upon the role of the university in training citizens, it is not surprising that the report considered the traditional examinations to be "formal and stereotyped," to encourage "conformity upon the part of teachers and students," and to stifle "freedom of inquiry and critical judgement, lending itself readily to manipulation by the authorities in the interests of a narrow bureaucracy rather than of society as a whole."[34] This final concern was subsequently heightened by Occupation surveys which reported an increase in politically oriented questions after the outbreak of war with China in 1937.³⁵ American concerns about the pedagogy of the examinations thus dovetailed rather nicely with the broader American belief that a few evil leaders had tricked a poorly educated public into an immoral war with the United States.

A counterattack began almost immediately. To begin with, by lowering the age at which students entered the new high schools (vs. higher schools) from seventeen to fifteen and by greatly increasing the number of such schools, the Occupation in effect switched the main "crunch" or competition for scarce spaces from getting into the new high schools to getting into the new universities. Here the American and Japanese authorities suggested that admissions decisions be decided now upon the basis of a high school transcript, less fearful achievement tests to be given by each faculty (*gakubu*) of each university, and a new standardized aptitude test known as the *shingaku tekisei kensa* (literally, investigation of the ability to proceed with schooling) or *shinteki* for short.³⁶ The test, Vivian Edmiston Todd reported at the time, was designed by a number of "outstanding Japanese psychologists," and took two and one-half hours to complete. Fifty percent of the test consisted of "disarranged sentences," vocabulary, mathematical reasoning, and "following directions." The rest consisted of passages testing literary and scientific comprehension.³⁷ Despite problems, some 129,966 students took the test in 1947 to loud Occupation claims that the newly designed university admissions system was ideal because it tested past performance (school record), present accomplishments (achievement exams), and future promise (the *shinteki*).³⁸

The new test rather quickly ran into the kinds of difficulties that have always plagued efforts to introduce any educational reforms. On the one hand, conservatives appear to have been upset that the test was conducted largely at the insistence of the Americans, and they hence wished to restore the traditional mode of achievement testing that had been so prominent in traditional Japanese pedagogy. Progressives, on the other hand, worried about surrendering any autonomy in testing to central authorities; reacting both to the abuse of academic freedom prior to 1945 and to the alleged American "reverse course" from at least 1947 on, faculties (*gakubu*) within the university structure insisted upon maintaining control over how student admissions would be decided. Both high school authorities and parents felt that students were studying for the new examination, thereby simply adding to already heavy burdens, and few could be found to defend the idea of aptitude testing. For a variety of reasons, then, the *shinteki* was dropped in 1954, a mere two years after the Occupation had officially ended.³⁹

Behind these immediate criticisms lurked the incredible pressures emanating from a rapid rise in the applicant pool. The number of applicants to the universities apparently rose from 176,125 in 1949 to 596,461 in 1954, the year in which the *shinteki* was dropped.⁴⁰ Economically, this great rise reflected both the gradual recovery of Japan from the hardships of the war and the increasing necessity of a good education for students wanting jobs in a steadily modernizing economy.

Educationally, the rise undoubtedly reflected some of the effects of single-track schooling, as well as a shift from the high schools to the universities as the point at which a really competitive admissions process occurred. While admission to the new high schools—as opposed to the older higher schools—could still be a tense and difficult process, particularly when Occupation efforts to make students attend school in this district largely fell apart, the growing social homogenization of the society, a tendency for women to begin competing for spaces in the university, and the increasing possibility and desirability of a university education made this process the key one in the educational ladder.

Compounding the difficulty was the fact that the Occupation reforms never effectively ended the domination of the traditional elite universities. The Occupation stripped the universities of their old imperial (*teikoku*) name, but it did not abolish either the particular institutions or the chair system (*koza*) under which these elite institutions received extra funds for prestigious faculty posts. Newer public universities were often hastily thrown together amalgamations of former higher schools and other institutions which had neither the facilities nor the prestige of their elite competitors. Private universities, meanwhile, got special encouragement from the Occupation but suffered heavily from a lack of endowment and a sharp postwar inflation.[41] By 1968, a government report tells us, private universities charged on an average five times as much as public institutions, but they spent one-half as much money per pupil ($611), had but one-third as much per pupil floor space, forced over 40 percent of their students to work part time, and had a student faculty ratio that was three times as large (1:37).[42] Not surprisingly, many of the students enrolled in private education expressed dissatisfaction with their education, thereby increasing the pressure to get into a few better *and* cheaper national institutions.[43]

The discrepancy between universities meant that increasing numbers of students simply would not accept the university to which they were admitted after high school. These students became known as *ronin,* a term that literally meant "masterless samurai," but in this case meant students studying for at least one postgraduate year to take the examinations again. By 1980, notes Rohlen, the number of seniors seeking a higher education had increased from the 596,461 figure quoted for 1954 to approximately 636,000; some 452,000 of these students were competing for places in the various four-year universities that now numbered roughly 412,000. The "fit" here would obviously not have been too bad, continues Rohlen, had there not been some 200,000 additional *ronin* trying for these same spaces. To put this another way, only one in three graduating seniors was able to get into the university faculty (*gakubu*) that he or she ("he" in 80 percent of the cases) wanted; 33 percent of the entering classes of these universities would consist of *ronin.*[44] The net effect of the postwar reforms was thus a tremendous increase in the number of students able and willing to take university examinations, a noticeable widening in the distance between high-quality and low-quality institutions, and consequently a greater tendency for students to take the examinations more than once before being admitted.

TOWARD THE FUTURE

Policies started in recent years to attack the examination problem have so far borne little fruit. After the university riots of the mid-1960s, for example, the ruling Liberal Democratic Party attempted to flatten the hierarchy of universities by beginning a new national university at Tsukuba Research City, which was to some extent patterned upon smaller American residential colleges, and by getting government aid to hard-pressed private universities. Both policies were no doubt helpful in checking a further widening of the gap between the most and least competitive universities, and yet the amount of money involved was nowhere near enough to give the traditional elite institutions such as Tokyo any real competition.[45] As one rather flippant Tsukuba University student told his teacher when asked an unusually hard question, "If I'd known the answer to that, I'd be at Tokyo."[46] The precedents of these two policies might be useful for future efforts, and yet the hierarchies remained.

Similarly, the decision in 1979 to begin a new preliminary screening examination known as the *kyōitsu shikken* or "first screening test" was a policy longer on promise than performance. Now required of all applicants wishing to take the particular tests of the various national universities, the new test has served as a useful screening examination, but it has not yet succeeded in substituting a more aptitude-oriented test for an achievement one, or in getting the various university faculties (*gakubu*) to drop their insistence upon giving their own examinations.[47] While it is important that such a test is in place should feelings change, the suspicion of the national government and the difficulties of cooperation between the various universities have still combined to make the *kyōitsu shikken* a test that has only a very limited value in reducing the tensions of examination hell.

The current situation is thus rather confused. On the one hand, an optimist might say, a blue-ribbon commission has been appointed to review the educational system as a whole. As noted earlier, this commission has argued that the "excessive competition" for university entrance is unhealthy, and it has suggested that an alarming increase in school bullying (*ijime*) reflects the fact that too many students are absorbed in the mindless quest for facts to be exposed to questions of basic human values. Japan has now largely caught up to Western levels of knowledge and technology, the report continues, and hence it is clearly time for the Japanese school system to worry about fostering creativity;[48] the suggestions for doing this take full note of the universities' need for autonomy, yet still stress the desirability of the optional use of a common test, the creation of more formal admissions offices capable of making significant distinctions between students, and the use of criteria other than achievement test scores.[49] The report thus goes well beyond the usual Japanese "tut-tutting" about the difficulties of examination hell—a response, it was suggested earlier, that really reflected an admiration for the character-building difficulties inherent in the system. To put this another way, the fact that Japanese young people now feel confident that they will get a decent enough job may encourage them to be less nervous about their chances of getting into a good university at precisely the time that the Japanese government is becoming concerned about the dangers of too much studying. Creativity and free time may become important to both students and educators for different yet equally compelling reasons.

Cynics, on the other hand, might suggest that too many people profit from the present system for it to change easily. Publishers selling examination guides, the lucrative "cram school" industry, and the universities which make money for themselves and their faculty from giving and correcting examinations simply have too much at stake to change. Even those who have no stake in the system, our cynic might continue, are convinced, despite evidence to the contrary, that objective factual testing gives any student a chance regardless of social class or wealth. Separate university achievement tests simply have too long a history and meet too many of the needs outlined in this chapter to disappear simply because a new generation is beginning to be truly worried about them. The growing crop of eighteen-year-olds (peaking in 1992) guarantees a fierce competition for places, particularly as long as the university system remains hierarchical. And what top education official, our cynic triumphantly concludes, could ever seek to dismantle the very system that propelled him and a few elite male students to the top?

Sadly enough, the cynics may well have the better of the argument. As this chapter has tried to suggest, the current university admissions system is a combination of traditional ideas about the value of rote learning, deep and quite legitimate concerns about objectivity in a highly particularistic society, and a university system in which it is quite clear exactly how good any particular institution is. Japanese parents have long schemed to get their children into the best of these institutions so that the children could then be assured of the most prestigious jobs and secure futures. Prior to World War II, this meant preparing a child for the tense higher school examinations; after the war, the most crucial bottleneck became the four-year university. If and when the Japanese economy becomes so sophisticated that ordinary jobs appear to have almost as much status as those jobs open only to elite university graduates, then increasing numbers of potential examination takers may well say, "Bye bye Tokyo U." Given the depth of this historical tradition, on the other hand, it seems that for some time to come, separate, difficult achievement examinations will continue to be a fiery rite of passage for Japanese high school students.

NOTES

1. Kyōgakusha, comp., '77 *Daigakubetsu nyūshiki shirizu; todai bunka* (Tokyo: Kyōgakusha, 1976), 51 *nendo*, 2. As will be made clear later, the publication of these yearly examination guides is a big business in Japan.

2. Masuda Seiichi, *Nyūgaku shikken: Kako kara genzai made* (Tokyo: Minshu Kyōiku Kyōkai, 1964), pp. 6ff.

3. Shimizu Yoshihiro, "Entrance Examinations: A Challenge to Equal Opportunity in Education," *Journal of Social and Political Ideas in Japan* 1, no. 3 (December 1963), p. 89.

4. Orihara Hiroshi, "Test Hell and Alienation: A Study of Tokyo University Freshmen," *Journal of Social and Political Ideas in Japan* 5, nos. 2–3 (December 1967), p. 232.

5. "Summary of First Report on Educational Reform" (no author or date). This is an English-language summary of the Japanese report that was distributed by the Japanese Embassy in the United States.

6. Omiya Tomonobu, *Sayonara, todai* (Tokyo: Bungei Shunju, 1987). The quotation comes from the jacket cover.

7. Ezra Vogel, *Japan's New Middle Class* (Berkeley: University of California Press, 1971), especially pp. 40–67.

8. Ezra Vogel, *Japan as Number One* (Cambridge, Mass.: Harvard University Press, 1979), especially pp. 163ff. It is worth noting that this book was very popular in Japan.

9. Christie Kiefer, "The Psychological Interdependence of Family, School and Bureaucracy in Japan," in T.S. Lebra and W. Lebra, eds., *Japanese Culture and Behavior* (Honolulu: University of Hawaii Press, 1974), p. 354.

10. Ronald Dore, *The Diploma Disease: Education, Quantification and Development* (Berkeley: University of California Press, 1976).

11. Ibid., pp. 35ff.

12. Edwin O. Reischauer, *The Japanese* (Cambridge, Mass.: Harvard University Press, 1979), p. 46.

13. *Kodansha Encyclopedia of Japan* (Tokyo: Kodansha, 1983), 7: 171–72.

14. William T. deBary, Donald Keene, and Tsunoda Ryusaku, *Sources of the Japanese Tradition* (New York: Columbia University Press, 1958), pp. 50–51.

15. Robert Borgen, *Sugawara no Michizane and the Early Heian Court* (Cambridge, Mass.: Harvard University Press, 1986), pp. 77, 78.

16. Ibid., p. 2. The question of *ema* has been discussed by my colleague Jennifer Robertson in a yet unpublished paper.

17. Ivan Morris, *The Nobility of Failure* (New York: Holt, Rinehart and Winston, 1975).

18. For a clear summary of educational changes in English, see Kobayashi Tetsuya, *Society, Schools and Progress in Japan* (Exeter, Eng.: Pergamon, 1976).

19. Daisetz T. Suzuki, *Zen and Japanese Culture* (New York: Pantheon, 1960), p. 31.

20. *Kodansha Encyclopedia of Japan* 6: 7–8.

21. deBary, Keene, and Tsunoda, *Sources of the Japanese Tradition*, p. 644.

22. Japanese National Commission for UNESCO, *The Role of Education in the Social and Economic Development of Japan* (Tokyo: Institute for Democratic Education, 1966), pp. 23ff.; Herbert Passin, *Society and Education in Japan* (Tokyo: Kodansha International, 1982), pp. 62ff.

23. For sophisticated commentary in English on this process, see Nagai Michio, *Higher Education in Japan: Its Take-Off and Crash,* trans. Jerry Dusenbury (Tokyo: University of Tokyo Press, 1971).

24. Japanese National Commission for Unesco, *The Role of Education*, p. 64. I have obviously simplified a complex set of statistics here, since, among other things, not all children who "attend" school do so regularly. Yet the pattern is clear.

25. Masuda, *Nyugaku shikken,* chart one (no page number).

26. Ibid., chart two.
27. Passin, *Society and Education*, p. 104.
28. Donald T. Roden, *Schooldays in Imperial Japan* (Berkeley: University of California Press, 1986), p. 55.
29. Masuda, *Nyugaku shikken*, pp. 19ff.; Zenkoku Shinro Shido Kenkyō-kai, comp., *Senbetsu no kyōiku to nyūshiki seido* (Tokyo: Minshusha, 1976), pp. 62ff.
30. Masuda, *Nyugaku shikken*, p. 51.
31. Thomas P. Rohlen, *Japan's High Schools* (Berkeley: University of California Press, 1983), p. 62. This is an excellent book for general background.
32. For detailed scholarship on this fascinating period, see Kaigo Tokiomi et al., *Kyōiku kaikaku; sengo nippon no kyōiku kaikaku* (Tokyo: Tokyo Daigaku Shuppankai, 1975) plus the other volumes in this series. The Kobayashi and Rohlen books cited above are useful English language works.
33. *Report of the United States Education Mission to Japan*, George Stoddard, chairman (Washington, D.C.: U.S. Government Printing Office, 1946), p. 47.
34. Ibid., p. 10.
35. Robert K. Hall, *Education for a New Japan* (New Haven, Conn.: Yale University Press, 1949), p. 117.
36. Nippon Kyōiku Shinri Gakkai, comp., *Daigaku nyūshiki o kangaeru* (Tokyo: Kinbidō, 1973), p. 12; for a participant's view, see Hidaka Daishiro, *Kyōiku kaikaku e no michi* (Tokyo: Yōyōsha, 1954), p. 314.
37. Virginia Edmiston Todd, "Selection of Students for Higher Schools in Japan," *Educational Administration and Supervision* 36 (October 1950), pp. 368ff.
38. Daishiro, *Kyōiku kaikaku e no michi*, p. 314; Mombusho, *"Showa niju nana nen ippohō no kaisetsu'.'* Mombujiho, no. 81, October 1949, p. 71.
39. For a sample of the controversy in the contemporary press, see "Shinteki o tesuto suru," *Shukan Asahi*, December 6, 1952, pp. 4ff.
40. Masuda, *Nyugaku shikken*, chart two.
41. These events are covered in detail in the Kaigo Tokiomi readings cited in note 32. In English, see the Nagai Michio book cited in note 23.
42. Mombusho, *Kōtō kyōiku no keikakuteki seibi ni tsuite* (Tokyo: n. p., 1976), p. 54.
43. For a vivid short description of the problems of private universities, see David A. Titus, "Comments on Frost," *Berkshire Review*, 1981, p. 123.
44. Rohlen, *Japan's High Schools*, p. 84. For disturbing evidence that those getting admitted come increasingly from the more well-to-do, see Thomas Rohlen, "Is Japanese Education Becoming Less Equalitarian? Notes on High School Stratification and Reform," *Journal of Japanese Studies* 3, no. 1 (1977), pp. 37–70; and Ronald Dore's review of Rohlen's book in the *Journal of Japanese Studies* 11, no. 1 (1985), pp. 183–88.
45. William Cummings, "The Conservatives Reform Higher Education," *Japan Interpreter* 4 (1974).
46. This story was told to me personally by a professor at Tsukuba University.
47. Rohlen, *Japan's High Schools*, p. 93.
48. See note 5.
49. See, for example, William K. Cummings, "Expansion, Examination Fever and Equality," in William K. Cummings, Amano Ikuo, and Kitamura Kazuyuki, eds., *Changes in the Japanese University: A Comparative Perspective* (New York: Praeger, 1979), especially pp. 101–6.

14

The Future of Japanese Higher Education

Kitamura Kazuyuki

THE GROWTH OF A "SELLER'S MARKET"

Japanese higher education as a whole has enjoyed continuous growth in both enrollment and the number of institutions since the new university system *(shnsei-daigaku seido)* was introduced under the influence of the American Occupation in 1949. During the Occupation period, radical educational reform was carried out, and the single-track (6-3-3-4) school ladder based on the American model was introduced. The prewar, multitrack system of higher education, characterized by a hierarchy of status, was integrated into two basic institutions called *daigaku* (universities) and *tanki-daigaku* (junior colleges). As a result of this reorganization, by the beginning of the 1950s, 201 new universities and 149 new junior colleges had been created in place of the 49 existing universities (9 imperial universities and 40 national, public, and private universities) and 391 various types of higher educational institutions composed of *koto-gakko* (higher schools), *semmongakko* (specialized technical schools), and *shihan-gakko* (normal schools), which had existed before the end of the World War II.[1]

In 1950, about 250,000 students were enrolled in the existing 350 institutions. By 1960 the number had increased to more than 1 million students in 525 institutions (245 universities and 280 junior colleges); by 1971, to 1.6 million students in 861 institutions (382 universities and 479 junior colleges); and by 1980, to 2.2 million students in 963 institutions (446 universities and 517 junior colleges). The admission rate to junior colleges and universities among eighteen-year-olds was less than 10 percent in 1950; but, by 1970, it had climbed to 23.6

percent (males, 29.2 percent and females, 17.7 percent), and by 1980, to 37.4 percent (males, 41.3 percent and females, 33.3 percent).

In addition to the traditional higher education sector, in 1980, 46,000 students were enrolled in sixty-two technical colleges (*koto-semmongakko*), and more than 150,000 students were enrolled in technical and vocational schools (*semmongakko*) at the postsecondary education level. If we add those students studying at technical and vocational types of postsecondary institutions to those attending universities and junior colleges, almost half of the nation's young people were receiving some sort of education beyond the secondary level.

In 1987, 1.9 million students were enrolled in 474 universities (95 national, 37 public, and 342 private), and 437,000 students were enrolled in 561 junior colleges (38 national, 53 public, and 470 private); the admission rate to junior college and universities was 36 percent. There were also 50,000 students in sixty-two technical colleges (fifty-four national, four public, and four private). In addition to the traditional higher education sector, 483,000 students were studying in 2,581 technical and vocational schools (159 national, 166 public, and 2,256 private) at the level of postsecondary education.

This dramatic expansion of higher education was accompanied by an unprecedented growth in secondary education. The rate of admission to senior high schools (grades 10 to 12) for those who completed compulsory schooling (grades 1 to 9) was 42.5 percent, when the new high school system started in 1948. It increased to 60 percent in 1961, jumped to 80 percent in 1971, and only five years later exceeded 90 percent. In 1980, the admission rate to senior high schools had climbed to 94.3 percent, lifting the educational level of the relevant age cohort well beyond the level of "semi-compulsory schooling."[2]

In terms of quantity, this demonstrates that Japanese higher education has, since the late 1940s, been a "high-growth industry." There has been a continuous increase in the "push" pressures for more educational opportunities from parents and students, stimulated by "pull" pressures from employers who need a greater number of college graduates. The continuing growth of Japanese higher education depends on the existence of a large pool of students seeking higher education.

Since 1951, Japanese higher education can be described as a "seller's market" in the sense that colleges (i.e., sellers of higher educational services) have always been flooded with applicants for admission (purchasers of higher education). Japanese colleges and universities were highly valued because of their screening function in which they selected potential young people, based on their academic abilities, and distributed them into various specialized fields according to the needs of the labor market.

For many large Japanese industries, this was a blessing since they were handicapped by a lack of college graduates during high economic growth periods. As a result, they urged universities to assume the important function of "sorting" potentially good students to meet their manpower needs according to the hierarchical rank of universities rather than to take on the role of trainers of students in terms of practical training. Industrial leaders believe that college graduates are much more effectively trained and socialized into good employees through strong in-service training programs conducted by the industry itself. Because of the lifelong employment system and an emphasis on seniority, most employees are expected to work for the same company until they retire, although this practice has gradually been changing during the past decade. For these reasons, both business and government have devoted substantial money and energy to their own in-service training programs in order to make their employees' skills directly relevant to their organizational needs. From this viewpoint, it is most important for employers to recruit potentially good young people who can be educated or trained by the company to meet its direct needs rather than look for "added-value," or, in other words, the value of any specialized academic or professional training obtained at the university.

As a result, it is believed that universities in Japan have a monopoly on human resources. The highest quality young people are those who are carefully selected through their university entrance examinations, a screening device which chooses those with the greatest potential to meet the needs of Japanese industry. In fact, no human resource pool has been available to employers other than that found in colleges and universities. Although conservative curricula and nonpractical teaching in colleges and universities have often been criticized by the business world, the lack of relevant training in higher education has been compensated for by the strong in-service training programs found in many large companies.

DEMOGRAPHIC CHANGE

Will colleges and universities in Japan continue to enjoy prosperity in the twenty-first century as they have during the high-growth period? Will they continue to be flooded with student applicants, and will their graduates continue to meet the needs of Japanese industry without changing their basic programs, curriculum, or teaching methods? Will the thousand colleges and universities in Japan be able to survive during the 1990s when a sharp decline in the college-age population is predicted?

One of the important changes in the next decade will be a demographic change. This is one of the very few trends that is clearly predictable. The eighteen-year-old population is expected to decrease by nearly one half million during the period from 1992 to 2000. Since the decline of the college-age population means the loss of the major customer of Japanese higher education (in Japan, 90 percent of college enrollments are drawn from the eighteen- to twenty-two-year-old population), it will certainly influence the financial condition of many tuition-dependent private institutions. One of the most significant aspects of Japanese higher education is the great share that is controlled by the private sector. In 1987, more than 70 percent of the institutions and the students in the nation were in the private sector, and most of the private institutions have very small endowments. Their financing, therefore, depends largely on revenues from tuition and fees paid by students and parents. Thus, this demographic trend is, perhaps, the single most critical factor affecting the future of colleges and universities in Japan.

Although Japanese higher education as a whole has enjoyed continuous growth since the mid-1970s, and, although, between 1980 and 1987, enrollment grew from 2.2 million to 2.3 million and the number of institutions increased from 961 to 1,035, the admission rate to higher education had dropped slightly from 37.4 percent in 1970 to 36.1 percent in 1987 (males, 37.1 percent and females, 35.1 percent). The admission rate has never surpassed the 38.6-percent rate of 1976 when it was at its highest.

At the beginning of the 1980s, the age cohort for elementary school fell to its lowest level since the World War II "baby booms." (The first baby boom occurred between 1947 and 1949, the second, between 1971 and 1974.) As a result, many kindergartens in Japan have canceled some of their classes; this so-called child shock has begun to affect the primary schools and, inevitably, will impact on secondary and higher education in the 1990s. According to the government's population statistics, the number of eighteen-year-olds decreased from 2.5 million in 1966 to 1.6 million in 1985. Since 1986, however, the number has increased dramatically and it is estimated that it will increase even further, from 1.85 million in 1986 to 2.05 million in 1992. From 1993, the number will again drop sharply from 1.9 million in 1993 to 1.5 million in 2000, a decrease of nearly half a million from the 1992 level. Therefore, the survival of institutions in a period with a sharply declining college-age population is, perhaps, one of the single most serious problems facing those concerned with higher education policy and institutional management.

In the face of these demographic changes, in 1984, the Ministry of Education, Science and Culture published *Higher Education Planning for the Period of Post-1986*. The ministry's plan estimated that an additional 86,000 enrollment places would be necessary between 1986 and 1992 to provide for the expected increase of eighteen-year-olds. But, because of the anticipated sharp decrease of eighteen-year-olds between 1992 and 2000, 44,000 student places out of the 86,000 will have to be eliminated by the year 2000.

As soon as the ministry's plan was published, and despite the prediction of a declining college-age population in the 1990s, there was a great "rush" to establish new institutions, new departments, and new programs in 1987 and 1988. During the 1987 academic year, nine new universities (one public and eight private) and fifteen junior colleges (one national, one public, and thirteen private) were established, and during the 1988 academic year, seventeen new universities (one national, one public, and fifteen private) and eleven new junior colleges (one national, two public, and eight private) were created.[3] In addition, a number of new departments and programs were added or expanded as a result of the predictions, and student places were greatly increased. The rush to establish these new institutions by university administrators was motivated by their belief that this was a final chance to expand higher education's capacity before the period of declining enrollment which will make expansion impossible. They seem to believe that the best strategy for their survival is to expand their institutional size, adding new departments and programs to attract prospective students.

As the 1990s approach, it is predicted that Japanese higher education will face a period of "institutional self-selection" in which a number of higher educational institutions could be closed or severely cut back. This scenario is being predicted by some pessimistic scholars and higher education planners, and serious discussions over how to react best to the potential crises are common. As a matter of historical fact, however, almost no universities were closed before World War II in Japan. Out of the 485 new universities established during the four decades since World War II, only two small private universities were closed and one national university, Tokyo University of Education, was closed but was later revived as the University of Tsukuba. Only 42 private junior colleges out of the 647 junior colleges established since 1951 had actually been closed by 1987.[4] Although there were dramatic fluctuations in the college-age population between the two baby booms following World War II, there has been no clear evidence to substantiate the fear that these demographic changes will be the death of Japan's colleges and universities.[5]

In the United States, the demise of colleges and universities has been commonplace throughout American history. For example, several hundred colleges were created and closed during the college movement prior to the Civil War.[6] More recently, during the decade of the 1960s, when the college-age population (eighteen- to twenty-one-year-olds) increased from 9.5 million to 15 million, 162 colleges and universities were created, and enrollments more than doubled from 3.6 million to 7.9 million, whereas 77 institutions (14 public and 63 private) were closed. During the decade of the 1970s, when the college-age population increased from 14.5 million to 17.1 million and the number of enrolled students increased from 7.9 million to 11 million, 429 new colleges and universities were created, whereas 153 other institutions (22 public and 131 private) were shut down.[7] It is significant to note that, even during a period with an increased college-age population, many institutions were still closed. During the 1980s, when the 18- to 21-year-old college-age population declined from 17.1 million in 1980 to 15.4 million in 1985, and in spite of predictions that at least 200 colleges would be closed,[8] only about 30 colleges had actually been closed by the middle of the decade. The total number of students enrolled in colleges and universities even increased, primarily because of a significant increase in the number of adult students who were aggressively recruited by colleges and universities.[9]

This might suggest that, although a potential problem is associated with demographic decline, institutions vital and flexible enough to seek out new sources of students (e.g., adults) can overcome the crisis. The fact that most of the 3,000 institutions of higher education in the United States have survived during the difficult decade of the 1980s suggests that institutions which respond to the social needs of the age will not only survive, but may even prosper.

EXTERNAL CHALLENGES

In the period from 1990 to 2000, Japanese higher education will face not only a declining college-age student pool, but also several fundamental structural changes in Japanese society. As was shown in the case of the American experience, demographic change, by itself, might not be a decisive factor in the institutional health of colleges and universities. However, if it occurs in conjunction with other external and internal changes, the aggregate of these changes may influence enormously the fate of higher education. This appears to be the situation in the Japanese case.

One of the most important external pressures is the so-called internationalization of Japanese society. Japanese industry and her commercial world have already faced internationalization; now Japanese colleges and universities are faced with an increasing number of foreign students, foreign teachers, and Japanese returnees from foreign countries who want to participate in Japanese higher education. The existence of the increasing number of foreign students and teachers requires a reexamination and reconstruction of the traditional Japanese higher education which has existed, ever since its creation during the Meiji period (1868–1912), as a purely indigenous institution. Although they became familiar with Western civilization by inviting foreign teachers to come to Japan and by encouraging Japanese students to study abroad, the Japanese leaders intended to build a "Japanese educational system for Japan's own sake" by modernizing Japan. After the complicated processes of Westernization and "Japanization,"[10] Japan has become a successful economic power in the world, and in the 1990s, in contrast with the Meiji period, Japanese colleges and universities are faced with the challenges of accepting an increasing number of non-Japanese students, more than 80 percent of them from developing countries in Asia. These students come with strong aspirations and diversified expectations. They are not always satisfied with the current living and academic environment or with the curriculum and teaching methods which are not designed to meet the needs of international students. They also find unsystematic Japanese language programs to be a problem.[11] In 1983 the Japanese government decided on a "ten-fold increase policy," which projected 100,000 foreign students by the beginning of the twenty-first century. If the plan is realized, the existence of that number of foreign students may have an enormous impact on the educational system of Japanese universities and colleges.

At the same time, Japanese colleges and universities will have to compete in the rising international market for students in an age of declining population. More and more Japanese students are opting to study in foreign countries rather than attend marginal Japanese institutions. In addition, all but the best Japanese colleges and universities will be forced to compete with increasing numbers of American universities which have begun to recruit Japanese students either by building branch campuses in Japan or by sending admissions officers to Japan.

These pressures toward internationalization will require Japanese colleges and universities not only to open their doors to foreign students, but also to be subject to international evaluation. They will have to demonstrate their academic quality and standard in order to show that they are comparable to overseas schools in terms of academic credibility and degrees.

The internationalization of Japanese society means that Japan's universities cannot survive without participating more fully in the international higher education community. The increase of international competition in the industrial world has also had a great effect on traditional Japanese employment practices. Structural changes are occurring in the traditional seniority and lifelong employment practices of Japanese industry when new college graduates are recruited. Since the 1980s, major companies, which had long recruited Japanese students only from prestigious Japanese universities, began to recruit foreign professionals and college graduates of foreign universities. They have also been recruiting part-time workers and well-trained adults rather than recent college graduates who require long and costly on-the-job training before they become valuable employees. Increasingly, employers have found an urgent need to recruit experienced and uniquely talented people who can compete internationally.

These changes in the employment market will force higher education to depart from traditional practices. In order to survive in a more internationally competitive world, Japanese industry needs dynamic, unique, and ambitious talents rather than the merely diligent, uniform, and bright young people who have traditionally been selected through higher education. Employers will come to expect colleges and universities to provide stronger education to students in areas relevant to their career needs. They will also demand that institutions of higher education strengthen their added-value function rather than merely provide a selection function.

In predicting future trends, several important external factors are not clear at this moment. One of these important factors is the direction of public policy. The fate of higher education in Japan is heavily dependent upon financial assistance from the central government. Private higher education, which accounts for more than 70 percent of both institutions and students, is largely dependent upon tuition revenue from students and upon institutional aid from the government.[12] Government subsidies to private institutions, initiated in the 1970s, now constitute around 20 percent of their total institutional expenditures.

During the period of declining college-age population, it is predicted that a substantial number of the private tuition-dependent institutions will suffer from decreasing revenues. More generous public subsidies to these institutions will be a critical factor in their survival. However, at least at the present time, neither the legislature nor the executive has published a clear policy statement about this key subject. At the time of nationwide campus unrest in the early 1970s, the leaders of the ruling Liberal Democratic Party and their cabinet decided to initiate institutional financial aid to private colleges and universities because they feared that a combination of student disturbances in national and public universities and a financial crisis in the private sector would cause more serious conflict and damage to Japanese higher education as a whole. This action was a dramatic reversal of the traditional policy of the Japanese government in which it concentrated human and financial resources only in national universities and ignored the financial needs of the private sector. It is not, however, clear that the government will increase the budget for higher education for the sake of helping struggling institutions in the 1990s. Indeed, the direction of public policy toward higher education may well depend on the degree of public confidence in higher education, and at present it seems doubtful that Japanese universities will be successful in winning public trust. Therefore, the future of the government's policy toward higher education seems to be problematic.

INTERNAL CHALLENGES

Following the unprecedented rapid expansion of higher education in the past two decades, a change in what student applicants were seeking began in the mid-1970s. Although the desire to attend colleges and universities is still strong (more than one out of three in the eighteen-year-old population goes on to traditional higher education), at the same time an increasing number of students are choosing to attend nonacademic types of postsecondary educational institutions such as specialized vocational and technical schools (*semmongakko*) and branch campuses of American universities in Japan. The diversification in high school students' college choices and career aspirations seems to be closely tied to such changes in society as the reform of the entrance examination system, shifts in the employment market, and the creation of popular departments and programs which reflect social and economic changes. In addition, after the mid-1970s and increasingly in the 1980s, it became much more difficult for Japan's universities to obtain sufficient resources from either public or private sources. In this generally unfavorable situation there is growing dissatisfaction on the part of college students. Several empirical findings suggest that many students spend most of their college days very passively, without any serious motivation for independent learning. They find their curriculum irrelevant and are disappointed by the classes and lectures at the universities to which they worked so hard to gain entrance.[13] For instance, a recent students' survey at the University of Tokyo showed that 37 percent of the students expressed dissatisfaction with the classes; more than 30 percent of the students at private universities also voiced dissatisfaction with their classes.[14] Thus, an increasing number of professors face the problem of how to deal with students who are poorly motivated, who have passive attitudes toward their classes, and who have unclear goals about both academic life and their future careers.

In spite of the fact that changes both in teaching methods and in the curriculum are clearly necessary due to the increasing diversity of student attitudes and needs, very little has been done in either the traditional practices of the universities or in the professors' attitudes toward teaching. Many professors fail to attract students to their traditional lectures, and they turn to research in order to find meaning in their professional lives. At the same time, students uninterested in the traditional curriculum and boring lectures attempt to find meaning in extracurricular activities.

The university has been slow to recognize that structural change in society requires corresponding change in curriculum, teaching, research, and governance. It appears that most members of the academic community have become so accustomed to a growth-oriented management style that they assume that student applications will continue to increase, and they have not begun to make the adjustments necessary to cope with an age of declining student enrollment and fewer available resources.

There are several strategies that university administrators can follow in the face of declining enrollments. Among them are the use of institutional recruitment campaigns, the application of marketing techniques, and the establishment of new departments and programs that will be popular among prospective students. Many new programs—computer science, information science, business management, biotechnology, international relations, and area studies—have been created, and some of them have been successful in attracting large numbers of student applicants. These approaches are, most often, based on the same assumptions as the traditional expansion model and have merely been "added on" to the existing structure of higher education. What is really needed is a basic structural change which will include significant innovations for strengthening the functions of education.

A COMPARATIVE PERSPECTIVE

Most non-Japanese scholars who look for an explanation of Japan's economic success, national efficiency, and high productivity, as well as the superior achievement of Japanese high school students on international mathematics and science tests, tend to believe that Japanese education must be the major source of the success. However, the general feeling of the Japanese people is that, if Japan's schools and colleges are so excellent and so effective, why is there such deep dissatisfaction with education among the public, and why are so many *juku* (private preparatory or remedial cram schools) and the examination industry—both of which are strong support systems to formal schooling—not only necessary but so prosperous? Finally, why is it necessary for most firms and the government to continue to invest such huge amounts of money in employee on-the-job training?

If we examine the evaluation of Japanese education by non-Japanese critics, we find a common theme: In sharp contrast to the high marks given to primary education, little evaluation has been undertaken on higher education either in terms of its quality or its efficiency.

As was mentioned, the reform of Japan's educational system carried out immediately after World War II was heavily influenced by the American educational system and its underlying principles. In the succeeding four decades,

Japan has continued to look to the U.S. system as its model. Today, as Japan endeavors to reform her educational system, the suitability of the American model is being reexamined, along with everything else.

The United States, meanwhile—motivated by the desire to discover the secret of Japan's vigorous economic growth and her success in technological innovation—is paying more attention to the Japanese educational system. That Americans, who have possessed unrivaled influence over world affairs, politically, economically, and culturally since the end of the war, should feel their position of prominence threatened by Japan, a vanquished nation, and try to find the source of Japanese strength in its education system, is among the great ironies of history.

In 1983, it was proposed that a cooperative study of education be undertaken in the two countries, and a study group was set up in Japan by the Ministry of Education, Science and Culture, and another group was established in the United States by the Department of Education. In January 1987, the respective teams released their reports.

The U.S. report is quite critical of Japanese higher education, calling it "the weakest part of the entire system."[15] The report states that higher education is far less efficient than any other part of the educational system, including the primary and secondary schools, *juku*, preparatory schools, and even corporate education. It observes the various negative effects that the university entrance examination system, with its intense competition, has on school education in general. The report also says that the undergraduate curriculum, especially for freshmen and sophomores, is seriously flawed, both in terms of the system as a whole and in the quality of instruction. Institutions of higher education are not open to adults who desire to further or continue their education, and they lag behind in the internationalization of faculties and campus facilities as well. Graduate schools, which ought to play a leading role in conducting basic research and developing technical expertise, are behind the times. It notes the consensus in Japan that the higher education system is neither meeting the needs of the people at a time when the world is in the throes of rapid change nor responding to the concerns of Japanese youth.

The report cites Edwin O. Reischauer's criticism: "The squandering of four years at the college level on poor teaching and very little study seems an incredible waste of time for a nation so passionately devoted to efficiency." Perhaps the "inefficiency" of Japanese higher education seems "incredible" because there is such a great gap between the quality of elementary and secondary education on the one hand and higher education on the other. Another reason may be that it is probably hard for Americans to understand how the whole of Japanese education, despite the poor quality of the postsecondary system, functions as well as it does and helps give Japan its prosperous society.

The American comments reveal a considerable gap in the American and Japanese views of education and of the role of the university. From the American viewpoint, to spend the first two years of college life relaxing is a waste of time.

Japanese traditionally view the early stage of higher education as a transition from "schooling" to "scholarship": The basic premise is that college students, who acquired the capacity to learn and to discipline themselves academically in high school, should be left free to study on their own initiative. They have entered university after twelve years of school education, during which they learned to endure intense competition, to study diligently, and to tolerate externally imposed restraints. It is only natural that they should seek some relief and freedom from restrictions after they enter university. Considering the even heavier demands awaiting them in full-time employment after they graduate, the opportunity to relax and enjoy life for a few years may be crucial to Japanese youth in adjusting to society.

Even though the first two years of university life are thought of as a period of relative ease and relaxation on the part of students, it does not mean that the faculty are lax or that the students learn little. Japanese universities, especially in the fields of social sciences and humanities, try to leave students as much free time as possible and avoid imposing restraints upon them so that they will learn to cultivate individual initiative and motivation. This, indeed, is considered the important function of the university. Japanese professors do not exert the kind of heavy pressure to study on students that their American counterparts do, and they keep their involvement with students to a minimum.

In fact, the greatest difference between Japanese and American education lies in which phase of the system—secondary or postsecondary—functions to provide the instruction and discipline that nurtures scholastic aptitude. In Japan, scholastic aptitude is instilled before—and in the United States, after—entering university. Nonscholastic aptitudes, which are allowed to develop during high school as well as in college in the United States, are in Japan at last given a chance to blossom only after the student has entered university. The quality and function of higher education cannot be appropriately discussed without considering the difference between the two educational systems and the roles they play in the two countries. When comparing high schools in Japan and the United States, a Japanese would probably cite the same criticism of American high schools that the Americans aim at the Japanese university system. The educational systems of both countries are determined by the particular traditions and the social conditions and needs of each country.

CONCLUSION

The changes described in this chapter are fundamentally new and different from what Japanese higher education experienced during the decades right after World War II. For the first time in the history of postwar higher education, Japanese universities have begun to move from a seller's market to a buyer's market, in which students will be "courted customers" rather than "supplicants for admission" in the term of David Riesman. This situation is similar to the American situation in the 1980s.[16]

In the coming age of declining enrollment, a substantial number of marginal institutions will be forced to make a strong effort to attract not only traditional full-time students but also nontraditional part-time students. In order to attract enough of these nontraditional clients, these institutions will have to develop new and flexible curricula and teaching methods to strengthen the added-value function. The days of simply emphasizing the traditional screening function are over for Japanese higher education.

All these changes will be taking place in Japan beginning in the 1990s. These changes will require Japanese institutions of higher education (for the first time since 1945) to overhaul their basic assumptions fundamentally and to pursue innovative approaches in both academic affairs and management. In one sense, this will be a serious challenge to traditional Japanese higher education, but the decade ahead will also be a time for opportunity. As Eric Ashby warned, the danger is "not that universities fail to respond adequately to the short-term demands of an age of technology," but "just the opposite danger: that in responding so readily and so efficiently they will run the risk of self-disintegration through too facile an adaptation to tomorrow's world."[17] Only those who understand the implication of the changes and are brave enough to take up these new challenges without losing their identity as universities will not only survive but may even prosper in a time of decline.

NOTES

1. Kitamura Kazuyuki and William K. Cummings, "The 'Big-Bang' Theory and Japanese University Reform," *Comparative Education Review* 16, no. 2 (June 1972), pp. 303–24.

2. These figures are based on the statistics of the Ministry of Education, Science and Culture, *Mombu tokei yoran* [Digest of Educational Statistics], annual editions.

3. Ministry of Education, Science and Culture, *Daigaku shiryo* [University Information Material], no. 100 (1987) and no. 106 (1988).

4. Statistics published by Mombusho, *Zenkoku daigaku ichiran* [National Directory of Universities] (1988), *Zenkoku tankidaigaku ichiran* [National Directory of Junior Colleges] (1988).

5. Kitamura Kazuyuki, *Gakko tota no kenkyu* [A Study of Institutional Selection of Educational Institutions] (Tokyo: Toshindo, 1989).

6. According to Donald Tewksbury, before the Civil War 516 colleges were founded in sixteen states and 412 of them died an institutional death; only 104 colleges survived (a mortality rate of 81 percent). Donald G. Tewksbury, *The Founding of American College in the United States* (New York: Columbia University, Teachers College Press, 1932). In 1982, Colin Burke, through a comprehensive historical search, found that only 241 institutions were established in thirty-two states during the period and 70 percent of them survived into the twentieth century; only forty institutions died; and the mortality rate during the period from 1800 to 1860 was only 17 percent. Colin B. Burke; *American-Collegiate Populations: A Test of the Traditional View* (New York: New York University Press, 1982).

7. *Digest of Education Statistics* (Washington, D.C.: National Center for Educational Statistics, annual editions).

8. *The Condition of Education, A Statistical Report*, 1980 Edition (Washington, D.C.: NCES, 1980), p. 98.

9. M. Breland Hunter, *Demographics, Standards, and Equity: Challenges in College Admissions—Report of a Survey of Undergraduate Admissions Policies, Practices, and Procedures*. (Washington, D.C.: American Association of Collegiate Registrars and Admission Officers, 1986).

10. Nagai Michio, "Westernization and Japanization: The Early Meiji Transformation of Education," in Donald H. Shively, ed., *Tradition and Modernization in Japanese Culture* (Princeton, N.J.: Princeton University Press, 1971), pp. 35–76.

11. Kitamura Kazuyuki, *Daigaku-kyōiku no kokusaika* [The Internationalization of Higher Education] (Tokyo: Tamagawa University Press, 1984); Kitamura Kazuyuki, "The Internationalization of Higher Education in Japan," *The Japan Foundation Newsletter* (May 1983), pp. 1–9, (August 1984), pp. 9–11.

12. Kitamura Kazuyuki, "Mass Higher Education," in William K. Cummings, Amano Ikuo, and Kitamura Kazuyuki, eds., *Changes in the Japanese University—A Comparative Perspective* (New York: Praeger Publishers, 1979), pp. 64–82. See also The Japan Association of Private Colleges and Universities, *Japan's Private Colleges and Universities*, (Tokyo: 1987).

13. Kitamura Kazuyuki, "Curriculum and Teaching at Japanese Universities—New Implications," in *Current Issues in University Education of Korea and Japan—Proceedings of the KCUE 6th International Seminar* (Seoul: Korean Council for University Education, 1987), pp. 65–75.

14. Amano Ikuo, "1988 Survey of Students at the University of Tokyo," *Gakunai koho* (University of Tokyo Newsletter), November 15, 1988. Ohyama Akio, "Student Images Seen from National Survey of Students Sponsored by the Japan Association of Private Colleges and Universities," *Daigaku jiho* 185, 186 (November 1985, January 1986).

15. OERI Japan Study Team; *Japanese Education Today. A Report from U.S. Study of Education in Japan*. (Washington, D.C.: U.S. Department of Education, 1987).

16. David Riesman, *On Higher Education: The Academic Enterprise in an Era of Rising Student Consumerism* (San Francisco: Jossey Bass, 1980).

17. Eric Ashby, *Technology and the Academics: An Essay on Universities and the Scientific Revolution* (New York: Macmillan Co., 1966), p. 88.

15

Postscript: What Can We Learn from Japan?

Edward R. Beauchamp

During the Meiji period (1868–1912), virtually all Western scholars analyzed Japan's institutions from the perspective of how the Japanese had borrowed or adapted Western ideas and culture. This situation existed through World War II and well into the postwar period. Only in the last two decades, primarily as a result of Japan's spectacular economic growth, have a significant number of Americans begun to look at Japan in a different way. Ezra Vogel's best-selling book, *Japan as Number One*,[1] is the most extreme example of this genre. It was clearly a step in the direction of redressing the patronizing view of Japan held by most Americans, but it was too one-sided in Japan's favor to be taken as an approximation of reality. Although Vogel got the attention of his fellow citizens, his approach has now outlived whatever usefulness it had when he published it.

This volume attempts to go beyond the "Japan as Number One" approach by presenting not only the considerable strengths of the Japanese educational enterprise, but some of its weaknesses as well. How well we have succeeded is, of course, in the eye of the beholder. In any event, the preceding chapters provide a rich source of information and analysis about Japanese education. One of the fascinations of studying a foreign educational system is to search for ideas and practices that might be relevant to one's own system. That approach is, however, fraught with danger and should be used cautiously. Recently, for example, it has become fashionable for some Americans to take a brief trip to Japan, visit a school or two, talk with a handful of Japanese educators, have lunch at a local sushi stand, and return home as "instant experts" advocating that the United States emulate all or part of the Japanese educational model. What these well-intentioned people forget is that an educational system is an organic outgrowth of a specific cultural context and that, removed from this context, elements of the educational superstructure lose their *raison d'être*. The Japanese system cannot be uprooted and planted successfully in a radically different American culture. If we wanted to adopt the Japanese system we would first have to restructure our cultural life completely.

The Japanese are essentially a group-oriented society (although not to the extent that some believe), and the United States honors the idea of individuality (again, often not to the extent we claim). Harmony and order, based on Confucian ideals, are important concepts in Japan, whereas Americans place great stress on the holy grail of creativity and participation. As a result, it should not surprise us that the Japanese system is among the most highly centralized in the world, and that this results in a subject-matter-oriented curriculum and teacher-centered classrooms. Neither should it surprise us that the American system tends toward decentralization, a fragmented curriculum, a greater emphasis on social concerns, and student-centered classrooms.

The Japanese, however, value education highly and support it in deeds as well as words. The idea that education is important is reflected in the respect accorded to teachers as well as the reasonably attractive salaries paid to them. Americans, on the other hand, often give little more than lip service to education. Rhetoric to the contrary, many Americans neither particularly value education nor are willing to pay higher taxes to improve it. American parents do not always insist that children do their homework, and the general level of parental participation in school activities is abysmal. This, at best, lukewarm attitude toward education is at the heart of our educational problems.

Japanese schools are demanding. Students are exposed to a much broader range of basic subjects, especially in mathematics and the sciences, and they study them in greater depth for a much longer period of time. The results of this rigorous approach are reflected not only in the superior performance of Japanese students on international achievement tests, but also in Japan's generally better educated work force. Indeed, after teaching in Japanese universities, I am no longer shocked when I find that Japanese students often know more about American history than do American students!

Further evidence that the Japanese take education seriously is illustrated by the fact that Japanese students attend school five and one-half days a week, or 240 days a year (as opposed to about 180 days a year in the United States). If one factors in this extra time, the Japanese high school graduate has spent the equivalent of sixteen years in school versus the American high school graduate's twelve years. Japanese students also spend several hours a night on homework, and have major projects to complete during their shorter summer holiday. Finally, although the period of compulsory education in Japan ends after ninth grade, almost 94 percent of Japanese youth attend full-time upper secondary school, and another 2 percent attend part time. Almost 95 percent of those entering the noncompulsory tenth, eleventh, and twelfth grades graduate.

In the United States the dropout rate is horrendous; only approximately 71 percent of entering high school students graduate. American elementary students do little or no homework (and when a conscientious teacher assigns some he or she is often criticized by parents). At the secondary level (with the exception of college preparatory classes), little homework is assigned. In fact, I know of teacher education courses in which future teachers are advised to give high school students time in class to read assignments, a recognition that the majority are simply not motivated enough to do outside work.

An important pedagogical dimension of the Japanese group orientation is an emphasis on the individual's responsibility to school and classmates. Where American schools are defaced with grafitti and campus guards (often armed) provide security for students and teachers, Japanese schools are generally calm, well-ordered environments for learning. This does not mean to suggest that all Japanese schools are problem free, only that the nature and magnitude of the problems are of a far less dangerous type than in the United States.

Closely related to this is the success of Japanese schools in establishing standards of classroom order and discipline which tend to encourage learning. Once more, being part of the group acts as a strong deterrent to antisocial behavior. Such behavior, of course, does occur upon occasion, but it is seldom as frequent or as serious as in the American context. In American schools, on the other hand, discipline is often problematic at best. When children are taught from an early age, implicitly as well as overtly, that individuality and freedom are absolute "goods," a "me" attitude often develops which is likely to result in a need for instant gratification. As a result, in many schools, chaos is not an unusual classroom condition, and cutting classes and absenteeism are seen as "no big deal."

Since the two very different cultures have given birth to two very different educational systems, one might ask is there anything that Americans might learn from the Japanese? In terms of borrowing or adapting specific elements of the Japanese system, my answer would be no. Yet there are some potentially important general lessons that we might learn from studying the Japanese system. The first of these is an attitudinal one, that is, developing a positive attitude toward education. Theodore Sizer observed, in his neglected *Places of Learning, Places of Joy*,[2] that Americans have the education system we want because, if we seriously wanted a different system, we would find a way to achieve it. In other words, our rhetoric is what we use to express our dreams and our ideals, but convenience and our wallets determine our actions.

What, then, can the United States learn from the Japanese system of education? It is clear that American policymakers and educators cannot borrow any ideas and practices from Japan that require a Japanese environment in order to flourish. More modest goals are, however, within the realm of possibility.

1. First and foremost, we can learn from the Japanese the true value of education, and we can begin to take it as seriously as they do. In today's increasingly global society we simply must prepare our youth for an increasingly complex and technologically oriented future in which our position in the world

will face even greater challenges than today. Too often we understand the nature of our educational problems, as well as the steps that must be taken to rectify them. When the solutions are economically expensive, politically undesirable, or too challenging to our comfortable status quo, we find that we lack the courage to do what needs to be done.

2. Much nonsense has been written about "basic" education over the past few years. Following the prescriptions of Allan Bloom and E.D. Hirsch[3] will not solve our problems and, indeed, would probably exacerbate them. Having said this, however, it is clear that much of Japan's educational success is based on its rigorous curriculum and on the high academic expectations that the system (supported by parents) places on youngsters. It is true that the high level of Japanese literacy is possible in a society that is essentially homogenous, monocultural, and monolingual, and a much more fragmented American society cannot hope to approach the same level. There is no reason why American academic standards cannot be significantly raised; however, in order to do so, we need to take education much more seriously than we do at the moment.

3. There has been a widespread view among American educators that more money is the answer to our educational problems. Since the early 1960s, we have spent enormous sums of money on our schools and, in the words of former Secretary of Education Lauro F. Cavazos, "Although we have had some laudable reform efforts during the past 15 years, it is clear that as a nation we are still not seriously committed to working for positive changes in our educational system." To support his contention, Mr. Cavazos provided the following data: The American high school graduation rate declined from 71.7 percent in 1987 to 71.1 percent in 1988; the average American College Testing Service (ACT) examination score declined by two-tenths of a point, to 18.6, out of a possible 36 from 1988 to 1989; average Scholastic Aptitude Test (SAT) scores declined from 904 out of a possible 1,600 in 1988 to 903 out of 1,600 in 1989; and the percentage of public high school graduates receiving a qualifying score on advanced placement examinations declined from 8.8 percent in 1988 to 8.6 percent in 1989.[4]

The Japanese spend significantly less money on public education than the United States but manage to do well with rather basic buildings, classrooms, and equipment. Perhaps we should reallocate our resources away from the "educational palaces" common to many school districts; money might be better spent on attracting and educating those talented young people to the teaching profession.

None of these proposals is especially radical; indeed, most of them are harmonious with traditional American values. Even if they were all implemented, however, they would not be a panacea to America's educational problems. They would, however, begin to move us in a promising direction and, perhaps, that is the best that we can hope to achieve at this point in our history.

NOTES

1. Ezra Vogel, *Japan as Number One* (Cambridge, Mass.: Harvard University Press, 1979).

2. Theodore Sizer, *Places of Learning, Places of Joy* (Cambridge, Mass.: Harvard University Press, 1973).

3. Allan Bloom, *The Closing of the American Mind* (New York: Simon and Schuster, 1987); E.D. Hirsch, *Cultural Literacy* (Boston: Houghton Mifflin, 1987).

4. "Students' Learning and Graduation Rates Slip," *New York Times*, May 3, 1990.

Index

Achievement: relationship to preschool attendance, 107–8; science, 175
Ad Hoc Reform Council, 27, 42, 51–52, 57, 58, 102, 275–77, 281
"Advanced nation disease," 45
Ainu, 108
Amano Ikuo, 44
Amano Teiyu, 32
Amaya Naohiro, 65
Amidism, 6
Ancient studies, 11–12
Arita Kazuhisa, 65
Asahi Cultural Center, 242
Ashby, Eric, 318
Ashikaga Gakkō, 6

Baby hotels (*bebi hoteru*), 104
Barbarian studies (*nambangaku*), 8, 296
Bead calculation. See Soroban
Becker, Gary S., 210
Bell, Terrel, *vii–viii*
Benedict, Ruth, 119
Birthrate, 34, 43–44
Blaug, Mark, 210
Bloom, Allan, 324
Board of Education Law (1948), 32
Borgen, Robert, 295
Boyer, Ernest, 119

Bryn Mawr, 232
Buddhism, 3, 4–6, 8, 294, 295
Budgetary system for education, 87–89
Burakumin, 108

Cavazos, Lauro F., 324
Central Council for Education (CCE), 42, 275
Child care, commercial, 103, 104, 106
Child Welfare Law (1947), 101, 104
Children's advocates, 119
Chosoren (Federation of North Korean Residents in Japan), 285–286
Christianity, 6–7, 8; closure of schools, 8–9
Chun Jeon, 283
Classical period, 3–5
Cold war, 31
Confucianism, 3, 6, 11, 14–15, 28, 39, 130–31, 261–62, 322
Cram schools. See Juku; Yobikō
"Creativity, problem of, 56, 57
"Crisis of structuration," 44
Cummings, William K., 32–33, 129
Curriculum, 68; control of, 56; revision of, 35, 68–69

Daigaku. See Universities
Day care, regional variations, 105–8

Day care institutions. *See* Hoiku-en
Denison, Edward, 219
Dewey, John, 147
Domain school (*hankō*), 9
Dore, Ronald, 9, 12, 39, 213, 293, 298
Duke, Benjamin, 209, 219
Dutch studies (*rangaku*), 8, 12, 14

Economic: development, 35–36; expansion, 37
Economic growth, 209–10; linkage with jobs, 219–22; role of education, 210–13, 214–19; role of intelligence, 212; vocational training, 220–21; vocational training and size of firm, 222
Economic Planning Agency (EPA), 37
Education: centralized system, 33, 179–80; child-centered, 18–19; compulsory, 192, 230, 234, 262; enrollments, 43, 78, 216, 230; expenditures, international comparisons, 85–86; expenditures, private, 80–81; expenditures, public, 78–81, 82–83; history, 29–30, 214–19; local funding responsibility, 83–84; medieval, 5–7; national funding responsibility, 84; prefectural funding responsibility, 85; preschool enrollments, 97–98; problems, 45–46, 51, 52–59, 63, 276
Education Act of 1880, 231
Education Reform Committee, 263, 264, 299. *See also* Ad Hoc Reform Council
Educational finance, 180–81; politics of, 90–93
Educational opportunity, expansion, 34, 35–36, 38, 78–79, 100, 178–79, 190, 192–93, 202, 312
Entrance examinations, 39–40, 56–57, 62, 64, 67–68, 188–90, 235, 237, 286; American influences, 299–301; Chinese influences, 294; competition, 301; cram schools, 40, 235; discourage creativity, 56, 302; European influences, 297–99; "examination hell," 291–92, 293; future prospects, 302–3; linkage to jobs, 58, 189–90, 302–3, 309; obstacles to reform, 39–41, 303; *rōnin*, 11, 238–39, 291, 301

Esaka Akira, 213
Ethnic schools, 281

Ferris Seminary, 231
Foreign employees (*oyatoi gaikokujin/yatoi*) 28, 128
Foreign students in Japan, 281
Fujisawa Rikitaro, 140
Fujiwara family, 295
Fundamental Code of Education: 1872, 14, 31, 214, 230, 234; 1879 revision, 14

Gakumonjo. See School for nobles
Gakusei. See Fundamental Code of Education
Gakushūin. See Peer's school
Gambaru. See Persistence
Glazer, Nathan, 41–42
Gluck, Carol, 21
Graduate education, 197–202
Great Principles of Education (1879), 15
Group harmony, 130
Group loyalty, 130
Group orientation, 130

Hankō. See Domain school
Hayashi Kimpō, 1
Hayashi Razan, 9
Hayashi School, 2
Hendry, Joy, 99, 111–12
Higher education: American influence, 307; comparison with U.S., 311, 315–16; demographic changes, 309–10, 311, 313, 317–18; domestic challenges, 314–15; enrollments, 307–8; expansion, 307–8; external challenges, 312; junior colleges, 307; new student pool, 312–13; number of institutions, 307–8
Higher Girls' School Law (1899), 232
Higher Girls' School Law Revision (1910), 232
Hirsch, E.D., 324
Hoiku-en, 99–100; behavior, 111; content, 101–2; enrollment, 100, 106; minority pupils, 108–9; social class, 107

Hoiku-jo: content, 101–2; public vs. private, 102–3
Home education, 10
Horio Teruhisa, 16

I Ching, 6
IEA (International Association for the Evaluation of Educational Achievement), 166, 169, 194
Ienaga Saburō, 17
Igakujo. See Medical school
Iijima Soichi, 65
Ijime. See School: bullying
Ikeda Hayato, 37, 190
Imperial Oath (1868), 13, 28
Imperial Rescript on Education (1890), 17, 20, 29, 31
Imperial Way, 262
Income doubling plan, 37, 190, 219
Industrial development, 177
Industrial Promotion Law (1952), 217
Inoue Kowashi, 15
Institutional self-selection, 311
Internationalization, 58–59, 70, 281, 312–13
Ishii Takemochi, 65
Itō Hirobumi, 15
Ito Ryoji, 219
Iwaki Hideo, 184

Japan as Number One. See Vogel, Ezra
Japan Federation of Employers, 33, 36
Japan Recruit Center, 252
Japan Teachers' Union (JTU), 33, 43, 61–62, 91, 180
Japan Teachers Union Association for Enlightenment, 19
Japan Women's University, 232
Jesuits, 7, 128; expulsion (1614), 8
Jinzai. See Talent, formation of
Jitsugaku. See Practical studies
Jiyū minken undō. See Popular rights movement
Joshi Bijutsu Gakkō. See Tokyo Women's College of Fine Arts
Joshi Eigaku Juku. See Tsuda College
Juku, vii–viii, 57, 167–69, 235, 291

Kaisei kyōikurei, 1880. See Revised Education Law of 1880
Kaneko Motohisa, 195
Kansei Reform, 1, 12
Key, Ellen, 110
Kiefer, Christie, 292–93
Kikokushijo. See "Returnee children"
Kindergarten, 100
Kinoshita Hiroji, 298
Kitamachi Junior High School, 155
Kitamura Kazuyuki, *viii*
Kobayashi Sosaku, 215
Kobayashi, Victor, 194
Kogaku. See Ancient studies
Koike Kazuo, 222
Kokusai-ka. See Internationalization
Korean residents in Japan, 108, 281–87; Chosoren ethnic schools, 285–86; education and ethnic identity, 283–87; ethnic education in public schools, 286–88; funding of ethnic schools, 285–86; future of ethnic schools, 288–90; intermarriage, 282–83; Mindan ethnic schools, 284–85; population, 282; problems, 281–82, 283–84
Koshiro Kazutoshi, 222
Koyama Kenichi, 63–64, 69
Koza (academic chair system), 301
Krupskaya, Nadezhda Konstantinova, 110
Kuroyanagi Tetsuko, 215
Kyogaku taishi. See Great Principles of Education (1879)
Kyōiku chokugo. See Imperial Rescript on Education (1890)
Kyōiku gi. See Opinion on Education

Labor standards law of 1947, 219
LaFleur, William, 6, 22
Lincoln, Edward, 219
Literacy, 3, 21; and Buddhism, 8; Tokugawa, 77

Manpower policy, 176
Marshall, Alfred, 210, 218
Mathematics: achievement, 321; classroom instruction, 165–67; outside of classroom, 167; problems, 143; textbooks, 155–56, 161, 166. See also

IEA (International Association for the Evaluation of Educational Achievement)
Mathematics, curriculum, 139–40, 151; elementary (1911), 144–45; elementary (1925), 146; future trends, 171–72; middle school (1912), 145–46; summary of curriculum changes (1872–1980), 164–65
Matsudaira Sadanobu, 1–2, 7–9, 11, 12, 13
Medical school, 14
Mental training, 129
Minzoku gakko. See Ethnic schools
Miscellaneous schools, 38
Mitogaku. See Mito learning
Mito learning, 12
Moore, Eliakim Hastings, 147
Moral education, 32, 60, 66, 260
Mori Arinori, 17, 214, 262
Morsbach, Helmut, 129
Mother-child relationships, 115–16, 129
Motivation, 130
Motoda Nagazane, 15–16, 261
Multitrack schools, 36

Nakae Chōmin, 17
Nakasone Yasuhiro, 27, 51, 52, 57, 59, 63–64
Nakayama Sohei, 65
Nara Women's University, 233
National Council on Educational Reform. See Ad Hoc Reform Council
National Institute for Educational Research (NIER), 167
National Women's Education Center, 241
Nativism, 14
Neo-Confucianism, 9, 11, 13; influence on teacher education, 9
Neoconservative reformers, 62–64, 67, 69
New Education Law of 1879, 15
New mathematics, 150
Nihon Joshi Daigakko.
Nihon Kyōin Kumiai Keimeikai. See Japan Teachers Union Association for Enlightenment

Nikkeiren. *See* Japan Federation of Employers
Nikkyoso. *See* Japan Teachers' Union

Occupation of Japan, 29–31, 181–88; allied goals, 30, 188–90; American influence, 299–301; failures, 44; mathematics reform, 147–50; reforms, 179, 181–82; reverse course, 33. *See also* Mathematics
Ochanomizu Women's University, 233
Office of Strategic Services (OSS), 29
Ohkawa Kazushi, 219
"Oil shock," 43
Okabe Susumu, 140
Omi Codes, 295
Opinion on Education, 15
Organization for Economic Cooperation and Development (OECD), 43
Orihara Hiroshi, 292

Passin, Herbert, 12, 298
Pearse, Arno, 219
Peer's school (*gakushūin*), 13
Perry, John, 147
Persistence (*gambaru*), 128
Pestalozzi, Johannes, 18
Popular rights movement, 16
Postwar reforms and educational structure, 175
Practical studies, 8, 12
Preschools, 97; content, 109, 110; control, 116–18; health problems, 114; minimum standards, 109; parental roles, 114–16; problems, 120–21; programs, 111–13; salaries, 114; teachers, 113–14; types, 99; working day, 114
Pressure groups, 92
Prewar schooling, aims of, 262
Private academies, 12, 16
Private School Promotion Foundation, 195
Progressive education, 19–20

Rangaku. See Dutch studies
Reischauer, Edwin O., 28, 316
Religious seminaries, 7; curriculum, 7
"Returnee children," 70, 281–82

"Reverse course." *See* Occupation of Japan
Revised Education Law of 1880, 15-17
Revised Japanese Nationality Act (1984), 282
Rinkyoshin. See Ad Hoc Reform Council
Risshisha. See Self-Help Society
Robins-Mowry, Dorothy, 231
Rohlen, Thomas P., 39, 40, 194, 221, 235
Rōnin, 11, 12

Saigo Revolt, 216
Saito Kimiko, 110
Samurai, 5, 6, 128
Sato Eisaku, 41
Sawada Toshio, 167
Saxonhouse, Gary, 219
School: bullying (*ijime*), 45, 51, 54, 59; dropouts, 44; violence, 45-46, 51, 54, 59, 60
School Education Law (1947), 31, 101, 234
School for nobles, 6
School refusal syndrome, 44
Schultz, Theodore, 210
Science Education Centers, 39
Science-technology assessment, 205-7
Science-technology policy, 202-5
Scott, Marion M., 261
Seki Kowa, 139
Self-Help Society, 16
Sex role differentiation, 115
Shigaki, Irene, 130
Shijuku. See Private academies
Shimahara Nobuo, 108
Shimizu Yoshihiro, 292
Shintō, 6
Shōheikō, 1, 9, 14
Shōtoku Taishi, 4, 294
Shūgiin, 14
Shushin. See Moral education
Shūyō. See Mental training
Smiles, Samuel (*Self-Help*), 297
Social education, 241
Soroban, 139, 140, 147
Stoddard, George, 299
Student-professor relations, 197-99

Student radicals, 41
Sugawara Mariko, 245
Sugawara no Michizane, 294-95
Suicides, 54-56, 59; and teachers, 260
Suzuki, D.T., 296

Taihō Code, 3, 4, 295
Talent, formation of, 12
Taoism, 6
Task persistence, U.S. and Japan compared, 131-37
Teacher education, 36, 37-38, 61; criticisms, 265-68; current, 260, 264-65; inservice, 270-72; institutions, 262; Occupation, 263-64; prewar, 259, 260-63
Teacher education reform, proposals, 275-77
Teachers: criticisms of, 60, 260; cultural expectations, 272-73; gender inequalities, 240-41; number of applicants, 259-60, 268-70; probationary period, 60-61, 66-67; salaries, 86, 180-81, 481, 596
temple schools, 6, 10, 128, 214
Terakoya. See Temple schools
Todd, Vivian Edmiston, 549
Tokugawa education, 7-12, 77-78; legacy of, 12-13
Tokugawa Ieyasu, 7, 128
Tokyo Joshi Igakku. See Tokyo Women's Medical College
Tokyo University Protest (1968), 41
Tokyo Women's College of Fine Arts, 232
Tokyo Women's Medical College, 232
Totman, Conrad, 4
Tsuda College, 232
Tsuda Umeko, 232
Tsukuba University, 302

United States Education Mission to Japan (1946), 30-31, 259, 263, 299
United States-Japan, comparisons, 194-202; secondary schools, 194-95; tertiary institutions, 195-202
Universities, 14, 38, 297; Confucian, 295; elite, 213; expansion, 37, 188; hi-

erarchy, 36, 44; imperial, 3, 13, 176, 177, 223–24, 301; private, 301, 302, 313; private, declining revenues, 313–14; weakening, 57–58, 71; women's, 217
University of the Air, 241

Values, 130
Vocational education, 220–22; legislation, 220; within firms, 221–22
Vogel, Ezra (*Japan as Number One*), vii, 292, 321

Watanabe Tsunehiko, 219
Women: access to education, 34–35; participation in social education, 241–42
Women and family: aging of society, 244, 246–47; divorce rate, 244; gender roles, 242–47; holder of family purse, 245; influence on children, 243; labor force participation, 247–53; leisure activities, 244; marriage, 242–43; working women, 245–46
Women's education: attendance rates, 230–31, 232, 233, 234–37; gender inequalities, 229–30, 233–41; prewar Japan, 230–33; sex-linked streaming, 237
Women's higher education: attendance at women's universities, 238; domination of junior colleges, 237–38; graduate studies, 239; most popular subjects studied, 239; parental attitudes toward, 235–36
Women's school, special status, 232
Women's universities: achievement of university status, 234; relationship to men's universities, 233
Work ethic, 59
Work force policy origins, 176

Yano Masakazu, 223
Yatoi. *See* Foreign employees
Yobikō, 237, 291
Yochien, Kindergarten, 99–100; enrollments, 100, 106; funding, 102; public vs. private, 102–3; size, 103
Yoshida Shigeru, 32
Yoshida Shōin, 13
Youth culture, 45

Zen, 6, 295–96

About the Contributors

EDWARD R. BEAUCHAMP is Professor of Historical and Comparative Educational Studies at the University of Hawaii.

PRISCILLA N. BLINCO is a Postdoctoral Scholar at Stanford University.

SARANE SPENCE BOOCOCK is Professor of Sociology at Rutgers—the State University of New Jersey.

WILLIAM K. CUMMINGS is associated with Project Bridges in the Graduate School of Education at Harvard University

ROBERT EVANS, JR., is Atran Professor of Labor Economics at Brandeis University.

PETER FROST is Professor of History at Williams College.

KUMIKO FUJIMURA-FANSELOW teaches at Toyo Eiwa Jogakuin's newly established four-year institution in Yokohama.

ANNE E. IMAMURA is Chair of Asian Studies in the Foreign Service Institute of the Department of State.

KITAMURA KAZUYUKI is Professor of Higher Education in the Research Institute for Higher Education at Hiroshima University.

MARK LINCICOME is Assistant Professor of History at Holy Cross College.

NOBUO SHIMAHARA is Associate Dean in the Graduate School of Education at Rutgers—the State University of New Jersey.

LEONARD SCHOPPA is Assistant Professor in the Woodrow Wilson Department of Government and Foreign Affairs at the University of Virginia.

ICHIKAWA SHOGO is Director of Research Department II at the National Institute for Educational Research in Tokyo.

UMAKOSHI TORU is Professor of Comparative Education at Japan's Nagoya University.

NANCY C. WHITMAN is Professor of Curriculum and Instruction at the University of Hawaii.